The Dictionary of Real Estate Appraisal

About the Appraisal Institute

As the world's leading organization of professional real estate appraisers, the Appraisal Institute has general appraisal members who hold the MAI, SRPA, or SREA designation and residential appraisal members who hold the SRA or RM designation. Identified by their experience and knowledge of real estate valuation, these members adhere to a strictly enforced Code of Professional Ethics and Standards of Professional Appraisal Practice. Currently, the Appraisal Institute confers one general designation, the MAI, and one residential designation, the SRA.

Users of this text may be interested in *The Appraisal of Real Estate,* tenth edition, *Appraising Residential Properties,* and the *Communicating the Appraisal* series of texts published by the Appraisal Institute.

For a catalog of Appraisal Institute publications, contact the PR/Marketing Department of the Appraisal Institute, 875 North Michigan Avenue, Chicago, Illinois, 60611-1980.

The Dictionary of Real Estate Appraisal

THIRD EDITION

APPRAISAL INSTITUTE

875 North Michigan Avenue

Chicago, Illinois 60611-1980

Acknowledgments

Vice President, Publications: Christopher Bettin

Manager, Book Development: Michael R. Milgrim, PhD

Editor: Stephanie Shea-Joyce

Graphic Designer: Julie Beich

For Educational Purposes

The opinions and statements set forth herein reflect the viewpoint of the Appraisal Institute at the time of publication but do not necessarily reflect the viewpoint of each individual member. While a great deal of care has been taken to provide accurate and current information, neither the Appraisal Institute nor its editors and staff assume responsibility for the accuracy of the data contained herein. Further, the general principles and conclusions presented in this text are subject to local, state and federal laws and regulations, court cases and any revisions of the same. This publication is sold for educational purposes with the understanding that the publisher is not engaged in rendering legal, accounting or any other professional service.

Nondiscrimination Policy

The Appraisal Institute advocates equal opportunity and nondiscrimination in the appraisal profession and conducts its activities without regard to race, color, sex, religion, national origin, or handicap status.

© 1993 by the Appraisal Institute, an Illinois Not for Profit Corporation.

Printed in the United States of America
98 97 96 95 94 93   7 6 5 4 3 2

Library of Congress Cataloging-in-Publication Data
The Dictionary of real estate appraisal. — 3rd edition.
       p.   cm.
     Includes bibliographical references.
     ISBN 0-922154-12-0
     1. Real property—Valuation—Dictionaries.   2. Real estate business—Dictionaries.
     3. Real property—Dictionaries.
I. Appraisal Institute (U.S.)
HD1387.D435   1993
333.33′2′03—dc20   93-25493
                                                        CIP

TABLE OF CONTENTS

ACKNOWLEDGMENTS

Many of the definitions in this dictionary were derived from material in other texts. Definitions quoted verbatim are followed by a source reference. A list of bibliographic sources and related texts can be found beginning on page 514. The following copyrights are herewith acknowledged:

- Definitions of *construction area* (gross building area), *rentable area, store area,* and *usable area* from the *1989 BOMA Experience Exchange Report: Income/Expense Analysis for Office Buildings.* Reprinted with permission of the **Building Owners and Managers Association International,** 1201 New York Avenue, NW, Suite 300, Washington, DC 20005. Copyright 1989.

- Definitions of *asset management, facilities management, property management, systems maintenance administration,* and *systems maintenance technician* are those recently adopted by the **Building Owners and Managers Institute International,** P.O. Box 9709, Arnold, MD 21012.

- Definitions of *fair value, initial investment, net realizable value, project cost, rental cost, sales value,* and *selling cost* from FASB Statement No. 66, *Accounting for Sales of Real Estate* and FASB Statement No. 67, *Accounting for Costs and Initial Rental Operations of Real Estate Projects.* Copyright by **Financial Accounting Standards Board,** 401 Merritt 7, P.O. Box 5116, Norwalk, CT 06856-5116. Reprinted with permission. Copies of the complete documents are available from FASB.

- Definitions for the following terms were extracted, with permission, from ASTM Standard E 1528-93, Practice for Environmental Site Assessments Transaction Screen Process, © **American Society for Testing and Materials,** 1916 Race Street, Philadelphia, PA 19103: *adjoining properties; environmental lien; environmental professional; environmental site assessment (ESA); fill dirt; hazardous waste/contaminated sites; landfill; pits, ponds, or lagoons.*

- All definitions with a Marshall & Swift source reference are reprinted from *Marshall & Swift Valuation Service, 1991,* with the permission of **Marshall & Swift,** 1200 Route 22, First Floor, Bridgewater, NJ 08807.

- All definitions with an R.S. Means source reference are reprinted from *Means Illustrated Construction Dictionary,* new unabridged edition, 1991, with the permission of **R.S. Means Company, Inc.,** 100 Construction Plaza, P.O. Box 800, Kingston, MA 02364.

The Appraisal Institute would also like to thank the **International Association of Assessing Officers (IAAO)** and the **Urban Land Institute (ULI)** for permission to reprint the definitions attributed to them.

T he Appraisal Institute is proud to present the long-awaited third edition of *The Dictionary of Real Estate Appraisal*. This expanded and updated edition reflects the vision of the Textbook and Dictionary Revision Committee, whose members endeavored to develop the *Dictionary* into a primary reference work. The *Dictionary* has been considerably enhanced by the committee's decision to introduce technical terms as defined by professionals in ancillary fields such as accounting, assessment, banking, construction, finance, and property management. The third edition also includes coverage of recent legislation, regulatory guidelines, and government agencies affecting real estate appraisal as well as many new entries relating to market analysis, special property types, and real estate organizations.

Several features contribute to the usefulness of this new edition. Extensive cross-references help the reader locate related entries and a topical index at the beginning of the addenda identifies terms that fall under specific subject classifications. The addenda provide a wealth of information, including the 14 FIRREA guidelines on review appraisal, summaries of relevant Supreme Court decisions, the Exam Content Outlines of The Appraisal Foundation, a list of license law officials, and numerous charts and graphs on the measurement and description of real estate.

The Appraisal Institute wishes to acknowledge the dedicated work of David A. Pearson, MAI, current Chair of the Textbook and Dictionary Revision Committee, and Paula O. Thoreen, MAI, the 1991-1992 Chair of the

Textbook and Dictionary Revision Committee, both of whom guided the project over the year and a half that it took to complete. The Appraisal Institute also wishes to express its gratitude to the following contributors, who read the manuscript and made extensive suggestions on new and existing entries: James C. Burge, MAI, SRA; M. Rebecca Carr, MAI; David W. Craig, MAI; Mary J. Dum; Alfred J. Ferrara, MAI, SRA; Kathryn Mason Gearheard, MAI; John J. Healy, Jr., MAI, SRA; Austin Jaffe, PhD; Jeffrey A. Johnson, MAI; George Raymond Mann, MAI, SRA; Patricia J. Marshall, MAI; Michael J. Martin, MAI; Thomas A. Motta, MAI; William Mount, SRA; Brent A. Palmer, MAI; C. Spencer Powell, MAI; James P. Ryan, MAI; Alan M. Schmook, MAI, SRA; George F. Silver, MAI; Tae-Sung (Mike) Song, MAI; Richard C. Sorenson, MAI; and Richard L. Stallings, MAI, SRA. Special thanks are due J.D. Eaton, MAI, who provided the summaries of Supreme Court decisions significant to the appraisal profession.

Bernard J. Fountain, MAI, SRA
1993 President
Appraisal Institute

The
Dictionary
of
Real Estate
Appraisal

THIRD EDITION

**APPRAISAL
INSTITUTE**

875 North Michigan Avenue

Chicago, Illinois 60611-1980

A

AAA tenant. A tenant who has a very good (AAA) credit rating according to a recognized rating bureau; also called *prime tenant* or *creditworthy tenant*.

AASHO. American Association of State Highway Officials.

abandonment. The relinquishing of all interests in real property and any fixtures thereon with no intention to reclaim or reuse.

abatement

1. An official reduction or invalidation of an assessed valuation after the initial assessment for ad valorem taxation has been completed.
2. The termination of a nuisance.
3. The correction of an unlawful building condition, i.e., asbestos abatement.

4. The encapsulation or removal of building materials containing asbestos to prevent the release of and exposure to fibers. (R.S. Means)
5. A reduction in the rent levels that a landlord charges tenants, sometimes brought about by a rent control program.

ABC roads. A collective term for federally aided primary and secondary roads and urban extensions of federal aid systems.

ABC soil. A soil with a complete soil profile, i.e., well-developed A, B, and C horizons.

above-grade living area (*AGLA*). Total area of finished, above-grade residential space. Unfinished attics are not considered a part of *AGLA*. *See also* gross living area (*GLA*).

abscissa. In the rectangular coordinate system, the horizontal distance from a point to the vertical axis (the y-axis); expressed as the first number in an ordered pair, e.g., in (3, 7), the abscissa is 3.

absentee landlord. An owner, lessor, or sublessor of income-producing, rental real estate who does not reside in the area where the real estate is located.

absolute assignment. An outright transfer of title, as opposed to a transfer by way of security.

absolute conveyance. An unqualified, unrestricted, unlimited, or unconditional transfer of property.

absolute owner. One who holds all the real property interests in a parcel of real estate.

absorption period. The actual or expected period required from the time a property is initially offered for purchase or use by its eventual users until all portions have been sold or stabilized occupancy has been achieved. Although marketing may begin before the completion of construction, most forecasters consider the absorption period to begin after the completion of construction.

absorption rate. The rate at which properties for sale or lease have been or are expected to be successfully marketed in a given area; usually used in forecasting sales or leasing activity. *See also* capture rate.

abstraction. *See* extraction.

abstract of title. A summary of property conveyances, transfers, and other facts used as evidence of title plus any other public documents that may impair title.

abut. To touch or border; to share a common boundary with another property.

abutment. The part of a structure that an object borders on or presses; the structural member that receives the pressure of an arch or strut, e.g., the supports at either end of a bridge.

abutter's rights. The right of visibility, i.e., the right to see and be seen from the street and to enjoy the flow of light and air from the street to the property.

accelerated cost recovery system (ACRS). A set of income tax rules established under the Economic Recovery Tax Act of 1981, which covers depreciation deductions and the computation of the tax basis for depreciable property. The 1986 Tax Reform Act maintained the ACRS, but lengthened cost recovery periods for many categories of depreciable assets and allowed only straight-line depreciation rather than accelerated depreciation for real estate placed in service after December 31, 1986.

accelerated depreciation. In tax accounting, a method of cost write-off in which the allowances made for depreciation of a wasting asset are greater in early years and decline in subsequent years according to a formula. Technically, the depreciation decelerates over time; the popular term *accelerated depreciation* refers to accelerated, or faster, recovery of capital during the early years of an investment. *See also* straight-line depreciation.

acceleration clause. A condition in a loan contract or mortgage note that allows the lender to demand immediate repayment of the entire balance if the contract is breached or other conditions for repayment occur, e.g., sale or demolition of the property.

acceleration lane. An additional traffic lane that permits entering traffic to merge with through traffic quickly and safely.

access. The path through a neighborhood by which a property is approached; the means of physical entrance into or upon a property.

accessibility. The relative degree of effort, i.e., time and cost, required to reach a site; indicates ease of entrance into or upon a property.

accession. Additional property rights that accrue to an owner when additions or improvements are attached to the property either naturally or by the labor or materials of another, e.g., tenant improvements at tenant cost.

accessory building. A building on the same property as a main building; any outbuilding used in connection with the main building, e.g., a garage, a pump house, a well house.

access rights
1. The right of ingress to and egress from a property that abuts an existing street or highway; an easement in the street that adjoins abutting property; a private right, as distinguished from public rights. *See also* landlocked parcel.
2. The right of a riparian owner to pass to and from the waters on which the premises border.

accommodated room night demand. The number of hotel and motel rooms within a market area that are actually occupied during a 12-month period; calculated by multiplying each competitive property's room count by its annual occupancy and then by 365.

accommodation. An obligation assumed without consideration.

accounting standards. *See* Financial Accounting Standards Board (FASB).

accretion. An increase in dry land created by the gradual accumulation of waterborne solid material over formerly riparian land, i.e., accretion by alluvion. *See also* alluvion; reliction.

accrual basis. A method of accounting in which income and expenses are recorded on the books in the fiscal period when they are earned or incurred regardless of when they are actually received or paid. *See also* cash basis.

accruals for depreciation. On accounting statements, the provisions made for anticipated depreciation, usually credits to reserves.

accrued depreciation
1. The difference between the reproduction or replacement cost of the improvements on the effective date of the appraisal and the market value of the improvements on the same date.
2. In accounting, the amount reserved each year or accumulated to date in the accounting system for replacement of a building or other asset.

acknowledgment. A declaration usually made before an official, e.g., a notary public, who attests to the validity of the declarer's signature.

ACMs. Asbestos-containing materials.

acoustical material. A substance with sound-absorbing qualities that can be applied to walls and ceilings and is usually made of mineral fiber or insulated metal materials, e.g., tile, fiber or mineral board, cork, special plaster.

acoustical tile. *See* acoustical material.

acquisition fee. Money paid for arranging for the acquisition of a property, e.g., for a property being syndicated.

acre. A land measure equal to 43,560 square feet.

acreage. Acres collectively, e.g., farm acreage, industrial acreage, residential acreage.

acreage controls. Limits set by the federal government on the number of acres that can be planted with price-supported crops.

acre-foot
1. A volume of water equal to the amount required to cover one acre of land to a depth of one foot; equal to 325,850 gallons or 43,560 cubic feet of water.
2. A measurement of coal in place; equal to a one-acre horizontal bed of coal that is one foot thick.

acre-inch
1. A volume of water equal to the amount required to cover one acre of land to a depth of one inch; equal to 27,154 gallons.
2. In irrigation, a flow of 450 gallons per minute is considered an acre-inch. This flow volume is called *one second-foot* or *one cubic foot per second.*

acres-in-crops. The area of land, exclusive of permanent pasture and woods, on which crops are either growing or harvested in a year.

acres-of-crops. The total acreage of crops growing or harvested in a year, exclusive of annual crops planted for harvest during the following year. It may be larger than the number of acres actually in crops because more than one crop may be produced on a part or all of the cropland.

across the fence method. A means of estimating the price or value of land adjacent to or "across the fence" from a railroad, pipeline, highway, or other corridor real estate; as distinguished from valuing the right-of-way as a separate entity. *See also* value for other use.

across the fence value (ATF). In the valuation of corridor real estate, the price or value of land adjacent to or "across the fence" from a railroad, pipeline, highway, or other corridor real estate.

ACRS. *See* accelerated cost recovery system.

action in rem. A legal action taken to effect a legal judgment against property to determine its status, e.g., an action to foreclose on a mortgage.

active market. A market characterized by growing demand, a corresponding lag in supply, and an increase in prices.

actual age. The number of years that have elapsed since construction of an improvement was completed; also called *historical* or *chronological age.*

ADA. *See* ADAAG; alteration; Americans with Disabilities Act of 1990; commercial facility; public accommodation; readily achievable; reasonable accommodation.

ADAAG. Americans with Disabilities Act Accessibility Guidelines on Buildings and Facilities. *See also* Americans with Disabilities Act (ADA) of 1990.

addition. Part of a building that has been added to the original structure.

additional commitment. The amount, if any, that each investor in a real estate syndication must pay in addition to the initial subscription.

adjacent. Describes property that borders or adjoins another property.

adjoining properties. Any real property or properties the border of which is contiguous or partially contiguous with that of the property, or that would be contiguous or partially contiguous with that of the property but for a street, road, or public thoroughfare separating them. (ASTM)

adjustable-rate mortgage (ARM). A debt secured by real estate with an interest rate that may move up or down following a specified schedule or in accordance with the movements of a standard or index to which the interest rate is tied. A limit upon how much the interest rate can be adjusted is called the *adjustment cap. See also* variable-rate mortgage (VRM).

adjusted basis. In accounting, the original cost of a property plus allowable additions, e.g., capital improvements, certain carrying costs, assessments, minus any depreciation taken and partial sales. *See also* basis; book value.

adjusted internal rate of return (AIRR). *See* modified internal rate of return (*MIRR*).

adjusted sale price. The figure produced when the transaction price of a comparable sale is adjusted for elements of comparison. When the appropriate sequence of adjustments is followed, several intermediate adjusted sale prices are calculated and used as the basis for subsequent adjustments. *See also* sequence of adjustments.

adjustment cap. *See* adjustable-rate mortgage (ARM).

adjustments

1. Mathematical changes made to basic data to facilitate comparison or understanding. When dollar adjustments are used, individual differences between comparables and the subject property are expressed in terms of plus or minus dollar amounts; with percentage adjustments, individual differences are reflected in plus or minus percentage differentials; in cumulative percentage adjustments, individual differences between comparables and the subject property are represented by plus or minus percentage differentials, cumulated by multiplication or division. The process assumes a causal relationship among the various factors for which adjustments are made.

2. Items that should be prorated or apportioned between the purchaser and the seller in a real estate transaction, e.g., taxes, rents, fuel. *See also* qualitative techniques; quantitative techniques.

administrative expenses. In real estate, those expenses incurred in property operation. The items in this category depend on the nature of the real estate, but usually include the salaries of property managers, rent of offices, office and general expenses, and costs for noncustodial personnel and the services needed to operate the property. *See also* property management.

administrator. A person appointed by the court to manage and settle the estate of a deceased person; a representative of limited authority who collects the assets of an estate, pays its debts, and distributes the residue to those entitled. An administrator provides security for the due administration of the estate by entering into a bond with sureties, called an *administration bond*. *See also* executor.

administrator's deed. A deed conveyed by an administrator, i.e., a person lawfully appointed to manage and settle the estate of a deceased person who has left no executor.

adobe. A heavy-textured soil that cracks deeply when dry and breaks into irregular, cubical blocks. (Marshall & Swift)

adobe construction. A building method featuring exterior walls built of blocks made from adobe soil mixed with straw and hardened in the sun.

ADR rate. *See* average daily room rate.

ADT. *See* average daily traffic.

ad valorem. According to value.

ad valorem tax. A real estate tax based on the assessed value of the property, which is not necessarily equivalent to its market value.

adverse possession. The actual, exclusive, open, notorious, hostile, and continuous possession and occupation of real property under an evident claim of right or title. The time required to obtain title legally by adverse possession varies from state to state.

aeolian soil. Soil developed from material transported and deposited by wind.

aeration zone. The upper ground water zone that retains water for plant use and permits excess water to seep into the saturation zone.

affidavit. A sworn or affirmed statement or declaration in written form.

affiliation agreement. A contract, such as that entered into by a local broadcasting company and a major network, that provides valuable advantages to both.

affirmative easement. The right to perform a specific action on a property owned by another; also called the *dominant estate. See also* negative easement.

affordability. The ability of prospective buyers to purchase a residential property. Affordability is reflected in the relationship between the median income of a family and its ability to qualify for a mortgage on a median-priced home. In the mid-1980s, an affordability crisis developed in specific market segments due to soaring housing prices and the depressed income levels of many younger households. The precipitous decline in interest rates during the early 1990s helped close the affordability gap.

affordability index. A measure that indicates potential buyers' ability to purchase a home; compiled by the National Association of Realtors. An affordability index of 100 indicates that a median-income family has sufficient funds to qualify for a mortgage on a median-priced home.

AFLM. Accredited Farm and Land Member, a designation conferred by the Realtors Land Institute (RLI).

after-completion costs. Costs incurred after construction of the primary improvements has been completed, e.g., leasing commissions, tenant alterations, extra interest to cover shortfalls on debt service.

after-tax cash flow (*ATCF*). The portion of pre-tax cash flow that remains after all income tax liabilities have been deducted.

after-tax equity yield rate. The annualized rate of return on equity after payment of income taxes, including those that are or will be incurred upon disposition of the investment; the internal rate of return after taxes. *See also* internal rate of return (*IRR*)

after-tax income. In accounting, the income that remains after deducting income tax liability from taxable income; not to be confused with *after-tax cash flow.*

after-tax net cash proceeds of resale. The after-tax reversion to equity; the estimated resale price of the property minus commissions and other expenses of sale, outstanding debt, and tax claims on the ownership interest.

AGC. Associated General Contractors of America.

age-life method. *See* economic age-life method; modified economic age-life method; physical age-life method.

agency. A fiduciary relationship in which one party, the agent, acts as a representative of the other, the principal, in matters specified in a contract between them.

agent. A person who has been given the authority to act for another. *See also* agency.

agents in production. The elements of labor, capital, coordination, and land, which together create wealth, income, or services.

aggregate
1. Materials used in the manufacture of concrete or plaster, except water and the bonding agents, e.g., sand, gravel, cinders, rock, slag. *See also* soil aggregate.
2. In statistics, the sum of all the varieties within a population, e.g., the aggregate sale price of all the houses sold in a given community.

aggregate of retail values (*ARV*). The sum of the appraised values of the individual units in a subdivision, as if all of the units were completed and available for retail sale, as of the date of the appraisal. The sum of the retail sales includes an allowance for lot premiums, if applicable, but excludes all allowances for carrying costs.

AGLA. Refers to either adjusted gross leasable area or above-grade living area. *See also* above-grade living area.

agreement of sale. A written contract of sale between a buyer and a seller, drawn up before the actual transfer of title or assumption of ownership, which states the conditions necessary for the transfer of ownership; also called *sale contract. See also* contract date.

agricultural districting. The designation of certain geographic areas for long-term agricultural use.

agricultural extension agent. A representative of the U.S. Department of Agriculture stationed in a county to advise the farming community on new agricultural developments and methods to improve farming and rural living. Synonymous with *county extension agent* and *county farm advisor.*

agricultural property. Improved or unimproved land that is devoted to or available for the production of crops and other products of the soil, e.g., fruits, timber, pasture, and buildings for livestock.

agricultural research administration. A major division of the U.S. Department of Agriculture which is responsible for coordinating most of the department's bureaus and offices engaged in experimental, demonstration, or research activities. The administration has direct responsibility for the department's special research funds and for departmental research laboratories.

agricultural research service. A major division of the U.S. Department of Agriculture engaged in experimental, demonstration, and research activities relating to the production and utilization of farm products. It is also responsible for the control and regulatory programs involving the enforcement of plant and animal quarantines, the eradication of animal and plant diseases, meat inspection, and related work. Projects are carried on at the Agricultural Research Center in Beltsville, Maryland, and elsewhere in the United States and abroad. Much of the research is performed in cooperation with state agricultural experiment stations.

agricultural use value. An estimate of value based solely on the property's agricultural productivity.

Agriculture, Department of. *See* Department of Agriculture.

A horizon. Upper horizon, surface soil from which material is removed by percolating water. *See also* B horizon; C horizon; D horizon.

AIA. American Institute of Architects.

AICPA. *See* American Institute of Certified Public Accountants.

AIHC. American Institute of Housing Consultants.

AIP. American Institute of Planners.

air-conditioning. A system designed to control room temperature and humidity through ventilation, air circulation, air cleaning, and air cooling.

air curtain. A device to protect an opening against heat loss or passage of insects by blowing a high-velocity flow of air across the opening. (Marshall & Swift)

AIRR. *See* adjusted internal rate of return.

air plenum. Any space used to convey air in a building or structure. The space above a suspended ceiling is often used as an air plenum.

airport zoning. A system that limits the height of structures and natural growth and controls land uses around an airport to eliminate hazards to aircraft, e.g., smoke, electronic interference, structural interference.

air quality control region. An area designated by the federal government that encompasses two or more communities that share a common air pollution problem.

air quality maintenance area. A geographical area designated by the Environmental Protection Agency for the administration of air quality standards; may include several municipalities and more than one state.

air quality standard. The prescribed level of air pollutants that cannot be lawfully exceeded during a specified time in a specified geographical area.

air rights. The right to undisturbed use and control of designated air space above a specific land area within stated elevations. Such rights may be acquired to construct a building above the land or building of another or to protect the light and air of an existing or proposed structure on an adjoining lot. *See also* transferable development right (TDR).

air-supported structure. A tent-like curved structure held up by air pressure with an airtight seal around its base perimeter. (Marshall & Swift)

Akerson format. A mortgage-equity procedure that substitutes an arithmetic format for the algebraic equation in the Ellwood formula; also called *Ellwood without algebra.*

alcove. A recessed area connected to a room or hallway.

ALDA. American Land Development Association.

alienation. A transfer of title from one person to another.

alkali. Describes certain soluble salts that are toxic to plant growth when high concentrations are present in soils.

alkaline soil. Any soil that has a pH above seven.

alley. A relatively narrow public or private way that serves as a secondary means of access and affords light and air to abutting properties.

alley influence. The effect of a side or rear alley on the value of abutting property, especially commercial property.

all-inclusive deed of trust. A junior deed of trust in which the beneficiary (lender or seller) agrees to pay one or more senior lienholders and the trustor (borrower or buyer) makes one payment to the beneficiary rather than separate payments to the junior and senior lienholders. *See also* deed of trust; wraparound mortgage.

all-inclusive mortgage. A junior mortgage in which the mortgagee agrees to pay one or more senior lienholders and the mortgagor makes one payment to the mortgagee, rather than separate payments to the junior and senior lienholders. *See also* wraparound mortgage.

allocation. A method of estimating land value in which sales of improved properties are analyzed to establish a typical ratio of site value to total property value and this ratio is applied to the property being appraised or the comparable sale being analyzed.

allodial. *See* alodial.

allotment

1. A tract of land that has been divided into smaller parts; a subdivision.
2. An allowance established by the U. S. Department of Agriculture designating the specific amount of crops that may be produced or the acreage that can be devoted to the production of a specific crop.

3. Funds allocated by an institutional investor to purchase mortgages for its portfolio within a designated period.

all risk insurance. An insurance policy that can be written separately to add coverage against certain specific risks of damage or loss from any number of potential events. These risks represent potential losses in excess of coverage provided by other forms of insurance purchased for the purpose of protecting the owner, design professional, and contractor during and after the construction process. (R.S. Means)

all-suite hotel. A hotel in which space that could be allotted to meeting, banquet, restaurant, and lounge facilities is instead allocated to guest suites that include separate living and sleeping areas. Most all-suite hotels offer free breakfast and an evening cocktail hour. With only limited food and beverage facilities, all-suite hotels are usually easier to operate and typically have higher profit margins.

alluvial. Deposits made by flowing water.

alluvial fan. A sloping, fan-shaped deposit of boulders, gravel, and sand left by a stream or river where it spreads out onto a level plain or meets a slower stream or river.

alluvial soil. An azonal, unstable soil formed from materials transported by flowing water.

alluvion. The addition to dry land produced by the washing of a sea, a navigable river, or another body of water; a gradual increase that cannot be perceived at any one moment in time. *See also* accretion.

alluvium. A fine material, e.g., sand, mud, carried by water and deposited on land.

alodial. Pertaining to an *alodium*, i.e., freehold property held in absolute independence and not subject to any rent, service, or acknowledgment of superior rights.

ALTA. American Land Title Association.

alteration. Under the Americans with Disabilities Act (ADA) of 1990, a requirement of employers to ensure accessibility ("path of travel") for people with disabilities to a major use area within a commercial facility when modifications are made to such areas. *See also* Americans with Disabilities Act (ADA) of 1990.

alternative mortgage instrument (AMI). Any mortgage that differs from the standard fixed-rate, level-payment mortgage instrument. *See also* flexible loan insurance plan (FLIP); graduated-payment mortgage (GPM); reverse annuity mortgage (RAM); variable-rate mortgage (VRM).

amenity. A tangible or intangible benefit of real property that enhances its attractiveness or increases the satisfaction of the user, but is not essential to its use. Natural amenities may include a pleasant location near water or a scenic view of the surrounding area; man-made amenities include swimming pools, tennis courts, community buildings, and other recreational facilities.

amenities index. *See* hedonic price index.

American bond. A masonry process in which every fifth, sixth, or seventh course of bricks is laid with the length perpendicular to the wall as a header course.

American Institute of Certified Public Accountants (AICPA). Professional organization of state-certified accountants that sets standards, develops guidelines for corporate financial statements, and prepares the national Uniform CPA Examination.

American National Standards Institute. *See* American standard.

American Real Estate and Urban Economics Association (AREUEA). Organization of university faculty and real estate professionals which promotes education and research into real estate, urban land economics, and related fields; publishes a quarterly journal.

American Real Estate Society (ARES). Professional society of university professors and practitioners involved in real estate finance, investment, valuation, marketing, consulting, management, law, and research. ARES offers an educational program and publishes a journal, a semiannual real estate bibliography, and a monograph series.

American Society for Testing and Materials (ASTM). An organization with a membership drawn from engineering, scientific, manufacturing, consumer, and governmental groups interested in establishing voluntary test standards for materials, products, systems, and services.

American standard. A system for measuring areas in buildings established under the auspices of the American National Standards Institute and participating organizations.

Americans with Disabilities Act (ADA) of 1990. A civil rights act passed by Congress guaranteeing individuals with disabilities equal opportunity in public accommodations, employment, transportation, government services, and telecommunications. Statutory deadlines become effective on various dates between 1990 and 1997. *See also* ADAAG; alteration; commercial facility; public accommodation; readily achievable; reasonable accommodation.

AMI. *See* alternative mortgage instrument.

AMO. Accredited Management Organization, a designation conferred by the Institute of Real Estate Management (IREM).

amortization. The process of retiring a debt or recovering a capital investment, typically through scheduled, systematic repayment of the principal; a program of periodic contributions to a sinking fund or debt retirement fund. *See also* negative amortization.

amortization factor. *See* partial payment factor $(1/a_n)$.

amortization rate. The ratio of the periodic amortization payment to the total principal amount to be amortized; corresponds to a sinking fund factor or rate; the difference between the mortgage (annual) constant (R_M) and the nominal rate of interest (I).

amortization schedule. A schedule of debt repayment specifying the timing and amount of payments; a program of retiring debt through the scheduled, systematic repayment of principal.

amortizing mortgage. A mortgage requiring periodic payments that include both a partial repayment of the debt and interest on the outstanding balance. *See also* fully amortizing mortgage loan.

amount of $1 ($S^n$). The compound interest factor that indicates the amount to which $1 will grow with compound interest at a specified rate for a specified number of periods. The amount of $1 factor is one of the "six functions of a dollar" found in standard financial tables. Also called the *future value of $1*.

amount of $1 per period ($S_n$). The compound interest factor that indicates the amount to which $1 per period will grow with compound interest at a specified rate for a specified number of periods. The amount of $1 per period factor is one of the "six functions of a dollar" found in standard financial tables. Also called *sinking fund accumulation factor* or *future value of $1 per period*. *See also* annuity.

analysis

1. The act or process of providing information, recommendations, and/or conclusions on diversified problems in real estate other than estimating value; often used interchangeably with *consulting*. *See also* evaluation.
2. Method of resolving a problem by determining the nature and relationship among the components, e.g., discounted cash flow analysis, market analysis.

anchor bolt. A bolt used to secure a structural member to a masonry support to prevent upward and lateral movements of the superstructure, e.g., a bolt set into a concrete foundation, extended up through the sill, and secured with a nut at the top.

anchor tenant. The major store within a shopping center that attracts or generates traffic for the facility, e.g. a supermarket in a neighborhood shopping center, a major chain or department store in a regional shopping center.

animal unit (AU). A unit of measure equivalent to an animal weighing 1,000 pounds; e.g., a 500-pound weaner calf represents one-half animal unit. The term is subject to some local variation.

animal unit month (AUM). The quantity of feed that one animal unit needs for one month to sustain life and achieve good growth.

annual constant. *See* mortgage constant (R_M).

annual debt service. *See* debt service (I_M).

annualizer (a). *See* conversion factor (a).

annual loan constant. *See* mortgage constant (R_M).

annual percentage rate (APR). The effective annual interest rate. Truth-in-lending legislation requires that loan instruments and advertising show the interest cost to the borrower in the form of an annual rate, as distinguished from the nominal rate.

annuals. A type of range vegetation in which annual forbs or annual grasses dominate.

annuity. An annual income; a program or contract of regular payments of stipulated amounts—e.g., forecast cash flows. *See also* annuity certain; annuity payable in advance; constant dollar change per period annuity; constant ratio change per period annuity; decreasing annuity; deferred annuity; increasing annuity; Inwood annuity; level annuity; life annuity; ordinary annuity; reverse annuity mortgage (RAM); step-up or step-down annuity; variable annuity.

annuity capitalization. *See* yield capitalization.

annuity certain. An annuity that is assured for a specified period of time, as distinguished from a life annuity, which terminates with the death of an individual.

annuity due. *See* annuity payable in advance.

annuity payable in advance. A type of level annuity; similar to an ordinary annuity except that payments are received at the beginning of each period.

anodized aluminum. Aluminum that is covered with a hard, corrosion-resistant, oxide film using an electrochemical process. (R.S. Means)

ANSI. American National Standards Institute. *See* American standard.

anticipated use method. *See* development procedure.

anticipated use procedure. *See* development procedure.

anticipation. The perception that value is created by the expectation of benefits to be derived in the future.

antilogarithm. The real number corresponding to a logarithm.

apartment. A dwelling unit of one or more rooms designed to provide complete living facilities for one or more occupants.

apartment building. A structure containing four or more dwelling units with common areas and facilities, e.g., entrances, lobby, elevators or stairs, mechanical space, walks, grounds. *See also* condominium; cooperative apartment unit; flat; high-rise apartment building; tenement.

apartment hotel. A furnished apartment building with more or less permanent tenants that offers hotel facilities, e.g., reception desk, telephone switchboard, maid service, utilities.

appeal. A process in which a property owner contests an assessment either informally or formally. (IAAO)

appliance allowance. This cost includes consideration for the residential appliances commonly found at different quality levels. Typically, ranges and ovens, garbage disposers, dishwashers and range hoods are included. The better qualities (higher cost ranks) have additional feature consideration for trash compactors, microwaves, built-in mixer units, etc. (Marshall & Swift) Appliances are generally considered items of personal property. An appliance allowance pertains to the cost incurred by the developers or owners of apartment buildings or condominiums to outfit the units with appliances.

applications software. Computer programs designed to solve specific problems or perform specified functions, e.g., a cost-analysis program, a lease-by-lease discounted cash flow analysis program, an electronic spreadsheet, a database. *See also* operating system.

appraisal

1. An analysis, opinion, or conclusion relating to the nature, quality, value, or utility of specified interests in, or aspects of, identified real estate. (Code of Professional Ethics of the Appraisal Institute) In this usage, *appraisal* covers a variety of assignments, including valuation, consulting, and review.

2. The act or process of estimating value; an estimate of value. (USPAP, 1992 edition). *See also* appraisal review; consulting; valuation.

appraisal date. *See* date of value estimate.

Appraisal Foundation, The. A not-for-profit educational foundation, organized in 1987 to foster appraisal professionalism through the establishment of uniform standards of appraisal practice and qualifications for the state certification and licensing of appraisers. The Appraisal Foundation has 19 sponsors, who include organizations representing appraisers, users of appraisal services, and academia. The Appraisal Foundation has a Board of Trustees composed of 32 individuals responsible for funding and appointing the members to The Appraisal Foundation's two independent boards, the Appraisal Standards Board (ASB) and the Appraiser Qualifications Board (AQB). The Appraisal Standards Board promulgates the generally accepted standards of the appraisal profession, the Uniform Standards of Professional Appraisal Practice (USPAP). The Appraiser Qualifications Board establishes minimum experience, education, and examination criteria for state licensing of appraisers and recommends such criteria for state licensing of appraisers. Through the enactment of the Financial Institutions Reform, Recovery and Enforcement Act of 1989 (FIRREA), Congress delegated significant responsibility to these boards and gave the Appraisal Subcommittee of the Federal Financial Institutions Examination Council authority to monitor and review the practices, procedures, and organizational strategy of The Appraisal Foundation.

appraisal process. *See* valuation process.

appraisal report. The written or oral communication of an appraisal; the document transmitted to the client upon completion of an appraisal assignment. Reporting requirements are set forth in the Standards Rules relating to Standards 2 and 5 of the Uniform Standards of Professional Appraisal Practice.

appraisal report forms. Report forms prepared and used by lending institutions, government agencies, and employee transfer firms which process large numbers of appraisals. Standardized forms allow users to compare many appraisals quickly, to discern immediately whether all required information has been supplied, and to analyze the reported data with computers. Appraisal report forms include the Uniform Residential Appraisal Report form, the Individual Condominium or PUD Unit Appraisal Report form, the Small Residential Income Property Appraisal Report form, and the Employee Relocation Council Residential Appraisal Report form.

appraisal review. The act or procedure of critically studying a report prepared by another appraiser. (USPAP, 1992 edition)

Appraisal Standards Board (ASB). *See* Appraisal Foundation.

Appraisal Subcommittee. A subcommittee designated by Title XI of the Financial Institutions Reform, Recovery and Enforcement Act (FIRREA) of 1989 to be composed of representatives of the regulatory agencies belonging to the Federal Financial Institutions Examination Council (FFIEC) and the Department of Housing and Urban Development. The Appraisal Subcommittee is empowered to monitor state certification and licensing requirements for appraisers, review appraisal regulations set by federal regulatory agencies, and review the procedures and activities of The Appraisal Foundation. The Appraisal Subcommittee maintains a national registry of state certified and licensed appraisers and reports to Congress annually on the implementation of Title XI. *See also* Appraisal Foundation; Federal Financial Institutions Examination Council (FFIEC); federally related transaction; Financial Institutions Reform, Recovery and Enforcement Act (FIRREA); transitional licensure.

appraisal update. *See* update of an appraisal.

appraised value. *See* estimate of value.

appraiser. One who performs an appraisal.

Appraiser Qualifications Board (AQB). *See* Appraisal Foundation.

appreciation (*app*). An increase in property value resulting from an excess of demand over supply. *See also* inflation.

approaches to value. Systematic procedures used to derive value indications in real property appraisal. *See also* cost approach; income capitalization approach; sales comparison approach.

approach nose. An area of land between highways that faces approaching traffic, which may pass on either or both sides of this land.

approach zone. The designated path or corridor of air space through which aircraft may legally descend to or take off from an airport.

appropriation
1. The taking of a public thing for private use, e.g., the appropriation of water from a stream for a beneficial use. *See also* condemnation; eminent domain.
2. The dedication of land for a particular use, e.g., a public park, a school.

appurtenance. Something that has been added or appended to a property and has since become an inherent part of the property; usually passes with the property when title is transferred. *See also* fixture.

appurtenant easement. *See* easement appurtenant.

APR. *See* annual percentage rate.

apron
1. A hard-surfaced entrance to a loading dock or portion of a building.
2. A portion of a private driveway or roadway that connects with a public street or road.
3. A portion of a wharf or pier lying between the waterfront edge and the buildings.
4. A wooden barrier along a sea wall or the face of a dam.
5. The inside wood finish piece of a window underneath the sill.

aqueduct. An artificial channel to convey water from place to place; a major conduit that may be open or covered.

ARA. Agricultural Research Administration.

arable. Describes land suitable for cultivation; tillable.

arbitration. A process in which one or more individuals are selected by opposing parties to settle a dispute out-

side of court. The decision of an arbitrator is generally binding.

arbitrator. A person who decides a dispute to avoid a court determination.

arcade

1. A series of open or closed arches on the same plane.
2. A walkway or passageway with an arched roof, which frequently has shops along one or both sides.
3. A passageway that is open on the street side and is usually colonnaded.

arch. A convexly curved vertical span of steel, concrete, stone, or wood; a structural section with end base supports designed to support itself, the superstructure, and the attached or suspended structure.

architect's approval. An architect's written or imprinted acknowledgment that the materials, equipment, and methods of construction are acceptable for use in the work; a statement that a contractor's request or claim is valid.

architect's punch list. A list of items to be completed that is prepared by the architect during final inspection of a structure.

architect's standard net assignable area (usable area) The area available for assignment or rental to an occupant, including every type of usable space; measured from the inside finish of outer walls to the office side

of corridors or permanent partitions and from the centerline of adjacent spaces; includes subdivided occupant space, but no deductions are made for columns and projections. There are two variations of net area: single occupant net assignable area and store net assignable area.

architectural area of buildings. The sum of the areas of several floors of a building, including basements, mezzanines, and intermediate floors and penthouses of headroom height, measured from the exterior walls or from the centerline of walls separating buildings; may include one-half the area of covered walkways, open roofed areas, porches, and similar spaces; does not include pipe trenches, exterior terraces or steps, chimneys, or roof overhangs.

architectural concrete construction. Concrete with little or no reinforcement poured against a form that bears a design to produce a decorative treatment simulating stone masonry.

architectural style. The character of a building's form and ornamentation.

architectural volume of buildings. The sum of the products of the architectural areas of a building and the height measured from the underside of the lowest floor construction system to the average height of the surface of the finished roof.

architecture. The art and science of building design and construction.

architrave. The molding above and on both sides of a door or other rectangular opening.

area. The surface extent of a building, a site, a neighborhood, a section of a city, a tract, or a region, measured in square units. *See also* architect's standard net assignable area; architectural area of buildings; architectural volume of buildings; construction area; gross area; gross building area (*GBA*); gross leasable area (*GLA*); rentable area; store area; usable area.

area controls. A zoning provision limiting use densities.

area sample. A limited number of observations selected from a full aggregate of phenomena based on geographical location.

areaway. An uncovered space next to a building that provides for light, air, or access. *See also* light well.

ARES. *See* American Real Estate Society.

AREUEA. *See* American Real Estate and Urban Economics Association.

arithmetic mean. The sum of a series of values divided by the number of values in the group. It is the simplest, most commonly used average, but its value may be distorted by extreme figures.

ARM. Accredited Resident Manager, a designation conferred by the Institute of Real Estate Management (IREM).

ARM. *See* adjustable-rate mortgage.

arm's-length transaction. A transaction between unrelated parties under no duress.

arpent. An old French land measure of area used in Canada and in some parts of the southern United States; varying slightly but approximating 0.84625 acre. The side of a square arpent equals 2.909 chains, or 191.994 feet.

array. The listing of a set of observations in a specific order, e.g., alphabetical, alphanumeric, chronological, order of magnitude.

arroyo. A dry gully that can become flooded without warning.

Art Deco. A decorative style popular in the 1920s and 1930s that is based on geometric forms and patterns, sometimes derived from nature. The style promoted the use of ornamentation in architecture, furnishings, textiles, and decorative arts.

arterial highway. A major highway usually on a continuous or through route; describes the character of the adjacent use, not the character of the highway itself. *See also* axial theory; beltway.

Art Nouveau. A decorative style popular in the late 19th and early 20th centuries characterized by asymmetric, curvilinear forms inspired by nature. The style was used in all the arts and crafts of the period, including architecture and interior design.

asbestos. A generic name given to a number of naturally occurring hydrated mineral silicates that possess a unique crystalline structure, are incombustible in air, and are separable into fibers; formerly used as an insulating material in building construction, but found to be a health threat.

as-built drawings. Record drawings made during construction. As-built drawings record the locations, sizes, and nature of concealed items such as structural elements, accessories, equipment, devices, plumbing lines, valves, mechanical equipment and the like. These records (with dimensions) form a permanent record for future reference. (R.S. Means)

ASCP. American Society of Consulting Planners.

ASCII. American Standard Code for Information Interchange; a widely used standard for character representation which facilitates communication among different brands of computers.

ashlar. Squared stone carefully laid in a wall with uniform joint thickness; further described by the coursing as range, broken range, or random. Stone more than 12 inches thick is called *rough ashlar.*

aspect
1. Position facing, fronting, or regarding a particular direction, e.g., a house with a southern aspect; the part so fronting; also called *exposure.*
2. In forestry, the direction toward which a slope faces according to the main points of the compass.

asphaltic concrete. Asphalt binder combined with stone or another aggregate and used to produce a hard surface for streets, airstrips, and other paved areas.

asphalt tile. A resilient floor covering of asphaltic composition laid in mastic.

ASPO. American Society of Planning Officials.

assart rent. Rent paid for land that has been deforested.

assemblage. The combining of two or more parcels, usually but not necessarily contiguous, into one ownership or use. *See also* plottage.

assemblage cost. The excess cost incurred to acquire individual adjacent parcels of real estate in a single ownership beyond the estimated cost of acquiring similar sites that do not form a specifically desired assemblage.

assess

1. To estimate property value as a basis for taxation.
2. To fix or determine, e.g., by a court or commission, the compensation due a property owner for the taking of real property.

assessable improvement. An improvement that increases the value of a property and should, in the absence of a contrary law, increase the assessment.

assessed value. The value of a property according to the tax rolls in ad valorem taxation. May be higher or lower than market value, or based on an assessment ratio that is a percentage of market value.

assessment

1. The official valuation of property for ad valorem taxation.
2. A single charge levied against a parcel of real estate to defray the cost of a public improvement that presumably will benefit only the properties it serves, e.g., assessment for the installation of sidewalks, curbs, or sewer and water lines. *See also* special assessment.
3. An official determination of the amount to be paid by or to the owners of real estate to defray the cost of a public improvement that is presumed to benefit the properties it serves in an amount at least equal to the cost of the improvement, e.g., assessment of benefits and damages for public sewer or water lines.

assessment base. *See* property tax base.

assessment district. A jurisdiction, e.g., a county, under the authority of an assessor; may be a single tax district or encompass several districts.

assessment map. *See* tax map.

assessment period. The period during which all property in the assessment district must be reassessed; also called *assessment cycle* or *assessment frequency.*

assessment process. The discovery, listing, and valuation of property for taxation purposes.

assessment ratio. The relationship between assessed value and market value. *See also* equalization.

assessment roll. A public record that shows how the property tax levy is allocated among the property owners in a jurisdiction with taxing powers; usually identifies each taxable parcel in the jurisdiction, the name of the owner of record, the address of the parcel or the owner, the assessed value of the land, the assessed value of the improvement(s), applicable exemption codes if any, and the total assessed value. Also called *cadastre, list, grand list, abstract of ratables,* and *rendition.* (IAAO)

assessment/sales ratio. The number derived by dividing the assessed value by the selling price; used as a measure of the relationship between a property assessment and market value.

assessor

1. The head of an assessment jurisdiction. Assessors may be either elected or appointed. The term is sometimes used collectively to refer to all administrators of the assessment function. (IAAO)

2. One who discovers, lists, and values real property for ad valorem taxation.

assessor's manual. A manual that lists specific requirements for property assessment; used as a guide to ensure uniform treatment of similar properties.

asset. Any owned property that has value, including financial assets (cash or bonds) and physical assets (real and personal property). *See also* capital assets; cash assets; current assets; diminishing assets; fixed assets; intangible assets; liquid assets; working assets.

asset management. The process of maximizing value to a property or portfolio of properties from acquisition to disposition within the objectives defined by the owner. Asset management utilizes strategic planning which includes investment analysis, operation analysis, and the positioning of a property in the marketplace in accordance with market trends and conditions. (BOMA)

assignee. A person or corporation to whom a contract is assigned.

assignment. A written transfer of the rights of use and occupancy of a property to be held by another legal entity or to be used for the benefit of creditors, e.g., assignments of mortgages, sales contracts, and leases.

assignor. A person or corporation from whom a contract is assigned.

assisted housing. Housing for which the government provides assistance to facilitate occupancy, construction, or financing.

assumable mortgage. A mortgage in which the existing debt may be transferred to a third party without the approval of the lender.

assumed mortgage. An existing mortgage for which a new owner becomes liable when the property is purchased and transferred.

assumption of mortgage. A purchase of mortgaged property in which the buyer accepts liability for existing debt. The seller remains liable to the lender unless the lender agrees to release the seller.

assumptions and limiting conditions. For appraisal or analysis purposes, a list of assumptions and limitations on which an appraisal or analysis is based.

ASTM. *See* American Society for Testing Materials.

atrium. An open central area in a structure, typically surrounded by corridors. Many atriums have ceilings of translucent material that admit sunlight.

atrium house. A dwelling with an interior court onto which rooms open; may be of one or more stories, freestanding or joined in rows, groups, or clusters; a variation of the patio house.

attachment. Seizure of property by court order.

attic. Accessible space between roof rafters and ceiling joists

attic ventilators. Openings in a roof or in gables that allow for air circulation.

attorney-in-fact. One who is authorized to act for another under a power of attorney; power may be general or limited to certain acts.

attributes. The positive and negative characteristics of real estate that determine its productivity. Property productivity depends on physical, legal or regulatory, and locational attributes. *See also* productivity.

AU. *See* animal unit.

AUM. *See* animal unit month.

Austrian school. *See* marginal utility school.

authority. A government agency, usually independent, which is established for a specific purpose, e.g., to construct and operate housing projects, toll roads, turnpikes, ports, or public transportation.

auxiliary lane. A portion of pavement adjoining the traveled way, which is designed for parking, acceleration, deceleration, or another use that facilitates traffic flow.

average. *See* mean.

average absolute deviation. In statistics, the sum of the absolute differences, both positive and negative, between the individual observations and the average of all the observations, divided by the number of observations.

average daily room rate (ADR). In hotel analysis, total guest room revenue divided by the total number of occupied rooms.

average daily traffic (ADT). The average traffic volume measured at a selected highway location on a single day; the sum of all traffic recorded for a given period of time divided by the number of days in that period.

average deviation. In statistics, the number obtained by subtracting the arithmetic mean of all the items from each item, adding up these differences without regard to sign, and dividing this sum by the number of items.

average household income. Estimated average income, or salaried income, per household.

avigation easement. The right, acquired by government through purchase or condemnation from the owner of land adjacent to an airport, to the use of the air space above a specific height for the flight of aircraft; may prohibit the property owner from using the land for structures, trees, signs, or stacks above a specified height. The degree of the restriction is dictated by the glide angle required to use the airfield's runway safely.

avulsion. The sudden removal of land from the property of one owner to that of another, e.g, by inundation or a change in the course of a river. The land so removed remains in the original ownership.

awning. A roof-like shelter extending over an area, e.g., the deck of a ship, a doorway, a window, a porch, that provides protection from the sun or rain.

awning window. A type of window that has a sash with hinges at the top, which permit the window to open horizontally, forming an awning over the opening.

axial growth. Urban growth that takes the form of finger-like extensions radiating out along major transportation routes.

axial theory. A theory of land use development that postulates that land uses tend to develop in relation to the time-cost functions of transportation axes that radiate out from the central business district. A beltway around the metropolitan area may link these arterial axes at or near the perimeter. Also called *radial corridor theory. See also* urban growth theories.

azimuth. The angle between an object and true north or true south. In surveying, the azimuth is measured clockwise from true north.

azonal soil. A soil without horizons, insufficiently developed, and lacking a definite soil profile.

B

back band casing. A common buttcasing with a molded and/or mitered trim piece around its outer edge.

backfill

1. To replace earth removed during excavation.
2. The subsurface material placed against structures, foundations, or footings.

backland theory. A legal theory which asserts that in a partial taking of a tract of land with different zones of value, compensation is based on the property of lower value (even if higher valued property is taken) provided the same amount of higher valued land can be reestablished after the taking. This theory is inherent in the federal before-and-after rule of appraisal. When the state rule is required, the backland theory is not usually applicable because the condemnor is required to pay the value of the property taken. *See also* before-and-after rule.

backup

1. The cheaper material in a masonry wall that is covered by more expensive, ornamental material, e.g., face brick, stone, marble, metal panels.
2. In computer usage, an extra copy of a program or data file stored in a safe place, usually on a diskette or magnetic tape, to be used in case the original is damaged.

backwater valve. An automatic valve set in the sewer lateral to prevent sewage from backing up during periods of flooding.

balance. The principle that real property value is created and sustained when contrasting, opposing, or interacting elements are in a state of equilibrium.

balanced operation

1. An enterprise in which the gross income produced either equals or exceeds the cost of production.
2. In ranching, a livestock enterprise that provides sufficient feed and forage resources in each season to sustain its livestock and game throughout the year.

balance outstanding (*B*)

1. The unpaid amount of a loan at any point in time.
2. The present value of the debt service on a level-payment loan over the remaining amortization period discounted at the interest rate.

balance sheet. An itemized listing of the total assets, total liabilities, and net worth of an entity.

balcony

1. A balustrade or railed platform that projects from the face of a building above the ground level; it has an entrance from the building interior and is usually cantilevered or supported by columns.
2. In a theater or auditorium, a partial upper floor furnished with seats.

balloon frame. In construction, a type of framing in which the studs extend from the sill to the roof. The second floor is supported by a horizontal ribbon or ledger board and joists that are nailed to the studs.

balloon mortgage. A mortgage that is not fully amortized at maturity, and thus requires a lump sum, or balloon, payment of the outstanding balance.

balloon payment. The outstanding balance due at the maturity of a balloon mortgage.

baluster. A short pillar or post that supports a rail and is usually circular and tapered at the top; the uprights supporting the handrail of a staircase.

balustrade. A row of balusters surmounted by a rail, coping, or cornice.

band of investment. A technique in which the capitalization rates attributable to components of a capital investment are weighted and combined to derive a weighted-average rate attributable to the total investment.

band sill. In the construction of pier-and-beam foundations, the two horizontal members that connect the pier to the floor joist. The boards are joined to create a right angle, and the joist is placed perpendicular to the upright board to give the foundation rigidity. Also called *box sill.*

banker's acceptance. A bank's obligation or promise to pay; similar to commercial paper in that it is a marketable, short-term obligation.

banking system. The institutions and agencies that oversee banking activity and regulate the money supply. In the United States, the banking system is under the direction of the Federal Reserve Bank, the Federal Deposit Insurance Corporation (FDIC), and the Office of the Comptroller of the Currency (OCC) of the Treasury Department. *See also* Federal Deposit Insurance Corporation (FDIC); Federal Reserve System; Office of the Comptroller of the Currency (OCC).

bar chart. A graphic method of presenting data in which bars of uniform width and varying height are used to indicate differences in the size of two or more variables.

bargain and sale deed. A deed that conveys real property from a seller to a buyer but does not guarantee clear title; used by court officials and fiduciaries to convey property they hold by force of law, but to which they do not hold title. *See also* deed; grant deed; quitclaim deed; warranty deed.

barn. A building specifically designed to house farm animals and store hay, grain, and equipment.

barrel. A unit of measure equal to 31½ gallons for liquids; 42 gallons for oil; or 376 pounds (4 sacks) of cement.

barren. A tract of land that has little or no natural vegetation, e.g., intermittent lake beds, saline flats, active sand dunes, shale, rock slides, lava flows.

basal area. In forestry, the cross-sectional area of a single tree or of all the trees in a stand, expressed in square feet.

basal area factor (BAF). The basal or stem area per unit of stand area for a given angle for each tree intercepted from a sampling point. The factor multiplied by the average number of trees counted per sample point yields the basal area in square feet per acre.

base

1. In compound interest tables, one plus the periodic rate; denoted by *S* in mortgage-equity formulas.
2. In building construction, the lowest part of a wall, pier, pedestal, or column.

base amount. Refers typically to the expense item or group of expense items that constitutes the base for escalation clauses in leases.

baseboard. A piece of finishing material placed at the bottom of interior walls to conceal the intersection of the wall and the floor.

baseboard heating. A system of perimeter heating with radiators, convectors, or air outlets located at the base of the wall where the baseboard would be; may be hot water, forced air, or electric. Also called *base panel heating.*

base line

1. In the government survey system of land description, a line running due east and west through the initial point of a principal meridian from which township lines are established.
2. The topographic centerline of a survey such as one to delineate the route of a highway.
3. In construction, an established line from which measurements are taken when laying out building plans or other working plans.

base map. A map with enough points of reference, e.g., state, county, or township lines, and other physical features to facilitate the plotting of data.

basement. The lowest story of a building, which may be partially or wholly below ground level. *See also* cellar.

base mold. A decorative strip of molded material laid along the top of a baseboard.

base periods. Time intervals or reference points used for business and economic data. In the formulation of index numbers, the figures for a base period are usually averaged and the average is represented as 100.

base plate. The horizontal member at the bottom of a column or post that transmits the column load to its foundation. *See also* anchor bolt.

base property. The private holdings of a stock raiser, i.e., fee-owned land, water sources, or private leased property, used as the base required to issue a grazing permit on public domain under the Taylor Grazing Act.

base rent. The minimum rent stipulated in a lease. *See also* rent.

base sale. In paired data set analysis, the sale against which other sales are compared.

base year. The year on which escalation clauses in a lease are based.

basic activities. In economic base analysis, activities that produce goods intended for export to other areas. *See also* economic base analysis; nonbasic activities.

basic building code. A performance-type building code prepared by Building Officials and Code Administrators International (BOCA) and adopted for use by a number of midwestern counties and cities. (Marshall & Swift)

basic capacity. The maximum number of automobiles that can pass a given point on a lane or roadway during one hour under the most ideal roadway and traffic conditions obtainable; often reported as automobile units of capacity.

basic crops. Staple commodities, e.g., corn, wheat, cotton, tobacco, rice, peanuts, that are often subject to price supports.

basic multiplier. The ratio of an area's total economic activity (total employment) to basic activities (basic employment).

basic rate (r). In yield capitalization, the portion of the overall capitalization rate that provides for all investment requirements except change in income (Δ_I) and value (Δ_O). The part of the mortgage-equity formula that corresponds to the basic rate is $Y_E - M(Y_E + P\, 1/S_n - R_M)$.

basis. In income taxation, the portion of total property value most likely to be affected by depreciation or capital improvement; the dollar amount attributed to a property from which capital gains or losses upon resale are computed. *See also* adjusted basis.

basis point. One one-hundredth of one percentage point; used to express changes in interest rates and in the yields of stocks and bonds, which must be expressed in fractions of a percent.

batch processing. A computer operation which involves the processing of a number of programs using the same database in a single, continuous run.

bathroom. A room containing a toilet, a lavatory, and a bathtub or shower.

batten. A narrow strip of wood used to cover a joint between boards or to simulate a covered joint for architectural purposes.

batter. The slope of a wall, terrace, pier, or bank from the perpendicular. The vertical incline is generally expressed in inches horizontal to inches vertical.

batture land. Land situated between the water's edge at low tide, or low water stage, and the river bank or levee; generally held in the same ownership as the abutting land, but it can be sold separately from the adjoining land.

Bauhaus. A school of design founded in Germany in 1919 by Walter Gropius to synthesize the fine and applied arts by incorporating architecture, painting, sculpture, and industrial arts into one curriculum; a style based on using then-current technology to meet utilitarian requirements and unify the design and materials.

bay. The interior building space between columns or piers.

bay depth. The distance from the tenant side of the corridor wall to the exterior wall of the structure.

Bayesian analysis. A statistical technique in which probabilities, called *prior probabilities,* are assigned to a set of mutually exclusive and exhaustive events on the basis of whatever evidence or information is currently available; when additional evidence is obtained, the initial prior probabilities are revised using Bayes Theorem. The probabilities resulting from the revision process are called *posterior probabilities. See also* posterior distribution.

Bayesian decision rule. A rule that states that one should choose the action that is expected to optimize the expected gain and minimize the expected loss, where gains and losses are defined in terms of utility or cash.

Bayes' theorem. A formula central to the Bayesian approach to statistical estimation which is used to incorporate sample information about a particular situation into the total amount of information available and revise prior probabilities.

bay window. A window that forms a bay in a room and projects outwardly from the wall. It is supported by its own foundation, as distinguished from an oriel or box bay window which lacks foundation support.

beam
1. A principal load-supporting member of a building, typically horizontal in position; may be made of wood, steel, or concrete.
2. The lumber in a rectangular cross section of a building, five or more inches thick and eight or more inches wide. *See also* bond beam; cantilever beam; constrained beam; grade beam.

beamed ceiling. A ceiling with exposed beams. A false beamed ceiling has ornamental boards (box beams) or timbers that are not load-bearing.

bearing
1. The position or horizontal direction of one point or object with respect to another object or to the points of the compass.
2. The portion of any building member that rests on its supports.

bearing capacity. *See* bearing value of the soil.

bearing partition. *See* bearing wall.

bearing value of soil. The ability of the soil and other underlying material to support a load, e.g., a foundation and a building.

bearing wall. A wall that supports part of a building, usually a floor or the roof above it. *See also* wall-bearing construction.

bed and breakfast. A house, generally an older renovated residence, where lodging and breakfast are provided to paying guests. *See also* boarding house; rooming house.

bed a tree. To prepare the path where a tree is to fall so that it will not shatter.

bed mold. An ornamental strip laid horizontally at the juncture of the frieze and cornice soffit. *See also* base mold.

bedrock. The solid rock underlying soils and other surface formations.

bedroom community. A suburban community where a large number of residents work in another location.

before-and-after rule. In eminent domain valuation, a procedure in which just compensation is measured as the difference between the value of the entire property before the taking and the value of the remainder after the taking. *See also* backland theory; state rule.

before-tax cash flow. *See* pre-tax cash flow (*PTCF*).

bellwether stocks. Stocks whose performance serves as an indicator of trends.

belt course. A continuous, horizontal layer of distinctive masonry usually, but not necessarily, of decorative natural or cast stone around an exposed wall or walls of a masonry building; laid at one or more levels between the water table and the cornice.

beltway. An arterial highway that carries traffic partially or entirely around an urban area and is connected with the city by principal streets or highways. *See also* arterial highway; axial theory.

bench mark. Identification symbols inscribed on stone, metal, or other durable objects permanently fixed in the ground from which differences in elevation are measured for tidal observations or topographical surveys.

benchmark. The standard or base from which estimates are made.

beneficial interests
1. Benefits, profits, or advantages resulting from a trust contract.
2. The equitable title in a property, as distinguished from the legal title.

beneficial use
1. The right to the enjoyment of property when legal title is held by one person and the right to use the property is held by another.
2. In water rights, the doctrine that holds that the water resources of the state must be put to their most beneficial use. In some states, this doctrine supersedes the doctrine of riparian rights. *See also* riparian rights.

beneficiary of trust deed. The lender, who is one of three parties in a trust deed agreement. The borrower, or trustor, gives the title to a third party, the trustee, who holds the title in trust for the benefit of the borrower and the lender.

benefit/cost ratio. *See* profitability index (*PI*).

benefits. In eminent domain valuation, the advantageous factors that arise from a public improvement for which private property has been taken in condemnation. *See also* general benefits; set-off rule; special benefits.

bent
1. A transverse frame designed to support horizontal or vertical loads, e.g., elevated railroad tracks.
2. A section of a tobacco shed.

BEPS. *See* Building Energy Performance Standard.

berm
1. A horizontal ledge or bench partway up a slope.
2. A mound of earth, sometimes paved, that is used to divert or control the flow of surface drain-

age, mark property boundaries, or alter topography.

3. The earthen or paved extension of a roadway; the shoulder along a highway.

Bernard Rule. A method of appraising corner lots in which each lot is assumed to be two identical lots (one facing each of the streets) and each is appraised using the appropriate average-unit-value rate. The values are then summed to yield the total value of the whole lot. (IAAO)

betterment. Substantial improvements to real property representing capital expenditures that constitute more than mere repairs.

beveled siding. Clapboard.

B horizon. The subsoil; a layer of deposit to which materials are added by percolating water; the horizon lying beneath the A horizon. *See also* A horizon; C horizon; D horizon.

bidet. A toilet-like bathroom fixture used for hygienic washing of the lower private part of the body. (Marshall & Swift)

bidirectional. In computer usage, the ability of a printhead to print right to left as well as left to right, which enables the printer to operate quickly.

bikeway. A continuous path designated for the use of bicycles and other self-propelled vehicles.

bilevel. A house built on two levels. In different parts of the country, *bilevel* may denote a two-story dwelling, a raised ranch (split-foyer), or a split-level (tri-level) dwelling. *See also* raised ranch; split-level house.

binary. In computer usage, a numbering system that uses combinations of only two numerals, 0 and 1. This numeric structure is employed by all computers. Also called the *base two system.*

binomial distribution. In statistics, a discrete distribution that characterizes situations in which samples are taken from a population of attributes with only two values, e.g., yes or no, success or failure.

birth rate. The number of births per 1,000 persons per year.

bit. In computer usage, a shortened term for binary digit; an electrical signal that represents either 0 or 1 in the binary system. Depending on the internal specifications of the computer, a group of eight, 16, 32, or even 64 bits may form one byte.

blacktop. Bituminous or asphaltic material used in hard surface paving.

blanket mortgage. A mortgage that covers more than one property; common in subdivision development and in situations where the equity in one property is insufficient to satisfy loan policy. Usually individual properties are released from the blanket mortgage as they are sold.

blended rate. An interest rate on a refinancing loan that is higher than the rate on the old mortgage but lower than the current market rate; found in wraparound mortgages.

blight

1. Decay caused by a failure to maintain the quality of real estate and public services in an area.
2. Describes plant diseases that cause withering and death of part or all of a plant.

blighted area. An area or district subject to detrimental influences, e.g., an adverse land use mix that is severe enough to undermine desirability and cause a decline in property values.

blind fund. *See* blind pool.

blind pool. An investment program in which monies are invested in an ownership entity by investors who do not know which properties will be purchased.

BLM. Bureau of Land Management.

block

1. A segment of a city; usually a square area lying between intersecting streets or other physical boundaries; the length of one side of such a square.
2. A preformed structural component made of concrete and used

in construction. *See also* concrete block.

blowdown. A tree or an area of trees blown down by the wind; also called *windslash.*

BLS. Bureau of Labor Statistics.

blueprint. A working plan used by workers on a construction job; an architectural drawing that is transferred to chemically treated paper using a strong light, which turns the paper blue and reproduces the drawing in white.

blue sky. The process of qualifying an issue, e.g., a real estate syndication, under a state securities act.

blue sky law. A state law that regulates the solicitation and sale of securities to protect investors.

board and batten. A type of siding, typically vertical, composed of wide boards and narrow battens. The boards are nailed to the sheathing with a space between them and the battens are nailed over these spaces.

board of equalization. A nonjudicial board that reviews assessments to see that all districts are assessed at a uniform level of value; authorized to raise or lower the assessments to achieve a uniform basis of taxation; also called *Board of Tax Review* or *Board of Appeals.*

board foot. A unit of lumber measurement that is one foot long, one foot wide, and one inch thick, i.e., one square foot, one inch thick (144 cubic inches). A board foot differs from a square foot in that it has depth and its dimensions are nominal, not actual, i.e., board measurements reflect size before dressing or planing.

boarding house. A house where lodging and meals are provided to paying guests. *See also* bed and breakfast; rooming house.

board measure
1. A system for measuring lumber. Quantities of lumber are designated and priced in terms of board feet. *See also* board foot.
2. The volume of logs, trees, or stands measured in terms of the estimated amount of lumber they will yield according to various log rules; usually abbreviated B.M. Larger quantities are stated in thousands of board feet and abbreviated M.B.M. or M. *See also* log rules.

boards. Yard lumber eight or more inches wide and less than two inches thick.

boatel. An adjunct to a marina that provides guests traveling by boat with accommodations and services comparable to those of a motel.

BOCA. Building Officials and Code Administrators International, Inc.

bog soil. An intrazonal group of marshy or swampy soils underlying peat; common to humid or subhumid climates.

bole. The trunk of a tree.

bolster. In construction, a horizontal timber on a post used to lessen the free span of a beam.

bolt
1. Any of several types of strong fastening rods, pins, or screws, usually threaded to receive a nut.
2. A movable bar or rod that fastens a door or gate when slid into a socket.

BOMA. *See* Building Owners and Managers Association.

BOMA standard. The standard method of floor measurement for office buildings as defined by the Building Owners and Managers Association.

BOMI. Building Owners and Managers Institute. *See* Building Owners and Managers Association.

bona fide sale. A sale made in good faith that represents an agreement between the buyer and the seller at the current market price. *See also* arm's-length transaction.

bond. A capital market instrument with a maturity of one year or more. *See also* convertible bond; zero-coupon mortgage.

bond beam. A continuous beam placed in masonry walls to tie them together, add lateral stability, and distribute concentrated vertical loads along the wall; usually made of re-inforced concrete, but sometimes of reinforced brick or concrete block.

bond for deed. An executory contract for the sale of property that provides that the title remain with the grantor until the purchase price is paid; or-dinarily binding on both parties.

bond risk rating services. Independent rating agencies that identify the rela-tive level of risk associated with bond issuers meeting the promises specified on the bond. Moody's and Standard and Poor's are two espe-cially prominent bond risk rating services.

book cost. The cost of acquisition as shown on the general ledger of an individual, a partnership, or a cor-poration; generally includes direct and indirect financing and all devel-opment costs and excludes prelimi-nary operating losses.

book depreciation. An accounting term that refers to the amount of capital recapture written off on an owner's books.

book value. The capital amount at which property is shown on the ac-count books. The net amount at which an asset is carried on the books or reported in the financial statements; the asset's cost at acqui-sition, reduced by the amount of ac-cumulated depreciation on the asset. *See also* adjusted basis. (R.S. Means)

boom
1. A period of rapid economic growth characterized by the ex-pansion of business facilities and activities.
2. In construction, a heavy crane or lift arm. *See also* log boom.

boot
1. Any asset or liability transferred as part of an exchange of realty and given to make up for any difference in the value of the re-alty exchanged. Typical forms in-clude cash and debt existing prior to the exchange, purchase-money mortgages created within the ex-change, and debt instruments transferred in lieu of cash. *See also* realized gain; recognized gain.
2. In computing, to execute a boot-strap program.

bootstrap program. A program used to start a computer, which usually in-volves clearing the memory, initial-izing peripheral devices, and load-ing the operating system.

BOP. Beginning of period; often used to describe when scheduled payments are due, as distinguished from EOP (end of period).

BOR. Bureau of Outdoor Recreation.

boring test. A study of the load-bear-ing qualities of a subterranean sur-face performed by analyzing bore or drilling residue, called *core samples*.

borrow. Soil or other suitable material brought from outside a construction project and used for fill, regrading, or backfilling.

borrow bank. The source from which borrow (fill) is obtained.

borrowed light. Glazing of an interior partition that allows outside light to enter interior areas.

borrow pit. In the construction of highways and railroads, land that is excavated to obtain dirt for making fills. Often land is condemned to make a borrow pit.

bottom land. Low land in a valley or dale or along a river or lake that is often inundated with water. *See also* wetlands.

bottom rail. A horizontal member that forms the bottom of a window or paneled door; also called *bottom stile.*

boulevard. A broad street or promenade that is often planted with trees or grass along its border or on a median strip.

boundaries. The lines demarcating a neighborhood or district, i.e., the physical area that exerts relevant influences on a subject property's value; may coincide with changes in prevailing land use, occupant characteristics, or physical characteristics.

boundary survey. A closed diagram that mathematically depicts the complete outer boundary of a site; shows dimensions, compass bearings, and angles. A licensed land surveyor's signed certification is required, and a metes and bounds or other written description is included. (R.S. Means)

bounded description. The earliest form of land description in which property boundaries were described in terms of impermanent features, e.g., features of the terrain, fences, the ownership of adjacent property.

bowstring truss. A steel or wooden truss with a top member that resembles a bow or an arch.

box culvert. A rectangular-shaped, reinforced concrete drainage structure either cast in place or precast in sections. (R.S. Means)

box construction. A construction system using horizontal framing members to which vertical siding is attached; frequently used for farm buildings.

box girder. A girder with a hollow cross section similar to a rectangular box.

BPO. *See* broker's price opinion.

BRAB. Building Research Advisory Board.

brace. A structural member that reinforces a frame or truss.

braced framing. A type of heavy timber framing in which posts, girts, and braces are used to reinforce the frame, forming a more rigid structure than balloon framing.

bracket. A horizontal projecting support that bears an overhanging weight, e.g., a cornice, eaves. *See also* bracketing.

bracketing. A process in which an appraiser determines a probable range of values for a property by applying qualitative techniques of comparative analysis. The array of comparables are divided into two groups—those superior to the subject and those inferior to the subject. The adjusted sale prices reflected by these two groups limit the probable range of values for the subject and identify a bracket in which the final value estimate will fall.

Bradley fountain. A large, circular basin featuring a central column equipped with faucets or spray heads to provide washing facilities for several persons at one time; frequently found in industrial buildings.

branch store. A secondary or outlying store owned, supplied, and operated by a main store, which is generally larger and more centrally located. Common in shopping centers.

breakdown method. A method of estimating accrued depreciation in which the total loss in the value of a property is estimated by analyzing and measuring each cause of depreciation (physical, functional, and external) separately.

breakeven point. In real estate investment analysis, the point at which the cumulative income (effective gross income) of an investment property equals its cumulative loss (normal operating expenses plus debt service). *See also* payback period.

breakpoint. A method of calculating the level of retail sales over which a percentage rent is paid by the tenant; calculated as the base rent divided by the overall percentage rate. *See also* base rent; overage rent; percentage rent.

breast-height. In forestry, a height 4½ feet above the average ground level or the root collar; the height at which the diameter of a standing tree is ordinarily measured. *See also* diameter-breast-high (DBH).

breather roof. A roof on a storage tank that rises and falls with the level of the stored material, which is usually liquid; prevents loss through rapid vaporization and the mingling of gases with the outside air.

breeding herd. In ranch operations, the livestock retained to provide for the perpetuation of the herd.

breezeway. A covered passage, open at each end, which passes between two structures. (Marshall & Swift)

brick cavity wall. A wall with a space between the inner and outer tiers of brick. The space may be filled with insulation.

brick masonry. The arrangement or overlapping of bricks, blocks, or stones that ties a masonry wall together and adds to its strength. *See also* header; stretcher.

brick veneer. A single tier of brick used as decorative facing on a wall of another material.

bridge crane. A crane often used in manufacturing or assembling heavy objects. A bridge crane requires a bridge spanning to overhead rails. A hoisting device moves laterally along the bridge while the bridge moves longitudinally along the rails. (R.S. Means)

bridge financing. Short-term financing between 1) the termination of one loan and the commencement of another; 2) the acquisition of a property and the improvement or rehabilitation that will make it eligible for a permanent mortgage; or 3) the maturity of a construction loan and the negotiation of permanent financing.

bridging. Small wood or metal structural members inserted between joists or studs to give them lateral rigidity.

broad-leaved trees. A type of vegetation that includes all deciduous trees, e.g., aspen, cottonwood, maple, oak.

broker. A person who acts as an intermediary, bringing together two or more participants in a market transaction.

broker's price opinion (BPO). An opinion of property value rendered by a broker.

brooder house. A heated building for raising young fowl.

brownstone. A term usually referring to houses built, until about 1900, with a brown-colored, quarried, sandstone which was laid up in mortar. (Marshall & Swift)

browse-shrub. A type of range vegetation that includes foothills or mountain ranges where browse, but not sagebrush, predominates; characteristically located in the transition zone between the lower foothills and mountain slopes.

Btu. British thermal unit; a standard unit for measuring heat equal to the amount required to raise the temperature of one pound of water by one degree Fahrenheit. In the United States, the rated capacity of furnaces and boilers is expressed in terms of Btus emitted per hour. All heat sources, e.g., fuel oil, natural gas, electricity, are measured in Btus.

buck

1. Wood framework for a door opening in a masonry wall to which jambs and casings are attached.
2. A fabricated steel frame prefitted for doors in a masonry wall; may include the entire assembly, except the door. The entire assembly may also be called the *door buck.*

bucked. Cut into log lengths.

budget motel. A motel that can offer substantially lower rates due to high volume, lower initial investment costs, and efficient operations. *See also* microtel; motel.

buffer. In computer usage, a block of memory where data or characters are stored until the computer or peripheral is ready to process them.

buffer strip. A parcel of land, usually unimproved except for landscaping and screening, that separates parcels with different land uses.

bug. In computer usage, a problem in a program that has not yet been fixed; typically causes erratic performance in a piece of software.

builder-seller sponsor. The sponsor of a project that is undertaken specifically to be sold, immediately upon completion, to a private, nonprofit organization at the certified cost of construction.

building. A structure, usually roofed and walled, that is erected for permanent use.

building automation system. A network of integrated computer components that automatically control a wide range of building operations such as HVAC, security/access control, lighting, energy management, maintenance management, and fire safety control. (R. S. Means)

building block. Any rectangular masonry unit (except brick) used in building construction. Typical materials are burnt clay, concrete, glass, gypsum, etc. (R. S. Means)

building capitalization rate (R_B)

1. The rate used in certain residual techniques or in a band of investment to convert building income into an indication of building value.
2. The ratio of building income to building value.

building code. A local or state ordinance or regulation that controls the design, construction, alteration, repair, quality of materials, use, and occupancy of all buildings in the jurisdiction; enforced by police power in the interest of public health, safety, and welfare.

building description. The analysis of a building's design, layout, construction details, size, condition, current use, and alternative uses that provides the basis for comparing the subject property's improvements and the improvements typically accepted in the subject property's market.

Building Energy Performance Standard (BEPS). A standard requiring that a building be designed to meet a specified level of energy use per year.

building envelope. The walls, roof, and floors which enclose a heated or cooled space. (Marshall & Swift)

building height. Generally, the greatest vertical distance measured from curb or grade level to the highest level of a flat or mansard roof, or to the average height of a pitched, gabled, hip, or gambrel roof. Penthouses and the like are usually excluded if they do not exceed a specified height or their projected area is less than a specified percentage of the main roof. (R.S. Means)

building inspector. An official employed by a municipal building department to review plans and inspect construction to determine if they conform to the requirements of applicable codes and ordinances, and to inspect occupied buildings for violations of the same codes and ordinances. (R.S. Means)

building line
1. A line established by ordinance or statute. Between this line and the street line no structure is permitted although exceptions may be made for terraces or uncovered porches.
2. The outermost dimension of a building, generally used for building placement in relation to zoning or plot restrictions. (R.S. Means)

building orientation. The direction that a building faces.

Building Owners and Managers Association (BOMA). National association of professionals involved in the office building industry. BOMA publishes annual statistics on office buildings, e.g., the average amount of space required by typical office employees. The Building Owners and Managers Institute (BOMI) is the educational arm of BOMA.

building paper. A heavy, waterproof paper used as sheathing in wall or roof construction.

building permit. Authorization granted by a local government for the erection, alteration, or remodeling of improvements within its jurisdiction.

building residual technique. A capitalization technique in which the net operating income attributable to improvements is isolated and capitalized by the building capitalization rate (R_B) to indicate the improvements' contribution to total property value. When the improvements' value is added to land value, a total property value estimate is produced.

building restrictions. Limitations on building imposed by codes, easements, deed restrictions, or statute.

building service systems. The systems and components that provide a building with plumbing, sewerage, heating, ventilation, air-conditioning, lighting, power, vertical transport, fire protection, and special services, e.g., public address.

building site. A parcel of land on which a building may be erected, including all surrounding land allocated to the improvement.

building standards. Specific construction features that an owner or developer chooses or is required to use throughout a building.

built-in appliances. Those appliances which are permanent fixtures generally found in a residence. They are not included in the base costs and should be added separately. (Marshall & Swift)

built-ins. Items that are permanently attached to the building structure and cannot be removed without leaving evidence of removal, e.g., cabinets, counters, desks, benches, shelving, equipment. *See also* fixture; trade fixture.

built-up method. A method of identifying the compensable elements in the development of a discount rate or capitalization rate. There are four basic components of a discount or capitalization rate: the pure or riskless rate, management, nonliquidity, and risk. *See also* built-up rate.

built-up rate. An overall capitalization rate or discount rate that represents the combination of a safe, or risk-free, rate and rates that reflect nonliquidity, management, and risk.

built-up roofing. Roofing that is applied by laying felt paper in overlapping sheets and sealing the seams with hot asphalt or roofing compound. The final coat may be asphalt or asphalt covered with small gravel.

bulb tee. A rolled steel shape with a cross section resembling a bulbous T; often used as a purlin.

bulkhead

1. A retaining wall that is backed with solid fill and erected along the water to extend the upland out to the bulkhead line; serves as protection against tidal or watercourse erosion of land.

2. The wall beneath a store display window.

bulkhead line. A line in navigable waters, established by the federal government through the Army Corps of

Engineers, beyond which no solid filling is permitted; can be either in-shore from the structure limit line or coincident with it.

bulk regulations. Zoning laws or other regulations that control the height, mass, density, and location of buildings, setting a maximum limit on the intensity of development to ensure proper light, air, and open space. *See also* zoning.

bullet loan. Gap financing for leased-up properties used when the construction loan has expired and acceptable permanent financing has not yet been found; typically an interest-only loan for two to 10 years which cannot be prepaid.

bumper strips. Material placed along the outer edge of a loading dock to protect it from damage during the loading and unloading of trucks.

bundle of rights theory. The concept that compares property ownership to a bundle of sticks with each stick representing a distinct and separate right of the property owner, e.g., the right to use real estate, to sell it, to lease it, to give it away, or to choose to exercise all or none of these rights.

burden

1. The loose material that overlays bedrock.
2. The depth of material to be moved or loosened in a blast. (R.S. Means)

Bureau of Public Roads. A unit of the Federal Highway Administration of the U.S. Department of Transportation that administers federal grants-in-aid to states for the construction and maintenance of major highways; cooperates with the U.S. Department of Agriculture and the U.S. Department of the Interior in the construction of roads in national forests, national parks, and elsewhere.

Bureau of Reclamation. A major bureau of the U.S. Department of the Interior that is engaged in irrigation projects and related activities, e.g., the construction of dams, reservoirs, power plants, transmission lines, canals, tunnels, and aqueducts; supplies water to arid sections of 17 western states.

burn off. Amortization of prepaid interest and other similar prepayments.

bus bar. A conductor or an assembly of conductors that collect and distribute electrical current to feeders.

bus duct. A conduit for a conductor or assembly of conductors that collect and distribute electrical current to feeders.

business cycle. A recurring cycle of economic activity that moves through prosperity, recession, depression, recovery, and back to prosperity. *See also* real estate cycle.

business valuation. The appraisal of a business, usually performed to determine the present and future monetary rewards of complete or partial ownership of the business.

business value. A value enhancement that results from items of intangible personal property such as marketing and management skill, an assembled work force, working capital, trade names, franchises, patents, trademarks, contracts, leases, and operating agreements. *See also* going-concern value.

business, types of. *See* generative business; shared business; suscipient business.

butt. A door hinge.

buttcasing. A very plain casing formed by installing a piece of material across the top of an opening and bringing up two side pieces to butt against it from beneath.

butterfly roof. An inverted gable roof with two sides that slope downward and inward, forming an inverted ridge in the center. The two gables resemble the wings of a butterfly.

butt joint. A joint formed when two timbers or members are joined by butting, or meeting end to end.

butt log. The log in a tree that is closest to the stump.

buttress. An external structure, usually of brick, stone, or concrete, that supports a wall or building by receiving lateral pressure at a particular point and in a single direction.

buy a job. Accept a construction contract at bare cost or below. (R.S. Means)

buydown. A lump-sum payment to the lender that reduces the interest payments of the borrower. The cost of the buydown is usually reflected in the price paid.

buyer's extras. Improvements not included in original plans or cost figures, but requested by the buyer.

buyer's market. A depressed market in which buyers have the advantage; exists when market prices are relatively low due to an oversupply of property.

buying power. *See* disposable income; purchasing power.

BX. Electrical cable consisting of two or more wires in a flexible metal covering.

bypass. *See* beltway.

byte. In computer usage, the smallest identifiable unit of information in a computer; consists of at least eight bits; equivalent to one alphanumeric or graphic character or to a single control code. *See also* kilobyte (K); megabyte.

C

CAA. Civil Aeronautics Administration.

CAB. Civil Aeronautics Board.

cabana. A small shelter of open, tent, or wood-grain construction placed near swimming pools or the shoreline. (R.S. Means)

cabin

1. A small, simple hut or house.
2. A rustic shelter often made of logs. (R.S. Means)

cabinet work. Any interior finish, usually in hardwoods, that involves the skills of cabinetmakers rather than carpenters; built-in fixtures, e.g., kitchen cupboards, counters.

CAC. Central air-conditioning.

cadastral map. A scale map showing the dimensions of each parcel and related information such as parcel identifier, survey lines, and easements. Annotations on recent sales prices and land values are sometimes added. (IAAO) *See also* tax map.

cadastre. An inventory of the land in an area by ownership, description, and value. (IAAO) *See also* assessment roll.

CAE. Certified Assessment Evaluator, a designation conferred by the International Association of Assessing Officers.

caisson. A large, strong, watertight box or casing in which work is done below water level, usually under artificial air pressure; also used as a retaining structure in an open excavation to prevent cave-ins; used as a supporting member of a structure when sunk to a high bearing stratum and filled with concrete.

caisson foundation. A foundation system in which holes are drilled into the earth down to bearing strata and then filled with concrete.

calcareous soil. A soil containing carbonate of calcium, or limestone.

calf crop. The number of calves produced by a given number of cows, usually expressed as a percentage of calves weaned of cows bred.

calibration. The process of estimating the coefficients in a mass appraisal model. (IAAO)

California ranch architecture. A modern residential style that originated in California and is characterized by a sprawling, one-story design that is easily adapted to floor plan variations.

call provision. A clause in a mortgage or deed of trust that gives the mortgagee or beneficiary the right to accelerate payment of the debt if the mortgage security is sold or transferred. *See also* due-on-sale clause.

CAM. *See* common area maintenance.

CAMA. *See* computer-assisted mass appraisal.

camber
1. In construction, slight, convex arching of a load-bearing beam, girder, or timber to compensate for, and thus eliminate, sagging or concavity due to superimposed weight.
2. The slight arching of a structure, e.g., a road, the deck of a ship.

campanile. A tall bell tower; usually detached from the building. (Marshall & Swift)

canal
1. An artificial, open watercourse that joins rivers, lakes, or seas for inland navigation.
2. A channel used in irrigation.

candle. A measure of light intensity approximately equal to the light from a 78-inch sperm candle burning at the rate of 120 grains per hour.

candle power. The luminous intensity of a light expressed in candles.

canopy
1. An overhanging shelter or shade covering.

2. An ornamental rooflike structure over a pulpit. (R.S. Means)

cantilever
1. The part of a structural member that extends beyond its support and is rigid enough to support loads and resist lateral pressure.
2. Either of two structural members that project from a pier and are joined directly or by a suspended span to form the span of a cantilever bridge.

cantilever beam. A beam with one end that projects beyond the point of support and is free to move under the influence of vertical loads placed between the support and the free end.

cantilever construction. A building technique in which a portion of the structure is supported by one or more cantilever beams.

cap
1. A ceiling, or limit, on monetary charges, e.g., rent, interest, escalation income.
2. The top part of a structural member, e.g., a column, a door, a molding; a cornice or lintel.
3. A threaded plumber's fitting used to close a pipe end.

capacity
1. In land utilization, the input of labor and capital expressed in terms of the number of dollar

units that can profitably be expended on any given area.

2. The ability of land to provide vegetation to support livestock; ordinarily expressed as the number of acres required to feed an animal unit continuously for one month (AUD) or for a year (CYL); the number of head a specific ranch will carry on a year-long basis. *See also* range capacity formula.

3. The ability of a roadway to carry traffic. *See also* basic capacity; possible capacity; practical capacity.

Cape Cod house. A residential architectural style, popular from the 1920s to the 1950s, that is a development of the one-story cottage; characterized by the main cornice line at the second-story level, a sloping roof, and dormer windows.

capital

1. Accumulated wealth; a sum of money available for investment.

2. In building construction, the uppermost part of a column, usually ornamented.

capital assets

1. Assets of a permanent nature used to produce income, e.g., land, buildings, machinery, equipment.

2. In accounting, the liquid or readily convertible assets of a corporation as of a certain date, e.g., cash, accounts receivable, merchandise inventories. *See also* current assets.

capital expenditure. Investments of cash or the creation of liability to acquire or improve an asset, e.g., land, buildings, building additions, site improvements, machinery, equipment; as distinguished from cash outflows for expense items that are normally considered part of the current period's operations.

capital expense. The amount required to satisfy the interest on and amortization of an investment; also called *capital charge.*

capital gain. The amount by which the net proceeds from the resale of an asset exceed the adjusted cost, or book value, of the item; used primarily in income tax computations; may be short or long term. The Tax Reform Act of 1986 eliminated the special treatment of capital gains. *See also* capital loss.

capital grant. A cash contribution to the cost of a project, usually supplied by government.

capital improvement plan. A schedule of capital improvement projects that the government intends to complete over a specified period of time; includes project descriptions, a schedule of priorities, cost estimates, and methods of finance.

capitalism. An economic system based on the principles of private property ownership and personal rights.

capitalization. The conversion of income into value. See also direct capitalization; yield capitalization.

capitalization in perpetuity. Capitalization in which the discount rate equals the overall cap rate. Capitalization in perpetuity is applicable when a property is expected to generate level net operating income for a finite period and then be resold at the original purchase price.

capitalization of ground rental. A procedure used to estimate the value of leased land.

capitalization rate *(R).* Any rate used to convert income into value.

capital loss. The amount by which the net proceeds from the resale of an asset fall short of the adjusted cost, or book value, of the item; used primarily in income tax computations; may be short or long term. *See also* capital gain.

capital market. The interaction of buyers and sellers trading long- or intermediate-term money instruments.

capital recapture. The return of equity in an investment as distinguished from the return on equity. Investment capital may be recaptured through annual income or it may be recaptured all or in part through resale of the property at the termination of the investment; also called *capital recovery.*

capital recovery. The return to investors of that portion of their property investment expected to be lost over the income projection period. Capital recovery may be viewed in either a physical sense, as reflected in the traditional physical residual techniques of capitalization, or in a financial sense as reflected in mortgage-equity analysis. Capital recovery is not interchangeable with the term *depreciation. See also* capital recapture.

capital recovery method. One of several alternative methods that provide for the recovery of capital, each of which can be expressed in the form of a sinking fund; also called *capital recapture method.*

capital recovery payments. Annual amounts to cover the anticipated decline in capital from the initial investment until the reversion; *also called* capital recapture payments.

capital recovery period. The period over which invested sums are returned to the investor.

capital recovery rate. The return of invested capital, expressed as an annual rate; often applied in a physical sense to wasting assets with a finite economic life; used interchangeably with *amortization rate* to express investors' desire to recover their equity investment over a specified time period; also called *capital recapture rate.*

capital requirements. The total monetary investment needed to establish and operate an enterprise; usually the appraised investment in plant facilities and normal working capital; may or may not include the appraised cost of business rights, e.g., patents, contracts.

capital stock. The permanently invested capital of a corporation contributed by the owners at the time the corporation is organized or afterwards. Capital stock is divided into shares, with each share representing a proportionate ownership interest in the corporation; shares are issued as stock certificates that usually can be transferred only by endorsement.

capture rate. The estimated percentage of the total potential market for a specific type of property, e.g., office space, retail space, single-family homes, that is currently absorbed by existing facilities or is forecast to be absorbed by proposed facilities. The capture rate of a retail center depends on the size of its trade area, the anchor tenants in the facility, competition within the trade area, and the relative position of the subject facility compared to the competition.

car float bridge. A landing place where railroad cars are transferred between tracks on the shore and tracks on floats; a movable section of a lighterage pier that accommodates itself to the change in water elevation and is used for the same purpose.

carport. A roofed auto shelter that is not completely enclosed.

carriage port/porch. A canopy structure that extends from the doorway of a building over a driveway. (R.S. Means)

carryback financing. *See* purchase-money mortgage (PMM).

carrying capacity. The maximum number of animals that can be grazed without damaging the forage production, quality, or soil of the range; expressed in AUs, AUMs, or CYLs.

carrying charges. Expenses incurred on idle property or property under construction, e.g., taxes, insurance premiums, standby water and sewer rents, security or protective service.

case. The framework of a structure; the external facing of a building that is made of material superior to the backing.

casement window. A type of window with a sash and side hinges.

cash. Money, especially ready money; money on deposit or due on demand.

cash assets. Cash on hand and working funds immediately available to satisfy current business needs.

cash basis. A method of accounting in which income and expenses are recognized when they are actually received or paid out. For income tax purposes, taxpayers use either a cash basis or an accrual basis and recognize and report their income accordingly. *See also* accrual basis.

cash crop. Farm crops grown for direct sale, as distinguished from those fed to farm animals.

cash equivalency analysis. The procedure in which the sale prices of comparable properties sold with atypical financing are adjusted to reflect typical market terms.

cash equivalent. A price expressed in terms of cash, as distinguished from a price expressed totally or partly in terms of the face amounts of notes or other securities that cannot be sold at their face amounts.

cash flow. The periodic income attributable to the interests in real property. *See also* after-tax cash flow *(ATCF)*; pre-tax cash flow *(PTCF)*.

cash flow analysis. A study of the anticipated movement of cash into or out of an investment. (USPAP, May 1992)

cash flow dividend. *See* equity dividend.

cash on cash. The ratio of annual equity income to the equity investment; also called *equity capitalization rate, cash flow rate,* or *equity dividend rate.*

cash rent
1. The amount of rent paid in money, not including services rendered in lieu of cash.
2. A fixed, negotiated money rent for a farm, usually in dollars per acre per year.

cash throw-off. Net operating income minus annual debt service; also called *before-tax cash flow. See also* equity dividend.

casing. A piece of trim material used around the sides and top of doors, windows, and other wall openings. *See also* back band casing; butt–casing.

casualty loss appraisal. An appraisal to estimate the decrease in property value resulting from a fire, storm, or some other casualty; usually performed for income tax or insurance claim purposes.

catena. A group of soils within one zonal region that developed from similar parent material but differ in solum characteristics due to differences in relief or drainage. *See also* solum.

cathodic protection. A form of protection against electrolytic corrosion of fuel tanks and water pipes submerged in water or embedded in earth. Protection is obtained by providing a sacrificial anode that will corrode in lieu of the structural component, or by introducing a counteracting current into the water or soil. This type of protection is also used for aluminum swimming pools, cast-iron water mains, and metal storage tanks. (R.S. Means)

catslide style. A regional name for salt box architecture used in the southern United States.

cattle guard. An opening in a fence that is closed, not by a gate, but by a ground grill that cattle will not cross.

cattle squeeze. A mechanism in a corral chute that closes on the animal and immobilizes it so that various treatments, e.g., branding, dehorning, can be performed.

catwalk. In construction, a narrow footing on a bridge or along a girder of a large building; a walkway strung from one girder to another or placed over uncovered attic joists.

caulking. A flexible material, e.g., sealant, putty, glazing compound, used to fill gaps at fixed joints in a building to reduce the passage of air and moisture; to apply such material. *See also* grout.

causeway. A raised roadway on fill material or a bridge-like structure over a low area, e.g., a swamp, a lake, a bay.

caveat. A formal notice, filed by an interested party with a court or official, requesting that a proceeding be postponed until he or she is heard.

caveat emptor. Let the buyer beware; a maxim of the common law stating that the buyer purchases at his or her own risk.

cavity wall. A wall, usually of masonry, that consists of two vertical components with air space between. An exterior masonry wall in which the inner and outer wythes are separated by an air space, but tied together with wires or metal stays. Also called *hollow masonry wall* or *hollow wall* (R.S. Means)

CBD. *See* central business district.

CCC. Community Credit Corporation.

CCIM. Certified Commercial Investment Member, a designation conferred by the Commercial Investment Real Estate Institute. *See also* Commercial Investment Real Estate Institute.

CC&R. *See* covenants and restrictions.

CCRC. *See* continuing care retirement centers (CCRC).

CD. *See* certificate of deposit (CD).

CEA. Council of Economic Advisors; Community Exchange Authority.

CEBA. *See* Competitive Equality Banking Act of 1987.

CED. Committee for Economic Development.

ceiling joists. The horizontal structural members to which the ceiling is fastened; may support a floor above.

ceiling loan. A part of a loan that will be disbursed when special requirements are met, e.g., rent roll achievement. *See also* floor loan.

cellar
1. A storage space usually, but not necessarily, below ground. *See also* basement.
2. An underground chamber.

cellular concrete. A lightweight, insulating concrete.

cellular steel deck. A structural floor system consisting of two layers of sheet metal shaped to form cells and welded together; the cells serve as electrical raceways.

cement. The binding agent in mortar and concrete. *See also* concrete.

cement blocks. Blocks composed principally of cement and gravel formed into shape under pressure; typically used for walls.

census tracts. Relatively uniform areas of approximately 4,000 residents into which large cities and adjacent areas are divided by the U.S. Census Bureau.

center line profile map. A type of right-of-way map that shows the center line elevation profile of a proposed roadway.

center to center. The measurement between the centers of two adjoining, parallel structural members. *See also* on center (O.C.).

central assessment. An assessment of property, e.g., railroads, public utilities, commercial and industrial property, held under a single ownership but located in more than one assessment district.

central business district (CBD). The core, or downtown area, of a city where the major retail, financial, governmental, professional, recreational, and service activities of the community are concentrated. *See also* node; uptown.

central city. The primary city in a standard metropolitan area, from which the name of the area is usually taken. *See also* metropolitan statistical area (MSA); primary metropolitan statistical area (PMSA).

central limit theorem. In statistics, a principle that identifies the tendency of the arithmetic mean to be normally distributed in a given number of size increases, almost without regard to the shape of the distribution of the original population.

central place theory. The theory that cities arise in response to the service needs of surrounding rural areas and that the location of urban settlements can be understood in terms of the functions they perform for these outlying areas. *See also* urban growth theories.

central processing unit (CPU). The intelligent component of a computer system containing circuitry to interpret and execute program instructions. The CPU includes a control unit, an arithmetic-logic unit, and an internal memory.

central tendency. In statistics, the tendency of samples to cluster around a central point, or representative value, in a frequency distribution. The measures of central tendency are the mean, the median, and the mode.

CEQ. Council on Environmental Quality.

CERCLA. *See* Comprehensive Environmental Response, Compensation, and Liability Act of 1980.

certificate. An instrument that formally assures the existence of a fact or set of facts; used as evidence of a right or obligation.

certificate of beneficial interest. A document that identifies an owner's interest in the assets and earnings of a business enterprise; may be issued to stockholders when the stock of a corporation is surrendered to a trustee or trustees.

certificate of deposit (CD). A financial instrument that represents a time deposit with a banking organization.

certificate of limited partnership. A summary of the major provisions of a limited partnership agreement, which is filed in the county recorder's office in the county where the partnership operates its business.

certificate of occupancy (C of O). A written document issued by the governing authority in accordance with the provisions of the building permit. The certificate of occupancy indicates that in the opinion of the building official, the project has been completed in accordance with the building code. This document gives the owner permission from the authorities to occupy and use the premises for the intended purpose. (R.S. Means)

certificate of reasonable value. A document required for a federally insured or guaranteed loan that states the value on which the loan amount may be granted.

certificate of title. A document, usually given to a home buyer with the deed, which states that the title to the property is believed to be clear;

usually prepared by an attorney or another qualified person who has examined the abstract of title for the property.

certification of value. A part of the introduction to an appraisal report in which the appraiser certifies that the statements of fact presented are correct to the best of his or her knowledge; that the analysis and conclusions are limited only by the reported assumptions and conditions; that the appraiser has no (or the specified) interest in the subject property; that the appraiser's compensation is not contingent upon any aspect of the report; that the appraisal was performed in accordance with the Code of Professional Ethics and Standards of Professional Practice of the Appraisal Institute, which may review the report; that the appraiser has (has not) satisfied continuing education requirements; that the appraiser has (has not) made a personal inspection of the property; and that no one, except those specified, has provided assistance in preparing the report.

certiorari

1. A writ from a superior to an inferior court officer, board, or tribunal directing that a certified record of its proceedings in a designated case be reviewed.
2. A remedy calling for judicial review of an alleged illegal or er-

roneous tax assessment of real estate.

cesspool. An underground catch basin for household sewage or other liquid waste. *See also* septic tank.

chain

1. A chainlike measuring instrument consisting of wire links.
2. A surveyor's chain is 66 feet long, each link being 7.92 inches long. A mile is 80 surveyor's chains; one acre is 10 square chains.
3. An engineer's chain consists of 100 wire links, each a foot long. A mile is 52.8 engineer's chains.

chain link fence. A fence made of steel wire fabric supported by metal poles. (R.S. Means)

chain of title. A historical record of all conveyances and encumbrances affecting a property title from the time the original patent was granted. *See also* abstract of title.

chain store. One of a number of retail stores or shops under the same ownership and management which sell uniform merchandise and follow a uniform policy.

chamfer. To bevel or round off a right-angle corner.

change. The result of the cause and effect relationship among the forces that influence real property value.

change order. A change in the original plan of construction due to the upgrading of material or the inclusion of additions.

channel

1. The bed of a stream; the deeper part of a river, harbor, strait, or bay where the main current flows; a ship's passageway.
2. A long gutter, groove, or furrow.
3. A closed course or conduit through which something flows or passes, e.g., a duct.

channelization. The direction of traffic flow into definite paths, accomplished with traffic markings, islands, or other means.

characteristic

1. In decimal arithmetic, the number or numbers to the left of the decimal point in a logarithm; as distinguished from the mantissa, the numbers to the right of the decimal point. *See also* mantissa.
2. *See* attribute.

chattel. In law, any property other than a freehold or fee estate in land; treated as personal property, although divisible into chattels real and chattels personal.

chattel interest. A nonownership right in real estate, such as a leasehold, easement, or lien.

chattel mortgage. A lien on chattels.

chattels personal. Tangible and movable items that generally constitute personal property.

chattels real. Intangible personal property rights that may be created by leases.

check rail. The horizontal members, or rails, that form the top of the lower sash and the bottom of the upper sash in a double-hung window; two rails in combination.

check row. A type of planting in which the plants are grown at the intersections of lines on a field resembling a checkerboard; frequently used for corn, melons, and tomatoes.

check valve. A plumbing valve that closes automatically, preventing the backflow of water or other liquids.

chernozem. A zonal group of soils with a deep, nearly black surface horizon, rich in organic matter, that grades into lighter-colored soils and finally into a layer of lime accumulation; developed under tall and mixed grasses in a temperate to cool, subhumid climate.

Chicago school. A school of architecture prevalent from 1875 to 1900 and noted for the development of the multistory commercial building with elevators, made possible by the new technique of riveted steel framing. The building exteriors were characterized by large areas of glass in indented bands of windows, terra-cotta facing, and elaborate projecting cornices. Among the leading exponents of the Chicago school were William Le Baron Jenney, Louis Sullivan, Daniel H. Burnham, and John Wellborn Root; the architects designed not only skyscrapers, but also residences, factories, railroad stations, theaters, museums, and churches.

chilled-water refrigeration system. A cooling system in which cold water is circulated to remote blower units. (R.S. Means)

chiller. A piece of equipment that utilizes a refrigeration cycle to produce cold (chilled) water for circulation to the desired location or use. (R.S. Means)

chimney. A stack of brick or other masonry that extends above the surface of the roof and carries smoke outside.

chimney back. The rear wall of a furnace or fireplace.

chimney cap. Ornamental stone or concrete edging at the top of the chimney stack that protects the masonry from the elements and improves the draft in the chimney.

chimney flashing. A strip of material, usually metal, placed where the chimney meets the roof to make the joint watertight; used wherever the slope is interrupted by a vertical structure.

chimney pot. A fire clay or terra-cotta pipe projecting from the top of the chimney stack which is decorative and increases the draft of the chimney.

chi-square (X^2) test. A statistical test used to determine the probability that observed frequencies differ from theorized expected frequencies.

chord
1. The top or bottom members of a truss (typically horizontal), as distinguished from the web members.
2. A straight line between two points on a curve. (R.S. Means)

C horizon. Soil layer of relatively unweathered material that lies below the B horizon; parent material; the substratum. *See also* A horizon; B horizon; D horizon.

chronological age. The number of years elapsed since an original structure was built. Also called *actual age* or *historical age*. (IAAO) *See also* effective age

cinder block. A building block similar to a concrete block which is made using cinders as the coarse aggregate to achieve a lighter weight.

cinder fill. In construction, a layer of cinder placed between the ground and the basement floor or between the ground and foundation walls to enhance water drainage.

circlehead window. A small, half-oval window often used as decoration over a door; resembles an open fan, with the ribs represented by the sash bars.

circuit breaker
1. In property taxation, a method used in some states to provide property tax relief for the elderly and poor by rebating, through income tax credits or cash payments, that portion of the taxpayer's payment that exceeds a certain percentage of his or her income; usually limited to residential property taxes paid by homeowners or renters.
2. A permanent electrical safety device that substitutes for a fuse by automatically turning off an electric circuit that is overloaded.

circuity of travel. Governmental changes in traffic patterns, street closures, the relocation of streets, or changes in roadway widths which have an adverse effect on access to or from a property, making access more roundabout or indirect than it was prior to the governmental action.

circulating capital. *See* current assets.

circulation pattern. The traffic pattern established in moving from one place to another on foot or by car, e.g., from home to business, to or past a specific location.

circulation system. A network of transportation modes that provides for the safe, efficient, and convenient movement of people and goods within a city or region.

circumferential highway. *See* beltway.

CIREI. *See* Commercial Investment Real Estate Institute.

cistern. An artificial reservoir or tank, often underground, that stores water, especially rainwater.

city. In the United States, a municipal corporation that occupies a definite area and is subject to the laws of the state in which it is located. In Canada, a municipality of the highest class.

city planning. The conscious control of growth or change in a city, town, or community, taking into account aesthetics, industry, utilities, transportation, and many other factors that affect the quality of life. (R.S. Means) Also called *urban planning*.

civic center. A building or place where a city's principal public and cultural institutions are concentrated.

civil law. A body of private law developed from Roman law; used in Louisiana and in many countries outside the English-speaking world. *See also* common law.

claims adjuster. *See* insurance claims adjuster.

clapboard. An exterior wood siding with one edge thicker than the other, which is laid so the thick edge of one board overlaps the thin edge of the board below.

Class A, B, C building. *See* class of building.

Class A, B, C, D, E (fire-resistance ratings). Fire-resistance ratings applied to building components such as doors or windows. Class A is an Underwriters' Laboratories classification for a component having a 3-hour fire endurance rating; Class B (interior component), a 1 or 1½ hour rating; Class C (interior component), a ¾ hour rating; Class D (exterior component), a 1½ hour rating; and Class E (exterior component), a ¾ hour rating. (R.S. Means) *See also* class of construction.

classical school. A school of economic thought that originated in England with Adam Smith's *Wealth of Nations* (1776) and included the writings of English economists such as David Ricardo, Thomas R. Malthus, and John Stuart Mill, as well as the French economist Jean Baptiste Say. In the writings of the classical economists, one's self-interest is assumed, and a person's economic behavior is generalized to reflect principles or laws which are believed to be universally applicable.

classical statistics. A theory of statistical inference in which the decision to accept or reject a hypothesis is based on sample information alone; distinguished from the Bayesian approach in which the analysis is extended to include the judgment of the decision maker and the economic payoffs involved.

classified basal area. In forestry, the grouping of the total land area tallied per sample point into diameter classes to record and describe forest growing stock.

classified property tax system

1. A system intended by law to tax various kinds of property at different effective tax rates. Thus two different kinds of property worth the same amount of money have different tax bills. Although this could be done by applying different tax rates to different kinds of property that share a common assessment ratio, the usual approach is to apply a uniform tax rate to all properties and establish by law what the assessment ratio should be for each class of property. (IAAO)
2. Loosely, by extension, a set of assessment practices that has this result contrary to laws requiring uniformity. (IAAO)

class of building. The classification of office buildings according to features such as location, construction, condition, management, tenants, and amenities. Class A space is characterized by superior location and access;

high-quality construction materials and condition; and professional management. Class A buildings are competitive with new buildings and attract high-quality tenants. Class B buildings have good location, management, and construction, but may suffer some physical deterioration or functional obsolescence. Tenant standards are high, but rents are below those charged for space in new or Class A buildings. Class C buildings are older (15 to 25 years) and may suffer notable physical deterioration and functional obsolescence. While Class C buildings are still a part of the active supply of office space, occupancy levels may be lower. Rehabilitated buildings constitute a separate class of office space.

class of construction. The classification of buildings according to the fire-resistance of the materials from which they are constructed, e.g., structural steel framing (Class A), reinforced concrete framing (Class B), masonry walls (Class C), wood or light steel framing (Class D). *See also* Class A, B, C, D, E (fire resistance ratings).

clay. Small mineral soil grains, less than 0.005 millimeter in diameter which are plastic when moist, but hard when baked or fired.

clay loam. A soil that contains a moderate amount of fine material mixed with coarser soil grains.

claypan. A dense, heavy soil horizon under the upper part of the soil that interferes with water movement and root development.

clean room. A special-purpose room that meets requirements for the absence of lint, dust, or other particulate matter. In a clean room the filter systems are high efficiency and the air exchange is one-directional laminar flow. (R.S. Means)

clearance. A type of urban renewal project in which the predominant activities are land acquisition, demolition and removal of structures, relocation of residents and businesses, and preparation of land for redevelopment.

clearance easement. A type of avigation easement that governs structure height to give aircraft an unobstructed view and a safety margin for descent.

clear cutting. A timber harvesting technique in which all growing stock is removed from the land.

clear headway. In construction, the vertical measurement from the floor of the structure to the lowest overhead framing member.

clear lumber. Lumber practically devoid of defects, e.g., knots.

clear span. A portion of a structure built without internal supporting columns.

clear title. A title free of any encumbrances or defects.

clerestory window. A window or series of windows placed at the top of a building that provide additional light and ventilation for the interior; usually found in churches and similar structures, but also used in modern residences.

client. Any party for whom an appraiser performs a service. (USPAP, 1992 edition)

climatic zone. A section of the country where residents experience similar climatic conditions as established by the number of heating and cooling degree days.

climbing crane. A hoisting device with a vertical portion that is attached to the structure of a building so that as the construction is built higher and higher, the crane rises along with it. (R.S. Means)

clock thermostat. A device designed to reduce energy consumption by regulating the demands on the heating or cooling system of a building. *See also* thermostat.

closed-end trust. A trust with a fixed number of shares that are traded on the open market like stocks and bonds, not sold and redeemed by the trust.

closing. A meeting of the parties to a real estate transaction held to execute and deliver mortgage or property title documents.

closing costs. The settlement costs incurred in the transferring of property ownership, e.g., recording fees, attorney fees, title insurance premiums.

closing date. The date on which ownership of a property is formally transferred from the seller to the buyer, i.e., the date on which the seller delivers title and the buyer pays the agreed-upon price for the property. *See also* contract date, date of value estimate.

closing statement. A listing of the debits and credits of the buyer and seller in the final financial settlement of a real estate transaction.

closure. In a metes and bounds description, the return to the point of beginning, which is necessary to ensure the accuracy of the survey.

cloud on title. An encumbrance that may affect the fee holder's ownership and the marketability of the title.

cloverleaf. A grade-separated intersection designed to eliminate all left-turn and cross-traffic conflicts and to accommodate turning movements from four directions; loops are used for left turns and outer connections facilitate right turns, or two-way ramps are provided for turning. A full cloverleaf has two ramps for turning movements in each quadrant.

cluster sampling. In statistics, a two-stage sampling procedure in which a population is divided into several groups or clusters; some of these clusters are drawn into the sample, and then a subsample of elements is selected from each of the specified clusters.

cluster zoning. A type of residential zoning designed to preserve open space by permitting houses to be built in groups or clusters on less land than would normally be permitted under the zoning ordinance.

CMO. *See* collaterized mortgage obligations.

CMS. Cadastral Mapping Specialist, a designation conferred by the International Association of Assessing Officers.

CMSA. *See* consolidated metropolitan statistical area.

coarse-textured soil. A soil that contains a preponderance of grains larger than 0.25 millimeter, e.g., sandy loams, gravelly sandy loams, loamy sands.

Coastal Zone Management Act. A nationwide land planning measure that gives the U.S. federal government control over virtually any large-scale development along the shorelines of 30 coastal and Great Lakes states.

coat. A single layer of paint, plaster, or other material.

coefficient

1. A dimensionless statistic used as a measure of change or relationship, e.g., coefficient of multiple regression, coefficient of determination.

2. A number, a letter, a group of letters, or a combination of numbers and letters that precedes another variable by which it is to be multiplied; e.g., 2 is the coefficient of X in the expression $2X$.

coefficient of correlation (r). In statistics, a measure of the relationship between variables and the degree to which they change together. The correlation coefficient can range in value from -1 (perfect negative correlation) to 0 (independence) to +1 (perfect positive correlation).

coefficient of determination (r²). In statistics, the proportion of the total variance in the dependent variable that is explained by the independent variables; the proportion of total variance explained by the regression. In business and economics, the coefficient of determination is preferred to the term *coefficient of correlation* because it states the proportion of the variance in the dependent variable more clearly.

coefficient of dispersion

1. In statistics, the ratio of a measure of absolute dispersion to an appropriate average, usually ex-

pressed as a percentage; computed from either the quartile or the mean deviation, but usually expressed as a ratio of the standard deviation to the mean; a measure of relative dispersion.

2. In assessment administration, the ratio of a measure of absolute dispersion to the median. Also called *index of assessment inequality* or *Russell index*. *See also* coefficient of variation.

coefficient of multiple correlation *(R)*. In statistics, the square root of the coefficient of multiple determination.

coefficient of multiple determination *(R²)*. In statistics, an indication of the proportion of total variance in the dependent variable explained by all independent variables in the regression equation; the ratio of explained variance to total variance.

coefficient of partial determination. In statistics, an indication of the increase in explained variance, relative to prior unexplained variance, produced by adding a given variable to the regression equation.

coefficient of performance. A measure of operating efficiency expressed as a ratio of useful energy output to input; indicates in percentage terms the portion of the fuel input that is converted to useful heating or cooling.

coefficient of skewness. In statistics, a measure expressed in standard deviation units that is used to compare distributions that differ in the unit of measurement or in average size; of limited practical use because skewness is ordinarily described, not measured.

coefficient of variation. In statistics, the standard error of the estimate divided by the mean value of the dependent variable; a measure of the relative chance for error in a forecast or estimate of the dependent variable. *See also* coefficient of dispersion.

cofferdam. A temporary, watertight enclosure from which water is pumped to expose underwater land so that work can be done there; a caisson; a similar structure on the side of a ship used in making repairs below waterline.

C of O. *See* certificate of occupancy.

COG. Council of Government.

cogeneration. The simultaneous production of electrical energy and low-grade heat from the same fuel.

cohort group. A demographic grouping based on a shared characteristic such as age, e.g., all people between the ages of 15 and 24.

coignes. In architecture, stone or contrasting material used at the corner of a masonry wall, normally of alternating size and larger units than the remainder of the wall.

coil. A term applied to a heat exchanger that uses connected pipes or tubing in rows, layers, or windings, as in steam heating, water heating, and refrigeration condensers and evaporators. (R.S. Means)

coinsurance. The amount of insurance an insurer requires a property owner to carry; equal to a specified percentage of the property's value.

cold cellar. An underground storage area where fruit and vegetables are stored during the winter. Constant ground temperatures keep the contents from freezing and retard rotting.

cold storage. Refrigerated storage of perishable commodities.

collar tie. *See* tie beam.

collateral. Security offered as a guarantee for the fulfillment of a financial obligation.

collaterized mortgage obligations (CMOs). Bonds issued and sold in capital markets on debt collaterized by pools of Ginnie Mae, Fannie Mae, Freddie Mac, and conventional institutional mortgages. CMOs are an important source of liquidity for the mortgage industry.

collinearity. In statistics, the relationship between independent variables in a multiple regression, which may affect the reliability of the net regression coefficients; affects the reliability of individual variables in a regression, but may not alter the predictive power of the total regression equation. *See also* multicollinearity.

colluvial soil. Soil material that has been transported by gravity or water; usually found at the base of a steep hill or slope.

colonnade. A group of columns at regular intervals, usually supporting an architrave.

column. A vertical structural member that supports horizontal members, e.g., beams, girders; designed to transmit a load to bearing material at its base.

column footings. Reinforced concrete footings that support load-bearing columns.

column lots. Small sections of land acquired with air rights for the placement of the columns, piers, and caissons needed to construct a foundation.

column steel. A vertical bar of reinforcing steel in a concrete column; an H-shaped, structural steel member used as a column.

combination door. An outer door frame with an inside removable section into which a screen panel is inserted in warm weather and a glass panel in winter.

combination sewer. A sewer that carries both sewage and surface water or rainwater.

combination windows. An outer window frame with an inside removable section into which a screen is inserted in warm weather and a glass storm panel in winter.

commensurability. The measure of a rancher's ability to take care of his livestock without using public land; the property so used is called *commensurate property. See also* base property.

commercial bank. A privately owned institution that offers businesses and individuals a variety of financial services; may be state or federally chartered and is subject to government regulation; managed by boards of directors who are selected by stockholders.

commercial condominium. The application of the condominium concept to commercial, industrial, or office space.

commercial facility. Defined under the Americans with Disabilities Act (ADA) of 1990 as a facility, intended for nonresidential use, whose operations affect commerce; broadly interpreted to include commercial establishments that do not fall under the definition of public accommodation, e.g., office buildings, factories, other places of employment. *See also* Americans with Disabilities Act (ADA) of 1990.

Commercial Investment Real Estate Institute. An affiliate of the National Association of Realtors which confers the CCIM (Certified Commercial Investment Member) designation.

commercial paper. A corporation's promissory notes used to borrow short-term funds for current operations; through trading, organizations with excess cash lend to those in need of money.

commercial property. Real estate used for business purposes, e.g., office buildings, stores, banks, restaurants, service outlets.

commission. An agent's compensation for performing his or her duties; in real estate, a percentage of the selling price of property or a percentage of rentals that is received by the agent.

commitment. For a mortgage, a promise or statement by the lender of the terms and conditions under which the loan will be made.

commitment fee. A fee paid by a borrower to a lender who agrees to make funds available at a future date; frequently expressed as a percentage of the expected loan.

committee deed. A deed by a committee or commission appointed by a court of competent jurisdiction to sell a property.

common area. The total area within a property that is not designed for sale or rental, but is available for common use by all owners, tenants, or their invitees, e.g., parking and its appurtenances, malls, sidewalks, landscaped areas, recreation areas, public toilets, truck and service facilities. (ULI)

common area charges. Income collected from owners or tenants for the operation and maintenance of common areas; typically specified in retail leases. (ULI)

common area maintenance (CAM). The expense of operating and maintaining common areas. *See also* common area.

common base. In construction, a single-member base, usually from four to six inches high.

common costs. Costs for items that benefit more than one portion of a project or more than one project within a development, e.g., hallways and elevators in a condominium, streets, parking areas, amenities.

common law

1. A body of customs, usages, and practices developed by the Anglo-Saxons; English law as distinguished from Roman law, canon law, and other legal systems.
2. An ancient, unwritten body of law founded on customs and precedents, as distinguished from statute law.

3. A system of elementary rules and judicial principles that is continually expanded in response to changes in trade, commerce, arts, inventions, and the needs of society.

common property. Land in general or a tract of land that is considered public property, in which all persons enjoy equal rights; property not owned by individuals or government, but by groups, tribes, or formal villages. In law, the incorporeal, heritable right of one person in the land of another, e.g., of estovers (to forage for timber), of pasture, of piscary (to fish).

common stock. A share of ownership that usually represents a voting interest in a corporation.

common wall. A single wall used by two buildings or two sections of a single building. *See also* party wall.

community associations. Organizations formed for the ownership, maintenance, and operation of commonly owned facilities. (ULI)

Community Development Corporation. A corporation set up within the U.S. Department of Housing and Urban Development in 1970 to administer the new communities program. The corporation establishes policy for new communities on a wide range of subjects including loan guarantees, project selection, and work-out problems.

community facilities
1. Facilities used in common by a number of people and often owned by the general public, e.g., streets, schools, parks, playgrounds.
2. Facilities owned and operated by nonprofit private agencies, e.g., churches, settlement houses, recreation and neighborhood centers.

community facility loan. A type of loan that the Farmers Home Administration offers to communities of less than 10,000 which can show that commercial credit is not available at reasonable terms. Long-term, low-interest loans are available for projects such as water and waste disposal systems, the relocation of roads, and the acquisition of land and rights of way for the development of community facilities, as well as for the purchase and construction of a wide range of equipment and buildings.

community property. Property acquired by either spouse during their marriage, excluding gifts or inheritances, which belongs to them as a unit and not individually. The death of either person results in full ownership for the other.

community reinvestment act. A provision of the Housing Act of 1977 requiring the Office of Thrift Supervision, the Federal Reserve Board, and the Federal Deposit Insurance Corporation to assess and periodically report to Congress on the ability of their constituent lending institutions to meet the credit needs of their communities, especially low-income neighborhoods.

community renewal program. An urban planning program under which governmental grants may be extended for preparing community-wide blueprints for urban renewal. The law specifically contemplates such broad activities as:

1. Identification of blighted or deteriorating areas in the community
2. Measurement of the nature and degree of blight and blighting factors in the areas
3. Determination of the financial, relocation, and other resources needed to renew the areas
4. Identification of potential project areas and types of urban renewal action contemplated
5. Scheduling of urban renewal activities

community shopping center. A shopping center of 100,000 to 300,000 square feet that usually contains one junior department store, a variety store or discount department store, a supermarket, and specialty stores. A community shopping center generally has between 20 and 70 retail tenants and the market support of more than 5,000 households.

comparables. A shortened term for similar property sales, rentals, or operating expenses used for comparison in the valuation process; also called *comps*.

comparative analysis. The process by which a value indication is derived in the sales comparison approach. Comparative analysis may employ quantitative or qualitative techniques, either separately or in combination.

comparative-unit method. A method used to derive a cost estimate in terms of dollars per unit of area or volume based on known costs of similar structures that are adjusted for time and physical differences. *See also* cost estimating.

comparison goods. Merchandise offered by department, apparel, furniture, and other stores in sufficient variety to permit a wide range of choice between the merchandise offered by each store.

comparison method. *See* sales comparison approach.

compatibility. The concept that a building is in harmony with its use or uses and its environment.

compensable damages. Damages for which a condemnor is legally required to compensate the owner or tenant of the property that is being wholly or partially condemned. In most jurisdictions, physical invasion of the property by a condemning authority or the taking of some property right must occur before damages are considered compensable. *See also* consequential damages; inverse condemnation.

compensable interest. A property right for which the owner would receive just compensation if it were acquired for public purposes.

compensation. *See* just compensation.

competition. Between purchasers or tenants, the interactive efforts of two or more potential purchasers or tenants to make a sale or secure a lease; between sellers or landlords, the interactive efforts of two or more potential sellers or landlords to complete a sale or lease; among competitive properties, the level of productivity and amenities or benefits characteristic of each property considering the advantageous or disadvantageous position of the property relative to the competitors.

Competitive Equality Banking Act (CEBA) of 1987. Legislation that paved the way for the Financial Institutions Reform, Recovery and Enforcement Act (FIRREA) of 1989 by establishing guidelines on appraisals performed for the five federal financial institutions regulatory agencies.

competitive supply. *See* supply.

competitive supply analysis. A market study that identifies the citywide supply of properties competitive with the subject property and rates these properties against the subject based on their locational and amenity attributes. Supply analysis is used to define the primary trade area for the subject property and to determine the amount of competitive space in this area.

compiler. In computer usage, a language translator that converts programs, commands, and statements expressed in high-level, English-like languages into machine language for execution.

complementary properties. A property or property type that is complementary to the subject; the users of the subject property benefit from access to complementary properties because the integration of properties with complementary uses often has a synergetic effect. Also called *support facilities.*

completed contract method. In accounting, a method of revenue recognition used in long-term construction contracts when the date of completion cannot be forecast. Revenue and related costs are recognized when the project is completed.

completion date. The date certified by the architect when the work in a building, or a designated portion thereof, is sufficiently complete, in accordance with the contract docu-

ments, so that the owner can occupy the work or a designated portion thereof for the use for which it is intended. (R.S. Means)

completion list (punch list). The final list of items of work to be completed or corrected by the contractor. (R.S. Means)

complex. In real estate, a group of buildings, site improvements, and support facilities designed to carry out related activities in a single location, e.g., apartment complex, office complex; a concentration of similar buildings in a given area such as a group of hospital buildings or an industrial park.

component. Construction elements, e.g., complete exterior walls, framing, floor and roof construction, interior finish, building service systems, that are considered individually.

component construction. *See* prefabrication.

component depreciation. Allocating the cost of a building to its various structural components and computing the depreciation in each component based on its useful life.

component (split) financing. Splitting a property into its fee and leasehold interests and financing each component separately to obtain optimum benefits from the financial package. Component financing is involved in financial packages such as sale leaseback and fee subordination combined with a leasehold mortgage.

component panel. A wall unit that is ready for installation and consists of a panel with finished inner and outer surfaces, or skins, framing, insulation, etc. Panels may be solid or include door and window framing.

composite rate. An overall rate; a blend or weighted average of several rates of return applicable to a single investment; represented by R in the Ellwood formulation. *See also* blended rate; weighted rate.

composition shingles. Shingles made from felt impregnated and covered with asphalt, then coated on the exposed side with colored granules. (R.S. Means)

composition siding. A manufactured exterior wall covering often finished to resemble brick.

compound amount of one. *See* amount of $1($S^n$)$.

compound amount of one per period. *See* amount of $1 per period (S_n).

compound discount. Successive deductions from a future sum or sums receivable at specified future dates to reflect present worth. Mathematically it is the obverse of compound interest. *See also* discounting.

compound interest. The continuous and systematic additions to a principal sum over a series of successive time periods so that previously earned interest earns interest.

compound slope. A slope made up of two or more slopes with different gradients.

Comprehensive Environmental Response, Compensation, and Liability Act (CERCLA) of 1980. Federal legislation providing for the establishment of a superfund to expedite the cleanup of contaminated sites. Under CERCLA, liability is adjudicated on a strict, joint, several, and retroactive basis.

comprehensive plan. An official document adopted by a local government that sets forth its general policies regarding the long-term, physical development of a city or other area.

Comptroller of the Currency. *See* Office of the Comptroller of the Currency (OCC).

computer-assisted mass appraisal (CAMA)

1. The application of computer technology and statistical techniques to the solution of appraisal problems; used in assessment administration to derive value indications in the cost and sales comparison approaches and to perform other functions, e.g., assessment ratio analysis.

2. A system of appraising property, usually only certain types of real property, that incorporates sta-

tistical analyses such as multiple regression analysis and adaptive estimation procedure to assist the appraiser in estimating value. (IAAO)

computer floor. A prefabricated floor system installed over pedestal grid supports to provide a raised or access floor. (Marshall & Swift)

computer program. *See* software.

concealed heating. *See* radiant heating.

concentrates. In agriculture, milled and blended high-protein feed used to supplement farm-grown forage.

concentric zone theory. A theory of urban growth, developed by Ernest W. Burgess in the 1920s, which holds that predominant land uses tend to be arranged in a series of concentric, circular zones around a city's central business district. *See also* urban growth theories.

concession

1. An inducement for a tenant to lease space, usually in the form of free rent, an additional tenant improvement allowance, moving costs, etc.

2. A franchise for the right to conduct a business, granted by a governmental body or other authority.

3. A lease which allows a tenant to conduct a business on the property of another.

conclusion of value. *See also* certificate; final value estimate.

concrete. A hard, stone-like material formed by mixing sand, cement, and an aggregate such as crushed stone or gravel with water and allowing the mixture to harden. *See also* cement; poststressed concrete; prestressed concrete.

concrete block. Concrete compressed into a block, hardened, and used as a masonry unit.

concrete construction. *See* architectural concrete construction; reinforced concrete construction.

concrete, foamed. Concrete to which a chemical foaming agent has been added. The result is a light, porous material, full of air holes, with low strength and good thermal properties. (R.S. Means)

concrete, prestressed. Concrete members with internal tendons that have been tensioned to put a compressive load on the members. When a load is applied to a prestressed member, compression is decreased where tension would normally occur. (R.S. Means)

concrete, reinforcement. Metal bars, rods, or wires placed within formwork before concrete is added. The concrete and the reinforcement are designed to act as a single unit in resisting forces. (R.S. Means)

concretion. Local concentrations of certain chemical compounds, e.g., calcium carbonate, compounds of iron, that form hard grains or nodules of mixed composition in various sizes, shapes, and colors.

concurrency. Pertaining to laws in certain states that hold developers financially accountable for the installation of infrastructure and the cost of any environmental remediation.

condemnation. The act or process of enforcing the right of eminent domain. *See also* eminent domain.

condemnation blight. The diminution in the market value of property due to pending condemnation action.

condemnation value. A misleading term for the value to be compensated in a condemnation. The value sought under the laws applicable in condemnation is market value. *See also* market value.

condemnee. The owner of the property right taken in eminent domain.

condemnor. The taking agency; a federal, state, county, or municipal government, another public authority or a utility vested with the right of eminent domain.

conditional probability. The probability of one event given the occurrence of another.

conditional sale. *See* contract sale.

conditions, covenants, and restrictions (CC&R). *See* covenants and restrictions; restrictive covenant.

condominium
1. A form of fee ownership of separate units or portions of multi-unit buildings that provides for formal filing and recording of a divided interest in real property.
2. A multiunit structure or property in which persons hold fee simple title to individual units and an undivided interest in common areas.

condominium conversion. Conversion of rental properties, e.g., residential, commercial, office, or industrial buildings, into condominium ownership.

conduction. Transmission through a conductor; the transfer of heat from one object to another, as distinguished from convection or radiation.

conductor
1. A substance or body capable of transmitting heat, electricity, etc.
2. A wire or cable through which electricity flows.
3. A rod used to carry lightning to the ground; a lightning rod.
4. A pipe that carries rainwater from the roof gutter to the drain pipe; a downspout.

conduit

1. An artificial or natural channel for the conveyance of water or other fluid, e.g., pipe, canal, aqueduct, flume.
2. A pipe or tube used to convey and protect electric wires or cables.
3. The conveyance of income from one entity to another so that the final recipient incurs tax liability.

conduit system. An electrical wiring system with conductors encased in metal tubing.

confidence interval. In statistics, the specification of a zone within a population, based on a sample mean and its standard error, within which one may be confident the true mean lies.

conformity. The appraisal principle that real property value is created and sustained when the characteristics of a property conform to the demands of its market.

congregate housing. Multiunit, often rental housing facilities for the elderly which provide an array of common services such as housekeeping, daily communal meals, transportation, organized activities, and security, but generally not health care. *See also* elderly housing.

conifer. Trees or shrubs that bear cones; as range vegetation, includes all rangeland dominated by coniferous timber with supporting grasses, forbs, or browse.

connection. A part that fastens, joins, links, or unites, e.g., bolted connections that unite structural steel columns, girders, and trusses in a building.

consequential damages. Damage to property caused by a taking or construction on other lands. Compensability varies from state to state.

conservation

1. As applied to real estate, the protection of neighborhoods and structures from blight or other influences that might affect their desirability or value adversely.
2. As applied to natural resources, the care and preservation of limited resources to prolong their use and effectiveness.

conservation easement. A restriction that limits the future use of a property to preservation, conservation, or wildlife habitat.

consideration. The recorded price for which title to a property is transferred.

consistent use. The concept that land cannot be valued on the basis of one use while the improvements are valued on the basis of another. The concept of consistent use must be addressed when properties are devoted to temporary interim uses. Improvements that do not represent the land's highest and best use, but have substantial remaining physical lives, may have an interim use of temporary value, no value at all, or even negative value if substantial costs must be incurred for their removal.

consolidated metropolitan statistical area (CMSA). A large geographic area that consists of two or more primary metropolitan statistical areas (PMSAs); designated under standards set in 1980 by the Federal Committee on MSAs. *See also* metropolitan statistical area (MSA); primary metropolitan statistical area (PMSA).

constant. A number, characteristic, or item that does not vary in value or amount. *See* mortgage constant (R_M).

constant amount change per period. A type of increasing or decreasing annuity or income/property model that increases or decreases by a fixed amount; also called *straight-line change per period.*

constant dollar change per period annuity. A type of increasing or decreasing annuity that increases or decreases by a fixed dollar amount.

constant dollars. Dollars that account for real growth only, not for inflation.

constant-payment mortgage. A mortgage that has an unvarying debt service, although the amortization and interest payments of which it is composed vary. If the debt service pays off the loan in full at maturity, the constant-payment loan is described as *self-liquidating. See also* variable-payment mortgage (VPM).

constant ratio change per period annuity. A type of increasing or decreasing annuity or income/property model that increases or decreases at a constant ratio and, as a result, the increases or decreases are compounded; also called *exponential curve change per period annuity.*

constrained beam. A beam that is rigidly fixed at one or both points of support.

construction. The process or manner of building an improvement; the completed building. *See also* proposed construction; new construction.

construction area. A measurement used primarily for determining building cost or value; not used for leasing purposes except when an entire building is leased to a single tenant. The construction area of a floor is computed by measuring to the outside finished surface of permanent outer building walls. The construction area of a building is computed as the sum of the construction area of all enclosed floors of the building, including basement floors, mechanical equipment floors, and penthouse floors. The American National Standards Institute equates construction area with gross building area. (BOMA)

construction cost. The cost to build, particularly an improvement; includes the direct costs of labor and materials plus the contractor's indirect costs.

construction loan. Financing arranged for the construction of real estate; generally a short-term, floating-rate debt repaid with the proceeds from permanent financing. Construction loans with a permanent financing commitment are designated as loans "with a takeout commitment"; those that do not have permanent financing are loans "without a takeout commitment." May include a very small permanent component to see the property from the post-construction phase through full absorption.

construction manager. One who directs the process of construction, either as the agent of the owner, as the agent of the contractor, or as one who, for a fee, directs and coordinates construction activity carried out under separate or multiple prime contracts. (R.S. Means)

constructive notice. The accessibility of public records; notice is assumed by the existence of the records. The law presumes that an individual has the same knowledge of all instruments properly recorded as if he or she were actually acquainted with them.

consulting. The act or process of providing information, analysis of real estate data, and recommendations or conclusions on diversified problems in real estate other than estimating value; also called *analysis* or *evaluation.* (USPAP, 1992 edition)

consumer good. A durable or nondurable economic good that satisfies a human want.

Consumer Price Index (CPI). A measurement of the cost of living determined by the U.S. Bureau of Labor Statistics; the principal cost of living index and measure of inflation.

contaminated sites. *See* hazardous waste/contaminated sites.

contemporary. A type of modern architecture designed to promote a close relationship with the outdoors, to incorporate new construction methods and materials, and to create new uses for old materials. The style is characterized by large windows, open planning, horizontal lines, and simple details.

contingency. An amount included in the construction budget to cover the cost of unforeseen factors related to construction. (R.S. Means)

contingent fees. Remuneration that is based or conditioned on future occurrences or conclusions or on the results of the services to be performed.

contingent interest. Interest that may be added to a loan's fixed interest rate. The loan commitment calls for an additional fixed interest rate, which is a percentage of the annual gross or net project income that exceeds a base amount to be paid to the lender.

continued occupancy clause. A lease provision that conditions the continued occupancy of one tenant upon the occupancy of another, usually an anchor tenant in a multitenanted retail center.

continuing care retirement center (CCRC). A newer, modified version of the lifecare center that is distinguished by its method of financing. Residents are charged either monthly maintenance and entrance fees or pay on a fee-for-service basis. A CCRC includes a residential complex, with units ranging from cottages to high-rise apartments; a common area including administrative, dining, and activities areas; and a health center with nursing beds and an infirmary or clinic. *See also* congregate housing; elderly housing; lifecare facilities.

continuous distribution. In statistics, a distribution in which the random variable can take on any value within the interval, rather than a restricted set of values, e.g., only integers.

continuous growth. Growth as it occurs in nature; in finance, growth at compound interest with instantaneous compounding or compounding at infinitely short time intervals.

continuous windows. Windows designed for sawtooth roofs or roof monitors of industrial buildings; usually top hinged and opened mechanically.

contour furrows. Furrows plowed at right angles to the direction of the slope, at a constant level, and usually at comparatively close intervals. The furrows and the ridges they produce intercept and retain runoff water, thereby facilitating erosion control, moisture distribution, penetration, and retention.

contour leveling. Land leveling in an area with little change in elevation, resulting in terraced land.

contour line. An outline of a figure, body, or mass; lines representing an outline such as the edge of a lake, e.g., on a topographic map or chart; a line connecting the points on a land surface that have the same elevation.

contour map. A map that shows the configuration of a surface with contour lines that represent regular intervals of elevation.

contract. An agreement between two or more persons that represents their promise to do or not to do a particular thing; where real property is concerned, a dated, written, signed statement between two or more competent parties who agree to perform or not to perform a legal act, for legal consideration, within a specified time. *See also* installment contract; land contract.

contract date. The date on which a buyer and a seller agree to the sale of a property. The contract date precedes the actual closing date. *See also* agreement of sale; closing date; date of value estimate.

contract for deed. *See* contract sale; land contract.

contractor. A constructor who is a party to the contract for construction, pledged to the owner to perform the work of construction in accordance with the contract documents. (R.S. Means)

contractor's overhead. The general and administrative costs, over and above the direct costs of material and labor, that are assumed by a contractor on any construction work. *See also* contractor's profit.

contractor's profit. The amount by which the fee received by a contractor for work performed exceeds the total direct costs of materials, labor, and overhead. *See also* contractor's overhead; developer's profit.

contract rent. The actual rental income specified in a lease.

contract sale. A sale in which the title to the property or goods remains with the seller until the buyer has fulfilled the terms of the contract, which usually call for payment in full. *See also* installment contract; land contract.

contribution. The concept that the value of a particular component is measured in terms of its contribution to the value of the whole property, or as the amount that its absence would detract from the value of the whole.

control data. A method of using real property transactions to adjust the market data used in the sales comparison approach to value. Control data are used to segregate certain influences that have caused changes in real estate values, either generally or specifically. For example, two or more sales of each of several properties could be studied, the first sales made during a certain period and the subsequent sales occurring after a lapse of time. Any trend shown by an increase or decrease in the prices of the properties between the two periods would indicate a change due to the time difference, assuming no other specific causes. Such changes in value could be used in making adjustments for time when only older sales of properties comparable to the subject property in the immediate area are available. Control data can be used to identify and segregate the value effect in a specific area of a public improvement such as a freeway.

controlled-access highway. A highway specially designed for through traffic.

Owners or occupants of abutting land may have no easement rights over, from, or to the highway or only controlled easement rights of access, light, air, or view.

convection. Motion within a fluid or gas that results in a difference in density and gravity. In heat transmission, convection includes both natural motion and forced circulation.

convector. A radiator designed to furnish a maximum amount of heat by convection; equipped with many fins or plates closely fitted on pipes that carry hot water or steam and heat the circulating air.

convenience goods. Commodities purchased frequently and without extensive comparison of style, price, or quality.

convenience shopping center. A planned development in which most retailers sell daily necessities.

convenience store. A retail outlet, typically located in proximity to a residential neighborhood, where convenience goods can be purchased; provides a convenient location and longer hours for the quick purchase of a wide array of consumable goods and services. Convenience stores have five identifiable formats: the mini-convenience store (800–1,200 square feet); the limited-selection convenience store (1,500–2,200 square feet); the traditional convenience

store (2,400–2,500 square feet); the expanded convenience store (2,800–3,600 square feet); and the hyper convenience store (4,000–5,000 square feet). (NACS)

conventional home. A home that is constructed totally on site, as distinguished from a factory-built or mobile home.

conventional loan. A mortgage that is neither insured nor guaranteed by an agency of the federal government, although it may be privately insured.

conversion. Transforming the use or ownership of property, generally income-producing real estate, e.g., converting a large residence into offices or apartments into condominiums. Conversion may involve remodeling or partitioning and relocating tenants who do not choose to buy their units. *See also* condominium conversion; cooperative conversion.

conversion factor (*a*). An element in yield and change formulas that converts the total change in capital value over the projection period into an annual percentage; varies with the pattern of the income stream and may be an annual sinking fund factor or an annual recapture rate; also called the *annualizer.*

conversion period. The interval of time considered in the computation of compound interest.

convertible bond. A bond that the holder can at any time exchange for other securities, usually common stock in the corporation, at a specified rate of exchange.

convertible debentures. Debentures that can be converted into stock in the issuing corporation, either directly or through the use of attached warrants or options.

convertible mortgage. A debt secured by real estate in which the lender may choose to change all or a portion of the debt into an equity interest in the property, thereby acquiring the right to a share of the property's cash flow and appreciation. Typically the lender advances more funds than would be indicated by conventional loan-to-value ratios and charges the borrower a face rate that is lower than conventional rates.

conveyance. A written instrument that passes an interest in real property from one person to another, e.g., a deed, a mortgage, a lease. Conveyances should specify any covenants attached to the property.

conveyor belt. A belt used to move items continually in the production process or to convey materials from their source to a place of transport or use.

cooling plant. The machinery that produces chilled water or cool refrigerant gas, such as the condenser, cooling tower, and condenser water pumps for water shed plants; air-cooled condensers for air-cooled systems; and chilled water pumps and expansion tanks for chilled water systems. (R.S. Means)

cooling tower. A tower designed to cool water by evaporation.

coop. Housing for chickens or other fowl.

cooperative. *See* cooperative ownership.

cooperative apartment unit. An apartment in a building owned by a corporation or trust, in which each owner purchases stock representing the value of a single apartment unit and receives a proprietary lease as evidence of title. Ownership is considered personal property, not real property.

cooperative conversion. Conversion of rental properties such as apartments into cooperative ownership.

cooperative housing (FHA Section 213). A section of Title II of the National Housing Act under which the Federal Housing Administration insures mortgages, including construction advances, on sales-type and management-type cooperative housing projects of eight or more units. Amended in 1990 by the Cranston-Gonzalez Program.

cooperative interest. The ownership interest component of the shares attributable to the cooperative unit, exclusive of the prorata share of the blanket mortgage or mortgages.

cooperative ownership. A form of ownership in which each owner of stock in a cooperative apartment building or housing corporation receives a proprietary lease on a specific apartment and is obligated to pay a monthly maintenance charge that represents the proportionate share of operating expenses and debt service on the underlying mortgage, which is paid by the corporation. This proportionate share is based on the proportion of the total stock owned.

coordinates. In graphic analysis, any of a number of magnitudes that determine position, e.g., points, planes, lines.

co-ownership. An undivided partial ownership interest as opposed to a fractional ownership arrangement.

coping. The covering course of a wall or roof which usually slopes downward to permit water runoff.

corbel. A beam or bracket that projects from a wall and supports another object or structural part of the building; may be decorative rather than structural.

cord. A cubic measure, especially of wood; the quantity of wood in such a measure; equal to a pile of cut wood eight feet long, four feet high, and four feet wide, totaling 128 cubic feet.

cordage. In forestry, a forest product measured in cords.

corn crib. A farm building designed to store harvested, unshelled, undried corn.

corner
1. The point or place where two converging lines or planes meet, e.g., where two streets intersect.
2. In surveying, a point marked by a monument.

corner influence. The effect on value produced by a property's location at or near the intersection of two streets; the increment of value or loss in value resulting from this location or proximity.

corner influence table. A table purporting to reflect the increment in value accruing to a parcel of land (usually commercial) because of its location on a corner; used primarily for mass appraising such as in assessment work.

corner lot. A lot abutting two intersecting streets at their point of intersection.

cornice
1. A horizontal projection, usually molded, that finishes or crowns an interior or exterior wall.
2. The enclosure at the roof eaves or at the rake of a roof, crown mold, fascia, soffit, or frieze.

corn suitability rating. A system used mostly in the Midwest to estimate a soil's capacity to produce primary crops. The various types of soil on a property are rated based on their potential for crop production; these ratings are converted into a single index which is used to compare or rate farms.

corporation. In law, an organization that acts as a single legal entity in performing certain activities, usually business for profit; also includes charitable, educational, and religious organizations.

corporeal. Pertaining to a visible and tangible right or group of rights.

corporeal property. Tangible property.

corral. A small enclosure for handling livestock in close quarters.

correction. A selloff of stock issues and a consequent decline in their price following excessive market activity that had resulted in overpricing.

correction lines. In the government survey system, east and west lines drawn on a map at intervals to account for convergence caused by the shape of the earth. *See also* standard parallels.

correlation. In statistics, estimation of the degree, or closeness, with which two or more variables are associated.

correlation analysis. A statistical technique that relates a dependent variable to one or more independent variables to determine the extent and direction of any change in the dependent variable associated with change in the independent variable or variables. Simple correlation involves one independent variable; multiple correlation involves more than one independent variable.

correlation coefficient. *See* coefficient of correlation (*r*).

correlation matrix. A table of numbers used to display the correlation coefficients for each pair of variables when three or more variables are thought to be correlated.

correspondent. *See* mortgage correspondent.

corridor
1. A passageway or hall that connects parts of a building.
2. A strip of land between two destinations where traffic, topography, environment, land uses, and other characteristics are evaluated for transportation purposes.

corrugated siding. Siding made of sheet metal or asbestos cement composition board used on industrial facilities and other inexpensive buildings. Corrugation increases the structural strength of the material.

corrugated wall tie. A piece of thin sheet metal about six inches long and one inch wide that is folded repeatedly and laid in the mortar courses between the bricks to bind a wall where a brick bond cannot be used.

cost. The total dollar expenditure for an improvement (structure); applies to production as distinct from exchange (price). Appraisers distinguish among direct (hard) costs, indirect (soft) costs, and the cost of entrepreneurship. *See also* construction costs; development costs; direct costs; entrepreneurial profit; indirect costs.

cost approach. A set of procedures through which a value indication is derived for the fee simple interest in a property by estimating the current cost to construct a reproduction of, or replacement for, the existing structure; deducting accrued depreciation from the reproduction or replacement cost; and adding the estimated land value plus an entrepreneurial profit. Adjustments may then be made to the indicated fee simple value of the subject property to reflect the value of the property interest being appraised.

cost/benefit ratio. The relationship between the benefits generated by an investment and the cost of that investment; must exceed 1:00 for the investment to be considered desirable; also called *benefit/cost ratio. See also* feasibility.

cost/benefit study. An examination of the economic benefits that will result from a proposed project. *See also* feasibility study.

cost effectiveness. The comparison of alternative courses of action in terms of their dollar costs and relative effectiveness in achieving a particular goal.

cost estimating
1. In appraising, estimation of the reproduction or replacement cost of an improvement by one or more methods. *See also* comparative unit method; quantity survey method; unit-in-place method.
2. In construction, the cost to build a structure based on the costs of all materials and labor to be employed and other essential expenses incurred in the process.

cost index. A multiplier used to convert a known historical cost into a current cost estimate.

cost of living index. An indicator of the current price level for goods and services related to a specified base year. *See also* Consumer Price Index (CPI).

cost of remodeling. Expenditures made or required for alterations to change the plan, form, or style of a structure or its potential use.

cost of repairs. Expenditures made or required to cure deterioration caused by decay, wear and tear, or partial destruction.

cost of replacement. *See* replacement cost.

cost of reproduction. *See* reproduction cost.

cost-plus contract. A contract in which the contractor's profit is a fixed percentage of the actual direct costs of labor and materials or a flat amount added to these costs.

costs incurred to rent real estate projects. Costs of model units and their furnishings, rental facilities, semipermanent signs, rental brochures, advertising, "grand openings," and rental overhead including rental salaries. (FASB)

costs incurred to sell real estate projects. Costs of model units and their furnishings, sales facilities, sales brochures, legal fees for preparation of prospectuses, semipermanent signs, advertising, "grand openings," and sales overhead including sales salaries. (FASB)

cost to cure. The cost to restore an item of deferred maintenance to new or reasonably new condition.

co-tenancy. Tenancy in common; joint or common ownership or possession.

coterminous. Having the same boundaries or expiration dates.

cottage. A small, single-family house; a small resort or summer house.

counseling. Providing competent, disinterested, and unbiased advice and guidance on diverse problems in the broad field of real estate; may involve any or all aspects of the business such as merchandising, leasing, management, acquisition/disposition planning, financing, development, cost-benefit studies, feasibility analysis, and similar services. Counseling services are often associated with evaluation, but they are beyond the scope of appraisal.

Counselors of Real Estate (American Society of Real Estate Counselors). A professional organization whose members have extensive experience in all phases of real estate and provide counseling services for a pre-set fee or salary; confers the CRE (Counselor of Real Estate) designation.

count plots. In forestry, sampling points at which tallied trees are counted by species to determine the average basal or stem area per unit of area.

county. The largest division of local government in all states except Louisiana and Alaska, where the comparable units are parish and borough, respectively.

county extension agent. *See* agricultural extension agent.

county highway. A road under the jurisdiction of a county; in many states, includes all rural public roads outside the state highway system.

course
1. A continuous, horizontal layer of bricks or masonry; one of a series of layers of material in construction.

2. The natural direction or path of a stream; a natural channel for water.

3. The direction between two points described in degrees, minutes, and seconds of the angle from north to south.

course provider. An entity that offers educational courses required for state licensure or certification.

court

1. An uncovered area bounded wholly or in part by buildings or walls.

2. An open space, e.g., a short street.

3. In law, the place where justice is administered; the persons duly assembled under the authority of law to administer justice; a tribunal established for the administration of justice; a session of a judicial assembly.

court award. Any decision resulting from a contested trial or hearing before a jury, commission, judge, or other legal entity with the proper authority.

cove. A concave molding; the edge of a ceiling that is curved or arched where it meets the side walls.

covenant. A promise between two or more parties, incorporated in a trust indenture or other formal instrument, to perform certain acts or to refrain from performing certain acts. *See also* full covenant and warranty deed; restrictive covenant.

covenants and restrictions. A list of expressed assurances and limitations on land use; often found in contracts between a land subdivider and a lot purchaser. Covenants and restrictions should be specified in the conveyance. Also referred to as *conditions, covenants, and restrictions (CC&Rs)*. *See also* restrictive covenant.

cover. In the restaurant business, one meal sold to one person; a unit of demand representing one patron dining at one mealtime.

coverage. The proportion of the net or gross land area of a site that is occupied by a building or buildings.

cover crop. A crop planted principally to control wind or water erosion during the dormant season; usually plowed under, not harvested.

cow unit. *See* animal unit (AU).

cow year long (CYL). The total number of cows that can be nourished properly for one full year on a given piece of land without harming the natural adult vegetative cover divided by the number of cows in that total that can produce calves. *See also* animal unit (AU); animal unit month (AUM).

CPI. *See* Consumer Price Index.

CPM. Certified Property Manager, a designation conferred by the Institute of Real Estate Management (IREM).

cps. In computer usage, characters per second; the amount specified is the rate at which a printer can imprint characters on paper; e.g., a 20-cps printer can operate at about 1,200 characters per minute.

CPU. *See* central processing unit.

cradle. A bed where large trees are felled to prevent breakage; the ground surface is prepared by excavating, filling, or both.

crane. A device for lifting and moving heavy weights, e.g., an overhead crane, a gantry crane, a one-leg gantry crane, a jib crane.

craneway. Column and girder supports of steel or concrete and rails on which a crane travels.

crawl space. An unfinished, accessible space below the first floor of a structure that is usually less than full story height.

CRB. Certified Real Estate Brokerage Manager, a designation conferred by the Real Estate Brokerage Managers Council of the Realtors National Marketing Institute (RNMI).

CRE. Counselor of Real Estate, a designation conferred by the Counselors of Real Estate (American Society of Real Estate Counselors).

credit report. A report on the credit standing of a prospective borrower, which is sent to a prospective lender.

creosote bush. A type of range vegetation that includes areas where creosote (*covillea*) constitutes the predominant vegetation.

crop. The harvest or yield of a single field or a single variety that is gathered in one season or a part of a season.

crop acres. *See* cropland.

crop allotment. The acreage allotted to farms under the federal government's Crop Production Program. *See also* acreage controls.

crop insurance. Programs designed to compensate farmers when they cannot plant or when yields are drastically reduced due to drought, flood, natural disaster, or other conditions beyond their control.

cropland. A portion of farm acreage normally used for the production of annual crops, summer fallow, or rotation pasture, as distinguished from wood lots, marshes, etc.

crop rotation. The practice of alternating food crops, e.g., corn or wheat, with legumes on an annual basis to maintain or improve the structure and productivity of the soil.

crop share rent. A rent set at a percentage of the crops grown by the tenant, which may vary depending on local custom and the landowner's contribution of seeds, fertilizer, harvesting costs, irrigation, water supply, etc.

cross-bridging. Cross-bracing between floor joists that provides rigidity, permits the transfer of an isolated, heavy-bearing weight to a broader supporting area, and prevents warping.

cross-connecting road. A connecting roadway between two nearby, generally parallel roads.

cross-easements. Reciprocal easements created by contract; an easement is granted in favor of the premises.

cross examination. The process of questioning a witness whose direct testimony is adverse to the position of the party undertaking the questioning. The purpose of cross examination is to dilute, neutralize, or completely destroy the effect of the witness's direct testimony.

cross fence. An interior fence on a farm or ranch that divides the property into fields or pastures. *See also* division fence.

crossover point. The point in the life of a real estate investment when a tax benefit is replaced by a tax burden.

cross section. A transverse section at a right angle to the longitudinal axis of a piece of wood.

cross tie. A lightweight structural member that is attached to rafters to brace them on opposite roof slopes.

CRS. Certified Residential Specialist, a designation conferred by the Residential Sales Council of the Realtors National Marketing Institute (RNMI)

cruise. A survey of land performed to locate standing timber and estimate its quantity by species, products, size, quality, or other characteristics; the estimate obtained in such a survey.

CSC. Civil Service Commission.

CSHA. Council of State Housing Agencies.

CTS System. A system for describing residential property by class, type, and style. Class refers to single-family, two-family, or three-family occupancy and whether the property is detached or separated by a party wall. Type designates the number of stories or levels; style describes the architecture.

cubic content. The cubic volume of a building, usually measured from the outer surfaces of the exterior walls and roof to the level of the lowest floor or six inches below the finished surface of the lowest floor.

cubic foot cost. The cost of a building divided by its cubic content.

cubic foot method. *See* comparative-unit method; quantity survey method; unit-in-place method.

cubic foot per second. A flow of water equal to a stream with a width and depth of one foot, or one square foot, that flows at the rate of one foot per second.

cubic yard. A measure of volume three feet wide, three feet high, and three feet deep; 27 cubic feet.

cuerda. A Spanish unit of land measurement.

cul-de-sac. A street with one open end and an enlarged turnaround at the closed end.

culvert. A generally small structure that provides drainage under a traveled way, parking lot, or other area.

cupola. A small structure built on top of a roof.

curable depreciation. Items of physical deterioration or functional obsolescence that are economically feasible to cure. Economic feasibility is indicated if the cost to cure is equal to or less than the anticipated increase in the value of the property. *See also* curable functional obsolescence; curable physical deterioration.

curable functional obsolescence. An element of accrued depreciation; a curable defect caused by a flaw in the structure, materials, or design.

curable physical deterioration. An element of accrued depreciation; a curable defect caused by deferred maintenance.

curb. The stone or concrete edge of a sidewalk or paved street; the raised edge of a floor or well opening.

curb line. The line that divides the roadway itself from the areas on either side of the roadway reserved for pedestrian use.

current assets. Assets that will most probably be realized in cash, sold, or consumed during the normal operation of a business.

current dollars. Dollars that account for both real growth and inflation.

current liability. A liability that will be paid in the normal operation of business; a short-term debt.

current value. In accounting, synonymous with *market value.*

current value accounting. The practice of showing both the book value and the current market value of assets on the annual financial statements of publicly owned real estate corporations.

current yield. In finance, the current dividend on an investment; current yield is the percentage of annual cash income to the investment cost; similar to a capitalization rate. *See also* yield to maturity.

cursor. In computer usage, a flashing bar, square, triangle, or other symbol that indicates where the next character on a video screen will be displayed.

curtain wall. An exterior wall that encloses, but does not support, the structural frame of a building. *See also* panel wall.

curtesy. In common law, the estate to which a husband is entitled in the lands of his deceased wife; varies with statutory provisions.

curtilage. Fenced-in ground surrounding a building.

curvilinear. Consisting of, or bounded by, curved lines, e.g., curvilinear streets.

custom-built house. A house sold before construction and built to the owners' specifications.

cut

1. The output of a sawmill over a given period of time; a season's output of logs.

2. Removal of earth to change the terrain.

cutover land. An area from which all or most of the salable timber has been removed by logging.

cuts. In highway construction, excavations to establish the grade of the right-of-way through lands of higher elevation.

cyclical fluctuation. Variations around a trend in activity that recur from time to time and are independent of seasonal factors.

cyclical movement. *See* business cycle.

CYL. *See* cow year long.

D

dam. A barrier across a watercourse that restricts or confines the flow of water, e.g., a simple earthen bank or masonry wall across a minor stream; a large engineering structure constructed across a river for a hydro-electric plant.

damages. In condemnation, the loss in value to the remainder in a partial taking of property. Generally, the difference between the value of the whole property before the taking and the value of the remainder af-ter the taking is the measure of the value of the part taken and the damages to the remainder. Three types of damages are recognized: consequential, direct, and severance.

damper. A hinged plate in the flue of a furnace or fireplace that functions as an air valve to regulate the draft; a device to deaden vibration.

dampproofing. To coat a surface to prevent the passage of moisture. *See also* waterproofing.

dark store clause. A clause in a lease that states that the tenant must do business at the site throughout the full term of the lease and cannot open a competitive store within six months prior to the expiration of the lease, which could put the subject property in a very poor re-leasing position; may also affect the rent payments of other tenants; vital in a straight percentage lease involving a major tenant. This type of clause may not be legal in all jurisdictions.

data. In statistics, information or facts, usually in numerical form, that can be classified by qualitative characteristics in ratios, by size in frequency distributions, or by time in time series or regression analysis. See also general data, specific data.

database

1. All data collected and stored for a given purpose or in a given location.
2. In computer usage, a set of related records structured so that various programs have access to the information contained in them, although each record is entered only once; in communications, an information utility, which may actually contain many separate databases.

data mode. In computer usage, the modem setting that permits information to be transmitted in digital form to other computers; distin-guished from talk, voice, or conversation mode, which is the normal operating mode of a telephone.

date of condition. The time prior to the development of a public project when the planned project has not yet been announced and has not had the effect of enhancing or depressing the value of the property being acquired or its surrounding neighborhood. *See also* condemnation blight; project enhancement.

date of opinion. The date for which an appraisal, analysis, or review is valid.

date of value estimate. The date for which an estimate of value is valid. The sale of a property may be negotiated months or even years before the closing or final disposition of the property. In this case, an adjustment for changes in market conditions between the date the contract is signed and the effective date of value may be appropriate. *See also* closing date; contract date; prospective value estimate; retrospective value estimate; value as is.

datum. In city planning, the horizontal baseline from which heights and depths are measured. The datum level adopted as a base or starting point for the grades or levels of the municipality is typically recorded in the codes that control building standards.

daylight factor. An indicator of the level of natural interior lighting established by British town and country planning authorities based on a ratio between the daylight available inside a building and the total light available outdoors on a clear day.

DBH. *See* diameter-breast-high.

DCF. *See* discounted cash flow analysis.

dead-end street. A street that is closed at one end.

dead load. The permanent, inert weight of a structure plus any fixed loads, e.g., boilers, heavy machinery, equipment; does not include variable, live loads, e.g., furniture, merchandise, people.

dead rent. A fixed, annual sum paid for the use of a mine or quarry in addition to the payment of royalties, which vary with the yield.

dead room. A room designed to have high sound-absorption properties. (R.S. Means)

dead storage. The storage of items not in use, as distinguished from live storage of items in active or daily use.

death loss. The number of range animals that die from natural causes, e.g., plant poisoning, accident, disease, as distinguished from the number lost due to other causes, e.g., straying, theft, sales.

death rate. The number of deaths per 1,000 persons annually. Also called the *crude death rate.* The refined death rate breaks down the number of people according to age groups.

debenture. An obligation that is not secured by a specific lien on a property, e.g., an unsecured corporation note.

debt
1. One of two characteristic types of investment, the other being equity. The debt investor expects a priority claim on investment earnings and looks for security in the form of a lien on the assets involved. Debt investors participate in bonds or mortgages and receive fixed or variable interest on investment with repayment of the principal upon maturity.
2. Money borrowed, usually for a specified period of time, which may be secured or unsecured.

debt coverage. The ability of a property to meet its debt service out of net operating income.

debt coverage ratio (DCR). The ratio of net operating income to annual debt service $(DCR = NOI/I_M)$; measures the ability of a property to meet its debt service out of net operating income; also called *debt service coverage ratio (DSCR).*

debt/equity ratio. The ratio between an enterprise's loan capital and its equity capital, i.e., the ratio between the amount owed to lenders and the capital account of shareholders or partners.

debt financing. Paying for all or part of a capital investment with borrowed funds; in real estate, the property itself may serve as security for the debt.

debt service (I_M). The periodic payment that covers the interest on, and retirement of, the outstanding principal of the mortgage loan; also called *mortgage debt service.*

debt service coverage ratio (DSCR). *See* debt coverage ratio *(DCR).*

decentralization
1. Dispersion from a center; movement of people, industry, and business away from the city and to suburbs, rural-urban fringe areas, or smaller cities.
2. In business, the construction of plants outside large cities and some distance from one another; dividing an existing business into smaller units or expanding a business by establishing separate business units.

decibel
1. The standard unit of measurement for the loudness of sound.
2. In closed-circuit television, a numerical unit used to express the difference in power levels, usually between acoustic or electric signals, equal to 10 times the common logarithm of the ratio of those two levels. (R.S. Means)

deciduous. Trees that shed their leaves annually.

decision trees. In statistics or decision theory, a method of analyzing problems that involve a sequence of decisions; alternative actions are represented as branches of the tree. *See also* flow chart.

deck. An open porch usually at the ground floor level or on the roof of a ground floor porch or wing. In modern architecture a deck may be supported by piers or cantilevers.

decking. The surfacing material applied to rafters or floor joists before the roof cover or floor cover material is applied.

deck roof. A nearly flat roof constructed without a fire wall.

declination. In surveying, the angle formed by the compass's magnetic needle and a geographical meridian.

decline. A stage of diminishing demand in a neighborhood's life cycle.

declining-balance depreciation. In accounting, a method of depreciating an asset by applying a fixed percentage rate to the successive balances remaining after previously computed amounts of depreciation have been deducted.

decomposition. The breaking down of complex chemical compounds into simpler ones; the breaking down of soil minerals by solution and chemical change.

decreasing annuity. An income stream consisting of evenly spaced periodic payments that decrease in a systematic pattern; also called *declining annuity.*

dedicated. Property in public use, e.g., a roadway, that was originally obtained from the fee owner; also describes land acquired and dedicated to burial purposes.

dedication. A voluntary gift of private property made by the owner for some public use, e.g., the dedication of land for streets and schools in a development.

deed. A written, legal instrument that conveys an estate or interest in real property when it is executed and delivered. *See also* administrator's deed; bargain and sale deed; bond for deed; committee deed; executor's deed; full covenant and warranty deed; general warranty deed; grant deed; mortgage deed; quitclaim deed; trust deed; warranty deed.

deed description. A recitation of the legal boundaries of a parcel of land as contained in a deed of conveyance.

deed in fee. Sufficient conveyance of a fee simple, free of all encumbrances with the usual covenants of the grantor.

deed in lieu. A deed given by an owner or debtor in lieu of foreclosure by the lender or mortgagee. *See also* foreclosure.

deed of release. A legal instrument, subscribed and acknowledged by the mortgagee, by which the mortgaged property is absolved from the lien of the mortgage.

deed of trust. A legal instrument similar to a mortgage which, when executed and delivered, conveys or transfers property title to a trustee.

deed restriction. A limitation that passes with the land regardless of the owner; usually limits the property's type or intensity of use. *See also* restrictive covenant; title defect.

defacto contract. A contract which purports to pass a property from the owner to another. A purchaser in good faith taking from such transferee obtains a good title.

default. The failure to fulfill a contractual agreement.

default ratio. The occupancy level at which the effective gross income from an income-producing property is insufficient to pay operating expenses and debt service, thus creating the risk of default; calculated by dividing effective gross income into operating expenses plus debt service.

defeasance. A legal instrument that defeats the force or operation of another deed or estate, e.g., when a mortgage loan is paid off, the defeasance clause in the mortgage loan agreement restores title from the lender to the borrower.

defeasible title. A title that can be annulled or made void, but not one that is already void or in absolute nullity.

deferred annuity. An income stream that begins at some time in the future.

deferred assets. In accounting, the portion of expense items applicable to the period subsequent to the closing date; also called *deferred charges* or *deferred expenses.*

deferred liability. Liability from transferred real property interests that does not become an obligation to the transferee until some time after the transfer.

deferred maintenance. Curable, physical deterioration that should be corrected immediately, although work has not commenced; denotes the need for immediate expenditures, but does not necessarily suggest inadequate maintenance in the past.

deferred payment sale. A sale in which the proceeds are to be received in more than one installment. The Internal Revenue Code provides for several methods of reporting such a gain.

deficiency. An inadequacy in a structure or one of its components.

deficiency judgment. Judgment granted in a suit initiated to recover the difference between a legally imposed indebtedness and the dollars received from a foreclosure sale of the debtor's assets.

deficit. An insufficiency of funds, e.g., a deficit in an expense fund; the amount by which the total assets of a business fall short of its total liabilities plus invested capital.

definition of value. A written statement specifying the type of value to be estimated; must be included in every appraisal report.

definitive loan. A loan secured by a long-term lease and made by an entity other than the legal seller to finance the purchase of a fee title. In urban renewal projects, definitive loans are made or guaranteed by the federal government.

deflation. A decrease in the general price level; a period in which the purchasing power of money rises. *See also* inflation.

degree day. A unit of fuel consumption equal to the number of degrees deviation from 65° F, usually totaled over a number of days, e.g., over a year or a heating season; used to project annual heating or cooling costs.

degrees of freedom *(DF)*. In statistics, the difference between the size of a sample and the number of variables used in arriving at an unbiased estimate or equation; as this number decreases, the related variance and standard deviation increase.

delphi survey. A survey of professionals who are especially knowledgeable about market conditions, economic trends, and governmental policies. Such a survey is used to develop a prognostication for a specific industry.

delta (Δ). The mathematic symbol for percent of change; used in yield and change formulas to represent the expected percentage change in the value or income of a total property or a specified interest in property over a projection period.

demand. The desire and ability to purchase or lease goods and services; in real estate, the amounts of a type of real estate desired for purchase or rent at various prices in a given market for a given period of time. *See also* effective demand; elasticity of demand; fall-out demand; forecast demand; induced demand; inferred demand; latent demand; marginal demand; move-up demand; pent-up demand; residual demand; supply and demand; unaccommodated demand.

demand deposits. Funds deposited in a bank that can be withdrawn at any time, e.g., money in checking accounts. Any deposit that is payable on demand and may be withdrawn by check, draft, negotiable order of withdrawal, or another similar instrument for payment to third parties. Money market accounts are excluded because they are considered acquisitions of shares.

demand unit. An economic unit that can or does express demand for a product. Representative demand units include the population of potential buyers or renters in a specific market area who are capable of purchasing or leasing the subject property, and the population of potential shoppers in a specific trade area who are likely to make purchases at a particular retail facility.

de minimis PUD. A category of planned unit development that was eliminated by Fannie Mae in 1989. Characteristically, de minimis PUDs included a minimal amount of common property and improvements that exerted little or no effect on the value of the property securing the unit mortgage.

de minimis requirement. A stipulation of Title XI of the Financial Institutions Reform, Recovery and Enforcement Act (FIRREA) of 1989, that federal agencies must retain state certified appraisers to perform appraisals of properties with values above a specified dollar amount.

demise. A lease or conveyance for life or years.

demising wall. A dividing wall in a building housing two or more tenants that separates the area leased by one tenant from that leased by the other(s).

demography. The study of population and population change.

demolition grant program. Established by the Housing and Urban Development Act of 1965, it authorizes federal grants to cities and other municipalities and counties to assist in financing the cost of demolishing structures which under state or local law have been determined to be structurally unsound or unfit for human habitation.

density. The number of items present per unit of area, e.g., dwellings per acre, persons per square mile. *See also* forage density; height density; traffic density; use density; vegetative density.

density zoning. A system of land use control in which residential occupancy is limited by the number of families per unit of land area, e.g.,

per acre, rather than the number of families per building.

Department of Agriculture. One of the more important administrative units of the U.S. Government with a secretary of cabinet rank. Created February 9, 1889, its prime objective has been to conduct education and research activities of immediate benefit to the farm community. In recent decades the department has acquired additional responsibilities of a regulatory and enforcement nature. It now has direct or indirect responsibility for the administration of many federal agricultural-aid programs, among them programs for the stabilization and extension of agricultural markets; the extension of various forms of credit to the agricultural community; the administration of agricultural price-support policies; the promotion of land resource conservation; and other programs designed to assist farmers and ranchers. Some of its principal subsidiary units are the Soil Conservation Service, the Forest Service, the Agricultural Marketing Service, the Farmers Home Administration, and the Commodity Credit Corporation.

Department of Housing and Urban Development (HUD). The department of the U.S. Government responsible for major housing and urban development programs, e.g., urban renewal, low-rent public housing, mortgage insurance, metropolitan planning; administers FHA mortgage insurance programs.

Department of Justice. A major administrative unit of the U.S. Government, headed by the attorney general, that has supervisory powers over federal prosecuting agencies and provides representation in court cases involving the federal government. The Department of Justice has an appraisal staff in its Land and Natural Resources Division, Land Acquisition Section.

Department of the Interior. A major administrative unit of the U.S. Government that controls many subsidiary agencies, including the Fish and Wildlife Service, the Bureau of Mines, the Reclamation Bureau, and the National Park Service.

Department of Transportation. *See* Federal Aviation Administration; Federal Highway Administration.

Department of the Treasury. The department of the U.S. Government that implements the fiscal policy shaped by Congress and the president. The Treasury Department mints currency, collects taxes, and borrows money through the sale of government debt instruments (bonds, bills, and notes).

Department of Veterans Affairs. The department of the U.S. Government entrusted with the execution of all laws that benefit war veterans; administers special compensation and allowances, pensions, vocational rehabilitation, education, insurance, loans, hospitalization, and medical care.

department store. A store selling general merchandise, apparel, furniture, and other goods arranged in different departments.

department store-type merchandise (DSTM). General merchandise, apparel, furniture, and other merchandise so defined by the Department of Commerce's *Census of Retail Trade;* also called *GAFO.*

departure provision. Specific requirements of the Uniform Standards of Professional Appraisal Practice that apply to an appraiser who performs an assignment that calls for something less than, or different from, the work that would otherwise be required. The appraiser must: 1) determine that the departure would not mislead the client or users of the report; and 2) advise the client that the assignment is less than, or different from, the work required by the specific guidelines, and that the resulting report will include a qualification stating the limitation. (USPAP, 1992 edition)

depletion. A reduction in the value of an asset due to the removal of ex-

haustible material assets or resources, e.g., the removal of trees
from a forest, the taking of minerals
from a mine, the pumping of oil
from a well.

depletion rate. The periodic percentage rate at which a quantity, usually
a natural resource, is exhausted; calculated as the amount of commercially recoverable reserves divided
by the volume of production contemplated; may be expressed in
monetary units.

deposition

1. A discovery device by which one
   party asks oral questions of the
   other party or of a witness for
   the other party. The person who
   is deposed is called the *deponent*.
   The deposition is conducted under oath outside of the court-
   room, usually in one of the
   lawyer's offices. The testimony
   of an appraiser in a deposition
   regarding his or her opinion
   about a parcel of real estate is
   considered an oral report.
2. A formal method of obtaining information relevant to a lawsuit
   by verbally asking an individual
   questions under oath prior to
   trial. (R.S. Means)

depreciated cost

1. Cost new less accrued depreciation as of the date of the appraisal.

2. Sometimes erroneously used in
   reference to cost new less deterioration, or physical wear and
   tear only.

depreciated value. Often used to describe cost less a single form of depreciation, or used synonymously
with sound value, or with replacement cost less depreciation. A very
nebulous term and purely a cost
concept which is frequently related
to book value. (Marshall & Swift)

depreciation

1. In appraising, a loss in property
   value from any cause; the difference between the reproduction
   or replacement cost of an improvement on the effective date
   of the appraisal and the market
   value of the improvement on the
   same date.
2. In regard to improvements, depreciation encompasses both deterioration and obsolescence.
3. In accounting, an allowance
   made against the loss in value of
   an asset for a defined purpose
   and computed using a specified
   method.

depreciation allowance. In accounting, the amount charged against
earnings to write off the cost of an
asset; used more properly in accounting for income tax purposes
than in appraising.

depreciation recapture. The difference
between the capital gain and the or-

dinary gain when real estate is sold at a gain. The difference between capital gain and the ordinary gain results from the different methods of estimating depreciation, i.e, straight-line basis vs. accelerated basis. When preferential treatment of capital gains was disallowed under the 1986 Tax Reform Act, all gain became taxable at ordinary rates. In the past, excess write-offs based on accelerated depreciation were used to shelter a portion of income from taxation at ordinary rates. For example, consider an office building, which had been depreciated to $6,000,000 on an accelerated basis for tax purposes and sold for $10,000,000. Had straight-line depreciation been used, the tax basis for the building would have been $7,000,000; the $1,000,000 difference in the depreciated tax bases would then be *recaptured* for tax purposes as ordinary income. *See also* accelerated depreciation; straight-line depreciation.

depreciation reserve. In accounting, the account on a business' books where accruals for depreciation are recorded.

depressed market. A market in which a drop in demand is accompanied by a relative oversupply and a decline in prices.

depression. A severe economic crisis in which business activity is depressed

for a long period, purchasing power is declining, and unemployment is high.

depth curve. A graph of depth factors that shows the estimated percentage relationships between the front foot values of lots of various depths and the front foot value of a lot of standard depth.

depth factor. A factor, or percentage, that represents the relative value of a lot of a given depth as compared to the value of a lot of standard depth. *See also* depth table.

depth influence. The effect of depth on the value of a lot or parcel with a given frontage; the increase or decrease in value arising from a depth that is greater or less than the standard.

depth table. A table of depth factors showing the estimated percentage relationship between the front foot value of a lot of a given depth and the front foot value of a lot of standard depth. *See also* depth factor.

descent. A transfer of property when the owner dies without leaving a will; transfer by inheritance.

description of the scope of the appraisal. Statement describing the extent of the process in which data are collected, confirmed, and reported.

descriptive statistics. A branch of statistics concerned only with characterizing, or describing, a set of numbers; the measures used to characterize a set of data, e.g., average, maximum, coefficient of dispersion. *See also* inferential statistics.

desert shrub. A type of range vegetation that includes areas where desert shrubs of unspecified type dominate, but pure types of each are too limited to characterize a separate type; includes blackbush (*coleogyne*), coffee berry (*simmondsia*), cat's claw (*acacia* and *mimosa*), gray molly (*kochia*), hopsage (*grayia*), horse brush (*tetradymia*), and little rabbit brush (*crysothamnus stenophyllus*).

desert soil. A zonal group of soils with a light-colored surface soil usually covering calcareous material and possibly hardpan; nurtures extremely scant shrub vegetation in dry, moderate climates.

design. An architectural drawing or draft of the plan, elevation, and sections of a structure.

desire. A purchaser's wish for an item to satisfy human needs (e.g., shelter, clothing, food, companionship) or individual wants beyond essential life-support needs. *See also* demand.

desk review. An appraisal review that is limited to the data presented in the report which may or may not be independently confirmed. A desk review is generally performed using a customized checklist of items. The reviewer checks the accuracy of the calculations, the reasonableness of the data and the appropriateness of the methodology as well as compliance with client guidelines, regulatory requirements, and professional standards. Also called *technical review*. *See also* field review; review.

destination resort. A vacation facility that caters to visitors from a wide geographical area who usually arrive by air.

deterioration. Impairment of condition; a cause of depreciation that reflects the loss in value due to wear and tear, disintegration, use in service, and the action of the elements. *See also* curable physical deterioration; depreciation; incurable physical deterioration.

developer's fee. A term subject to various interpretations. Many appraisers associate a developer's fee with payment for overseeing the development of a project from inception to completion and include it among the direct and indirect costs of development. Others use the term interchangeably with *entrepreneurial profit*, equating it with compensation for the time, energy, and experience a developer invests in a project as well as a reward for the risk the developer takes.

developer's profit. The profit anticipated by the developer of a subdivision. *See* developer's fee; entrepreneurial profit.

development. The transformation of
formerly raw land into improved
property through the application of
labor, capital, and entrepreneurship.
Development may also include the
marketing of the real estate product.

development cost. The cost to create
a property, including land costs, and
bring it to an efficient operating
state, as distinguished from the cost
to construct the improvements.

development exaction. A requirement
imposed by a local government that
a developer contribute to the community by providing an amenity,
paying an impact fee, or making
some other monetary contribution
as a condition for the right to construct the development. For example, a residential developer may
be required to dedicate a park to
serve the development's residents
or to improve the roadway that provides access to the development.

development fund. A syndication
formed solely to develop real estate
projects.

development procedure. A technique
for valuing undeveloped acreage
which involves discounting the cost
of development and the probable
proceeds from the sale of developed

sites. *See also* subdivision development method.

development right. The right to build
on or beneath a property, subject to
local zoning, building codes, etc.
The right to development is fundamental to private property in the
United States and was reaffirmed in
the *Nollan v. California Coastal Commission* decision (1987). See also
transferable development right
(TDR).

deviation. In statistics, the difference
between one number in a set of
numbers and the mean of the set. *See
also* average deviation; coefficient of
dispersion; standard deviation.

devise. A gift or transfer of real property by the owner's last will and tes-
tament; an estate so transferred.

DF. *See* degrees of freedom.

D horizon. Calcareous material beneath
the C horizon that shows some oxi-
dation. *See also* A horizon; B horizon;
C horizon.

diagram rules. Full-sized circles of
various diameters drawn to represent the top ends of logs. On these
cross sections, the boards that could
be sawed from each log are drawn,
leaving between each board a space
equal to the width of the saw kerf.

diameter-breast-high *(DBH)*. The diameter of a tree at breast height, i.e.,
4½ feet above the average ground

level. The abbreviations *o.b.* and *i.b.* indicate whether the diameter is measured outside or inside the bark. *See also* breast-height.

differential assessments. Assessments in a system of law that requires different classes of property to be assessed with different assessment ratios; usually used where the classes are easily divisible, e.g., classified property tax systems, use value farmland assessment systems. A similar effect is achieved by partial homestead exemptions and temporary exemptions to encourage rehabilitation.

digital. Refers to communications equipment and procedures in which information is represented in binary form (1 or 0), as opposed to analog form (variable, continuous wave forms). (R.S. Means)

dike. An embankment that restrains the waters of a sea or river; a levee; a causeway.

diluvion. The gradual washing away of soil along the banks of streams. *See also* alluvion.

dimension lumber. Lumber as it comes from the saw; all yard lumber, except timbers, strip, and board, of two to five inches in depth and of any width.

dimension shingles. Shingles cut to a uniform size.

diminishing assets. Assets that are periodically reduced by exhaustion, lapse of time, etc., so that their value must also be reduced; include mineral deposits, copyrights, franchises for limited terms, and similar wasting properties in which value loss cannot be arrested by expenditures, e.g., maintenance of tangible fixed property.

diminishing returns. *See* law of decreasing returns.

diminishing utility. The concept that the consumption of each succeeding unit of an economic good yields less satisfaction than the preceding unit although satisfaction continues to increase at a positive rate. Thus, total utility increases at a decreasing rate.

direct capitalization

1. A method used to convert an estimate of a single year's income expectancy into an indication of value in one direct step, either by dividing the income estimate by an appropriate rate or by multiplying the income estimate by an appropriate factor.

2. A capitalization technique that employs capitalization rates and multipliers extracted from sales. Only the first year's income is considered. Yield and value change are implied, but not identified.

direct compensation. *See* just compensation.

direct costs
1. Expenditures for the labor and materials used in the construction of improvements; also called *hard costs. See also* indirect costs.
2. The labor, material, subcontractor, and heavy equipment costs directly incorporated into the construction of physical improvements. (R.S. Means)

direct examination. The process in which an attorney questions a witness whom he or she has called to elicit testimony favorable to his or her client's interest.

direct-indirect lighting. A lighting system employing diffused light luminaries that emit little or no light horizontal to the lighting unit. (R.S. Means)

direct labor. Labor costs that are directly connected with a specific product or project, as distinguished from indirect labor, e.g., overhead, management.

direct lighting. A lighting system in which all or most of the light is directed toward the surface to be illuminated. (R.S. Means)

direct reduction mortgage. A debt secured by real estate that is repaid in periodic, usually equal, installments that include repayment of part of the principal and the interest due on the unpaid balance; in general, an ordinary, fixed-rate, level-payment, fully amortizing mortgage.

direct sales comparison approach. A term formerly used to refer to the sales comparison approach.

direct steam system. A heating system in which steam or vapor is delivered from the boiler to room radiators through piping, e.g., a one-pipe gravity system for smaller installations, a two-pipe system for larger installations.

dirt tank. A small reservoir with an earth-filled dam that collects natural runoff to provide water for livestock.

disaggregation. The differentiation of a subject property from other properties on the basis of subclassifications with differing product characteristics. *See also* market segmentation.

disappearing stair. A hinged stair, usually folding, that is attached to a trap door in the ceiling and can be raised out of sight when not in use. (R.S. Means)

disclaimer. A denial or disavowal of any interest in or claim to the subject of an action, such as renunciation of any title, claim, interest, estate, or trust. The owner of a subdivision, the map of which has been filed in a county clerk's office, may disclaim and abandon the subdivision after five years have elapsed by filing an appropriate instrument of record. Thereafter, for the purpose of taxation, the tract is considered to be one parcel of land (New York State Law). Also, a statement of limiting conditions in an appraisal report.

discontinuous easement. A right of accommodation (for a specific purpose) requiring action by one of the parties, such as a right-of-way. (R.S. Means)

discount

1. Conversion of future payments to present value.
2. Money paid at the beginning of a time period for the use of capital during that period; commonly deducted from the principal when the funds are advanced.

discounted cash flow (DCF) analysis. The procedure in which a discount rate is applied to a set of projected income streams and a reversion. The analyst specifies the quantity, variability, timing, and duration of the income streams as well as the quantity and timing of the reversion and discounts each to its present value at a specified yield rate. DCF analysis can be applied with any yield capitalization technique and may be performed on either a lease-by-lease or aggregate basis.

discounted rate of return. *See* internal rate of return (*IRR*).

discount house. A retail store that can offer merchandise at a price below the usual or advertised price through self-service shopping and other low-overhead methods.

discounting. A procedure used to convert periodic incomes, cash flows, and reversions into present value; based on the assumption that benefits received in the future are worth less than the same benefits received now.

discount points. A percentage of the loan amount that a lender charges a borrower for making a loan; may represent a payment for services rendered in issuing a loan or additional interest to the lender payable in advance; also called *points*.

discount rate. A yield rate used to convert future payments or receipts into present value. See also risk rate; safe rate; yield rate (*Y*).

discovery

1. The process whereby an assessor identifies all taxable property in a jurisdiction and ensures that it is included on the assessment roll. (IAAO)
2. The process in which lawyers prepare their cases for trial by

requiring, with court authority, that witnesses from the opposing side answer a number of written questions.

discretionary commingled fund. A mix of investment properties or investment monies combined in a common fund. The fund trustee has, within specified limitations, the authority to buy, sell, or retain assets of the fund at times and in amounts the trustee deems in the best interest of the investors(s). *See also* blind pool; mixed fund; real estate investment trust (REIT).

disintermediation. The transfer of money from low interest-bearing accounts to higher interest-bearing accounts.

dispersion. In statistics, the degree of scatter in a set of terms or observations, usually measured from a central value, e.g., the mean, the median.

disposable income. The personal income remaining after deducting income taxes and all other payments to federal, state, and local governments.

disposal field. An area where waste or effluent from a septic tank is dispersed, draining into the ground through a tile and gravel leaching field.

disposition value. The most probable price which a specified interest in real property is likely to bring under all of the following conditions:

1. Consummation of a sale will occur within a limited future marketing period specified by the client.
2. Actual market conditions are those currently obtaining for the property interest appraised.
3. The buyer and seller is each acting prudently and knowledgeably.
4. The seller is under compulsion to sell.
5. The buyer is typically motivated.
6. Both parties are acting in what they consider their best interests.
7. An adequate marketing effort will be made in the limited time allowed for the completion of a sale.
8. Payment will be made in cash in U.S. dollars or in terms of financial arrangements comparable thereto.
9. The price represents the normal consideration for the property sold, unaffected by special or creative financing or sales concessions granted by anyone associated with the sale.

This definition can also be modified to provide for valuation with specified financing terms. (The above definition, proposed by the Appraisal Institute Special Task Force on Value Definitions, was adopted by the Appraisal Institute Board of Directors, July 1993.) *See also* distress sale; forced price; liquidation value; market value.

distemper. A composition of pigments mixed with size, glue, egg whites, or egg yolks that is used for painting walls and murals.

distress sale. A sale involving a seller acting under duress. *See also* disposition value; forced sale; liquidation value.

distributed cash flow. Revenue from any source that is or can be distributed to the investor.

distributed load. Weight that is evenly spread over an entire surface or along the length of a girder or beam; measured in pounds or tons per square or lineal foot.

distribution box
1. A fuse box; a metal box containing fuses and circuit breakers that provides access to connecting branch circuits.
2. An underground box that receives waste from a septic tank and distributes it to the laterals of a disposal field.

distribution method. *See* extraction.

distribution panel. An insulated board from which electrical connections are made between the main feed circuit and branch distribution circuits.

distribution tile. Concrete or clay tile laterals leading from a septic tank distribution box; laid with open joints through which effluent drains and seeps into the soil. *See also* leaching trenches.

district
1. A type of neighborhood characterized by homogeneous land use (e.g., apartment, commercial, industrial, agricultural).
2. A unit of local government with the authority to levy taxes and issue bonds to finance schools, parks, sewers, etc.

district mutation. A phenomenon observed frequently in rapidly growing cities in which the centers of various types of districts, e.g., retail districts, financial districts, move in the direction of city growth.

ditch. A man-made or natural small surface drain; a narrow, open excavation.

diversified farming. A type of farming in which farm income is derived from several sources.

divided interest. An interest in part of a whole property, e.g., a lessee's interest.

dividends. The income earnings on an equity investment.

division fence. A cross fence used to divide a ranch into various pastures. *See also* drift fence; line fence; snow fence.

Division of Liquidation (DOL). *See* Federal Deposit Insurance Corporation (FDIC).

division wall. An interior, load-bearing wall that divides a structure into rooms; a load-bearing or self-sustaining masonry wall that separates two abutting buildings.

dock

1. An elevated floor or platform used to facilitate the transfer of goods to or from a vehicle.
2. A structure extending from the shore into the water that permits the mooring of vessels; a wharf.
3. A slip or waterway that extends between two piers to receive ships; such a waterway, closed or open, and any surrounding piers and wharves.

documentation. In computer usage, written information describing the specifications and proper operation of a piece of hardware or software.

dog. A metal gripping or fastening implement used to bind timbers or other materials.

dollar adjustments. Adjustments for differences between the subject and the comparable properties expressed in dollars; often used to reflect differences in financing terms or physical characteristics. *See also* percentage adjustments.

dollar reward. *See* net present value.

dolphin. A post or pile cluster that is used to moor a boat; also, a bumper that protects the dock or wharf from vessels or floating objects.

dome. A hemispherical roof or ceiling constructed to exert equal, oblique thrust in all directions.

domestic hot water heater. A packaged unit that heats water for household purposes. (R.S. Means)

domicile. The locality where a person or corporation has legal residency.

dominant estate. *See* affirmative easement.

door. A unit of measure in truck terminal valuation; rentals are frequently related to $/door/month and sales comparisons may be made on the basis of $/door. Two cross-dock doors may be referred to as a *double door unit.*

door stop. A trim piece placed around the inside face of side and top door jambs to prevent damage from the door swinging too far.

dormer. A window set upright in a sloping or pitched roof; also the roofed structure in which such a window is set.

DOS. Disk operated system.

DOT. Department of Transportation.

double-declining balance method of depreciation. A method formerly used to calculate depreciation in which the initial cost of a capital asset is spread over time by deducting, in each period, twice the percentage recognized by the straight-line method, and applying this double percentage to the undepreciated balance at the start of each period. Since 1986 depreciation allowance tables have been used in place of this method. Also called *200% declining balance.*

double floor. Wood construction using a subfloor and a finished floor.

double framing. A building technique using double joists, trimmers, and other structural members for reinforcement.

double-gabled roof. *See* butterfly roof; M roof.

double glazing. Two glass panes hermetically sealed with an air space in between to provide insulation.

double house. A dwelling separated by party walls and designed for use by two families; also called a two-family house. *See also* duplex.

double-hung window. A window with two movable sashes that slide vertically.

double pitch. Sloping in two directions.

double-pitch roof. A roof that slopes in two directions. *See also* butterfly roof.

double plate. In construction, two horizontal boards that cover and connect the studs; serves as a foundation for the rafters.

double window header. Two boards laid on edge to form the upper portion of a door or window.

dovetail. An interlocking joint commonly used in carpentry, e.g., in drawers, cases.

dowel. A wooden or metal pin used to hold or reinforce the juncture of two timbers.

dower. The portion of, or interest in, a deceased husband's real estate that the law gives to the widow for life; varies with statutory provisions.

down payment. Cash a buyer pays at the time of purchase; usually includes the earnest money deposit. *See also* earnest money.

downspout. A pipe that carries rainwater from roof gutters to the ground or the storm sewer system; also called a *leader* or *rain leader.*

downzoning. A public action in which the local government reduces the allowable density for subsequent development, e.g., fewer housing units, fewer stores, or changes the allowable use from a high use to a low use, e.g., multifamily to single-family.

drainage. A system of drains, e.g., tiles, pipes, conduits, designed to remove surface or subsurface water or waste water and sewage.

drainage district. A unit of local government set up to construct and operate a drainage system for the area, usually to achieve a higher and better use of the land.

drainage ditch. An open watercourse other than a gutter.

drainage easement. *See* drainage right-of-way.

drainage right-of-way. The right to drain surface water from one owner's land over the land of one or more adjacent owners.

drain field. An area with a system of underground lateral pipes to drain septic systems of liquid overflow.

drain tile. A specially designed pipe used in a drainage system.

draw. A natural path of drainage on land, usually not of great depth.

drawings
1. Graphic illustrations depicting the dimensions, design, and location of a project. Generally including plans, elevations, details, diagrams, schedules, and sections.
2. The term, when capitalized, refers to the graphic portions of a project's contract documents. (R.S. Means)

draw request. Schedule prepared by the borrower requesting construction funds from the lender at specific points in the construction process; based on the percentage of work completed.

dress. The planing and finishing of a wood surface; to cut, trim, and smooth a material.

dressed and matched boards. Boards that are finished on one or two sides with tongue and groove edges.

dressed lumber. Lumber machined and surfaced on all four sides at a mill.

drift. Material moved from one place and deposited in another. Glacial drift includes glacial deposits and unstratified till as well as stratified glacial outwash materials.

drift fence. A partial fence open at both ends to keep stock from grazing in an area. *See also* division fence; line fence; snow fence.

drill track. A rail track serving industrial property from which individual industry tracks branch off to plant sites; track kept open for the movement of locomotives in sorting cars or moving them to and from yards; a track on which a locomotive works, not one on which cars stand; also called *lead track*.

drip

1. A projecting structural member that throws off rainwater and protects structural parts below; a channel cut underneath a sill.
2. Describes the part of a piping system that conveys condensation from the steam pipes to the water or return pipes.
3. A type of easement or servitude derived from civil law that grants permission for the falling or dripping of water from the roof of one property owner onto the estate of a neighbor.

drop. In air conditioning, the vertical distance that a horizontally projected air stream has fallen when it reaches the end of its throw. (R.S. Means)

drop ceiling (dropped ceiling). A nonstructural ceiling suspended below the structural system, usually in a modular grid pattern. A drop ceiling usually contains a lighting system. (R.S. Means)

drop panel. In reinforced concrete slab construction, an area around a column head or mushroom column where the slab is deeper.

drop siding. A type of tongue and groove weatherboard applied to the exterior of frame structures. *See also* lap siding.

drought. Lack of rain; a relatively long period without rainfall, causing crop damage and the depletion of moisture in the soil.

droughty soil. A loose-textured soil with poor water-holding capacity due to the presence of sand or gravel subsoil.

drumlin. A long, narrow hill or ridge of unstratified glacial drift, normally compact, positioned with its length parallel to the movement of the ice responsible for its deposition. Because parallel ridges give the land poor drainage, drumlins are frequently surrounded by swampy terrain.

dry dock. An artificial basin for the reception of vessels from which water can be removed; used to repair ships below waterline.

dryer. In agriculture, a facility used to dry or dehydrate farm crops prior to storage or milling.

dry farming. Cultivation under semi-arid conditions.

dry-pipe sprinkler system (dry sprinkler). A sprinkler system with pipes that remain empty of water until the system is activated.

dry rot. A decay of seasoned wood caused by a fungus.

drywall. Interior walls made of gypsum board; walls constructed not of plaster, but of materials such as wood paneling, plywood, hardboard, or any other type of wallboard are broadly referred to as dry-wall. *See also* gypsum wallboard; Sheetrock.

drywall construction. A type of interior wall construction using wood paneling, plywood, plasterboard, or any other type of wallboard instead of plaster as the finish material.

dry well. A drainage pit lined or filled so that roof runoff, liquid effluent, or other sanitary wastes will leach or percolate into the surrounding soil.

DSTM. *See* department-store type merchandise.

ducts

1. In construction, conduits used to transmit and distribute warm or cooled air from a central unit to the rooms.
2. The space in an underground conduit that contains electrical cables or conductors.

due diligence

1. A stated or assumed requirement that the party to a contract make a reasonable, good-faith effort to perform his or her obligations under the contract.
2. Refers to a legal obligation, e.g., in connection with the public sale of securities in real estate syndicates or corporations, of the underwriting or selling group to ensure that the offering statement or prospectus does not misstate or omit material information.

due-on-sale clause. A clause in mortgage contracts that provides that the outstanding loan balance is due when the mortgaged property is sold or transferred; precludes loan assumption by a new buyer.

dumbwaiter. A small hoisting mechanism or elevator in a building used for hoisting materials only. A small elevator used for conveying dishes and food in a restaurant or house. (R.S. Means)

dumpster. Portable container box normally placed on a construction site for the disposal of job-generated refuse. (R.S. Means)

duplex. A house containing two separate dwelling units, side by side or one above the other; also describes apartments that occupy two levels or a portion of two floors.

durable capital goods. Goods that can be used repeatedly, e.g., machinery, as distinguished from raw material.

durable goods. Consumer goods that can be used repeatedly, e.g., a refrigerator, as distinguished from short-lived goods, e.g., bread.

Dutch colonial architecture. A residential style of architecture characterized by gambrel roofs, exterior walls of masonry or wood, and side porches.

Dutch door. A door divided horizontally in the middle so that the bottom half can remain closed while the top is open.

dutchman. A piece of wood or other material used to conceal a defect, strengthen a weak part, or fill an opening.

dwelling. A structure designed or occupied as the living quarters of one or more households; usually equipped with cooking, bathing, toilet, and heating facilities, where necessary.

DWV. Drain, waste, and vent system.

E

earnest money. A part of the purchase price given to bind a bargain. In real estate transactions, this deposit is frequently used as an initial payment.

earning power. The capacity to generate income.

earnings. *See* income.

earnings approach. *See* income capitalization approach.

earthquake load. The total force that an earthquake exerts on a given structure. (R.S. Means)

easement. An interest in real property that conveys use, but not ownership, of a portion of an owner's property. Access or right-of-way easements may be acquired by private parties or public utilities. Governments dedicate conservation, open space, and preservation easements. *See also* reciprocal easement.

easement appurtenant. An easement that is attached to, benefits, and passes with the conveyance of the dominant estate; runs with the land for the benefit of the dominant estate and continues to burden the servient estate, although such an estate may be conveyed to new owners.

easement by prescription. The right to use another's land, which is established by exercising this right over a period of time. Such an easement is not specifically granted; it is understood. Also called *prescriptive easement.*

easement in gross. An easement that is not attached or appurtenant to any particular estate; does not run with the land nor is it transferred through the conveyance of title.

eaves. The lower or outer edge of a roof that projects over the side walls of a structure.

econometrics. The application of mathematics and statistics to the interpretation of economic data, testing of economic theories, and solution of economic problems. *See also* economics; graphic analysis; isoquant; statistical analysis.

economic age-life method. A method of estimating accrued depreciation in which the ratio between the effective age of a building and its total economic life is applied to the current cost of the improvements to obtain a lump-sum deduction.

economic approach. *See* income capitalization approach.

economic base. The economic activity of a community that enables it to attract income from outside its borders. A single activity may constitute the economic base of a community.

economic base analysis. A survey of the industries and businesses that generate employment and income in a community as well as the rate of population growth and levels of income, both of which are functions of employment. Economic base analysis is used to forecast the level and composition of future economic activity. Specifically, the relationship between basic employment (which brings income into a community) and nonbasic employment (which provides services for workers in the basic employment sector) is studied to predict population, income, or other variables that affect real estate values or land utilization. *See also* basic activities; nonbasic activities; nonbasic income.

economic base multiplier. *See* basic multiplier.

economic enterprise. In agriculture, a business of sufficient resources to provide an accepted standard of living for a family; also called an *economic unit.*

economic feasibility. The ability of a project or an enterprise to meet defined investment objectives; an investment's ability to produce sufficient revenue to pay all expenses and charges and to provide a reasonable return on and recapture of the money invested. In reference to a service or residential property where revenue is not a fundamental consideration, economic soundness is based on the need for and desirability of the property for a particular purpose. An investment property is economically feasible if its prospective earning power is sufficient to pay a fair rate of return on its complete cost (including indirect costs), i.e., the estimated value at completion equals or exceeds the estimated cost.

economic impact statement. A report detailing a major real estate project's potential impact on the local economy, which may include estimates of the project's market value and potential gross sales as well as indications of its business, occupational, and tax impact on the community.

economic indicator. Any of a group of statistical parameters (e.g., trade/payment balance, currency exchange rates, commodity prices, CPI, wage levels, interest rates, production levels, GNP, volume of retail sales, unemployment rate) that, taken together, provide an indication of the health of the economy. There are lagging, leading, and roughly coincident economic indicators.

economic life. The period over which improvements to real property contribute to property value.

economic obsolescence. *See* external obsolescence.

economic rent
1. In appraisal, a term sometimes used as a synonym for *market rent*.
2. In economics, the surplus payment in excess of the amount necessary to justify the development of a property or to attract any factor of production into an enterprise.

economics. A social science concerned with the description and analysis of the production, distribution, and consumption of goods and services. *See also* econometrics; economic base analysis; investment analysis; macroeconomics; microeconomics.

effective age. The age indicated by the condition and utility of a structure.

effective area
1. The net area of an air inlet or outlet system through which air can pass. The effective area equals the free area of the device multiplied by the coefficient of discharge.
2. The cross-sectional area of a structural member, calculated to resist applied stress. (R.S. Means)

effective demand. The desire to buy coupled with the ability to pay. When the term *demand* is used in economics or real estate analysis, effective demand is usually presumed. *See also* effective purchasing power.

effective gross income *(EGI)*. The anticipated income from all operations of the real property after an allowance is made for vacancy and collection losses. Effective gross income includes items constituting other income, i.e., income generated from the operation of the real property that is not derived from space rental (e.g., parking rental or income from vending machines).

effective gross income multiplier *(EGIM)*. The ratio between the sale price (or value) of a property and its effective gross income; a single year's *EGI* expectancy or an annual average of several years' *EGI* expectancies *(EGIM = V/EGI)*.

effective interest rate *(i)*. Interest per dollar per period; the nominal annual interest rate divided by the number of conversion periods per year; also, the lender's yield to maturity, which in many instances is equivalent to the lender's internal rate of return; also called *effective rate*. *See also* nominal interest rate *(I)*.

effective purchasing power. The ability of an individual or group to participate in a market, i.e., to acquire goods and services with cash or its equivalent. *See also* effective demand.

effective rent. The rental rate net of financial concessions such as periods of no rent during the lease term; may be calculated on a discounted basis, reflecting the time value of money, or on a simple, straight-line basis.

effective tax rate

1. The ratio between the annual property tax on real estate and its market value; the tax rate times the assessed value divided by the market value; the official tax rate times the assessment ratio; the actual income tax paid per period divided by the taxable income for the period.

2. The tax rate expressed as a percentage of market value; this will be different from the nominal tax rate when the assessment ratio is not equal to 1. (IAAO). *See also* marginal tax rate.

efficiency ratio

1. In appraising, the ratio between the net rentable area of a building, i.e., the space used and occupied exclusively by tenants, and its gross area, which includes the building's core.

2. In land utilization, the ratio between the value of the product flowing from the site and the expense of the labor and capital that produced it; refers to the average amount of net product, e.g., rent, returned per unit of labor and capital applied.

3. In economics, the ratio between the ends produced, or output, and the means used, or input.

efflorescence. A white powder on brick or stone that forms as a result of a chemical action and can be washed off without damage; deposits of soluble salts on the surface of masonry.

effluent. Liquid sewage that has passed through any stage of purification.

egress. A way out; an exit or outlet.

EIS. *See* environmental impact study.

elastic. In economics, the responsiveness of prices to changes in the supply or demand for a good.

elasticity of demand. The tendency for the price of real estate to vary directly with shifts in demand. Prices tend to increase if demand increases and other factors remain constant; conversely, prices tend to decrease if demand decreases and other factors remain constant.

elastomeric roofing. Single sheet (ply) of rubber-like, layered membrane consisting of several combinations of plastics and synthetic rubber stretched into place as a roof cover. It may be loosely laid, ballasted, mechanically fastened or fully adhered. Also used to describe a single component liquid or spray applied to the roof surface to yield elastomeric films (hypalon-neoprene, silicone) for high-strength, waterproof membranes. (Marshall & Swift)

elderly housing. *See* congregate housing; continuing care retirement center (CCRC); empty nester; lifecare facilities; nursing home; retirement community.

electrical outlet. A point on the wiring system where current is available to activate equipment.

electric heating. Any of several methods that convert electrical energy into usable heat.

eleemosynary. Of or pertaining to a charitable institution or a not-for-profit corporation.

elements of comparison. The characteristics or attributes of properties and transactions that cause the prices of real estate to vary; include real property rights conveyed, financing terms, conditions of sale, market conditions, location, physical characteristics, and other characteristics such as economic characteristics, use, and non-realty components of value.

elevated floor. Any floor system not supported by the subgrade. (R.S. Means)

elevated slab. A floor or roof slab supported by structural members. (R.S. Means)

elevation

1. A geometric projection of a vertical plane perpendicular to the horizon, e.g., of the external, upright parts of a building from a front, side, or rear view.
2. Altitude; the height of a place or point above mean sea level.

elevator

1. A raising and lowering mechanism that moves on tracks up and down a shaft between the floors of a building and is equipped with a car or platform to transport passengers and freight.
2. A farm storage building in which a commodity such as wheat is stored.

elevator car. That part of an elevator that includes the platform, enclosure, car frame, and gate or door. (R.S. Means)

elevator pit. That part of an elevator shaft that extends from the threshold level of the lowest landing door down to the floor at the very bottom of the shaft. (R.S. Means)

elevator shaft. A hoistway through which one or more elevator cars may travel. (R.S. Means)

Ellwood formula. A yield capitalization method that provides a formulaic solution for developing a capitalization rate for various combinations of equity yields and mortgage terms. The formula is applicable only to properties with stable or stabilized income streams and properties with income streams expected to change according to the *J*- or *K*-factor pattern. The formula is:

$$R_O = \frac{Y_E - M\,(Y_E + P\,1/S_n - R_M) - \Delta_O\,1/S_n}{1 + \Delta_I\,J}$$

where:

R_O = overall capitalization rate

Y_E = equity yield rate

M = loan-to-value ratio

P = percentage of loan paid off

$1/S_n$ = sinking fund factor at the equity yield rate

R_M = mortgage capitalization rate or mortgage constant

Δ_O = change in total property value

Δ_I = total ratio change in income

J = J factor

Also called *mortgage-equity formula*.

embankment. A ridge constructed of earth, fill rocks, or gravel and used most commonly to retain water or to carry a roadway. The length of an embankment exceeds both its width and its height. (R.S. Means)

emergency exit. A door, hatch, or other device leading to the outside of the structure and usually kept closed and locked. This exit is used chiefly for the emergency evacuation of a building, airplane, or other occupied space when conventional exits fail, are insufficient, or are rendered inaccessible. (R.S. Means)

emergency lighting. Temporary illumination provided by battery or generator and essential to safety during the failure or interruption of the conventional electric power supply. (R.S. Means)

emergency power. Electricity temporarily produced and supplied by a standby power generator when the conventional electric power supply fails or is interrupted. Emergency power is essential in facilities like hospitals, where even relatively short power outages could be life-threatening to certain individuals. (R.S. Means)

eminent domain. The right of government to take private property for public use upon the payment of just compensation. The Fifth Amendment of the U.S. Constitution, also known as "the takings clause," guarantees payment of just compensation upon appropriation of private property.

Employee Relocation Council (ERC). A nonprofit organization founded in 1964 whose members include corporations, relocation service companies, brokers, and appraisers involved in the transfer of corporate employees. The ERC provides relocation assistance to transferred employees who wish to sell their homes and acquire new ones.

employment base. The number of gainfully employed persons in a community or city.

employment density. The ratio between the number of employees actually working in the largest, normal daily shift at a plant site and the land area of the site.

empty nester. A pre-retiree, generally 55 years old or older, who is seeking to move from a large, single-family home to a smaller home, condominium, or townhouse. Most empty nesters are married couples who currently have no dependents.

encapsulation. A technique for trapping asbestos fibers in a dense chemical substance. (R.S. Means)

enclosed stair. An interior staircase that has a closed string on each side, often encased in walls or partitions. There are also door openings at various floor levels, thus making it accessible to hallways of living units. (R. S. Means)

enclosure. Land enclosed with a visible or tangible obstruction, e.g., a fence, a hedge, a ditch, to protect the premises from encroachment by animals.

encroachment
1. Trespassing on the domain of another.
2. Partial or gradual displacement of an existing use by another use, e.g., locating commercial or industrial improvements in a residential district.

encumbrance. An interest or right in real property that may decrease or increase the value of the fee estate but does not prevent its conveyance by the owner. An encumbrance effects a permanent reduction in an owner's property rights, while a lien represents a claim against the owner's property rights which may or may not become permanent. Mortgages, taxes, and judgments are liens; restrictions, easements, and reservations are encumbrances.

energy audit. An inventory of the physical characteristics of a building that affect thermal efficiency; conducted to identify appropriate energy conservation measures, estimate the cost of these measures, and calculate the savings they are likely to produce.

energy efficiency. The ability of an appliance or a building's energy system to produce a given effect with minimum effort, expense, and waste; quantitatively, the ratio between an output and the energy expended to achieve that output. *See also* energy efficiency ratio *(EER)*.

energy efficiency ratio *(EER)*. A measure of the efficiency of an electric heat pump, air conditioner, or vapor compressor heating or cooling device; the ratio between output, expressed in Btus per hour, and energy input, expressed in watts.

engineering breakdown method. *See* breakdown method.

engineer's scale. A straightedge on which each inch is divided into uniform multiples of ten, thus enabling drawings to be made with distances, loads, forces, and other calculations expressed in decimal values. (R.S. Means)

English architecture. A residential architectural style incorporating the features of Elizabethan, Tudor, Cotswold, and other English architectural styles; characterized by large, stone houses with slate shingles on gable roofs, mullioned casement windows, wainscoted interiors, and sometimes exposed timbers. *See also* English Cotswold architecture; English half-timbered architecture; Tudor architecture.

English Cotswold architecture. A residential architectural style patterned after English country houses and characterized by sills, mullions, porches, stone chimneys, heavy details, and a roof of irregularly shaped, variegated slates.

English half-timbered architecture. A rustic, informal, residential architectural style characterized by exterior ornamentation of half-timber and plaster, carved wood, stone, and brick, and steep roof slopes that end in barge boards rather than cornices; also called *Elizabethan architecture.*

ensilage. Green fodder that is chopped or shredded and preserved in a silo or pit.

entrepreneur. One who assumes the risks and management of a business or enterprise in exchange for possible gains; a promoter who initiates development.

entrepreneurial incentive. *See* entrepreneurial profit.

entrepreneurial profit

1. A market-derived figure that represents the amount an entrepreneur expects to receive for his or her contribution to a project; the difference between the total cost of a property (cost of development) and its market value (property value after completion), which represents the entrepreneur's compensation for the risk and expertise associated with development. In the cost approach, expected profit is reflected as entrepreneurial profit.

2. In economics, the actual return on successful management practices, often identified with coordination, the fourth factor of production following land, labor, and capital; also called *entrepreneurial return* or *entrepreneurial reward*. *See also* developer's fee; project profit.

envelope

1. A term used to denote the extreme outside surface and dimensions of a building. (R.S. Means)

2. An assembly of planes representing the limits of an area that may house a structure, i.e., a zoning envelope. (R.S. Means) *See also* building envelope.

environment. The social, physical, political, and economic characteristics of the area surrounding a property, which can affect its value.

environmental deficiency. Conditions, circumstances, and influences that surround an area and promote blight and deterioration, e.g., overcrowding or improper location of structures on the land, excessive dwelling unit density, conversion of buildings to incompatible uses, the presence of obsolete buildings, detrimental land uses, unsafe or congested streets, inadequate utilities or community facilities.

environmental impact study (EIS). An investigation to assess the comprehensive, long-range environmental impact of a proposed land use, including both direct and indirect effects over all phases of use.

environmental lien. A charge, security, or encumbrance upon title to a property to secure the payment of a cost, damage, debt, obligation or duty arising out of response actions, cleanup or other remediation of hazardous substances or petroleum products upon a property, including (but not limited to) liens imposed pursuant to CERCLA 42 USC 9607 (1) and similar state or local laws. (ASTM)

environmental obsolescence. *See* external obsolescence.

environmental professional. A person possessing sufficient training and experience necessary to conduct site reconnaissance, interviews, and other activities... and from the information generated by such activities, having the ability to develop conclusions regarding recognized environmental conditions in connection with the property in question. An individual's status as an environmental professional may be limited to the type of assessment to be performed or to specific segments of the assessment for which the professional is responsible. The person may be an independent contractor or an employee of the user. (ASTM)

environmental property assessment (EPRA). A procedure commonly conducted at commercial and industrial sites to identify potential environmental problems prior to the transfer of the property. EPRAs are performed in phases. A phase one audit focuses on evidence of potential contamination; a phase two audit confirms the presence of contamination; and a phase three audit describes its extent. Also called *environmental site assessment, environmental survey,* or *transactional audit.*

Environmental Protection Agency (EPA). An independent agency of the executive branch of the U.S. Government with broad powers to control and prevent water, air, and noise pollution and to protect the nation's environment in general.

environmental site assessment (ESA). The process by which a person or entity seeks to determine if a particular parcel of real property (including improvements) is subject to recognized environmental conditions. . . An environmental site assessment is both different from and less rigorous than an environmental audit. (ASTM) *See also* environmental property assessment (EPRA)

EOP. End of period; often used to describe when scheduled payments are due; as distinguished from BOP (beginning of period).

EPA. *See* Environmental Protection Agency.

EPA identification number. A number assigned to each generator of hazardous waste that notifies the EPA of its activity. (R.S. Means)

EPRA. *See* environmental property assessment.

Equal Credit Opportunity Act. Federal legislation effective in 1992 that entitles borrowers to receive, upon written request to their lender, a copy of the appraisal report used in connection with their mortgage application.

Equal Employment Opportunity Commission (EEOC). A government agency under the administration of the Department of Labor. This agency is dedicated to enforcing the provisions of Title IV of the Civil Rights Act of 1964, which forbids discrimination by an employer based on the race, color, religion, sex, or national origin of a potential employee. (R.S. Means)

equalization. The process by which an appropriate governmental body attempts to ensure that all property under its jurisdiction is assessed equitably at market value or at a ratio or ratios as required by law. (IAAO)

equalized values. Assessed values after they have been multiplied by common factors during equalization. (IAAO)

equilibrium. *See* market equilibrium.

equipment. Fixed assets other than real estate, e.g., office equipment, automotive equipment; as distinguished from fixtures, which are assets that are physically or legally attached to the real estate. *See also* chattel.

equipment and mechanical systems. Equipment and mechanical systems are divided into two categories: those needed to provide for human comfort, such as plumbing, heating, air-conditioning, and lighting, and process-related equipment and mechanical systems. *See also* process-related equipment and mechanical systems.

equitable ownership. The estate or interest of a person who has a beneficial right in property that is legally owned by another, e.g., the beneficiary of a trust has an equitable estate or interest in the trust property.

equitable right of redemption. *See* equity of redemption.

equity

1. The ownership claim on property. Total property value is obtainable by adding equity to the debt claim. Equity investors assume greater risk and their earnings are subordinate to operating expenses and debt service. They are compensated with dividends (cash flows) and possible appreciation in the value of their investments. Equity includes the residual claim to the assets, which is solely possessed by the owners.

2. In regard to a specific property, equity refers to the net value of the property obtained by subtracting from its total value all liens or other charges against it; the value of an owner's interest in property in excess of all claims and liens.

3. In regard to social, economic, or political issues, equity refers to the fairness or justness of a program or policy.

equity buildup. An increase in the equity investor's share of total property value that results from gradual debt reduction through periodic repayment of principal on a mortgage loan, an increase in total property value, or both.

equity capitalization rate (R_E). An income rate that reflects the relationship between a single year's pre-tax cash flow expectancy and the equity investment; used to convert pre-tax cash flow (equity dividend) into an equity value indication; also called the *cash on cash rate, cash flow rate,* or *equity dividend rate.* (R_E = pre-tax cash flow/equity invested)

equity-debt ratio. The ratio of the equity value or equity capital invested in a property to the amount of debt incurred on that property.

equity dividend. Cash flow after debt service but before income and capital gains taxes. *See also* pre-tax cash flow *(PTCF).*

equity dividend rate. *See* equity capitalization rate *(R_E).*

equity fund. A limited partnership or real estate investment trust (REIT) formed to purchase equities in real estate; typically formed to develop projects and purchase equity in existing projects.

equity kicker. An interest in the equity of a property given to the mortgage lender to increase the lender's yield.

equity of redemption. The right of a mortgagor by absolute deed to redeem the property by paying the debt; exercised after forfeiture, but before sale under foreclosure, transfer of title, or expiration of this right under the statute of limitations; also called *equitable right of redemption.*

equity participation. The right of a lender to receive a share of the gross profit, net profit, or cash flow from or appreciation of a property on which it has made a loan as an additional return to the lender. *See also* equity participation mortgage; income participation.

equity participation mortgage. A mortgage in which the lender receives a share of the income and sometimes a share of the reversion from a property on which the lender has made a loan; also called *participation mortgage.*

equity ratio (1 - *M*). The ratio between the down payment paid on a property and its total price; the fraction of the investment that is unencumbered by debt.

equity residual technique. *See* residual techniques.

equity value. Market value less all encumbrances on the property. (Marshall & Swift)

equity yield rate (Y_e). A rate of return on equity capital as distinguished from the rate of return on debt capital (the interest rate); the equity investor's internal rate of return. The equity yield rate considers the effect of debt financing on the cash flow to the equity investor.

ERC. *See* Employee Relocation Council.

erosion. The wearing away of surface land by natural causes, e.g., running water, winds. *See also* gully erosion; rill erosion; sheet erosion.

errors and omissions insurance (E&O). Insurance to cover errors or omissions in the performance of professional services. *See also* insurance, professional liability.

ESA. Economic Stabilization Agency.

escalation. An increase in the cost of performing construction work, resulting from performing the work in a later period of time and at a cost higher than originally anticipated in the bid. (R.S. Means)

escalation clause. A clause in an agreement that provides for the adjustment of a price or rent based on some event or index, e.g., a provision to increase rent if operating expenses increase; also called *expense recovery clause.*

escalation income. Income generated from an escalation clause in a lease.

escalator lease. A lease that requires the lessor to pay expenses for the first year and the lessee to pay any necessary increases in expenses as additional rent over the subsequent years of the lease.

escape clause. A provision that allows a tenant to cancel a lease.

escarpment. A long, precipitous face of rock or land.

escheat. The right of government that gives the state titular ownership of a property when its owner dies without a will or any ascertainable heirs.

escrow. Property or evidences of property, e.g., money, securities, instruments, deposited by two or more persons with a third person to be delivered under a certain contingency or on the completion of specified terms. An escrow account is generally held to cover taxes and insurance.

esker. A ridge of sandy or gravelly material deposited in a stream channel beneath a glacier, which indicates the meandering course of the stream.

established business value. *See* going-concern value.

estate. A right or interest in property.

estate at will. The occupation of lands and tenements by a tenant for an unspecified period, which can be terminated by one or both parties.

estate for years. A leasehold interest in land established by a contract for possession for a specified period of time.

estate in land. The degree, nature, or extent of interest that a person has in land.

estate in possession. An estate that entitles the owner to the immediate possession, use, and enjoyment of the property.

estate in reversion. The residue of an estate left by operation of law in the grantor, the grantor's successors, or the successors of a testator, who can possess the estate on the termination of some particular estate granted or devised.

estate of inheritance. An estate that can be passed on to heirs, i.e., all freehold estates except estates for life.

estate tax. A tax on the estate or wealth of a deceased person that is usually computed as a percentage of the market value of the assets of the estate.

estimate. A preliminary opinion of the cost of performing work.

estimate of value. In appraising, an opinion based on an analysis of adequate data by one qualified to develop such an opinion.

estimator. One who is capable of predicting the probable cost of a building project. (R.S. Means)

estoppel. A legal doctrine under which one is precluded and forbidden from denying his or her own act or deed.

estoppel certificate. A statement of material facts or conditions on which another person can rely because it cannot be denied at a later date. In real estate, a buyer of rental property typically requests estoppel certificates from existing tenants.

estovers. The right of a tenant to use timber from the leased premises to the extent deemed necessary to promote husbandry, e.g., the building and maintaining of feed bunks, storage cribs, and loafing sheds.

Eurodollars. Monies such as U.S. dollars deposited outside their countries of origin and used in foreign money markets, especially markets in Europe and the Far East.

evaluation
1. A study of the nature, quality, or utility of a parcel of real estate or interests in, or aspects of, real property in which a value estimate is not necessarily required; sometimes used to denote consulting. *See also* analysis.

2. The Office of the Comptroller of the Currency distinguishes between "appraisals" undertaken for any real estate-related financial transaction involving loans of amounts more than the federal de minimis and "evaluations" required for real estate collateral for loans of amounts equal to the federal de minimis or less. The OCC specifies that like appraisals, evaluations are used to validate real estate values that serve as collateral to support a borrower's credit capacity. Further, the OCC states that an evaluation may be required to determine the appropriate carrying value, and probable sales price, for foreclosed properties. (Banking Issuance regarding 12 CFR 34)

evaporative cooling. Cooling achieved by the evaporation of water in air, thus increasing humidity and decreasing dry-bulb temperature. (R.S. Means)

evaporator. The part of a refrigeration system in which vaporization of the refrigerant occurs, absorbing heat from the surrounding fluid and producing cooling. (R.S. Means)

eviction. The ouster of one or more persons from a property; a legal process for the recovery of property by virtue of a paramount right recognized by law or for a default.

exactions. *See* development exaction.

examination of title. An interpretation of the condition of the title to real property based on a title search or abstract.

exception. In contracts, a clause in which the maker denies or negates something granted elsewhere in the contract; the exclusion of something from the effect or operation of the contract that would otherwise be included.

excess condemnation. The policy on the part of the condemnor of taking, by right of eminent domain, more property than is physically necessary for the public improvement.

excess frontage table. A table of factors that reflect the decrease in unit front foot value of a parcel of land (usually residential) attributable to an excess of frontage; applies to land held in one ownership with more lot frontage than is typical or standard in the area.

excess income. *See* excess rent.

excess land. In regard to an improved site, the land not needed to serve or support the existing improvement. In regard to a vacant site or a site considered as though vacant, the land not needed to accommodate the site's primary highest and best use. Such land may be separated from the larger site and have its own highest and best use, or it may allow for future expansion of the existing or anticipated improvement. *See also* surplus land.

excess rent. The amount by which contract rent exceeds market rent at the time of the appraisal; created by a lease favorable to the landlord (lessor) and may reflect a locational advantage, unusual management, unknowledgeable parties, or a lease execution in an earlier, stronger rental market. Due to the higher risk inherent in the receipt of excess rent, it may be calculated separately and capitalized at a higher rate in the income capitalization approach.

excess value. Value over and above market value which is ascribable to a lease that guarantees contract rental income in excess of market rent at the time of the appraisal.

exchange. The trading of equities in certain types of properties, usually to defer the capital gains tax liability incurred in an outright sale.

exchange value. The value of a commodity in terms of money to persons generally; as distinguished from use value to a specific person.

exclusive agency listing. A contract to sell property which states that only one agent has been hired to sell the property, but the seller may sell through his or her own efforts without paying a commission; also, a property so listed.

exclusive right to sell listing. A contract to sell property which states that the agent, or listing broker, is entitled to the commission regardless of who sells the property, including the owner.

exculpatory clause. A provision in an agreement that limits the recourse of one party against the other party in the event of default; e.g., a nonrecourse mortgage limits recovery to the property itself.

execution sale. A legal procedure that enforces a payment judgment; property is sold to obtain the amount owed.

executor. An individual or trust institution designated in a will or appointed by a court to settle the estate of a deceased person.

executor's deed. A transfer of real estate in which the grantor is the executor of the granting estate.

exemption. *See* tax exemption.

exhaust fume hood. A prefabricated hood unit that serves to confine noxious or toxic fumes for subsequent exhausting or filtration. (R.S. Means)

existing building. In codes and regulations, an already completed building or one that prior laws or regulations allowed to be built. (R.S. Means)

expanded metal. A type of open-mesh metal lath made by slitting and stretching sheet metal. Comes in different patterns and thicknesses. (R.S. Means)

expansion joint. In a building structure or concrete work, a joint or gap between adjacent parts which allows for safe and inconsequential relative movement of the parts, caused by thermal variations or other conditions. (R.S. Means)

expected value. A measure of investment risk that employs weighted probabilities. An event is weighted based on the probability of its occurrence.

expense ratio. The ratio of total expenses, excluding debt service, to either potential or effective gross income. *See also* operating expense ratio.

expense recovery clause. *See* escalation clause.

expenses. *See* operating expenses.

expense stop. A clause in a lease that limits the landlord's expense obligation because the lessee assumes any expenses above an established level.

expert. One who is presumed to have special knowledge of, or skill in, a particular field due to education, experience, or study.

expert testimony. Testimony of persons who are presumed to have special knowledge of, or skill in, a particular field due to education, experience, or study.

expert witness. One qualified to render expert testimony.

exponent. A number that indicates the number of times another value (the base) is to be used as a factor; e.g., in x^3, x is the base and 3 is the exponent. Thus, $x^3 = (x)(x)(x)$.

exponential-curve (constant-ratio) change per period. Refers to a type of annuity or income/property model that increases or decreases at a constant ratio and, as a result, the increases or decreases are compounded.

exponential smoothing. An exponentially weighted moving average applied to a time series. *See also* moving average; smoothing; time series.

exponential weighting. The simplest form of exponential smoothing.

exposure
1. The time a property remains on the market.
2. The estimated length of time the property interest being appraised would have been offered on the market prior to the hypothetical consummation of a sale at market value on the effective date of the appraisal; a retrospective estimate based upon an analysis of past events assuming a com-

petitive and open market. Exposure time is always presumed to occur prior to the effective date of the appraisal. The overall concept of reasonable exposure encompasses not only adequate, sufficient and reasonable time but also adequate, sufficient and reasonable effort. Exposure time is different for various types of real estate and value ranges and under various market conditions. (Appraisal Standards Board of The Appraisal Foundation, *Statement on Appraisal Standards No. 6*, "Reasonable Exposure Time in Market Value Estimates," October 1992) *See also* marketing period.

expressway. A highway with full or partial control of access where major crossroads are separated in grade from the roads for through traffic of all types.

expropriation. A British or Canadian term synonymous with *eminent domain* as used in the United States.

extended-stay hotel. A hotel designed for travelers who must stay in an area for a prolonged period, typically seven or more days; differs from a standard hotel in that rooms and amenities have a more residential atmosphere. Guestrooms have large living areas and full, eat-in kitchens; some have two separate sleeping areas, individual dining rooms, and separate baths. The exterior of an extended-stay hotel is similar to that of a garden apartment complex with recreational facilities and even barbecue grills. Since extended-stay travelers stay over the weekend, these hotels do not suffer normal weekend declines in occupancy. Some enjoy occupancy levels above 80%. Offering limited food and beverage service, extended-stay hotels are usually easy to operate and have higher profit margins. *See also* hotel.

extension agreement. An instrument that grants further time to pay an obligation or to fulfill the requirements of a contract.

extensive farming. The use of comparatively small amounts of labor and working capital to farm each acre of land.

exterior description. The part of a building description that provides information about the details of the building's substructure, superstructure, and exterior components.

exterior finish. The outside finish of a structure which includes roof and wall covering, gutters, and door and window frames; any protective outer cover.

exterior fixture. An outside item, e.g., an areaway, a canopy, a marquee, a platform, a loading dock, that is permanently attached to and part of the building structure.

exterior wall. Any outer wall, except a common wall, that serves as a vertical enclosure of a building.

external conformity. The compatibility between a property and its surroundings.

externalities

1. The principle that economies outside a property have a positive effect on its value while diseconomies outside a property have a negative effect upon its value.
2. Costs or benefits accruing to a property for which compensation or remuneration cannot be handled through normal, contractual procedures.

external obsolescence. An element of accrued depreciation; a defect, usually incurable, caused by negative influences outside a site and generally incurable on the part of the owner, landlord, or tenant.

extraction. A method of estimating land value in which the depreciated cost of the improvements on the improved property is estimated and deducted from the total sale price to arrive at an estimated sale price for the land; most effective when the improvements contribute little to the total sale price of the property.

extrapolation. Calculating or estimating a quantity beyond the range of the data on which the calculation or estimate is based; projections into the future that presume a continuation of observed trends, patterns, or relationships.

F

FAA. *See* Federal Aviation Administration.

facade. The principal, exterior face of a structure; usually the front face or front elevation of a building.

facade easement. A restriction that prohibits the fee owner of a property from altering the facade or exterior of an existing improvement on his or her land; generally imposed on historically significant structures to ensure their preservation.

face
1. The most important side of a structure; the front or facade.
2. The exposed surface of an object, e.g., the earth, a structure, a wall, a panel.

face block. *See* facing block.

face brick. A better grade of brick used for an exterior wall of a building, often only on the facade.

faced wall. A wall, usually of masonry, that has an exterior face of a different material. The two materials are bonded so that they serve as a single load-bearing unit.

face value. The stated price of securities or sale/rent transactions, e.g., bonds, stocks, mortgages, contracts for deed, purchase agreements, or leases as set forth in the documents themselves. Face value may not equal the cash equivalent value of the security or sale/rent transaction. (Marshall & Swift)

facilities management. The process of coordinating the physical work place with the people and the work of an organization. The primary function of facilities management is to plan, establish and maintain a work environment that effectively supports the goals and objectives of the organization. (BOMA)

facility audit
1. An assessment of the physical condition and functional performance of an organization's facilities.
2. A review of activities at a facility or location, the purpose of which is to identify the improper storage, handling, or disposal of hazardous materials or waste. (R.S. Means)

facing block. A concrete masonry unit having a decorative exterior finish. (R.S. Means)

factor
1. One of the elements that contributes to a given result, e.g., land

as a contribution to the value of an improved property.

2. An organization such as a finance company or commercial bank that lends money to dealers and producers and operates by discounting accounts receivable.

3. One of two or more numbers that, when multiplied together, produce a given number, e.g., 2 and 5 are factors of 10; also, a divisor.

4. Arithmetically, the reciprocal of a rate; a multiplier or coefficient. *See also* multiplier.

factors in production. *See* agents in production.

factory and shop lumber. Lumber that is cut for use in manufacturing; graded on the basis of the percentage of area that will produce a limited number of cuttings of a specified or given minimum size and quality.

factory-built. A reference to a construction, usually a dwelling, that is built, or at least partially preassembled, in a factory rather than on site. Most factory-built units are constructed in two or more modules, often complete with plumbing, wiring, etc. The modules are delivered to a building site and assembled there. Finish work is then performed. Factory-built houses are generally less expensive to build and quicker to erect because of savings gained through mass production and factory efficiencies. (R.S. Means)

fair housing laws. Federal, state, and local laws that guarantee persons the right to buy, sell, lease, hold, and convey property without discrimination on the basis of race, color, religion, gender, sexual preference, or national origin.

fair rental. *See* market rent.

fair value

1. A concept that was developed in the 1970s to address specific concerns which have since been satisfied by the evolution of the market value concept in the 1980s. *See also* market value; value.

2. The following definition is used by the Office of the Comptroller of the Currency (12 CFR Part 34, 42f [Docket No. 90-0016]): The cash price that might reasonably be anticipated in a current sale under all conditions requisite to a fair sale. A fair sale means that buyer and seller are each acting prudently, knowledgeably, and under no necessity to buy or sell—i.e., other than in a forced or liquidation sale. The appraiser should estimate the cash price that might

be received upon exposure to the open market for a reasonable time, considering the property type and local market conditions. When a current sale is unlikely—i.e., when it is unlikely that the sale can be completed within 12 months—the appraiser must discount all cash flows generated by the property to obtain the estimate of fair value. These cash flows include, but are not limited to, those arising from ownership, development, operating, and sale of the property. The discount applied shall reflect the appraiser's judgment of what a prudent, knowledgeable purchaser under no necessity to buy would be willing to pay to purchase the property in a current sale.

3. The amount in cash or cash equivalent value of other consideration that a real estate parcel would yield in a current sale between a willing buyer and a willing seller (i.e., selling price), that is, other than a forced sale or liquidation sale. The fair value of a parcel is affected by its physical characteristics, its probable ultimate use, and the time required for the buyer to make such use of the property considering access, development plans, zoning restrictions, and market absorption factors. (FASB)

fairway

1. The part of a golf course between the tees and putting greens where the grass is kept very short.
2. An unobstructed, navigable channel in a river or harbor for the passage of vessels; the usual course taken by ships.

falling ground. The ground where trees land after they are felled. Its condition, slope, and configuration must be considered in making a millcut cruise of redwood timber because the trees are large and the timber is brittle.

fall-out demand. In markets characterized by increasing rents, office building tenants who "fall out" of the market for Class A space to Class B space or from Class B to Class C space. *See also* move-up demand.

fallow

1. Land, ordinarily used for crops, that is allowed to lie idle during the growing season.
2. The tilling of land without sowing it for a season.

false ceiling. A ceiling suspended a foot or more below the actual ceiling to provide space for and easy access to wiring and ducts, or to alter the dimensions of a room. (R.S. Means) *See also* drop ceiling.

false front. A wall that extends beyond the sidewalls and/or above the roof

of a building to create a more imposing facade.

family room. An informal living room,
usually the center of family activities.

fan-coil unit. An air-conditioning unit
that houses an air filter, heating or
cooling coils, and a centrifugal fan,
and operates by moving air through
an opening in the unit and across
the coils. (R.S. Means)

Fannie Mae. *See* Federal National
Mortgage Association (FNMA).

fan window. *See* circlehead window.

FAR. *See* floor area ratio.

farm. A tract of rural land devoted to
agriculture; also, a tract of land or
water used for industrial purposes
such as a tank farm.

farm budget. The plan for the financial organization and operation of a
farm for a specified period of time;
includes a detailed statement of anticipated gross income, expenses,
and net income.

Farm Credit Administration (FCA). An
independent agency of the executive
branch of the U.S. Government
which provides a comprehensive
credit system for agriculture, including long-term, intermediate, and
short-term credit to farmers and
farmers' organizations.

**Farmers Home Administration
(FmHA).** An agency within the U.S.
Department of Agriculture established in 1933 to provide credit to
farmers to supplement commercial
credit. The FmHA interprets Congressional directives affecting its
lending policies and establishes
lending procedures. There are three
categories of FmHA loans: direct
loans, insured loans, and guaranteed loans. FmHA loans may be
used for rural housing, farm businesses (e.g., land purchases, refinancing debts, constructing or repairing farm buildings, improving
farm land, developing irrigation facilities, establishing farm-based
businesses, expenses incurred in operating a farm business), or a variety of other purposes (e.g., rebuild-
ing after natural disasters, resource
conservation and development, self-
help technical assistance).

farm expenses. The costs incurred in
operating a farm which include annual cash operating expenses, the
value of unpaid family labor, any
decrease in farm inventory, depreciation, and the value of living on
the farm furnished to hired laborers.

farm income. The income produced by
farm operations, which includes annual receipts from sales, miscella-
neous farm receipts, any increase in
farm inventory, and the value of living on the farm furnished to the operator, the operator's family, and
hired laborers.

farm labor and management wage. The name applied to a measure of overall operating success derived from farm account or survey records. Theoretically, it represents the income left to pay the farm operator for his labor and management after all deductions are made for operating costs, including taxes and insurance, and deductions for the recapture of and return on invested capital.

farmland. Land devoted to agricultural production; usually refers to the land comprising a farm, including tillable areas, untillable areas, and woodlots.

farm production. Productivity of a specific farm unit, usually measured by percentage of tillable land or per acre yield of various crops grown.

farm size. Total acres in the farm unit measured in terms of acres of cropland or number of livestock units.

farmstead. The site and location of farm buildings; the focal point of farm operations.

farm-to-market road. A road outside the primary state highway system which connects farms with towns or primary highways.

farrowing house. A building used for housing hogs that are giving birth.

FASB. *See* Financial Accounting Standards Board.

fascia. A long, flat construction member or band; the horizontal division of an architrave; the finishing board used to conceal the ends of rafters.

fashion shopping center. A concentration of apparel shops, boutiques, and custom quality shops selling high-quality merchandise at high prices. (ULI)

fast-food restaurant. A restaurant, generally part of a chain operation, that specializes in the rapid preparation and service of a specialty food, e.g., fried chicken, hamburgers, pizza.

fatigue. The weakening of a material caused by repeated or alternating loads. Fatigue may result in cracks or complete failure. (R.S. Means)

FCA. *See* Farm Credit Administration.

FCC. *See* Federal Communications Commission.

FCDA. Federal Civil Defense Administration.

FDA. Food and Drug Administration.

FDIC. *See* Federal Deposit Insurance Corporation.

f-distribution. In statistics, a distribution used to analyze variability within sampling groups. A statistical test to determine the *variance* between different sets of data is called an *f-test*. An f-ratio is the ratio between the two *variance* estimates. *See also* t-distribution.

FDPA. *See* Flood Disaster Protection Act.

FEA. *See* Federal Energy Administration.

feasibility. An indication that a project has a reasonable likelihood of satisfying explicit objectives. *See also* economic feasibility.

feasibility analysis

1. A study of the cost-benefit relationship of an economic endeavor. (USPAP, May 1992)
2. An analysis undertaken to investigate whether a project will fulfill the objectives of the investor. The profitability of a specific real estate project is analyzed in terms of the criteria of a specific market or investor.

feasibility study. *See* feasibility analysis.

Fed. A shortened term for the Federal Reserve System.

Federal Advisory Council. A committee of the Federal Reserve System that advises the Board of Governors on major developments and activities.

Federal Aviation Administration (FAA). An agency in the U.S. Department of Transportation that regulates civil aviation to promote its development and safety and provide for the safe and efficient use of the airspace by both civilian and military aircraft. The FAA acquires in fee or by lease many sites on which navigational aids are placed. Appraisals of these sites are commissioned at the time of land acquisition.

Federal Communications Commission (FCC). A government agency that regulates interstate and foreign commerce by wire and radio and consults with other government agencies and state regulatory commissions on matters involving telegraph, telephone, and radio communications. Its jurisdiction now includes radio, television, wire, cable, microwave, and satellite communication.

federal debt limit. A legal ceiling on the aggregate face amount of outstanding obligations issued, or guaranteed as to principal and interest, by the U.S. Government. Guaranteed obligations held by the Secretary of the Treasury are exempt.

federal deficit. A public or federal debt; the difference between government revenue and expenditures.

Federal Deposit Insurance Corporation (FDIC). A government body that insures the deposits of all banks entitled to insurance under the Federal Reserve Act, including all national and state banks that are members of the Federal Reserve System and many mutual savings banks.

Since 1989, the FDIC has assumed the assets of the defunct Federal Savings and Loan Insurance Corporation (FSLIC). The FDIC Division of Liquidation (DOL) establishes national policies and procedures for managing and liquidating the assets of failed banks.

federal discount rate. The interest rate charged by the Federal Reserve for funds borrowed by member banks.

Federal Emergency Management Agency (FEMA). A federal agency established by the Flood Disaster Protection Act to provide directives on where and where not to build in coastal and floodplain areas.

Federal Energy Administration (FEA). A federal agency under the Department of Energy that develops and implements federal energy policy, including the allocation of resources. The FEA regulates aspects of the electrical power and natural gas industries, deals with nonfederal hydroelectric power projects, and establishes rates for transporting oil by pipeline.

Federal Farm Loan Act. Legislation that provides long-term credit and capital for agricultural development, creates standard forms of investment based on farm loans, establishes a market for U.S. bonds, and creates government depositories and financial agents for the United States.

Federal Financial Institutions Examination Council (FFIEC). A group consisting of the heads of the five federal agencies regulating financial institutions in the United States. *See also* Appraisal Subcommittee; Federal Financial Institutions Regulatory Agencies (FFIRA); Financial Institutions Reform, Recovery and Enforcement Act (FIRREA).

Federal Financial Institutions Regulatory Agencies (FFIRA). The five federal financial regulatory agencies of the U.S. Government, i.e., the Federal Reserve Board, the Office of Thrift Supervision, the Office of the Comptroller of the Currency, the Federal Deposit Insurance Corporation, and the National Credit Union Administration.

federal funds. Funds available at a Federal Reserve Bank, including excess reserves of member banks and checks drawn to pay for purchases of government securities by the Federal Reserve Bank. Member banks may borrow these funds to meet Federal Reserve requirements.

federal funds rate. The interest rate charged on loans made by banks with excess reserve funds to banks with deficient reserves; an early indication of major changes in the national economy.

federal government securities. All obligations of the U.S. Government. *See also* Treasury bills.

Federal Highway Administration. Administers federal-aid highway programs in all 50 states; works with state highway departments to plan, design, fund, and administer highway projects.

Federal Home Loan Bank. Any of 12 regional banks established in 1932 to encourage local thrift and home financing during the Depression; now owned jointly by various savings and loan associations. Formerly monitored by the now-defunct Federal Home Loan Bank Board, the Federal Home Loan Bank is now overseen by the Housing Finance Board.

Federal Home Loan Bank Board (FHLBB). The entity formerly responsible for regulating the thrift industry; abolished by FIRREA in 1989. *See also* Office of Thrift Supervision (OTS).

Federal Home Loan Bank System. A system established in 1932 to serve as a mortgage credit reserve system for home mortgage lending institutions; members may obtain advances on home mortgage collateral and may borrow from home loan banks under certain conditions.

Federal Home Loan Mortgage Corporation (FHLMC). An agency that facilitates secondary residential mortgages sponsored by the Veterans Administration and the Federal Housing Administration as well as residential mortgages that are not government protected; also called *Freddie Mac.*

Federal Housing Administration (FHA). An agency of the U.S. Department of Housing and Urban Development that carries out the provisions of the National Housing Act by promoting home ownership and the renovation and remodeling of residences with government-guaranteed loans to home owners.

Federal Housing Administration (FHA) insured loans. Insured mortgages from private lending institutions designed to provide home ownership and rental opportunities for American families. The interest rates on these loans are set by the FHA.

Federal Housing Administration (FHA) mortgage. A mortgage made in conformity with the requirements of the National Housing Act and insured by the Federal Housing Administration.

Federal Interagency Real Property Appraisal Committee (FIRPAC). A committee made up of various federal agencies, many of which do not fall under FIRREA. FIRPAC is headed by the Office of Management and Budget and is currently drafting uniform standards for appraisals submitted to federal agencies.

Federal Intermediate Credit Banks. Regional banks created by Congress to provide intermediate credit for ranchers and farmers by rediscounting the agricultural paper of financial institutions.

Federal Land Bank (FLB). Any of 12 banks that offer long-term credit to farmers and are supervised by the Farm Credit Administration. Strictly speaking, these banks compete with thrift institutions, but regulations limit their participation in housing loans to 15% of their total investments and their money is available only to farmers and ranchers.

federally related transaction (FRT). Under Title XI of the Financial Institutions Reform, Recovery and Enforcement Act (FIRREA), any real estate-related financial transaction which a Federal Financial Institutions Regulatory Agency (FFIRA) engages in, contracts for, or regulates, and which requires the services of an appraiser. *See also* real estate-related transaction.

Federal National Mortgage Association (FNMA). A quasi-governmental agency that purchases mortgages from banks, trust companies, mortgage companies, savings and loan associations, and insurance companies to help distribute funds for home mortgages; also called *Fannie Mae.*

Federal Open Market Committee (FOMC). A committee composed of the Federal Reserve's Board of Governors, the president of the New York Federal Reserve Bank, and four district reserve bank presidents, which buys and sells government securities in the open market to regulate the money supply and interest rates. As the Federal Reserve System's most important policy-making group, the FOMC creates policy for the system's purchase and sale of government and other securities in the open market.

Federal Power Commission (FPC). An agency that regulates the interstate operations of private utilities, i.e., the issuance of securities, setting of rates, and location of sites.

federal rectangular survey system. *See* rectangular survey system.

Federal Reserve Bank. One of 12 Federal Reserve District Banks created and regulated by the Federal Reserve System. The 12 districts are: 1st District, Boston; 2nd District, New York; 3rd District, Philadelphia; 4th District, Cleveland; 5th District, Richmond; 6th District, Atlanta; 7th District, Chicago; 8th District, St. Louis; 9th District, Minneapolis; 10th District, Kansas City; 11th District, Dallas; and 12th District, San Francisco.

Federal Reserve Bank account. An account kept by all member banks, as required by Federal Reserve regulations, which clears the banks with a Federal Reserve Bank in their districts; shows the cash balance due from the reserve bank to guarantee that the member bank has sufficient reserves on hand.

Federal Reserve Bank collections account. An account that shows all monies for out-of-town checks distributed for collection by a Federal Reserve check collection system; the funds are not presently available in reserve but are being collected.

Federal Reserve Board. The seven-member governing body of the Federal Reserve System that regulates all national and state-chartered banks belonging to the Federal Reserve System, has jurisdiction over bank holding companies, and sets national money and credit policy; the governors serve for 14 years and are appointed by the President of the United States, subject to Senate confirmation.

Federal Reserve Board Bank. *See* Federal Reserve Bank.

Federal Reserve Bulletin. A monthly journal, issued by the Board of Governors of the Federal Reserve System, that deals with banking and financial issues.

Federal Reserve Chart Book. A quarterly publication of the Board of Governors of the Federal Reserve System that contains charts of interest to the financial community.

Federal Reserve credit. The credit supply that Federal Reserve Banks have added to member bank reserves; composed primarily of earning assets of the Federal Reserve Banks.

Federal Reserve notes. Notes issued by the Federal Reserve Banks when certain areas require large volumes of currency or when the public demand for currency is very heavy. As the need for currency relaxes, Federal Reserve Banks retire these notes. Federal Reserve notes are issued to member banks in denominations of $1 to $10,000, providing elastic currency with full legal tender status.

Federal Reserve notes of other banks. The total amount of Federal Reserve notes held by reserve banks other than the bank that issued them.

Federal Reserve System. The central banking system of the United States, which was created in 1913 to manage money and credit and to promote orderly growth of the economy. The Federal Reserve System operates independently of Congress and the president. The Federal Reserve regulates the money supply, determines the legal reserve of member banks, oversees the mint, effects transfers of funds, promotes and facilitates the clearance and collection of checks, examines member banks, and serves other functions; consists of 12 Federal Reserve Banks, their 24 branches, and national and state banks that are members of the system. All national banks are stockholding members of the Federal Reserve Bank of their district; membership is optional for state banks and trust companies.

federal rule. *See* before-and-after rule.

Federal Savings and Loan Association. One of the associations, established by the Home Owner's Loan Act of 1933 and amended in the Home Owners Loan Act of 1934, that brought existing and newly formed mutual savings banks and building and loan associations under a federal charter.

Federal Savings and Loan Insurance Corporation (FSLIC). A former division of the now-defunct Federal Home Loan Bank Board that insured the shares and accounts of all federal savings and loan associations and any state-chartered savings and loan associations that applied for insurance and met the requirements of the corporation. Abolished in 1989, its assets have been assumed by the Federal Deposit Insurance Corporation.

fee. *See* fee simple estate.

fee appraiser. An appraiser who is paid a fee for the appraisal assignments he or she performs. *See also* institutionally employed appraiser; staff appraiser.

feed bunk. A wooden or concrete trough from which livestock and poultry eat.

feeder. A prefabricated container from which animals or birds eat.

feeder cattle. A market classification for cattle raised on feed, from yearlings to mature cattle, which have not reached a finished or prime condition for slaughter.

feedlot. An enclosed area where feeder cattle are finished for the market; usually equipped with feed/hay bunks or self-feeders, watering facilities, paving, and adjacent shelter.

feed value. The amount of nutrients found in dairy cattle feed, usually measured in total digestible nutrients (TDN), digestible energy (DE), metabolizable energy (ME), or net energy (NE). To calculate these measures of energy, the energy content of the feed and the feces, urine, gases, and heat produced by the animal are measured.

fee on condition. *See* fee simple conditional.

fee on limitation. A fee simple estate that is automatically terminated when a specified event occurs, which may be at any time or not at all.

fee owned timber. The timber that is presently owned free and clear. The term fee comes from the legal phrases fee simple and fee simple absolute. A company's fee owned timber includes timber on land owned by the firm and also may include the timber that is owned by the firm but is on land owned by another party. (R.S. Means)

fee simple conditional. A fee simple estate that may be terminated when a specified event occurs, which may be at any time or not at all. The condition does not automatically terminate the estate; the grantor, the heirs, or a designee must act to terminate it.

fee simple estate. Absolute ownership unencumbered by any other interest or estate, subject only to the limitations imposed by the governmental powers of taxation, eminent domain, police power, and escheat.

fee simple title. A title that signifies ownership of all the rights in a parcel of real property, subject only to the limitations of the four powers of government.

fee timesharing. *See* timesharing.

felt. A nonwoven fabric of wool, fur, hair, or vegetable fibers that are matted together by heat, moisture, and pressure.

felt and gravel roofing. A continuous roof covering made up of various plies or sheets of saturated or coated felts cemented together with asphalt; also called *composition roofing* or *gravel roofing*. (R.S. Means) *See also* built-up roofing.

felt paper. Paper used as sheathing on walls and roofs to serve as a barrier against heat, cold, and dampness; covered with tar or asphalt and surfaced with gravel on certain types of roofs, e.g., flat roofs.

FEMA. *See* Federal Emergency Management Agency.

fenestration. The design and arrangement of windows and other openings in a building wall.

festival shopping center. A type of specialty shopping center designed to create a special retailing experience; characterized by a high percentage of *GLA* devoted to specialty restaurants and food vendors that emphasize ethnic authenticity and uniqueness of offerings, a wide selection of impulse and specialty retail goods, and a strong entertainment theme; e.g., Quincy Marketplace in Boston, South Street Seaport in Manhattan.

FF&E. Furniture, fixtures, and equipment.

FFIEC. *See* Federal Financial Institutions Examination Council.

FFIRA. *See* Federal Financial Institutions Regulatory Agencies.

FFLS. Federal Farm Loan System.

FHA. *See* Federal Housing Administration.

FHLBB. *See* Federal Home Loan Bank Board.

FHLMC. *See* Federal Home Loan Mortgage Corporation.

fiberboard. A prefabricated building material made of wood or other plant fibers compressed and bonded into a sheet.

fiberglass. Finespun filaments of glass that are made into yarn and used in batts as insulation; added to gypsum or concrete products to increase tensile strength.

fiduciary

1. Describes a relationship between two individuals in which one has a duty to act for the benefit of the other, e.g., between guardian and ward; the person so charged.
2. An individual or agency such as a bank that is given certain property to hold in trust under a trust agreement. Executors of estates and trustees serve as fiduciaries.

field appraiser. An appraiser who conducts primary and secondary research, analyzes researched data,

forms opinions, and prepares appraisal reports.

field box. In agriculture, a unit of measure applicable to harvested fruit crops; quantity varies with the variety and locality; also called *field lug.*

field crop. In agriculture, an annual crop that is planted and harvested by mechanical means.

field lug. *See* field box.

field review. An appraisal review that includes inspection of the exterior and sometimes the interior of the subject property and possibly inspection of the comparable properties to confirm the data provided in the report. A field review is generally performed using a customized checklist which covers the items examined in a desk review and may also include confirmation of market data, research to gather additional data, and verification of the software used in preparing the report. *See also* desk review; review.

field tile

1. Porous tile placed around a building's foundation to drain off excess water and prevent seepage into the foundation.
2. A system of drain tiles buried well below the field's surface or ground to drain the subsoil.

fill. The use of added material to equalize topography or raise land to a desired grade; in highway construction, the use of stones and earth to fill low sections of the right-of-way; the material used for this purpose.

fill dirt. Dirt, soil, sand or other earth, which is obtained off-site, that is used to fill holes or depressions, create mounds, or otherwise artificially change the grade or elevation of real property. It does not include material that is used in limited quantities for normal landscaping activities. (ASTM)

fill slope. The portion of a roadway that lies between the outer edge of the road's shoulder and the top of the slope at a different elevation.

final acceptance. The formal acceptance of a contractor's completed construction project by the owner, upon notification from an architect that the job fulfills the contract requirements. Final acceptance is often accompanied by a final payment agreed upon in the contract. (R.S. Means)

final reconciliation. *See* reconciliation.

final value estimate. The range of values or single dollar figure derived from the reconciliation of value indications and stated in the appraisal report.

financed out. Describes a property that is 100% financed.

Financial Accounting Standards Board (FASB). The agency of the Financial Accounting Foundation that is responsible for establishing financial accounting standards.

financial corporation. A corporation engaged primarily in some form of banking, e.g., a bank, a trust company, an insurance company, a savings and loan association.

Financial Institutions Reform, Recovery and Enforcement Act (FIRREA). Legislation enacted in 1989 to bail out the savings and loan industry; FIRREA created the Office of Thrift Supervision (OTS) under the Treasury Department. The OTS was charged with assuming the functions of the defunct Federal Home Loan Bank Board (FHLBB) and supervising all federal and state savings and loan associations. FIRREA also set up the Resolution Trust Corporation (RTC) to dispose of the assets of insolvent thrift institutions, and the Appraisal Subcommittee to implement Title XI of FIRREA mandating state certification and/or licensing of appraisers who perform assignments for Federal Financial Institutions Regulatory Agencies (FFIRA) as well as all federal and state savings and loan institutions. *See also* Appraisal Subcommittee; Federal Financial Institutions Examination Council (FFIEC); federally related transaction; temporary practice.

financial management rate of return (FMRR). A measure of investment performance; a specialized after-tax version of the modified internal rate of return which takes into account the prevailing rate of return on representative real estate projects of a particular risk class. *See also* internal rate of return *(IRR);* modified internal rate of return *(MIRR).*

financial statement. A statement that reflects the economic status of an individual or entity.

financial structure. The character and extent of distributed ownership and control of assets in a corporation, particularly the structuring of bonds, preferred stock, and common stock under qualified rights.

financing costs. The cost of acquiring capital to finance a project.

financing statement. An instrument that conveys a security interest in chattels and equipment, recorded in chattel records and indexed in land records.

finder's fee. A fee, usually expressed in points, that is paid to a banker, a broker, or an intermediary who locates debt or equity capital for a developer.

fine sandy loam. A soil containing much sand, but enough silt and clay to make it cohesive; contains more fine sand than sandy loam.

fine-textured soil. A soil with a high percentage of fine particles, 0.005 millimeter or smaller in diameter; also called *clay soils.*

finish
1. The texture of a surface after compacting and finishing operations have been performed.
2. A high-quality piece of lumber graded for appearance and often used for interior trim or cabinet work.

finish floor. Flooring of hardwood, linoleum, terrazzo, or tile laid over the subfloor.

finish hardware. All of the exposed hardware in a structure, such as door knobs, door hinges, locks, and clothes hooks, etc. (Marshall & Swift) *See also* hardware.

fire alarm system. An electrical system, installed within a home, industrial plant, or office building that sounds a loud blast or bell when smoke and flames are detected. Certain alarms are engineered to trigger sprinkler systems for added protection. (R.S. Means)

fireback. *See* chimney back.

firebrick. A brick made of fire clay that can resist high temperatures and is used to line heating chambers and fireplaces.

fire cut. A diagonal cut made across a horizontal, wood-supporting member at the end that is framed into a masonry wall. The cut, made from the top of the member and slanted toward the outside wall, allows the member to collapse in the event of failure from fire or any other cause without causing the wall to collapse as well.

fire detection system. A series of sensors and interconnected monitoring equipment which detect the effects of a fire and activate an alarm system. (R.S. Means)

fire division wall. A wall that subdivides one or more floors of a building to discourage the spread of fire. (R.S. Means)

fire doors and walls. Doors and walls constructed of fire-resistant materials and designed to prevent the spread of fires. (R.S. Means)

fire-extinguisher system. An installation of automatic sprinklers, foam distribution system, fire hoses, and/or portable fire extinguishers designed for extinguishing a fire in an area. (R.S. Means)

fireproof construction. *See* fire-resistive construction.

fireproofing. The use of incombustible materials to protect the structural components of a building so that a complete burnout of the contents of the building will not impair its structural integrity.

fire-protection sprinkler system. An automatic fire-suppression system, commonly heat-activated, that sounds an alarm and deluges an area with water from overhead sprinklers when the heat of a fire melts a fusible link. (R.S. Means)

fire-resistive construction. Construction designed to withstand a complete burnout of the contents of the structure without impairing its structural integrity. Such a structure is not combustible at ordinary fire temperatures and can withstand ordinary fire conditions for at least one hour without serious damage.

fire-retarding material. Material that tends to inhibit combustion.

fire stops. The use of incombustible material to block air spaces in a structure through which flames could travel.

fire wall. An incombustible wall built between two buildings, or between two parts of one building, as a fire stop.

FIRPAC. *See* Federal Interagency Real Property Appraisal Committee.

FIRREA. *See* Financial Institutions Reform, Recovery and Enforcement Act.

first bottom. The normal plane of a stream, part of which may be flooded at times. *See also* floodplain; second bottom.

first floor
1. In the U.S., the floor of a building at or closest to grade.
2. In Europe, the floor of a building above the ground floor. (R.S. Means)

first in, first out (FIFO). A type of accounting for inventory in which items purchased first are assumed to be sold first. An accountant will compute the cost and profit on the oldest or first items in the inventory.

first mortgage. A mortgage that has priority over all other liens on a property.

first-user depreciation. In taxation, a determination as to whether a property in the possession of the taxpayer is considered new or used.

fiscal year. Any 12 months selected as an accounting period; may or may not coincide with the calendar year.

fixed assets. Permanent assets that are required for the normal operation of a business, e.g., furniture, land, building, machinery; usually not converted into cash after they are declared fixed assets. *See also* liquid assets.

fixed capital. Capital invested in a stationary form that may be used many times in production; permanent assets, such as land; ordinarily, but not necessarily, tangible assets.

fixed capital goods. *See* durable capital goods.

fixed disbursement schedule. A disbursement system on a construction loan in which the lender and borrower agree on the number and timing of payments to be made during the construction period; as distinguished from the voucher system, in which only actual costs are reimbursed.

fixed expenses. Operating expenses that generally do not vary with occupancy and which prudent management will pay whether the property is occupied or vacant.

fixed-fee contract. A type of construction contract in which the contract price is a specific sum.

fixed liabilities. Long-term debts; debts payable more than one year hence, as distinguished from current liabilities

fixed-rate mortgage (FRM). A conventional mortgage with an interest rate that does not vary over the life of the loan.

fixed window. A window that does not open, e.g., a fixed bay window, a fixed bow window, a picture window.

fixture. An article that was once personal property, but has since been installed or attached to the land or building in a rather permanent manner so that it is regarded in law as part of the real estate. *See also* appurtenance.

flagstone. A flat, irregular slab of stone, usually sandstone or shale, used for paving walks, patios, terraces, and planter boxes.

flange. A projecting edge, ridge, rim, or collar used to attach an object to another object to keep it in place, e.g., the projecting horizontal portions of an I beam.

flank. The side of a building or arch.

flashing. Strips of sheet metal, copper, lead, or tin used to cover and protect structural angles and joints from water seepage.

flat
1. A floor or story of a building.
2. An apartment on one floor.
3. A multifamily, residential structure containing a limited number of units, each with a separate, outside entrance.

flat coat. The first coat of paint applied to a finished surface.

flat cost. In the building trades, the cost of labor and materials only.

flat rental lease. A lease with a specified level of rent that continues throughout the lease term; also called *level payment lease.*

flat roof. A roof with just enough slope to provide for proper drainage; one with a pitch that does not exceed 20 degrees.

flat slab construction. A method of construction in which a concrete floor slab is supported by columns, not beams; requires a thicker slab.

FLB. *See* Federal Land Bank.

flexible conduit. Conduit made of flexible material, such as fabric or spiral metal strips.

flexible loan insurance plan (FLIP). An alternative mortgage instrument; a graduated-payment mortgage that combines graduated payments for the home buyer, level payments for the lender, and conventional underwriting. In the FLIP mortgage program, a portion of the home buyer's down payment is deposited in a pledged interest-bearing savings account and serves as cash collateral for the lender and as a source of supplemental payments for the borrower during the first few years of the loan.

flex space. Space that is adaptable to various uses. *See also* research and development space.

flight pattern. The zone of approach or departure for aircraft from airport runways.

FLIP. *See* flexible loan insurance plan.

flitch beam. A beam consisting of an iron plate between two timber beams.

float. A valve-like device, often a hollow ball, whose buoyancy automatically regulates the supply, outlet, and level of a liquid, e.g., in a toilet tank.

float finish. A concrete surface that is finished by continuously spreading the material with a flat board.

floating capital. Capital invested in current assets, e.g., inventory, receivables.

floating foundation. A mat, raft, or rigid foundation consisting of concrete slabs four to eight inches thick over the entire foundation area with reinforcing bars closely spaced at right angles to each other within the slab; used when the bearing power of the soil cannot support spread footings and the use of piles is not advantageous or necessary.

floating rate. A variable interest rate charged for the use of borrowed money; set at a specific percentage above a fluctuating base rate, usually the prime rate of major commercial banks.

floating zone. A provision in a zoning ordinance that permits the planned development of a tract of land, usually subject to binding, prearranged controls, for a use not formally permitted in the zone where the land is located; ordinarily requires the approval of a regulatory body, but does not constitute an exception, variance, or change in zoning.

Flood Disaster Protection Act (FDPA). Federal legislation enacted in 1973 to broaden the National Flood Insurance Act of 1968. The FDPA set up the National Flood Insurance Program and led to the creation of the Federal Emergency Management Agency (FEMA).

flood irrigation. An irrigation method in which water is allowed to flow directly across the land surface.

floodplain. The flat surfaces along the courses of rivers, streams, and other bodies of water that are subject to overflow and flooding.

floor

1. The lower, horizontal surface of a specific floor.
2. The different stories of a structure, e.g., ground floor, first floor.
3. The horizontal structure dividing a building into various stories.

floor area. The total horizontal surface of a specific floor; the total area of all floors in a multistory building, computed from the outside building walls of each floor with balcony and mezzanine areas computed separately and added to the total. *See also* area.

floor area ratio (FAR). The relationship between the above-ground floor area of a building, as described by the building code, and the area of the plot on which it stands; in planning and zoning, often expressed as a decimal, e.g., a ratio of 2.0 indicates that the permissible floor area of a building is twice the total land area; also called *building-to-land ratio. See also* land-to-building ratio.

floor furnace. A metal, box-like, warm air furnace installed directly under the floor so that its grilled upper surface is flush with the finished floor of the room above.

floor joists. Horizontal framing lumber to which flooring is attached.

floor load. The live weight-supporting capabilities of a floor, measured in pounds per square foot; the weight, in pounds per square foot, that can be safely placed on the floor of a building if it is uniformly distributed. *See also* dead load; live load.

floor loan. A part of a total loan that is disbursed when the physical improvements are complete. The balance of the loan is disbursed when the other requirements of the lender are met, e.g., rent roll achievement. *See also* ceiling loan.

floor of forest. The dead vegetative matter on the ground in a forest, including litter and unincorporated humus. In fire control, it is called *duff. See also* litter.

flowage easement. The perpetual right, power, and privilege to overflow, flood, and submerge land owned by another, reserving for the landowner all rights and privileges that do not interfere with or abridge this right; may be either permanent or occasional.

flow chart. A diagram of symbols and connecting lines that illustrates the successive steps in a system or procedure. *See also* decision trees.

flow line. A profile of the low point of a drainage channel or structure, measured at the low point of the inside of the watercourse.

flue. A passage that removes smoke from a chimney; any duct or pipe for the passage of air, gases, smoke, etc.

flue lining. The tile or pipe inside a chimney.

flume. An artificial open channel used to carry water, e.g., a channel by which logs are transported; may or may not be supported by a trestle at points in its course.

fluorescent lighting. Lighting fixtures consisting of glass tubes with an inside coating of fluorescent material that produces light when subjected to a stream of electrons from the cathode.

flush siding. A level siding of tongue-and-groove boards laid flush on the sidewalls of a structure.

FMRR. *See* financial management rate of return.

FNMA. *See* Federal National Mortgage Association.

foam concrete. A lightweight, cellular concrete made by infusing an unhardened concrete mixture with prepared foam or by generating gases within the mixture. (R.S. Means)

foamed-in-place insulation. A plastic foam employed for thermal insulation, prepared by mixing an insulation substance with a foaming agent just before it is poured or sprayed with a gun into the enclosed receptacle cavities. (R.S. Means)

fodder. Coarse food for horses, cattle, or sheep.

folding door. An assembly of two or more vertical panels hinged together so they can open or close in a confined space. A floor or ceiling mounted track is usually provided as a guide. (R.S. Means)

folding partition
1. Large panels hung from a ceiling track, sometimes also supported by a floor track, which form a solid partition when closed, but stack together when the partition is maneuvered into an open position.
2. A partition, faced with fabric and hung from a ceiling track, that folds up flexibly when opened like the pleated balloons of an accordion. (R.S. Means)

FOMC. *See* Federal Open Market Committee.

footcandle. A measure of the amount of illumination produced by a lighting fixture, recorded at desk level using a light meter.

footings. The supporting parts of a foundation that prevent excessive settlement or movement by distributing building loads directly to the soil.

forage. All browse and herbaceous food that is available to livestock or game animals; used for grazing or harvested for feeding.

forage acre. A unit of measure equal to an acre totally covered with vegetation that is usable to livestock. This factor times the number of surface acres indicates the total forage acres in a plot.

forage-acre factor. A factor obtained by multiplying the weighted-use factor by the forage density; a forage index indicating the part of a range that is covered with available vegetation that can be entirely eaten by livestock without causing damage to the range. *See also* weighted-use factor.

forage crop. A member of the grass family, e.g., corn or grain sorghum; often harvested and stored in silos as reserve food for livestock.

forage density. The part of the total vegetative density that is within reach of livestock, generally four feet for sheep and five feet for cattle.

forbearance. Refraining from taking legal action on a mortgage that is in arrears; usually granted when a mortgagor makes a satisfactory arrangement to pay the arrears at a future date.

forbs. Herbs other than grass.

forced air heating. A warm air heating system in which circulation of air is effected by a motor-driven fan. Such a system includes air cleaning devices. (Marshall & Swift)

forced price. The price paid in a forced sale or purchase, i.e., a sale in which a reasonable time was not allowed to find a purchaser or the purchaser was forced to buy. *See also* disposition value; distress sale; liquidation value.

forced sale
1. Offering and transferring property for a valuable consideration under conditions of compulsion.
2. A sale at public auction made under a court order. *See also* distress sale; forced price.

force majeure. An unavoidable cause of failure to perform a contract obligation within the time specified.

forecast demand. In-depth analysis of anticipated demand, which involves the collection and organization of extensive data, consideration of the perceptions of market participants, and assessment of the likelihood that current trends will continue; also called *fundamental demand. See also* inferred demand.

forecasting. Predicting a future happening or condition based on past trends and the perceptions of market participants, tempered with analytical judgment concerning the continuation of these trends and the realization of these perceptions in the future.

foreclosure. The legal process in which a mortgagee forces the sale of a property to recover all or part of a loan on which the mortgagor has defaulted.

foreclosure sale. The optional right of the mortgagee or lending institution to sell mortgaged property if the mortgagor fails to make payment, applying proceeds from the sale toward the outstanding debt. (R.S. Means)

foreshore. The land between mean high water and mean low water along a shore in its natural condition.

forest. A large tract of land covered with trees.

forestation. The establishment of a forest in an area where no forest existed before, e.g., abandoned or submarginal farmland.

forest land. As defined by the U.S. Forest Service, land at least 10% stocked with live trees, or land formerly having such a tree cover and not currently developed for nonforest use. The minimum area of forest land recognized is one acre. (R.S. Means)

forest permit. A permit issued by a government agency that permits the use of cabins, access, wood cutting, and grazing.

forfeiture. A means by which the property of a citizen reverts back to the state through the violation of law.

formal architecture. Architecture identified by its conformity to aesthetic and functional criteria recognized by persons trained in architectural history. *See also* vernacular architecture.

formal review. A systematic review of each part of an appraisal report to confirm the accuracy of the data, provide additional documentation where needed, and verify the methodology and procedures applied.

form class. In forestry, the relationship between the diameter outside a tree's bark at breast-height *(DBH)* and the diameter inside the bark at the top of the first 16-foot log; represents a percentage of taper or form; e.g., if *DBH* is 24 inches and top diameter is 12 inches, the form class is 12 divided by 24, or 0.5 times 100, indicating form class 50.

Formica. A trade name for a plastic material used primarily on countertops, but also on wallcovering, plywood panels, and wallboard, where a fire-resistive material is desirable; similar materials are produced under other trade names.

form report. A limited appraisal report presented on a standard form such as those required by financial institutions, insurance companies, and government agencies. The reporting requirements for form reports, which are the same as for other types of reports, are set forth in the Standards Rules relating to Standards 2 and 5 of the Uniform Standards of Professional Appraisal Practice and the Appraisal Institute's Guide Note 3.

forms. Temporary panels, usually of wood, plywood, or steel, that form the shape of poured concrete while it hardens.

formula rules. Formulas used to estimate the number of board feet in a log given its diameter and length, allowing for waste in saw kerf and slabs; must be used very carefully. *See also* Humboldt rule; log rules; Scribner rule; Spaulding rule.

foundation. The base on which something is built; the part of a structure on which the building is erected; the part of a building that is below the surface of the ground and on which the superstructure rests.

foyer. The lobby of a theater or hotel; an entrance hall in a house.

FPC. *See* Federal Power Commission.

fractional assessment. A property's assessed value, computed by multiplying its full or market value by a specified percentage.

fractional interest. *See* partial interest.

fractional quarter. A section of land of irregular size. Theoretically, a section of land contains 640 acres, but due to the convergence of lines and surveying errors not all sections contain this exact amount. To avoid small errors in all sections, all shortages or surpluses are assigned to the north and west sections in each township. Hence, remaining quarter sections are described as fractional sections.

fractional rate. *See* split rate capitalization.

fractional reserve banking. An arrangement in which member banks in the Federal Reserve System are required to maintain reserves equal to a specified percentage of their deposits.

frame. The load-bearing skeleton of a building. The three types of framing are platform, balloon, and post-and-beam. *See also* framing.

frame construction. *See* wood frame construction.

framing. A system of joining structural members that provides lateral, longitudinal, transverse, and vertical support for a building. The framing of steel and precast concrete joists allows for curtain-wall construction. *See also* posttensioned concrete.

framing line. The outside, vertical plane of exterior wall framing.

franchise. A privilege or right that is conferred by grant on an individual or a group of individuals; usually an exclusive right to furnish public services or to sell a particular product in a certain community.

f-ratio. *See* f-distribution.

FRB. *See* Federal Reserve Board.

Freddie Mac. *See* Federal Home Loan Mortgage Corporation (FHLMC).

free and clear. Describes the title to a property that is unencumbered by mortgages or other liens.

free board. An allowance of land outside the property fence that may be claimed by the owner. In some places, the area extends $2^1/_2$ feet outside the boundary or enclosure.

free good. A useful thing so plentiful that it can be obtained without any effort, e.g., climate, fresh air, sunshine.

freehold. *See* fee simple estate.

free rent. The occupancy of premises with no rental obligation; typically offered as a rental concession and inducement during periods of oversupply. Free rent may be offered at beginning or end of a lease term, or staggered through the term.

free switching. The handling of freight by a railroad for no charge in certain switching districts or in areas where reciprocal switching is provided.

free switching limits. The specified boundaries that designate an area where a railroad will switch carloads of freight on which it receives a line haul, without further charge, to or from private spur tracks or its own team tracks; also, competitive traffic on which the line haul carrier absorbs the charge of the switching line.

freeway. A multilane highway with full control of access where intersecting roads are separated in grade from the road for through traffic. *See also* expressway; superhighway; toll road; turnpike.

French architecture. Any of several styles of architecture that originated in France. A common example is the small, formal house, perfectly balanced, with steep roof hipped at the ends, plastered walls on the first floor, and second-floor dormer windows. The French farmhouse style is informal, of stone, painted brick, or plaster, and sometimes accented with half-timbering. Norman French architecture is large scale and distinguished by the use of a round tower.

french curve. A stencil-like device used by a draftsman to draw curves other than circles or arcs.

French doors or windows. A pair of glazed doors that are hinged at the jamb and function as both doors and windows.

french drain. A drainage ditch containing loose stone covered with earth. (R.S. Means)

Freon. A trade name for a group of nonflammable refrigerants used in air-conditioning systems; a managed hazardous substance.

frequency distribution. In statistics, a system for analyzing data that condenses them into a more easily interpreted form. The formation of a distribution involves three steps: 1) determine the range of the data, 2) divide the range into a workable number of class intervals of a standard size, and 3) determine the number of observations falling into each interval using a tally or score sheet.

fresco. A method for painting a mural using watercolors on freshly plastered walls.

friable. Easily crumbled; not plastic.

frictional vacancy. Vacancy unrelated to disequilibrium in supply and demand, but rather due to tenant relocations as leases roll over and expire. Frictional vacancy is considered the normal vacancy rate in any given market. *See also* vacancy.

frieze. A horizontal trim piece immediately below the cornice soffit.

FRM. *See* fixed-rate mortgage.

front. The primary face of a structure, which usually contains the principal entrance. *See also* facade.

frontage. The measured footage of a site that abuts a street, stream, railroad, or other facility.

frontage road. A local street that parallels a limited-access highway, services abutting properties, and gathers and controls vehicles entering or leaving the major traffic artery.

front elevation. The front view of a building.

front foot. A land measure one foot in width taken along the road or water frontage of a property.

front-foot cost. The cost of a parcel of real estate expressed in terms of front-foot units.

front money
1. The cash outlay required to launch a project.
2. Money that must be spent before financing is available.

frost line. The depth of frost penetration in the soil, which varies throughout the United States. Footings should be placed below this depth to prevent movement of the structure.

FRT. *See* federally related transaction.

FSA. Federal Security Agency.

FSLIC. *See* Federal Savings and Loan Insurance Corporation.

FTC. Federal Trade Commission.

f-test. *See* f-distribution.

full covenant and warranty deed. A deed conveying real property in which the grantor usually warrants the title, making the five covenants of ownership, of quiet enjoyment, against encumbrances, of further assurances, and of warranty or defense.

full-cut lumber. Lumber that is cut to full dimension.

full-value assessment. An assessment that is theoretically based on 100% of the property's market value.

fully amortizing mortgage loan. A loan with equal, periodic payments, usually on a monthly basis, that provide for both a return on investment, or interest, and a return of investment, or recovery of principal, over the term of the loan.

functional inutility. Impairment of the functional capacity of a property or building according to market tastes and standards; equivalent to functional obsolescence because ongoing change renders layouts and features obsolete.

functional obsolescence. An element of accrued depreciation resulting from deficiencies or superadequacies in the structure. *See also* curable functional obsolescence; incurable functional obsolescence.

functional replacement. The replacement of real property, either lands or facilities or both, acquired as a result of a transportation-related project, with lands or facilities or both land and facilities that will provide equivalent utility.

functional utility. The ability of a property or building to be useful and to perform the function for which it is intended according to current market tastes and standards; the efficiency of a building's use in terms of architectural style, design and layout, traffic patterns, and the size and type of rooms.

fundamental analysis. Investment analysis that investigates both basic economic factors and conditions affecting specific sectors and industries. *See also* technical analysis.

fundamental demand. *See* forecast demand.

fungible. Capable of being exchanged or interchanged; a fungible commodity is relatively indistinguisable from other items within the same category, e.g., units of currency.

furnace
1. The part of a boiler or warm-air heating plant in which combustion takes place.
2. A complete heating unit that transfers heat from burning fuel to a heating system. (R.S. Means)

furring. Strips of wood or metal applied to a rough wall or other surface to form an air space or to provide a level surface for the application of a finish material.

fuse. An electrical safety device consisting of or including a wire or strip of fusible metal that melts and interrupts the circuit when the current exceeds a particular amperage.

fuse box. The container housing the fuses that control the electric circuits of a structure.

future value. *See* prospective value estimate.

future value of $1. *See* amount of $1 ($S^n$).

future value of $1 per period. *See* amount of $1 per period ($S_n$)

G

gable. The end of a building, generally triangular in shape; the vertical plane that lies above the eaves and divides the slope of a ridged roof.

gable roof. A ridged roof, the ends of which form a gable.

GAFO. General merchandise, apparel, furniture, and other retail goods; identifies the type of retail goods sold in regional and superregional shopping centers.

gallery
1. A covered walk or corridor that extends from an upper story of a building and runs along the exterior or interior wall.
2. The highest balcony in a theater.
3. A room for art exhibitions.

gallery apartment house. An apartment house whose individual units can be entered from an exterior corridor on each floor. (R.S. Means)

gallons per minute. A measurement of flow.

gambrel roof. A ridged roof with a side that has two slopes, with the lower slope the steeper.

Gantt chart. A form of bar chart used in project management. Each element (task) of a project is represented by a horizontal bar. The bars are placed on the chart according to a time scale. The left end of each bar indicates when the task is to begin. The length of each bar indicates the duration of the task. The right end of each bar indicates when the task is to be completed. (IAAO)

GAO. General Accounting Office.

gap loan. An interim loan.

garden apartments. An apartment development of two- or three-story, walk-up structures built in a garden-like setting; customarily a suburban or rural-urban fringe development.

garden city. A residential development with significant plantings and trees composed largely of single-family, detached houses and providing vehicular parking. (R.S. Means)

garnishment. A statutory proceeding in which the property, money, or credits of a debtor in the possession of another are seized and applied to pay the debt.

garret. *See* attic.

garrison house. A style of house whose second story overhangs the face of the first story on one or more walls. (R.S. Means)

gathering pen. A corral or pen that is usually constructed on the range at some distance from the ranch headquarters to facilitate the gathering of herds for shipping, branding, or other purposes.

GBA. *See* gross building area.

GDP. *See* gross domestic product.

general benefits. In eminent domain takings, the benefits that accrue to the community at large, to the area adjacent to the improvement, or to other property situated near the taken property. *See also* benefits; set-off rule; special benefits.

general conditions. The portion of the contract document in which the rights, responsibilities, and relationships of the involved parties are itemized. (R.S. Means)

general contractor. A person or business entity that supervises the erection of structures or other improvements.

general data. Items of information on value influences that derive from social, economic, governmental, and environmental forces and originate outside the property being appraised.

general industrial occupancy. The designation of a conventionally designed building that can be used for all but high-hazard types of manufacturing or production operations. (R.S. Means)

general obligation bonds. Instruments of obligation which, by permission of the public through a referendum, are issued to investors by a government entity. These bonds promise investors incremental payment of principal and interest from revenues collected annually by the government. The funds supplied by investors are used to pay for the construction of publicly owned buildings or other public works projects.

general partner. The entity or individual in a limited partnership who has full management responsibility and assumes all personal liability for partnership debt. *See also* limited partner.

general partnership. An ownership arrangement in which all partners share in investment gains and losses and each has personal and unlimited responsibility for all liabilities. *See also* limited partnership.

general warranty deed. A covenant of warranty inserted in a deed which binds the grantor and heirs to defend the title conveyed to the grantee and his or her heirs against the lawful claims of all persons. *See also* quitclaim deed; special warranty deed.

generative business. A retail enterprise that exerts strong drawing power on shoppers in a given location. Anchor department stores, prestigious specialty stores, and supermarkets are generative businesses. *See also* shared business; suscipient business.

genesis of soil. The origins of the soil, particularly the processes responsible for developing the solum from unconsolidated parent material.

geodesic dome. A stable, dome-shaped structure fabricated from similar lightweight members connected to form a grid of interlocking polygons. (R.S. Means)

geological map. A map showing the character and distribution of outcrops of strata or igneous rocks, including faults, anticlines, and other sizable formations. Some such maps show only the solid outcrops excluding the overlying drift. (R.S. Means)

gentrification. A neighborhood phenomenon in which middle- and upper-income persons purchase neighborhood properties and renovate or rehabilitate them.

geocode. A code used to locate or identify a point geographically, e.g., the center of a parcel of real estate; usually expressed in coordinates relative to a standard point of reference.

geodetic survey program. The program conducted by the U.S. Coast and Geodetic Survey and the U.S. Geological Survey which, in support of the rectangular survey system, publishes more elaborate maps (quadrangles) that take into account the curvature of the earth.

geodetic system. The United States Coast and Geodetic Survey System; a network of benchmarks located throughout the United States and identified by latitude and longitude; initially established to identify tracts of land owned by the federal government, but gradually extended across the nation.

geographical sequence. A method for filing appraisal data by location; in assessing, the system in which property record cards are filed first by lot number, then by block, and finally by subdivision.

Geographic Information Systems (GIS). A communications technology that combines spatial information from a national database compiled by the 1990 census with computer mapping and modeling capabilities.

geometric average. The *nth* root of the product of *n* items; depends on the size of all values, but less affected by extreme values than the arithmetic average; useful in computing index numbers when all values are positive; also called *mean average.*

geometric progression. A sequence in which the ratio of any item to the preceding item is constant, e.g., 1, 4, 16, 64, 256.

geomorphic. Resembling the earth in form; describes architectural designs or forms that fit into the landscape where they are built.

Georgian architecture. An architectural style, popular in the 18th century and still used in residences, that is a combination of popular English styles; characterized by regularity of form, horizontal lines, and classical proportions and featuring pitched roofs, central entrances, balanced windows, doors, and chimneys, and first-floor windows that extend to the ground.

gift deed. A deed given without consideration.

gift tax. A graduated tax, imposed by the federal government and some states, on gifts of property during the donor's lifetime; under the law, gifts may include irrevocable living trusts.

GI loan. A mortgage loan granted to veterans that is guaranteed by the Veterans Administration and subject to its restrictions.

gingerbread work. Describes excessive ornamentation in architecture, especially in a house.

Ginnie Mae. *See* Government National Mortgage Association (GNMA).

girder. A principal, horizontal structural member or beam that supports lesser beams, joists, or walls.

girt. A horizontal framing member that extends between columns or studs to stiffen the framework or carry the siding material.

GLA. *See* gross leasable area; gross living area.

glacial soil. Parent material of soil that has been moved and redeposited by glacial activity.

glass. A hard, brittle, generally transparent or translucent substance produced by the fusion of components such as silica, soda, and lime. *See also* plate glass; wire glass.

glass block. A hollow building block of translucent glass that admits light, but provides privacy and sound-insulating qualities; not intended for use in a load-bearing wall.

glass wool insulation. Material made of glass fibers, usually in the form of blankets wrapped in heavy, asphalt-treated or vapor-barrier paper. *See also* mineral wool.

glaze. To fit, furnish, or cover with glass; to produce a glassy or glossy surface.

glazed brick. A dress brick with a glossy surface made of glass.

glazed facing tile. A hollow, clay tile with one or two glazed surfaces.

glean. The gathering of grain or other produce left in fields by combines;

accomplished by grazing livestock or hand picking.

GNMA. *See* Government National Mortgage Association.

GNP. *See* gross national product.

going-concern value. The value created by a proven property operation; considered as a separate entity to be valued with a specific business establishment; also called *going value. See also* business value.

going value. *See* going-concern value.

good. In economics, a material or immaterial thing that satisfies human desire and is external to humans; divided into two categories—free goods and economic goods.

goodwill. A salable business asset based on reputation, not physical assets.

gore. A small, triangular piece of land.

government lots. In the government survey system, land areas that are not divided into quarter quarters due to location or size; usually lie along the northern and western borders of townships and along the edge of rivers or lakes, and extend from the border or waterline to the first quarter quarters.

Government National Mortgage Association (GNMA). A federally owned and financed corporation under the Department of Housing and Urban Development that subsidizes mortgages through its secondary mortgage market operations and issues mortgage-backed, federally insured securities; also called *Ginnie Mae. See also* Federal National Mortgage Association (FNMA).

government survey system. A land survey system used in Florida, Alabama, Mississippi, and all states north of the Ohio River or west of the Mississippi River except Texas; divides land into townships approximately six miles square, each containing 36 sections of 640 acres. *See also* legal description.

GPM. *See* graduated-payment mortgage.

GPO. Government Printing Office.

grace period. A period of time, usually measured in days, during which the borrower under a mortgage or other debt instrument may cure a default without incurring a penalty or triggering foreclosure or other remedies by the creditor.

grade

1. The slope of a surface such as a lot or road, with the vertical rise or fall expressed as a percentage of horizontal distance; e.g., a 3% upgrade indicates a rise of three feet for each 100 feet of horizontal distance.

2. The level or elevation of a lot; e.g., rough grade is the level, slope, or general elevation of the

land surface on which topsoil will be placed in landscaping; finish grade is the final level, slope, or elevation of a lot.

3. Sometimes used to mean on or at the same level, e.g., a crossing at street grade, a lot at street grade.

4. To provide a parcel of land with the desired contour and drainage.

5. A letter, number, or word that denotes the quality of construction materials.

grade beam. A horizontal, load-bearing foundation member that is end-supported like a standard beam, not ground-supported like a foundation wall.

graded tax. A local tax designed to impose an increasing burden on land values and a decreasing burden on improvements; differential is achieved by varying the assessment or the tax rate.

grade separation. A structure used to separate two intersecting roadways vertically; permits traffic on one road to cross traffic on the other without interference.

gradient. The rate of the rise or fall of land, i.e., the degree of inclination.

graduated-payment adjustable mortgage loan. A mortgage instrument, approved for use by federal savings and loans, that is a combination of the graduated-payment mortgage and the adjustable mortgage loan. Monthly payments increase over the graduation period, which is limited to 10 years, and the interest rate changes with the movement of a specified index. No limits are placed on the frequency of payment adjustments over the graduation period or on the frequency or amount of interest rate changes over the term of the mortgage.

graduated-payment mortgage (GPM). A debt secured by real estate in which mortgage payments are matched to projected increases in the borrower's income. The periodic payments start out low and gradually increase.

graduated rental lease. A lease that provides for specified changes in rent at one or more points during the lease term; e.g., step-up and step-down leases.

grain elevator. *See* elevator.

grand list. In New England, the tax roll or assessment list of a community.

grant. The act of transferring property or an interest in property.

grant deed. A deed in which the grantor warrants that he or she has not previously conveyed or encumbered the property; does not ensure that the grantor is the owner of the property or that the property is unencumbered; conveys any after-acquired title of the grantor, unless a different intent is expressed. *See also* bargain and sale deed; deed; quitclaim deed; warranty deed.

grantee. A person to whom property is transferred by deed or to whom property rights are granted by a trust instrument or other document.

grant-in-aid. The allowable contribution made by local parties, in cash or its equivalent, as part of the local share in an urban renewal project.

grantor. A person who transfers property by deed or grants property rights through a trust instrument or other document.

granular structure. Soil aggregates of up to two centimeters in diameter that are of medium consistency and are somewhat rounded. Coarse granular describes aggregates close to maximum size; fine granular refers to aggregates under five millimeters in diameter

graph. A diagram that represents the variation of a variable in comparison with one or more other variables; the collection of all points whose coordinates satisfy a given functional relationship.

graphic analysis. Quantitative techniques used to identify and measure adjustments to the sale prices of comparable properties; a variant of statistical analysis in which an ap-praiser interprets graphically displayed data visually or through curve fit analysis.

grassland. A type of range vegetation that includes all lands bearing grasses—i.e, plants with hollow, jointed stems and parallel-veined leaves that grow in two rows on the stems; perennial grasses predominate, but forbs and browse may be present.

gray scale. A series of achromatic samples that vary discretely from white to black. (R.S. Means)

grazing capacity. The maximum number of animals that can feed in an area without damaging the vegetation or related resources; also called *grazing potential.*

grazing land. Rangeland with an understory of vegetation that provides forage for grazing animals; includes natural grasslands, shrublands, savannas, most deserts, tundra, coastal marshes, and wet meadows.

grazing license or permit. Official, written permission to graze a specified number, kind, and class of livestock for a specific period on a defined allotment.

grazing season. A period of grazing that makes optimum use of forage resources; on public lands, an established period for which grazing permits are issued.

grazing unit. An area of public or private rangeland that is grazed as a single entity.

greasewood. A type of range vegetation where greasewood (*sacrobatus*) predominates.

great soil group. A group of soils with common internal characteristics; includes one or more families of soil.

greenbelt. A band of countryside surrounding a development or neighborhood on which building is generally prohibited; usually large enough to protect against objectional property uses or the intrusion of nearby development.

green lumber. Lumber that has more moisture than air- or kiln-dried lumber; unseasoned lumber.

grid
1. A grating of crossed bars.
2. A pattern composed of parallel lines that intersect at right angles.
3. A chart used to rate a property, a neighborhood, comparables, etc.

grid ceiling
1. A ceiling with apertures in which luminaries are inserted for lighting purposes.
2. Any ceiling hung on a grid framework. (R.S. Means)

gridiron. The rectangular pattern of streets in a city or subdivision development.

grid system. The rectangular subdivision of property used in many American cities; designed to make a minimum amount of road surface accessible to a maximum number of individual parcels.

grillage. A system of beams laid crosswise to form a foundation that evenly distributes imposed loads.

GRM. *See* gross rent multiplier.

groin
1. A structure placed on a beach to act as a breakwater; usually made of piling, sometimes with a stone apron at the end.
2. In architecture, the curved line or edge formed by the intersection of two vaulted or arched surfaces.

gross adjustment. The total adjustment to each comparable sale price calculated in absolute terms. All the adjustments, both positive and negative, are added together to determine the gross adjustment to a comparable sale price. *See also* net adjustment.

gross area
1. The total area of a structure without deducting for holes or cutouts.
2. The entire area of a roof.
3. In construction, the entire area of a shingle, including any parts that might have had to be cut out.
4. The total enclosed floor area of a building. (R.S. Means)

gross building area *(GBA)*. The total floor area of a building, including below-grade space but excluding unenclosed areas, measured from the exterior of the walls. *See also* area.

gross domestic product (GDP). The monetary value of all goods and services produced by a nation's economy during a year, valued at market prices; the gross national product of a country less net payments on foreign investment. GDP became the official measure of the U.S. economy in 1991. *See also* gross national product (GNP); national income.

gross floor area. The total area of all the floors of a building, including intermediately floored tiers, mezzanine, basements, etc., as measured from the exterior surfaces of the outside walls of the building. (R.S. Means)

gross income. Income from the operation of a business or the management of property, customarily stated on an annual basis. *See also* effective gross income *(EGI)*; potential gross income *(PGI)*.

gross income multiplier. *See* effective gross income multiplier *(EGIM)*; potential gross income multiplier *(PGIM)*.

gross leasable area *(GLA)*. The total floor area designed for the occupancy and exclusive use of tenants, including basements and mezzanines, and measured from the center of interior partitioning to outside wall surfaces; the standard measure for determining the size of shopping centers where rent is calculated based on the *GLA* occupied. *See also* area.

gross lease. A lease in which the landlord receives stipulated rent and is obligated to pay all or most of the property's operating expenses and real estate taxes.

gross living area *(GLA)*. The total area of finished, above-grade residential space excluding unheated areas such as porches and balconies; the standard measure for determining the amount of space in residential properties. *See also* above-grade living area *(AGLA)*.

gross national product (GNP). The monetary value of all final goods and services produced by a nation's economy during a year, before deducting depreciation and allowances for the consumption of durable capital goods. The GNP includes any income accruing to residents of the country from investments or other earnings abroad, but excludes any income earned in the domestic market by investments owned by foreigners abroad. *See also* gross domestic product; national income.

gross output. The number of Btus available at the outlet nozzle of a heating unit for continuously satisfying the gross load requirements of a boiler operating within code limitations. (R.S. Means)

gross rental basis. Refers to a lease which stipulates that the lessor pays all operating expenses of the real estate.

gross rent multiplier *(GRM).* The relationship or ratio between the sale price or value of a property and its gross rental income. *See also* effective gross income multiplier (*EGIM*); potential gross income multiplier (*PGIM*).

gross retail value. *See* aggregate of retail values (*ARV*).

gross sale price. The total consideration paid before professional fees, commissions, advertising, or other marketing expenses are deducted.

gross sales. The total amount of invoiced sales, before deducting returns, allowances, etc.

gross up method. A method of calculating variable operating expenses in income-producing properties when less than 100% occupancy is assumed. The gross up method approximates the actual expense of providing services to the rentable area of a building given a specified rate of occupancy.

ground area. The area in a building computed from the exterior dimensions of the ground floor; also called *building footprint* or *plot coverage. See also* ground coverage.

ground beam. In construction, a horizontal member of iron, steel, or stone that is located on or near the ground and used to support the superstructure and distribute its load.

ground coverage. The percentage of ground area covered by ground floor building improvements. *See also* ground area.

ground fault circuit interrupter. A circuit breaker that is sensitive to very low levels of current leakage from a fault in an electrical system.

ground fault interrupter. A device that automatically de-energizes any high-voltage system component that has developed a fault in the ground line.

ground floor. The floor of a building that is approximately level with the ground.

ground lease. A lease that grants the right to use and occupy land. Improvements made by the ground lessee typically revert to the ground lessor. *See also* master lease.

ground rent. The rent paid for the right to use and occupy land according to the terms of a ground lease; the portion of the total rent allocated to the underlying land.

ground rent capitalization. A method of estimating land value that is applicable when the ground rent corresponds to the owner's interest in the land, the leased fee interest; applied by capitalizing ground rent at a market-derived rate. This method is useful when comparable rents, rates, and factors can be developed from an analysis of sales of leased land.

grounds. Strips of wood placed around wall openings to indicate the finish level for plaster or concrete.

ground water. All water that has seeped down beneath the surface of the ground or into the subsoil; water from springs or wells.

ground water table. The top elevation of ground water at a given location and at a given time. (R.S. Means)

grout. A thin, fluid mortar used to fill small joints and cavities in masonry work. *See also* caulking; tuck-pointing.

grove. A planting of uniformly spaced fruit- or nut-bearing trees; commonly applied to citrus plantings, but also applicable to plantings of walnuts and other specialty nut crops.

growth. A stage in a neighborhood's life cycle in which the neighborhood gains public favor and acceptance.

GSA. General Services Administration.

guaranteed mortgage. A mortgage in which a party other than the borrower assures payment in the event of default, e.g., a VA-guaranteed mortgage.

guaranteed title. A title whose validity is insured by an abstract, title, or indemnity company.

guide meridian. *See* meridian.

gully erosion. Rill erosion that continues over a period of time, cutting through the soft, tilled earth and into the firm, subsoil structure. In time its depth becomes a barrier that is not easily crossed with farm tools or normal equipment. *See also* rill erosion.

gumbo soil. A silty, fine-textured soil that becomes very sticky and greasy when wet.

Gunite. A trade name for a cement-like compound that is dispensed from a gun under pneumatic pressure.

gutter
1. A channel running along the length of a building that carries off rainwater, usually by means of downspouts.
2. A ridge formed where the edge of a street meets a raised sidewalk, or a depressed ridge on the shoulder of a road, which controls the flow of storm water.

gypsum. A common mineral, hydrated calcium sulphate, in the form of colorless crystals or masses that are easily crumbled; an ingredient in plaster of paris and Keene's cement.

gypsum blocks. A friable building material that is not suitable for load-bearing walls.

gypsum sheathing board. A prefabricated material made of set gypsum covered with water-repellent paper; replaces sheathing and sheathing paper in construction.

gypsum wallboard. A type of wallboard used as a substitute for plaster in drywall construction; a prefabricated sheet of gypsum covered with paper to which paint or wallpaper can be applied. *See also* drywall; Sheetrock.

H

habendum clause. A clause in a real estate document that specifies the extent of the interest to be conveyed, e.g., life, fee.

half shrub. Semiwoody perennials of low stature, e.g., *aplopappus, gutierrezia, artemisia frigida, eriogonum wrightii*; a woody caudex that produces herbaceous stems that die back each year.

half-timbered. Describes house construction with exposed timber wall framing over masonry or lath and plaster; simulated half-timbering uses boards on plaster walls. Half-timbering is a distinguishing characteristic of Elizabethan architecture. *See also* English half-timbered architecture.

hall
1. A room at the entrance of a building or a passage that provides access to various parts of a building.
2. A large room used for public gatherings.

halon fire extinguisher. A suppressing system for use on all classes of fires. Its extinguishing agent is bromotrifluoromethane, a colorless, odorless, and electrically nonconductive gas of exceptionally low toxicity. Considered to be the safest of the compressed gas fire-suppressing agents. Although often used in computer equipment rooms, the use of halon is severely restricted because of its properties (which destroy the ozone layer). (R.S. Means)

hand. A linear measure of four inches.

handicap door opening system. A door equipped with a knob or latch and handle located approximately 36 inches from the floor, and an auxiliary handle on the other side at the hinge edge, for convenience to persons in wheelchairs. (R.S. Means)

handicap water cooler. A water cooler set low and operated by push-bars or levers for convenience to persons in wheelchairs. (R.S. Means)

hand-move sprinkler. Portable irrigation sprinkler system constructed from aluminum pipe and moved by hand to provide irrigation in various settings.

hard copy. In computer usage, any data or text printed on paper.

hard costs. *See* direct costs.

hard disk. In computer usage, a rigid, magnetic storage medium that holds a great deal of information which can be accessed more quickly than data on a floppy disk.

hard dollars. The portion of the total, initial consideration paid for the acquisition of property that cannot immediately be deducted by the buyer for income tax purposes.

hard finish. The smooth, finished coat of plaster that is applied over rough plastering.

hard goods. A class of merchandise composed primarily of durable items, e.g., hardware, machines, heavy appliances, electrical and plumbing fixtures, farming machinery and supplies; also called *hardlines.*

hardpan. Silt, clay, or any other soil material that is cemented together; a hardened soil horizon that will not dissolve in water; may be of any texture, compacted by iron oxide, organic material, silica, calcium carbonate, or other substances.

hardware
1. The metal fittings of a building, e.g., hinges, locks, lifts, doorknobs; also called *builders' hardware* or *finish hardware.*
2. In computer usage, the physical components or equipment that make up a computer system.

hardwood. Lumber cut from broadleaved trees, e.g., oak, mahogany, walnut, birch, that is used for interior finishing and flooring; refers to a type of tree, not the hardness of the wood.

hatchway. A lifting or sliding door in a ceiling that provides access to an attic; a similar door in a floor, providing access to a cellar; also called *scuttle.*

hay. Meadow grasses, e.g., clover, alfalfa, that are cut and cured for livestock feed.

haymow. The part of a barn where hay or straw is stored.

hazardous waste/contaminated sites. Sites on which a release has occurred, or is suspected to have occurred, of any hazardous substance, hazardous waste, or petroleum products, and which release or suspected release has been reported to a government entity. (ASTM)

H beam. An H-shaped, steel structural member frequently used as a column.

head
1. A body of water kept in reserve at a height, including the containing bank, dam, or wall.
2. The difference in elevation between two points in a body of fluid; the resulting pressure of the fluid at the lower point expressed as this height.
3. The source of a river or stream.
4. The topmost framing member of a window or door.

header. In masonry, a brick or stone laid across the thickness of a wall with one end toward the face of the wall; in carpentry, a wood beam set at right angles to the joists to provide a seat or support; a wood lintel.

head jamb. A piece of finish material placed across the underside of the top of a door or window opening.

head room. The distance between the top of a finished floor and the lowest part of the floor structure above.

headship rate. The ratio between the number of households headed by a person of a particular subgroup (e.g., unmarried males, aged 25-29) and all the persons in that subgroup (58.1% of unmarried males are heads of households). *See also* household.

headway. The time interval between two vehicles traveling in the same direction on the same route.

health-related facility. A facility designated, staffed, and equipped to accommodate individuals who do not need hospital care and are generally ambulatory, but require a minimum amount of supervision and assistance.

hearth. The floor of a fireplace. The front hearth extends out into the room and may be of brick or decorative stone; the back hearth is inside the fireplace and is usually made of firebrick.

heat exchanger. A device designed to transfer heat between two physically separated fluids. The fluids are usually separated by the thin walls of tubing. (R.S. Means)

heating plant. The entire heating system of a building or complex, including either a boiler, piping, and radiators, or a furnace, ducts, and air outlets. (R.S. Means)

heating system. Any device or system for heating a building; usually, a furnace or boiler used to generate steam, hot water, or hot air; a burner or air device that uses coal, oil, gas, or electricity to heat water or air which is then circulated through the system. Types of heating systems include warm air, hot water, direct steam, radiant, and electric.

heating, ventilation, and air-conditioning system (HVAC). A unit that regulates the distribution of heat and fresh air throughout a building.

heat loss
1. The net loss in Btus within a given space due to heat transmission through spaces around windows, doors, etc.
2. The loss by conduction, convection, or radiation from a solar collector after its initial absorption. (R.S. Means)

heat pump. A reverse-cycle refrigeration unit that can be used for heating or cooling.

heat recovery. The extraction of heat from any source not primarily designed to produce heat, such as a chimney or light bulb. (R.S. Means)

heavy industry. Industries that are physically extensive or complex and usually require large tracts of land, e.g., steel mills, refineries, foundries, packing plants; also, industrial operations that produce hazards or nuisances, e.g., objectionable fumes, pollution, noise, vibration.

heavy soil. A clay soil. *See also* clay; fine-textured soil.

heavy steel frame. A building with framing members of heavy steel, e.g., beams, girders, columns, that can carry heavy loads and absorb shocks and vibrations.

hectare. A metric unit of land measurement.

hedgerow planting. The planting of trees or vines in rows with little space between individual plants to increase production or decrease costs; usually facilitates mechanization in harvesting, pruning, or other operations; may affect the economic life of the trees or vines involved.

hedging. In agriculture, the trimming or mechanical pruning of permanent plantings, e.g., orchards, groves.

hedonic price index. An analytical model used to quantify the pricing tradeoff between measurable product capacity and intangible attributes such as an amenity feature, design, or reputation. *See also* isoquant.

heel. In construction, the part of a framing member that rests on the wall plate or top horizontal member.

height density. A zoning regulation that controls use or occupancy within a given area by designating the maximum height of structures.

heir. A person who inherits real or personal property; a person legally designated to inherit the estate of one who has died intestate.

hereditaments. All inheritable property, e.g., real, personal, corporeal, incorporeal.

HEW. Department of Health, Education, and Welfare. The duties of this now defunct government agency have been divided between the U.S. Department of Health and Human Services and the U.S. Department of Education.

highest and best use. The reasonably probable and legal use of vacant land or an improved property, which is physically possible, appropriately supported, financially feasible, and that results in the highest value. The four criteria the highest and best use must meet are legal permissibility, physical possibility, financial feasibility, and maximum profitability.

highest and best use of land or a site as though vacant. Among all reasonable, alternative uses, the use that yields the highest present land value, after payments are made for labor, capital, and coordination. The use of a property based on the assumption that the parcel of land is vacant or can be made vacant by demolishing any improvements.

highest and best use of property as improved. The use that should be made of a property as it exists. An existing property should be renovated or retained as is so long as it continues to contribute to the total market value of the property, or until the return from a new improvement would more than offset the cost of demolishing the existing building and constructing a new one.

high rise
1. An indefinite term for a multistory building that is serviced by elevators.
2. A building with upper floors higher than fire department aerial ladders, usually ten or more stories. (R.S. Means)

high-rise apartment building. An imprecise term used since World War II to distinguish a modern elevator apartment building from its prewar counterpart; usually a tall building, but this standard varies in different areas.

high technology. Commonly used to describe the industrial market segment that deals in or is related to technologically advanced products, e.g., computers, electronics, semiconductors. New variations include robotics, the use of computer-controlled robots to perform tasks once done by humans, and biotechnology in the life sciences, e.g., genetic engineering and the synthesis and manufacture of biological products; also called *high tech.*

high water line. The point on the shore to which the tide normally rises; varies with seasons, time, wind, and other causes. *See also* mean high water line.

highway capacity. The amount of traffic a roadway can accommodate; controlled by the types of vehicles using the highway, the number and width of travel lanes, the allowable speed, road curvature and topography, and the access limitations and development controls of adjacent real estate.

highway easement. A right granted or taken for the construction, maintenance, and operation of a highway; in the case of a public thoroughfare, the abutting landholders are ordinarily assumed to own the fee to the center line of the right-of-way.

highway frontage. Land that is adjacent to and abuts a highway right-of-way.

highway line. The outside limits of a highway right-of-way, as distinguished from the limits of actual construction, e.g., curbs, shoulders, slopes; also called *right-of-way line.*

hilly land. Uneven land with dominant slopes between 16% and 30%.

hindsight rule. A rule that permits the admission of evidence relating to events subsequent to the date of taking to prove or disprove the validity of any claim of value.

hip. The inclined ridge formed by the intersection of two sloping roof surfaces with unparallel eave lines.

hip roof. A roof with sloping sides and end slopes that are connected by a ridge, the length of which is called a *run*; distinguished from a pyramid roof in which all slopes meet so that virtually no ridge remains.

histogram. A set of vertical bars that are proportionate in size to the frequencies represented. *See also* frequency distribution.

historical cost. The cost of a property when it was originally constructed.

historic district. An area designated to retain and preserve its historic quality. The 1966 Historic Preservation Act defined the involvement of the federal government in historic preservation. The authority to create local historic districts usually comes from state legislation authorizing municipalities or counties to establish historic districts under their general zoning powers. *See also* National Register of Historic Places.

historic preservation. The preservation of historic sites, structures, and districts by regulation or rehabilitation.

Historic Preservation Act of 1966. *See* historic district; National Register of Historic Places.

historic site. A parcel that is distinguished because an important historic event occurred on or near the site.

historic value. *See* retrospective value estimate.

hog factory. In agriculture, a hog-feeding facility where hogs are confined to grow from farrowing to slaughter size under controlled conditions.

hogwallows. Describes the surface microrelief of a body of soil containing a series of rounded, low mounds with diameters up to 40 feet and variable heights up to about three feet.

holdback. A portion of a loan commitment that is not funded until an additional requirement is met, e.g., completion and rental of a project.

hold harmless agreement. A legally binding agreement in which the liability of one party is assumed by another.

holding period. The term of ownership of an investment. *See also* projection period.

holding period yield. The total yield on an investment, particularly a bond held for less than full term, including the gains or losses from resale as well as regular earnings; the sum of all current yield and deferred yield; sometimes a shortened term for the *holding period yield rate* which is analogous to the equity yield rate and internal rate of return.

holdover tenant. A tenant who remains in possession of the leased real estate after the lease has expired; in many states the lease is automatically renewed if the lessor accepts a rent payment after the expiration of the lease.

hollow-newel stair. A circular stairway with a well hole in the middle.

hollow wall. A wall, usually of masonry, that consists of two vertical components with an air space in between.

homestead. The fixed residence or dwelling of the head of a family, including the principal house, any other buildings, and the surrounding land.

homestead exemption
1. The lawful withdrawal of a property occupied by the head of a family from attachment by the occupant's creditors or forced sale for general debts.
2. A release from assessment or property tax on, or the application of a lower tax rate to, property designated as a family homestead.

homogeneous. Describes an area or neighborhood where the property types and uses are similar and the inhabitants have compatible cultural, social, and economic interests.

hood. A canopy over a casement window; the part of a fireplace that projects over the hearth; a chimney cap that eliminates down draft; a canopy over a cooking appliance that is usually ventilated to control and disperse heat or offensive odors.

hopper. A device used on the sides of hospital windows to prevent drafts.

hopper window. *See* hospital window.

horizon. A layer of soil approximately parallel to the land surface that has more or less well-defined characteristics produced through soil-building processes *See also* A horizon; B horizon; C horizon; D horizon.

horizontal control network. A national system of interrelated monument points that is used primarily to survey extremely large areas of land.

horizontal subdivision. The division of a tract of land into smaller parcels for sale or lease.

Hoskold factor. A multiplier calculated from special tables and used to capitalize the income produced by a wasting asset; provides for recapture with actual or hypothetical contributions to a sinking fund that grows with compound interest at a safe rate, and for return on the in-

vestment at a higher, speculative rate.

Hoskold premise. An assumption that the present value of an income stream is based on a combination of two separate rates: a "speculative" rate for risk and a "safe" rate for the sinking fund. The Hoskold premise applies to income in the form of an ordinary level annuity of limited duration which is sufficient to pay a fair return on capital at the speculative rate and to contribute necessary installments to a sinking fund. This sinking fund will grow with interest at a safe rate and repay the investor in full at the termination of the investment.

hospital. An institution where ill or injured persons receive short-term medical, surgical, or psychiatric treatment, nursing care, food, and shelter; provides complete medical and surgical services.

hospital window. A window that is hinged at the bottom and opens inward with hoppers on the sides to prevent drafts.

hostel. A facility that provides lodging, generally for younger travelers.

hotel. A facility that offers lodging accommodations and a wide range of other services, e.g., restaurants, convention facilities, meeting rooms, recreational facilities, commercial shops. *See also* all-suite hotel; budget motel; extended-stay hotel; lodging; microtel; resort hotel.

hotel/motel unit. The smallest accommodation that can be sold to a patron; must contain a full bath, sleeping accommodations, and an entrance door with a key.

hot water system. A heating system consisting of a boiler, radiators, an expansion tank, and interconnected piping filled with water that circulates from the boiler through pipes to radiators where heat is released before the water returns to the boiler; classified as gravity or forced circulation systems, with one or two pipes and open or closed expansion tanks.

hour-inch. A measure that equals water flowing at a miner's inch for one hour; 1/50th of a cubic foot per second in southern California, Arizona, Montana, and Oregon.

house. A dwelling; may be single or double, e.g., a duplex, a townhouse, a row house, a split-level ranch.

household. A number of related or unrelated people who live in one housing unit; all the persons occupying a group of rooms or a single room that constitutes one housing unit. A single person, a couple, or more than one family living in a single housing unit may make up a household. *See also* headship rate; living unit; ownership rate.

household size. The total number of related or unrelated persons residing in a household unit.

house sewer. The drain pipe system or the pipes that connect with the main sewer in the street. *See also* lateral.

housing. Residential property including categories that are owner-occupied (houses, condominiums) and tenant-leased (apartments, houses).

Housing and Urban Development, Department of. *See* Department of Housing and Urban Development.

housing starts. Newly constructed housing units; includes both single-family and multifamily domiciles.

housing stock. The total inventory of owned and rented dwelling units. Housing stock is determined by new construction, the number of demolitions, and the number of conversions to and from a residential use. *See also* living unit.

HUD. *See* Department of Housing and Urban Development.

human ecology. The study of the relationship between man and the environment. When focused on the urban environment, human ecology involves the spatial distribution of people, groups, and institutions in a community, the relationships among them, and the changes in the distribution caused by adaptation, competition, and accommodation.

Humboldt rule. A form of the Spaulding rule that measures old growth redwood logs and provides for their numerous invisible defects with a blanket 30% deduction; can produce a large overrun if the amount of defects is small. The Humboldt rule is sometimes used to scale Douglas fir, although this practice is not recommended. Also called *Humboldt scale. See also* log rules.

hummocks. Low mounds in swamp soils formed by the wind or by pasturing.

humus. The well-decomposed, relatively stable part of the soil's organic matter; keeps the soil soft and granular and increases its capacity to hold water and plant food.

hundred percent location. Describes a location in the central business district that commands the highest land value or rent.

hunting leases. Agreements in which a private property owner grants the right to hunt natural game on his or her land; sometimes necessitate additional land management.

hutch. A type of housing used for domestic rabbit production.

HVAC. *See* heating, ventilation, and air-conditioning system.

hydraulic cement. A type of cement that hardens under water.

hydroelectric plant. A plant designed to generate and distribute electrical power produced by falling water; includes buildings, engines, dynamos, etc.

hydrograph. A chart that shows the quantity of water flowing in a stream at specific intervals over a period of time.

hydroponics. The science of growing plants in liquid mineral solutions that provide all plant nutrients artificially.

hypothecate. To pledge as security while retaining possession.

hypothesis. In inferential statistics, a statement to be proved. One begins with a null hypothesis, a statement of what one chooses to accept in the absence of sufficient evidence to the contrary, specifies the alternative hypothesis to be proved, and analyzes the available data to determine if the null hypothesis can be rejected and the alternative hypothesis accepted with some confidence.

I

IAAO. *See* International Association of Assessing Officers.

I beam. A steel beam that resembles the letter I in cross section.

ICSC. International Council of Shopping Centers.

igneous rock. A rock created by the cooling of melted mineral material; also called *fire rock.*

illiquidity. Describes the condition of assets that are not readily converted into cash.

illuviation. The process in which soil material from an upper horizon is deposited in the horizon below.

immature soil. A young or imperfectly developed soil without individual horizons.

impact study. An investigation to determine the effect of development upon the environment. *See* environmental impact study (EIS).

impervious soil. Soil that does not allow for the passage of water, air, or plant roots.

impounds. Payments made to a fiduciary, usually a lender, for items such as property taxes, as-sessments, and insurance; often imposed by government agencies on the sale of interests in real estate syndications. The agency may require that subscription funds be placed in a special escrow account until a specific number of subscriptions have been paid. Then the funds are returned to the syndicate for use in purchasing the subject property or other activities defined in the offering circular and application for qualification.

improved land

1. Land that has been developed for some use by the construction of improvements; also, land that has been prepared for development by grading, draining, installing utilities, etc., as distinguished from raw land.
2. Land prepared for cultivation.

improvements. Buildings or other relatively permanent structures or developments located on, or attached to, land.

improvements to land. Usually additions to land to make property usable, such as curbs, sidewalks, street lights, sewers, drains, fills. *See also* site improvements.

imputed income. Income attributable to owner-occupied income properties equal to the amount of rent saved or not paid by the user. The funds that would otherwise have to be paid as rent are used to support ownership. Income allocated to land and/or buildings in the physical residual techniques is sometimes called *imputed income.*

inadequate improvement. *See* underimprovement.

incentive zoning. An agreement between public officials and private developers concerning rentable building area and the minimum building bulk specified by the zoning ordinance. In this arrangement, a desirable public improvement or open-space objective is established by government officials, and developers are offered greater usable building area as an incentive to provide the desired amenity. Planned unit developments and voluntary cluster developments are forms of incentive zoning.

incinerator. A device that burns waste material and rubbish.

income. Money or other benefits that are assumed to be received periodically.

income approach. *See* income capitalization approach.

income capitalization approach. A set of procedures through which an appraiser derives a value indication for an income-producing property by converting its anticipated benefits (cash flows and reversion) into property value. This conversion can be accomplished in two ways. One year's income expectancy can be capitalized at a market-derived capitalization rate or at a capitalization rate that reflects a specified income pattern, return on investment, and change in the value of the investment. Alternatively, the annual cash flows for the holding period and the reversion can be discounted at a specified yield rate.

income model. A formula developed to project a pattern of periodic income. Income models can be applied to level income with no change in value, level income with changing value, income and value that change by fixed amounts per period (straight-line), income and value that change at a constant ratio (exponential-curve), and variable or irregular income with changing value.

income multiplier. *See* gross income multiplier; multiplier; net income multiplier.

income participation. The right of the mortgagee to share some portion of the future income generated by the property, usually over the term of the mortgage. *See also* equity participation; equity participation mortgage.

income-producing life. A period of time that begins when a plant or crop achieves peak production and ends when production declines; refers specifically to orchard or vineyard crops that require a long start-up period before cash flow is realized; varies with the type of crop and the effectiveness of management.

income-producing property. A type of property created primarily to produce monetary income.

income rate. A rate that reflects the ratio of one year's income to the value of the property; includes the overall capitalization rate (R_O), the equity capitalization rate (R_E), and the mortgage constant (R_M); also called *cash flow rate.*

income stream. A steady flow of payments or benefits from an investment or property. *See also* annuity.

income tax liability
1. An obligation to federal, state, or local government based on the marginal tax rate and taxable income of an individual or corporation.
2. For income-producing properties, net operating income less deductible items, e.g., interest on debt, allowable depreciation,

times the appropriate marginal tax rate.

increasing and decreasing returns. The concept that successive increments of one or more agents of production added to fixed amounts of the other agents will enhance income, in dollars, benefits, or amenities, at an increasing rate until a maximum return is reached. Then, income will decrease until the increment to value becomes increasingly less than the value of the added agent or agents; also called *law of decreasing returns* or *law of increasing returns.*

increasing annuity. An income stream of evenly spaced, periodic payments that is expected to increase in a systematic pattern.

incremental demand. *See* marginal demand.

incubator building. An industrial property that is subdivided into low-rent space and leased to fledgling business or manufacturing firms in the hope that they will grow and require additional space.

incurable depreciation. *See* incurable functional obsolescence; incurable physical deterioration.

incurable functional obsolescence. An element of accrued depreciation; a defect caused by a deficiency or superadequacy in the structure, materials, or design, which cannot be practically or economically corrected.

incurable physical deterioration. An element of accrued depreciation; a defect caused by physical deterioration that cannot be practically or economically corrected.

indemnity. The recovery of a sustained loss by a party that has incurred loss or damage as the result of the actions of another party who must make restitution.

indenture. A deed or other instrument involving two or more parties that enumerates the reciprocal and paralleling rights and obligations of each party.

indexed mortgage. *See* price level-adjusted mortgage (PLAM).

index lease. A lease, usually for a long term, that provides for periodic rent adjustments based on the change in an economic index, e.g., a cost-of-living index.

index number. A measure of the differences in the magnitude of a group of related variables compared with a base period, which is typically valued at 100; usually index numbers show the change in the prices of specific commodities or group averages over a period of time.

indirect costs. Expenditures or allowances for items other than labor and materials that are necessary for construction, but are not typically part of the construction contract. Indirect costs may include administrative costs; professional fees; financing costs and the interest paid on construction loans; taxes and the builder's or developer's all-risk insurance during construction; and marketing, sales, and lease-up costs incurred to achieve occupancy or sale. Also called *soft costs. See also* direct costs.

indirect gain/loss. In passive solar design, heat gain or loss that occurs at the surface of a thermal storage wall. Typical materials include brick, concrete, and water. (R.S. Means)

indirect heating
  1. A method of heating areas removed from the source of heat by steam, hot air, etc.
  2. Central heating. (R.S. Means)

indirect lighting. Reflected or diffused lighting achieved by directing the light toward the ceiling, the walls, or some other surface.

indirect system. A system of heating, air-conditioning, or refrigeration whereby the heating or cooling of an area is not accomplished directly. Rather, a fluid is heated or cooled and then circulated to the area requiring the conditioning, or the fluid is used to heat or cool air which then is circulated to achieve the same end.

induced demand. A component of latent demand created by aggressive marketing efforts, the opening of a major demand generator, or the provision of new amenities. *See also* latent demand.

industrial park. A controlled, parklike development that is designed to accommodate specific types of industry; provides the required appurtenances, e.g., public utilities, streets, railroad sidings, water and sewage facilities.

industrial plant. A single location where industrial operations are performed; includes all structures on the site.

industrial property. Land and/or improvements that can be adapted for industrial use; a combination of land, improvements, and machinery integrated into a functioning unit to assemble, process, and manufacture products from raw materials or fabricated parts; factories that render service, e.g., laundries, dry cleaners, storage warehouses, or those that produce natural resources, e.g., oil wells.

industrial siding. A spur track running along an industrial site where a railroad delivers and removes freight cars.

industrial tax exemption. An exemption from local property taxes granted for a specific period to attract new industries to the community or to encourage the expansion of existing industry.

industry standard. Readily available information in the form of published specifications, technical reports and disclosures, test procedures and results, codes and other technical information and data. Such data should be verifiable and professionally endorsed, with general acceptance and proven use by the construction industry. (R.S. Means)

inferential statistics. A branch of statistics that attempts to predict the values of many observations of a variable from a few observations of that variable and related facts; the statistics calculated in such predictions. *See also* descriptive statistics.

inferred demand. Demand projected on the basis of current market conditions, rates of change, and absorption patterns. *See also* forecast demand.

inflation. An erosion of the purchasing power of currency characterized by price escalation and an increase in the volume of money, i.e., the proliferation of monetary units and consequent decline in the value of each unit. Inflation tends to increase discount rates because investors require a higher nominal rate of return to offset the loss in value due to inflation. Investors often include an additional risk premium in the required rate of return on investments that do not respond well to unexpected inflation. *See also* appreciation (*app*).

infrared heater. A source of heat-producing wavelengths, longer than visible light, which do not heat the air through which they pass, but only those objects in the line of sight. (R.S. Means)

infrastructure
1. In a group of buildings or a complex, the core of development that is the source of all utilities and support services, e.g., gas and electric lines, streets, curbs.
2. In planning, used to describe services and facilities that are integral parts of urban community life.

ingress. A means of entering; an entrance.

inheritance tax. A tax on the right to receive property by inheritance; as distinguished from estate tax.

initial investment. A buyer's initial investment shall include only: a) cash paid as a down payment, b) the buyer's notes supported by irrevocable letters of credit from an independent established lending institution, c) payments by the buyer to third parties to reduce existing indebtedness on the property, and d) other amounts paid by the buyer that are part of the sales value. The buyer's initial investment shall be adequate to demonstrate the buyer's commitment to pay for the property and shall indicate reasonable likelihood that the seller will collect the receivable. (FASB)

in lieu tax. A tax that substitutes for property taxes; also called *in lieu payments* or *payments in lieu of taxes.*

inner court. An outdoor area which is open above, but surrounded on four sides by the exterior walls of a building or structure. (R.S. Means)

in-personam. Against a person, not a thing.

in rem. Against a thing, not a person.

in rem note. A nonrecourse note.

inside lot. A lot that is removed from a street intersection and therefore not affected by corner influence.

inspection list. A list of incomplete or incorrect work items that must be addressed by the contractor before final payment can be issued. (R.S. Means) Many appraisers use a type of inspection list when inspecting or evaluating a property.

installment contract. A type of purchase contract in which payment is made in prescribed installments that are usually forfeited if default occurs; in the sale of real property, title is not normally transferred until all payments under the contract are made. *See also* contract; land contract.

installment note. A promissory note that provides for payment of the principal in two or more specific installments at stated times. *See also* installment contract.

installment sale. A sale in which the proceeds are to be received in more than one payment. *See also* installment contract.

Institute of Real Estate Management (IREM). An organization of real estate professionals concerned with property management which confers the following designations: AMO (Accredited Management Organization), ARM (Accredited Resident Manager), and CPM (Certified Property Manager).

institutionally employed appraiser. An appraiser who works as a staff appraiser or a review appraiser for a financial institution or government agency. *See also* fee appraiser; staff appraiser.

institutional property. Property of a public nature owned and operated by the government or by a non-profit organization; e.g., hospitals, orphanages, private and public

educational facilities, correctional facilities, museums; also certain private properties, e.g., banks, insurance companies.

instrument. In real estate, a formal, legal document, e.g., a contract, a deed, a lease, a will.

instrumentalities. Often applied to agencies of the federal government whose obligations are not the direct obligation of the federal government; however, there is an implied support; e.g., Federal Land Bank bonds.

insulate. To provide with special features and/or materials which afford protection against wound, moisture, heat, or heat loss. (R.S. Means)

insulating board. A building board made of compressed plant fibers, e.g., wood, cane, corn stalks, dried and pressed to a specified thickness.

insulation. Any material used to reduce the transfer of heat, cold, or sound.

insulation batt. Flexible insulation of loosely matted plant or glass fibers faced on one or both sides with kraft paper or aluminum foil and usually available in specifically sized sections. (R.S. Means)

insulation blanket. Usually composed of the same materials and the same widths and thicknesses as batts, but is available in rolls. (R.S. Means)

insurable value

1. The portion of the value of an asset or asset group that is acknowledged or recognized under the provisions of an applicable loss insurance policy.

2. Value used by insurance companies as the basis for insurance. Often considered to be replacement or reproduction cost less deterioration and non-insurable items. Sometimes cash value or market value but often entirely a cost concept. (Marshall & Swift)

insurance. A personal contract to indemnify the insured for a potential loss; specific coverages relate to the asset insured or the potential hazard, e.g., property insurance, boiler insurance, storm insurance, title insurance, mortgage insurance, rent loss insurance, fire insurance, plate glass insurance, extended coverage insurance, contents insurance, comprehensive insurance, scheduled insurance. *See also* all risk insurance; errors and omissions insurance; insurance, builder's risk; insurance, comprehensive general liability; insurance, contractor's liability; insurance, extended coverage; insurance, loss of use; insurance, owner's liability; insurance, personal liability; insurance, professional liability; insurance, property; insurance, property damage; insurance, public liability; insurance, special hazards; liability; title insurance.

insurance, builder's risk. A specialized form of property insurance that provides coverage for loss or damage to the work during the course of construction. (R.S. Means)

insurance claims adjuster. An insurance agent who investigates damage to personal and real property and estimates the value loss to reach a monetary settlement with the insured.

insurance companies. Companies that offer various types of insurance coverage; traditionally large suppliers of real estate mortgage credit as well as sources of real estate equity investment.

insurance, comprehensive general liability. A broad form of liability insurance covering claims for bodily injury and property damage that combines, under one policy, coverage for all liability exposures, (except as specifically excluded), on a blanket basis and automatically covers new and unknown hazards that may develop. Comprehensive general liability insurance automatically includes contractual liability coverage for certain types of contracts. Products liability, completed operations liability, and broader contractual liability coverages are available on an optional basis. This policy may also be written to include automobile liability. (R.S. Means)

insurance, contractor's liability. Insurance purchased and maintained by the contractor to protect the contractor from specified claims which may arise out of, or result from, the contractor's operations under the contract, whether such operations are by the contractor or by any subcontractor, or by anyone directly or indirectly employed by any of them, or by anyone for whose acts any of them may be liable. (R.S. Means)

insurance, extended coverage. An endorsement to a property insurance policy which extends the perils covered to include windstorm, hail, riot, civil commotion, explosion (except steam boiler), aircraft, vehicles, and smoke. (R.S. Means)

insurance, loss of use. Insurance protecting against financial loss during the time required to repair or replace property damaged or destroyed by an insured peril. (R.S. Means)

insurance, owner's liability. Insurance to protect the owner against claims arising out of the operations performed for the owner by the contractor and arising out of the owner's general supervision. (R.S. Means)

insurance, personal liability. Bodily injury, and also injury or damage to the character or reputation of a person. Personal injury insurance includes coverage for injuries or damage to others caused by specified actions of the insured such as false arrest, malicious prosecution, willful detention or imprisonment, libel, slander, defamation of character, wrongful eviction, invasion of privacy, or wrongful entry. (R.S. Means)

insurance, professional liability. Insurance coverage for the insured professional's legal liability for claims for damages sustained by others allegedly as a result of negligent acts, errors, or omissions in the performance of professional services. (R.S. Means) *See also* errors and omissions insurance (E&O).

insurance, property. Coverage for loss or damage to the work at the site caused by the perils of fire, lightning, extended coverage perils, vandalism and malicious mischief, and additional perils (as otherwise provided or requested). (R.S. Means)

insurance, property damage. Insurance covering liability of the insured for claims for injury to or destruction of tangible property, including loss of use resulting therefrom, but usually not including coverage for injury to, or destruction of, property which is in the care, custody, and control of the insured. (R.S. Means)

insurance, public liability. Insurance covering liability of the insured for negligent acts resulting in bodily injury, disease, or death of persons other than employees of the insured, and/or property damage. (R.S. Means)

insurance rate. The percentage relationship between the insurance premium and the coverage it buys.

insurance, special hazards. Insurance coverage for damage caused by additional perils or risks to be included in the property insurance (at the request of the contractor, or at the option of the owner). Examples often included are sprinkler leakage, collapse, water damage, and coverage for materials in transit to the site or stored off the site. (R.S. Means)

insured mortgage. A mortgage in which a party other than the borrower assures payment on default by the mortgagor in return for the payment of a premium, e.g., FHA-insured mortgages, private mortgage insurance (PMI).

intangible assets
1. Nonphysical items of personal property, e.g., franchises, trademarks, patents, copyrights, goodwill.
2. Deferred items such as a development or organization expense.

intangible property. *See* intangible assets.

intangible value. A value that cannot be imputed to any part of the physical property, e.g., the excess value attributable to a favorable lease or mortgage, the value attributable to goodwill.

integrated building (smart building). A building that contains some degree of automation, such as centralized control over HVAC systems, fire safety and security access systems, telecommunication systems, and so forth. (R.S. Means)

integrated building system. A building designed to efficiently use climatic resources for heating, cooling, lighting, and electric power generation. (R.S. Means)

intensity. In agricultural land use, a reflection of the amount of labor and capital applied per unit of land area; relates to physical development, not maximum economic potential or the highest and best use of the land.

intensive farming. The use of comparatively large amounts of labor and working capital per acre of land; generally implies maximum productivity.

intercept. In graphic analysis, the point at which a line, e.g., the regression line, intercepts the axis on which the dependent variable is plotted; the value of the predicted variable when the value of the predictor variable is zero

interchange. A system of underpasses and overpasses that routes traffic on and off highways without disrupting through traffic; may link two or more highways.

interchange ramp. A traveled way that allows traffic to change from one roadway to another.

interest. Money paid for, or earned by, the use of capital; a return on capital as distinguished from a return of capital.

interest-only mortgage. A nonamortizing loan in which the lender receives interest only during the term of the loan and recovers the principal in a lump sum at the time of maturity.

interest rate. The price of money; the level of market interest carried by a debt instrument from the day it is created over the duration of its life. The rate of return or yield rate on debt capital, usually expressed as the nominal annual percentage of the amount loaned or invested.

interim financing. A temporary or short-term loan that is secured by a mortgage and generally paid off from the proceeds of permanent financing. *See also* construction loan.

interim use. The temporary use to which a site or improved property is put until it is ready to be put to its future highest and best use.

Interior, Department of the. *See* Department of the Interior.

interior description. The part of a building description that includes all information about the interior walls of a structure and the areas between them, including how the space is divided and finished.

interior lot. *See* inside lot.

interior trim. The finish on the interior of a building, e.g., casing, molding, baseboard.

interjurisdictional equalization. The application of multipliers or factors to each assessment comprising the assessment base to ensure a common level of assessment in all taxing jurisdictions in a state or county; may include the adjustment of individual assessments and the ordering of reassessments.

internal conformity. The condition that exists when labor, capital, coordination, and land are appropriately combined in a property.

internal rate of return (*IRR*). The annualized yield rate or rate of return on capital that is generated or capable of being generated within an investment or portfolio over a period of ownership. The *IRR* is the rate of discount that makes the net present value of the investment equal to zero. The *IRR* discounts all returns from the investment, including returns from its termination, to equal the original capital outlay. This rate is similar to the equity yield rate. As a measure of investment performance, the *IRR* is the rate of discount that produces a profitability index of one and a net present value of zero. It is often used to measure profitability after income taxes, i.e., the after-tax equity yield rate. *See also* equity yield rate (Y_E); financial management rate of return (*FMRR*); modified internal rate of return (*MIRR*); yield rate (*Y*).

internal supports. A structure's beams and columns, flooring system, and ceilings.

International Association of Assessing Officers (IAAO). A professional organization for property tax assessors; confers the following designations: CAE (Certified Assessment Evaluator), CMS (Cadastral Mapping Specialist), PPS (Personal Property Specialist), and RES (Residential Evaluator Specialist).

International style. An architectural style popular from 1930 to 1970 and characterized by skyscraper construction with no cornices, ornamentation, or terra-cotta exteriors; emphasized a streamlined appearance with curtain wall construction and flush windows.

interpolation. The calculation or estimation of a quantity within the range of data on which the calculation or estimate is based; the approximation of a value that falls between the tabular entries in a set of tables.

interrogatories. A discovery device consisting of written questions about the case submitted by one party to the other party. The answers to the interrogatories are usually given under oath, i.e., the person answering the questions signs a sworn statement that his or her answers are true.

intersection. The point at which two lines cross; the crossing of two streets at grade.

interstate highway system. A network of limited-access, divided highways within the United States that link principal metropolitan areas and industrial centers, serve the national defense, and connect with principal intercontinental routes in Canada and Mexico.

interstitial space. The area enclosed within the building components.

intestate. The condition of dying without leaving a valid will.

intractability. The characteristic that describes a soil that is difficult to work.

intrinsic value. The inherent worth of a thing.

inventory approach to value. Synonymous with the cost approach; frequently applied by purchasers who assign separate values in use to buildings and land.

inventory control
1. A management plan designed to minimize the number and quantity of hazardous substances on a construction project.
2. A managerial process to control the quantity of items in storage. (R.S. Means)

inventory value. *See* book value.

inverse condemnation. A legal process in which an owner can claim damages from a loss in property value and receive compensation when the damaging condition has not been instituted by the condemning body, e.g., damages caused to private property by a public works project where no condemnation action was taken by a governmental agency.

invested capital. The original capital, or equity, invested in an enterprise plus any accumulated profits that are not withdrawn but allowed to remain and augment the initial investment.

investment. Monies placed in a property for long-term use, usually with the expectation of producing a profit; assumes a reasonable degree of safety and the ultimate recovery of principal.

investment analysis. A study that reflects the relationship between the acquisition price and anticipated future benefits of a real estate investment. (USPAP, 1992 edition) Any study of the performance of a capital investment. *See also* fundamental analysis; technical analysis.

investment builder. A company primarily engaged in the construction of residential, commercial, and industrial buildings to be retained as investments.

investment proceeds per dollar invested. A simple reflection of investment performance calculated as the anticipated total proceeds returned to the investment position divided by the amount invested. *See also* profitability index (*PI*).

investment property. Property that constitutes a business enterprise consisting of all tangible and intangible assets assembled and developed as a single unit of utility for lease or rental, in whole or in part, to others for profit; normally purchased in expectation of annual net income and/or capital gain; also called *income-producing property.*

investment tax credit. A direct credit against federal income tax, equal to a percentage or portion of the investment in a qualified property, that can be taken when certain depreciable property with a useful life of at least four years is placed in service during the taxable year. The Tax Reform Act of 1986 rescinded investment tax credit except for certain properties under transition rules.

investment trust. A type of investment company that raises capital through the sale of its own stock and invests the money received almost exclusively in the stocks and bonds of other companies, mainly common stocks. Such companies purchase stock as an investment, rather than as a means of controlling the policies of the companies in which they invest. Investment trusts are of two kinds: closed-end and open-end. Open-end trusts do not have a fixed number of shares and continuously sell new shares and redeem those offered for purchase. In contrast, closed-end trusts have a fixed number of shares,

which are traded on the open market like stocks and bonds, not sold and redeemed by the trust. *See also* real estate investment trust (REIT).

investment value. The specific value of an investment to a particular investor or class of investors based on individual investment requirements; distinguished from market value, which is impersonal and detached. *See also* market value.

investment yield. *See* internal rate of return (*IRR*).

invitation to bid. A written notice of an owner's intention to receive competitive bids for a construction project wherein a select group of candidate constructors are invited to submit proposals. (R.S. Means)

involuntary conversion. The conversion of property when it is destroyed, in whole or in part, stolen, seized, requisitioned, condemned, or threatened by imminent requisition or condemnation; as a result, property is converted into money or other, similar property through insurance proceeds or condemnation awards.

Inwood annuity. An ordinary level income stream.

Inwood annuity capitalization. A traditional technique in which present value factors, or Inwood coefficients, from standard compound interest tables are used to discount a stream of level income to present worth.

Inwood factor. A factor that reflects the present worth of $1 per period for a given number of periods, discounted at a given discount rate; obtained by calculation or from standard compound interest tables and used to discount an annuity to present worth; also called *Inwood coefficient.*

Inwood premise. An assumption that the present value of an income stream is based on a single discount rate; applies to income in the form of an ordinary level annuity.

IREM. *See* Institute of Real Estate Management.

iron, cast. An iron alloy usually containing 2½% to 4% carbon and silicon, possessing high compressive but low tensile strength, and which, in its molten state, is poured into sand molds to produce castings. (R.S. Means)

iron, wrought. The purest form of iron metal, which is fibrous, corrosion-resistant, easily forged or welded, and used in a wide variety of applications, including water pipes, rivets, stay bolts, and water tank plates. (R.S. Means)

IRR. *See* internal rate of return.

irregular curve. *See* french curve.

irrigation. The artificial application of water to the soil for full crop production; used in arid regions or when rainfall is not sufficient.

irrigation district. An agency established by local government that has the authority to implement and operate an irrigation system for the district and to levy taxes to finance its operations.

IRS. Internal Revenue Service.

island

1. A land mass surrounded by water.
2. In highway construction, the land area between opposing traveled ways that is set aside for their separation or for the safety of pedestrians.

island zoning. In planning and zoning, the placement of a property or a small group of properties in a permitted use category that does not conform to the zone classification and general character of the neighborhood; substantially equivalent to the legal concept of spot zoning.

isohyetal line. An imaginary line that connects areas on the earth where the quantity of annual rainfall is about the same; delineates zones of different rainfall.

isoquant. A simple curve used in econometric analysis to describe the pricing tradeoff between quantifiable product capacity and intangible attributes such as an amenity feature, design, or reputation. *See also* hedonic price index.

Italianate style. An architectural style popular from 1850 to 1870 and often used in urban commercial buildings; characterized by flat roofs with projecting cornices, arches and columns framing windows, cast iron ornamentation on the facade, and red S-shaped roof tiles.

iteration. A series of repetitive computations; a mathematical process used to solve for an unknown quantity by trial and error. Starting with a trial quantity, various quantities are tested in a series of repetitive calculations until the error in the result is negligible.

iterative routine. A computer subroutine that establishes a repeated calculation; used to derive a required value through repeated approximations.

J

jack rafter. A short roof rafter that extends from another structural framing member, not from the top of the exterior wall.

jack stud. An extra vertical supporting member in a frame wall or partition over a door, window, or archway.

jalousies. Adjustable glass louvers in doors or windows that regulate light and air or keep out rain.

jamb. The side framing or finish of a doorway or window.

jetty
1. A structure of stones, piles, etc., that projects into a body of water to protect a harbor, e.g., a pier.
2. In construction, the projecting parts of a structure, e.g., a bay window, a balcony.

J factor. An income adjustment or stabilization factor used to convert a stream of income changing on a curvilinear basis into its level equivalent. The J factor provides for the determination of a stabilizer $(1 + \Delta_i J)$.

job (job site)
1. Term commonly used to indicate the location of a construction project.

2. An entire construction project or any component of a construction project. (R.S. Means)

jobber

1. A person reasonably knowledgeable and somewhat skilled in most of the more common construction operations, such as carpentry, masonry, or plumbing.

2. In construction, a jack-of-all trades. (R.S. Means)

3. A skilled worker employed in building and maintaining an oil-drilling rig.

job condition. Those portions of the contract documents that define the rights and responsibilities of the contracting parties and of others involved in the work. The conditions of the contract include general conditions, supplementary conditions, and other conditions. (R.S. Means)

joint. The point where two objects or surfaces meet; the space between the units in a masonry wall that is occupied by mortar or bonding material. *See also* butt joint; lap joint.

joint and several obligation. An arrangement in which each signing party is liable for his or her share of a debt or obligation plus the shares of all other signing parties; as distinguished from several obligation, in which each signatory is responsible only for his or her own liabilities.

joint probability. The probability that two or more events will both occur.

joint tenancy. Joint ownership by two or more persons with the right of survivorship.

joint venture. A combination of two or more entities that join to undertake a specific project.

joists. Horizontal timbers, beams, or bars supporting a floor.

judgment creditor. A person who has received a decree or judgment from the court against his or her debtor for money due.

judgment debtor. A person against whom a judgment has been issued by the court for money owed.

judgment lien. A statutory lien on the real and personal property of a judgment debtor; created by the judgment itself.

judgment sampling. A sample selected according to personal judgment; subjective, but often less costly than probability samples and, sometimes superior, e.g., in small-scale surveys, in pilot studies, in constructing index numbers.

judicial sale. A court action that enforces a judgment lien by selling property to pay a debt.

junction box. A box in an electrical system where main circuits are connected or smaller circuits join the main circuit.

junior department store. A store that is classified between a full department store and a variety store in terms of its size and selection of merchandise.

junior lien. A lien placed on property after a previous lien has been made and recorded; a lien made subordinate to another by agreement; e.g., second and third mortgages; also called *second lien* or *third lien*.

junior mortgage loan. *See* junior lien.

junior mortgage originators. Private lenders such as real estate investment trusts (REITs), financing companies, and factoring organizations that provide secondary financing as a regular line of business; thrift institutions may also be included, but the funds used for such financing usually may not exceed 3% or 4% of their assets.

jurisdiction. The extent or range of power, authority, or control; the physical territory over which power, authority, or control is exercised.

just compensation. In condemnation, the amount of loss for which a property owner is compensated when his or her property is taken; should put the owner in as good a position pecuniarily as he or she would be if the property had not been taken; generally held to be market value, but courts have refused to rule that it is always equivalent to market value. *See also* before-and-after rule.

Justice, Department of. *See* Department of Justice.

K

Kalamein. Trade name for the galvanized sheet steel that covers solid core wooden doors.

kame. A short, irregular ridge, hill, or hillock of stratified glacial drift; usually hilly and interspersed with depressions, providing no surface drainage.

Keene's cement. A white, hard-finished plaster that sets quickly and produces an extremely durable wall; used for bathrooms and kitchens; made of plaster of paris soaked in a solution of borax or alum and cream of tartar.

keystone. A wedge-shaped or trapezoidal structural piece that forms the center unit at the top of a masonry arch.

K factor. An income adjustment or stabilization factor used to convert a stream of income changing at a constant ratio into its stable or level equivalent.

kicker. Payments made to a lender over and above the nominal interest rate and amortization payments; also called *contingent interests*. *See also* equity participation.

kick plate. A metal strip placed at the lower edge of a door to protect the finish.

kiln. An oven-like chamber that bakes, hardens, or dries material, e.g., green lumber, bricks.

kiln-dried lumber. Lumber that is dried in a kiln to reduce its moisture content.

kilobyte (K). In computer usage, 1,000 bytes in the base two numbering system; actually, 1024 bytes. *See also* byte.

kilogram. One thousand grams, which is 2.204 pounds avoirdupois weight.

kilometer. A linear unit of 1,000 meters.

kilowatt-hour (kwh). A common unit of electrical energy consumption equivalent to the total energy consumed when 1,000 watts are drawn for one hour.

king post. The vertical member at the center of a triangular truss.

kip. A unit of weight equal to 1,000 pounds that is used to express dead load.

kite winder. A triangular or kite-shaped step in a circular stairway placed where the direction of the stairway changes.

knee. A brace placed diagonally at the juncture of a post and a beam to provide rigidity.

knob insulator. A porcelain knob to which electric wires may be fastened in a single-line, open wiring system; rarely used in buildings, but common on pasture fences that carry low voltage current to confine animals.

knock down. Describes prepared construction materials that are delivered to the building site unassembled, but complete and ready to be assembled and installed, e.g., a window.

knot. A defect in lumber caused by cutting through a limb where it joins the trunk or cutting through a knot embedded in a tree.

L

laborer. Ordinarily denotes a construction worker who has no specific trade and whose function is to support the activity of the licensed trades. (R.S. Means)

laches. An established doctrine of equity in which courts discourage delay in the enforcement of rights and decline to try suits that are not brought within a reasonable time, regardless of statutory limitations.

lacustrine soil. Soils formed from materials deposited by the waters of lakes and ponds; usually fine-textured and heavy.

lagging economic indicators. A set of data used to analyze the peaks and troughs of a business cycle several months after the changes in economic activity have occurred. Lagging economic indicators may exert a significant influence on coincident or leading economic indicators. The U.S. Bureau of Economic Analysis uses the following six lagging economic indicators to compile its composite index: the average duration of unemployment, the ratio of manufacturing and trade inventories to sales, labor cost per unit of manufacturing output, the average prime rate charged by banks, outstanding commercial and industrial loans reported on a weekly basis, and the ratio of consumer installment credit to personal income.

laissez-faire. Let things proceed without interference; a doctrine opposing government interference in economic affairs beyond the minimum necessary for the maintenance of peace and property rights; the belief that an individual is most productive when allowed to follow his or her own interests without external restrictions.

lally column. A steel column, usually filled with concrete, that supports beams and girders.

lambing ground. In sheep raising, a specific area where ewes are held for grazing at lambing time; usually offers good protection and fresh water.

lamella roof structure. An arched, roof-framing structure composed of planking arranged in diamond shapes.

laminate. To build up with layers of wood that are held together in a single unit; used to produce plywood and laminated beams. A single layer is called a *lamination* or *ply.*

laminated floor. A floor deck made by gluing or spiking two-by-fours or planks together.

laminated wood. Wood that is laminated with the fibers or grains of the plies running parallel; as distinguished from plywood in which the grains of the plies run crosswise and only the fibers of the exterior plies are parallel.

land

1. The earth's surface, both land and water, and anything that is attached to it whether by the course of nature or human hands; all natural resources in their original state, e.g., mineral deposits, wildlife, timber, fish, water, coal deposits, soil.
2. In law, the solid surface on the earth, as distinguished from water.

land bank. A stockpile of land; created when an investor or developer buys land and holds it for future use.

land/building ratio. *See* land-to-building ratio.

Land Capability Classification System. A system developed by the Soil Conservation Service to classify agricultural land use based on a soil's limitations, not on its potential yield; indicates risk of damage to soil, soil needs, and response to management. The system includes land capability classes that group soils with similar limitations and restrictions in use, but different productive capabilities; subclasses that identify important limitations such as wetness or climate; and capability units that identify soils within a subclass that have similar risks and productivity and require similar management.

land capitalization rate (R$_L$).
1. The rate used to convert land income into an indication of land value when certain residual or band-of-investment techniques are applied.
2. The ratio of land income to land value.

land classification. *See* Land Capability Classification System.

land contract. A contract in which a purchaser of real estate agrees to pay a small portion of the purchase price when the contract is signed and additional sums, at intervals and in amounts specified in the contract, until the total purchase price is paid and the seller delivers the deed; used primarily to protect the seller's interest in the unpaid balance because foreclosure can be exercised more quickly than it could be under a mortgage; also called *contract for deed* or *installment (sale) contract.*

land court. A court that has jurisdiction over issues concerning real property and interests in real property.

land development. The improvement of land with utilities, roads, and services, which makes the land suitable for resale as developable plots for housing or other purposes.

land economics. A branch of economics that deals with the use of land resources in attaining objectives set by society; study of how land resources are allocated among alternative uses.

landfill. A place, location, tract of land, area, or premises used for the disposal of solid wastes as defined by state solid waste regulations. The term is synonymous with the term *solid waste disposal site* and is also known as a *garbage dump, trash dump* or similar term (ASTM)

land grant. *See* land patent.

L and H hardware. Door hinges and latches in L and H patterns designed to create a colonial atmosphere.

land improvements. Relatively permanent structures built on, or physical changes made to, a property to increase its utility and value.

landing
1. An intermediate platform between flights of stairs, or the platform at the top or bottom of a staircase; used to break the rise or change the direction of the stairway. (R.S. Means)
2. A place or platform where goods or persons land, e.g., from a boat.

land loan. A loan made to finance the purchase of raw land.

landlocked parcel. A parcel of land that has no access to a road or highway.

landlord. The owner of real estate that is leased to others.

landmark. A monument or erection that serves as a boundary dividing two adjoining parcels.

land or site analysis. A careful study of factual data relating to the neighborhood characteristics that create, enhance, or detract from the utility and marketability of the land or site as compared with competing, comparable land or sites.

land or site description. A compilation of detailed factual data, including a legal description, other title and record data, and information on the pertinent physical characteristics of a parcel of land or a site.

landowner's royalty. An interest in unsevered oil, gas, coal, and other mineral rights that is retained or reserved by the landowner when he or she relinquishes interest in the real property involved.

land patent. A legal document in which the federal government conveys the title to land to an individual.

land planner. An individual who studies and evaluates the appropriateness of a property's location within the larger community, integrates a development and its facilities into the larger community, and makes recommendations concerning various development standards, e.g., density, community service, functional design, environmental safety and health.

land planning. The discipline concerned with the design of land area uses, road networks, and utility layouts to ensure the efficient use of real estate resources.

land reclamation. Adaptation of land to a more intensive use by changing its character or environment through drainage, irrigation, etc.

land registration. The recording of deeds, mortgages, and other instruments in a public office as evidence of one's rights in real property and to protect against fraud and questions regarding the title to or interest in property. *See also* Torrens system.

land residual technique. A method of estimating land value in which the net operating income attributable to the land is isolated and capitalized to produce an indication of the land's contribution to the total property.

landscape

1. A relatively extensive view of rural scenery.

2. The natural or man-made elements that characterize an area of land.

3. To improve the natural environment by modifying its features

to achieve beautiful or unusual effects.

4. The natural setting for a structure.

landscape architect. One who designs ground forms by selecting plant materials, creating open space areas around buildings, and planning areas for recreation and other uses.

landscaping. Modifying an area or tract of land by adding land improvements, e.g., trees, shrubs, lawns, paths, gardens; the improvements so added.

land service road. A road that is used primarily for access to land.

land survey. *See* boundary survey.

land surveying. The location and identification of a parcel of land by a professional surveyor or engineer.

land surveyor. A person (usually registered in the state where the survey is being done) whose occupation is to establish the lengths and directions of existing boundary lines on landed property, or to establish any new boundaries resulting from division of a land parcel. (R.S. Means)

land tile. Clay tile laid with open joints and usually surrounded by porous materials. (R.S. Means)

land-to-building ratio. The proportion of land area to gross building area; typical land-to-building ratios for

properties combine land and building components into a functional economic unit.

land treatment area. A defined parcel of land on which wastes are deposited for the purpose of allowing natural cleansing actions to occur. (R.S. Means)

land trust. A legal vehicle for partial ownership interests in real property in which independently owned properties are conveyed to a trustee; may be used to effect a profitable assemblage or in some cases to facilitate the assigning of property as collateral for a loan.

land use. The employment of a site or holding to produce revenue or other benefits; also, the designation by a governing authority of the use to which land may be put to promote the most advantageous development of the community, e.g., designation of industrial, residential, commercial, recreational, and other uses under a master plan.

land use analysis. A systematic study of an area or region that documents existing conditions and patterns of use, identifies problem areas, and discusses future options and choices. As part of the general planning process, such an analysis might cover topics such as traffic flow, residential and commercial zoning, sewer services, water supply, solid-waste management, air and water pollution, or conservation areas. In short, any factors that could affect how particular areas of land should or should not be used. (R.S. Means)

land use capabilities. The various limitations on land use, usually determined by soil classifications; based on soils, relief or slope, and the amount of top soil, which affect crop rotation, cropping practices, and erosion control.

land use map. A comprehensive map of a community or a section of a community that shows the character of all land uses and the extent and density of each use.

land use model. A simplified representation of a planner's understanding of the land development process, normally in the form of mathematical models or sets of equations.

land use planning. The development of land use plans that will best serve the general welfare over the long term and the formulation of ways and means to implement these plans.

land use regulation. Any legal restriction, e.g., a zoning ordinance, that controls the use to which land may be put; may include controls established by restrictive covenants or

contained in redevelopment or urban renewal plans approved by local governing bodies.

land use study. A complete inventory of the land parcels in a given community or area, classified by type of use; may include an analysis of the patterns of use revealed by the inventory.

land utilization and marketability study (LUMS). An analysis of the potential uses of a parcel of land that is to be acquired in an urban renewal project; considers the entire market to be served and the effect of the project on the area; used to determine what the highest and best use of the land will be when the development project is completed.

land value map. An assessment map that shows the value of land by location, expressed as value per square foot, per acre, etc., depending on the type of land involved.

lap joint. The overlapping of two adjoining pieces of timber, wallpaper, or other material. *See also* butt joint.

lap siding. Siding applied horizontally to finish the exterior surface of a house or other structure; also called *ship lap siding*.

large-lot zoning. The practice of zoning large lots for single-family residences only; used mainly in rural and suburban areas to control the local environment and protect existing real estate values.

larger parcel

1. In condemnation, that tract or tracts of land which are under the beneficial control of a single individual or entity and have the same, or an integrated, highest and best use. Elements for consideration by the appraiser in making a determination in this regard are contiguity, or proximity, as it bears on the highest and best use of the property, unity of ownership, and unity of highest and best use.

2. In condemnation, the portion of a property that has unity of ownership, contiguity, and unity of use, the three conditions that establish the larger parcel for the consideration of severance damages in most states. In federal and some state cases, however, contiguity is sometimes subordinated to unitary use.

last in, first out (LIFO). A method of accounting for inventory in which it is assumed that goods bought last are sold first. This allows automatic updating of inventory values. (R.S. Means)

late charge. A penalty that a borrower or tenant must pay for failing to make a regular payment when it is due.

latent defects. Physical weaknesses or construction defects that cannot be detected in a reasonably thorough inspection of the property.

latent demand. Demand that is present in the market but not accommodated by existing facilities; consists of unaccommodated demand and induced demand. *See also* induced demand; move-up demand; unaccommodated demand.

lateral. Of or pertaining to a side; anything situated at, proceeding from, or directed to a side; any line that branches off or extends from a main line; e.g., the laterals of a septic system, an irrigation distribution ditch or pipe.

lath. Material used as a base for plaster, e.g., wood lath, gypsum lath, wire lath, metal lath.

latitude. The distance of a point on the earth's surface north or south of the equator; measured on the meridian through that point and expressed in degrees.

lattice. An openwork screen made of crossed strips, rods, or bars of wood or metal.

lavatory. A place where washing is done; a wash bowl; also, a room fitted with a wash bowl and toilet facilities.

law of decreasing returns. The premise that additional expenditures beyond a certain point (the point of decreasing returns) will not yield a return commensurate with the additional investment.

law of diminishing returns. Another term for the law of decreasing returns.

law of increasing returns. The premise that larger amounts of the agents of production produce greater net income up to a certain point (the point of decreasing returns).

layout. An arrangement or plan of the details of a room; the partitioning of areas that constitutes the floor plan of a building.

leaching. Removal of material from the soil by percolating liquid.

leaching field. Ground area through which septic waste liquids percolate, breaking down into soluble components. *See* septic system.

leaching trenches. Trenches that carry waste liquids from sewers; may be constructed in gravelly or sandy soils that allow liquids to percolate into surrounding soils, or dug into firm ground and filled with broken stones, tile, gravel, and sand through which liquids leach.

leach line. In sewage disposal, a loose tile or perforated pipeline used to distribute sewage effluent throughout the soil.

leader. *See* downspout.

leading economic indicators. A set of data analyzed from one month to a year in advance of the economic activity and used to forecast changes in the economy. The U.S. Bureau of Economic Analysis uses the following 12 leading economic indicators to compile its composite index: the average workweek of production workers in manufacturing, the average initial claims for state unemployment insurance filed weekly, new orders for manufactured consumer goods, vendor performance and deliveries, the index of net business formation, contracts and orders for plant equipment, the index of new building permits, change in inventories, change in crude material prices and the producer price index, the price index of 500 common stocks, change in total business credit, and the money supply (M-2).

lean-to. A small structure with a pitched roof, usually erected against the outside wall of a larger structure.

lean-to roof. A sloping roof that is supported on one side by the wall of an adjoining building.

lease. A written document in which the rights to use and occupy land or structures are transferred by the owner to another for a specified period of time in return for a specified rent. *See also* escalator lease; flat rental lease; graduated rental lease; gross lease; index lease; net lease; percentage lease; revaluation lease.

leaseback. An arrangement in which the seller of a property is obligated to lease the property from the buyer under terms and conditions that are not negotiable. *See also* sale-leaseback.

lease-by-lease analysis. *See* discounted cash flow (DCF) analysis.

leased fee. *See* leased fee estate.

leased fee estate. An ownership interest held by a landlord with the rights of use and occupancy conveyed by lease to others. The rights of the lessor (the leased fee owner) and the leased fee are specified by contract terms contained within the lease.

leasehold. *See* leasehold estate.

leasehold estate. The interest held by the lessee (the tenant or renter) through a lease conveying the rights of use and occupancy for a stated term under certain conditions.

leasehold improvements. Improvements or additions to leased property that have been made by the lessee.

leasehold loan. A loan received by the lessee on improvements and the leasehold interest in leased property.

leasehold mortgaging. A type of mortgage-equity financing in which a mortgage is secured by the tenant's leasehold interest subordinate to the leased fee interest; in other words, a lessee or tenant agrees to subordinate the leasehold interest to a mortgage that covers the leasehold; arranged for lessee developers who, with the lessor's consent, subordinate their leasehold interest to any mortgage covering the cost of the improvements they build on the property.

lease interest. One of the real property interests that results from the division of the bundle of rights by a lease, i.e., the leased fee estate or the leasehold estate.

lease rollover. The expiration of a lease and the subsequent re-leasing of the space.

leasing commissions. Fees paid to an agent for leasing tenant space. When leasing fees are spread over the term of a lease or lease renewal, they are treated as a variable operating expense. Initial leasing fees usually fall under capital expenditures for development and are not included among periodic expenses.

leasing fees. *See* leasing commissions.

leaves. The sliding, hinged, or detachable parts of a folding door, window, shutter, or table top.

left on the table. The dollar difference between the low bid and the next bid above. (R.S. Means)

legal access. The right of an adjacent owner whose property abuts a highway to use the highway for property ingress and egress. *See also* access rights.

legal description. A description of land that identifies the real estate according to a system established or approved by law; an exact description that enables the real estate to be located and identified.

legally nonconforming use. A use that was lawfully established and maintained, but no longer conforms to the use regulations of the current zoning in the zone where it is located. *See also* special use permit; variance.

legal notice

1. Notice to be given in a particular circumstance, as required by a statute, e.g., notice required prior to a public sale of foreclosed real estate.
2. Notice that is legally considered to have been given as a result of specified circumstances, although there is no proof that the involved parties were actually notified, e.g., recording a deed in the proper records office constitutes public notice of the facts contained in the deed.

legal owner. The owner of title, as distinguished from the holders of other interests, e.g., beneficial or possessory interests.

legal rate of interest. The maximum rate of interest that may be charged under state law.

lender. Any individual or institution that extends funds at interest; any institution that invests funds in mortgages; e.g., a mutual savings bank, a life insurance company, a pension or other trust fund, a commercial bank, a savings and loan association.

lender participation. A financing arrangement in which the mortgage lender shares in the income or ownership of a real estate venture as a condition of the loan. *See also* convertible mortgage; participation mortgage.

lender's yield. The monetary benefits accruing to the lender, i.e., periodic income from debt service and the reversion represented by the outstanding principal paid off prior to or at maturity. The lender's yield is calculated with discounting formulas.

lessee. One who has the right to use or occupy a property under a lease agreement; the leaseholder or tenant.

lessee's interest. *See* leasehold estate.

lessor. One who holds property title and conveys the right to use and occupy the property under a lease agreement; the leased fee owner or landlord.

lessor's interest. *See* leased fee estate.

letter of credit. A letter issued by a financial institution that certifies that the person named is entitled to draw on the institution up to a stipulated sum.

letter of intent. An instrument that expresses the intent to invest, buy, or lease, conditioned on the receipt and approval of further documentation or the issuance of a qualification permit. A letter of intent is not a binding agreement.

letter report. A limited appraisal report that contains only the conclusions reached in the appraiser's investigation and analysis. Most letter reports must be several pages long to ensure compliance with reporting requirements, which are the same as those applied to other types of reports. Reporting requirements are set forth in the Standards Rules relating to Standards 2 and 5 of the Uniform Standards of Professional Appraisal Practice.

levee. An embankment that prevents a river from overflowing; one of the small, continuous ridges that surround irrigated fields.

level
1. A term used to describe any horizontal surface that has all points at the same elevation and thus does not tilt or slope.
2. In surveying, an instrument that measures heights from an established reference.
3. A spirit level, consisting of small tubes of liquid with bubbles in each. The small tubes are positioned in a length of wood or metal which is hand-held and, by observing the position of the bubbles, used to find and check level surfaces. (R.S. Means)

level annuity. An income stream in which the amount of each payment is the same; a level, unchanging flow of income over time.

leverage. The effect of borrowed funds, which may increase or decrease the return that would be realized on equity free and clear.

LHA. *See* local housing authority.

liability. In appraisal, a legal obligation to render services in compliance with professional standards and to refrain from malpractice, which includes negligence, misrepresentation, fraud, and breach of contract. *See also* errors and omissions insurance; insurance, professional liability.

LIBOR. *See* London interbank offered rate.

license

1. A formal agreement from a lawful source that allows a business or profession to be conducted, e.g., a franchise.
2. Government permission to conduct an activity.

licensee. A person or corporate body that is granted a license or franchise to conduct a business or profession.

lien. A charge against property in which the property is the security for payment of the debt. *See also* specific lien.

lien date. The date on which an obligation, such as a property tax bill (usually in an amount yet to be determined), attaches to a property and the property thus becomes security against payment. The term is usually synonymous with *appraisal date,* but is not necessarily so. (IAAO)

lien release. Written release given by laborers, materialmen, and subcontractors to the developer waiving their rights under any mechanic's lien laws; usually given at the time of progress payments and upon completion of their work.

life annuity. An annuity that continues only during the lifetime of the recipient; as distinguished from an annuity certain, which continues for a specified period of time.

lifecare facilities. Housing facilities for elderly individuals who require services such as cooking, housecleaning, and sometimes nursing care. Such facilities foster the independence of residents while offering a continuum of care, i.e., a spectrum of services and facilities to meet the needs of seniors of varying capabilities. Residents pay an endowment fee guaranteeing lifetime residence and medical care as well as a monthly maintenance fee. *See also* continuing care retirement center (CCRC); elderly housing.

life-cycle cost. The total cost of owning, operating, and maintaining a building or item of capital equipment over its useful life, including its fuel and energy costs.

life-cycle costing. An analysis of the cost of an investment over its economic or useful life; often related to building energy costs. Life-cycle costs are based on the discounted present value of the aggregate future payments or benefits derived from current investments. Life-cycle costing illustrates the trade-offs between additional dollars invested today and reduced costs incurred in the future.

life estate. Total rights of use, occupancy, and control, limited to the lifetime of a designated party, often known as the *life tenant.*

life interest. *See* life estate.

life tenant. One who owns an estate in real property for his or her own lifetime, the lifetime of another person, or an indefinite period limited by a lifetime.

lift slab. A method of construction in which the floor and roof slabs are cast on top of one another at ground level, raised into position, and fastened to columns.

light
1. A fixture that provides illumination.
2. A window pane; a section of a window sash; a single pane of glass.

lighter. A large boat that is usually flat-bottomed and used in loading or unloading ships.

lighterage. The transfer of freight between a railroad terminal and various points by barges, floats, or lighters.

lighterage limits. Points in a harbor beyond which railroad companies will not deliver merchandise by lighter as part of the service included in the freight charge.

lighterage pier. A structure, e.g., a dock, a wharf, a quay, equipped with railroad tracks to facilitate the direct transfer of freight between railroad cars and lighters, barges, or floats.

light industry. Industries with less extensive physical plant requirements than heavy industry and less objectionable operations. *See also* heavy industry.

light-textured soil. Describes sandy or coarse-textured soil.

light well
1. A well-like, open area within a building that provides light and ventilation to inside rooms.
2. An open, subsurface space around a basement window that provides light and air.

lime. One of the ingredients used in making plaster, mortar, and cement and produced by burning limestone; also, any calcium compounds used to improve lime-deficient soils.

limen. *See* threshold.

limestone. A sedimentary deposit formed by the accumulation of the calcareous remains of organisms, e.g., shells; composed essentially of calcium carbonate and used extensively for building and the production of lime.

liming. The application of ground limestone to an agricultural field.

limited-access highway. *See* controlled-access highway.

limited assignment. An assignment that calls for something less than, or different from, the work that would otherwise be required. A limited assignment that complies with Uniform Standards of Professional Appraisal Practice rules governing the development of appraisal assignments and meets the Departure Provision is considered a conforming appraisal assignment.

limited-equity housing. Generally lower-income housing that is financed based on household income.

limited-market property. A property that has relatively few potential buyers at a particular time.

limited partner. A passive investor in a limited partnership who has no personal liability beyond his or her investment. *See also* limited partnership.

limited partnership. An ownership arrangement consisting of general and limited partners. General partners manage the business and assume full liability for partnership debt, while limited partners are passive and liable only to the extent of their own capital contributions. *See also* general partnership.

limited report. A report communicating a limited appraisal or consulting assignment. A limited report must comply with the reporting

rules set forth in the Uniform Standards of Professional Appraisal Practice and the Departure Provision, and contain sufficient information to lead to the appraiser's conclusions. The two types of limited reports most frequently requested are letter reports and form reports.

limiting conditions. *See* assumptions and limiting conditions; other limiting conditions.

limit of liability. The greatest amount of money that an insurance company will pay in the event of damage, injury, or loss. (R.S. Means)

linear programming. A method that employs a linear equation to subject variables to inequality constraints; used to optimize the allocation of resources.

linear regression. In quantitative analysis, a function that uses one independent variable to reflect a relationship that changes on a straight-line basis.

line fence. A fence on the boundaries or perimeter of a property, e.g., a farm, a ranch.

line of credit. A fixed amount of credit granted to cover a series of transactions. (R.S. Means)

line-of-sight easement. A right that prohibits using lands within the easement area in any way that obstructs the view of some distant area or object.

lining. A layer of material within another layer; the covering on the interior of a building, as distinguished from the covering on the exterior, i.e., the casing.

linkage

1. Time and distance relationship between a particular use and supporting facilities, e.g., between residences and schools, shopping, and employment.

2. The movement of people, goods, services, or communications to and from the subject site, measured by the time and cost involved.

linoleum. A floor covering made of burlap or canvas coated with a combination of powdered cork, powdered wood, linseed oil, pigments, and rosins, smoked and glazed under pressure and cured by baking.

lintel. A piece of wood, stone, or steel placed horizontally across the top of a door or window opening to support the wall immediately above the opening.

liquid assets. Assets that can be immediately converted into cash and are immediately available to pay debts; also called *quick assets. See also* fixed assets.

liquidated damages. An amount to be paid for a breach of contract; agreed upon by the parties in advance.

liquidation

1. Forced or voluntary cash realization; the selling of real estate, stocks, bonds, or other investments, either to take profits and limit losses or in anticipation of declining prices.

2. The termination or conclusion of a business or real estate operation by converting its assets into cash. The proceeds from liquidation are distributed first to creditors in order of preference, and the remainder, if any, is allocated to the owners in proportion to their holdings.

liquidation price. A forced price obtained without reasonable market exposure to find a purchaser.

liquidation value. The most probable price which a specified interest in real property is likely to bring under all of the following conditions:

1. Consummation of a sale will occur within a severely limited future marketing period specified by the client.

2. Actual market conditions are those currently obtaining for the property interest appraised.

3. The buyer is acting prudently and knowledgeably.

4. The seller is under extreme compulsion to sell.

5. The buyer is typically motivated.

6. The buyer is acting in what he or she considers his or her best interests.

7. A limited marketing effort and time will be allowed for the completion of a sale.

8. Payment will be made in cash in U.S. dollars or in terms of financial arrangements comparable thereto.

9. The price represents the normal consideration for the property sold, unaffected by special or creative financing or sales concessions granted by anyone associated with the sale.

This definition can be modified to provide for valuation with specified financing terms. (The above definition, proposed by the Appraisal Institute Special Task Force on Value Definitions, was adopted by the Appraisal Institute Board of Directors, July 1993.) *See also* disposition value; distress sale; forced price; market value.

liquidity. An entity's cash position, based on assets that can be readily converted into cash.

LIS. Land Information System. *See also* Geographic Information Systems (GIS).

lis pendens. Notice of a suit pending.

listing. A written contract in which an owner employs a broker to sell his or her real estate.

listing contract. A written agreement between an owner and a broker under which the broker attempts to sell the real estate of the owner in return for a specified commission when a sales contract is signed.

litter. The uppermost layer of organic debris; composed of freshly fallen leaves or slightly decomposed organic material; commonly designated by the letter *L*.

littoral. Pertaining to the shore or the area between high and low water levels.

littoral rights. The right of an owner of land with a contiguous shoreline to use and enjoy the shore without a change in its position created by artificial interference; as distinguished from riparian rights and water rights.

live load. Any moving or variable superimposed load; expressed in pounds per square foot of floor and roof areas for various types of building occupancy; e.g., weight of people, merchandise, or stock on a floor, snow load or wind pressure on a roof. Measurement of live load may vary with local building code requirements. *See also* dead load; floor load; total load.

livestock share rent. A form of rent in which the landlord and the tenant are equal owners of the livestock and share equally in the proceeds from sale; similar to crop share rent.

living trust. A trust that becomes effective during the lifetime of its creator; as distinguished from a trust under a will.

living unit. An apartment, condominium, house, or other residential property occupied by one household. *See also* household; housing stock.

load
1. The weight supported by a structural part or member.
2. The power delivered by a motor, transformer, generator, or power station.
3. The electrical current carried through a circuit.

load-bearing wall. *See* bearing wall.

load factor
1. In structural design, the factor applied to the working load to determine the design's ultimate load.
2. In a drainage system, the percentage of the total flow that occurs at a particular location in the system.
3. A ratio of the average air-conditioning load on a system to the maximum capacity. (R.S. Means)

loading chute. An inclined chute attached to a holding pen or corral to permit livestock to walk from ground level to the dock where they are loaded onto trucks or rail cars.

loading dock leveler. Typically, an adjustable mechanized platform built into the edge of a loading dock. The platform can be raised, lowered, or tilted to accommodate the handling of goods or material to or from trucks. (R.S. Means)

loading platform (loading dock). A platform adjoining the shipping and receiving door of a building, usually built to the same height as the floor of the trucks or railway cars on which shipments are delivered to and from the dock. (R.S. Means)

loafing shed. An open shed that provides shelter for livestock.

loam. A soil that is a mixture of different grades of sand, silt, and clay in which no one characteristic predominates; mellow with a gritty feel and slightly plastic when moist. *See also* clay loam; fine sandy loam; sandy loam; silt clay loam; silt loam.

loan commitment. A written promise from a lender to loan a specified sum at a certain rate of interest for a specified term; usually a fee is paid for this commitment.

loan constant. *See* mortgage constant (R_M).

loan fee. The fee paid to a lender for the use and forbearance of money or for service in making the loan; generally a percentage of the face amount of the loan; also called *points*.

loan servicing. The administration and collection of monthly mortgage payments from home owners and other borrowers; usually performed by a bank, mortgage broker, or real estate company acting for itself or the mortgagee.

loan-to-value ratio (*M*). The ratio between a mortgage loan and the value of the property pledged as security; usually expressed as a percentage.

loan value. A value which lending institutions will accept as a basis for a mortgage or trust deed; a nebulous value defined differently by various lending institutions; an underwriting concept, not value. (Marshall & Swift)

lobby. An interior entranceway to a theater, public building, hotel, or office building.

local housing authority (LHA). A government entity or public body authorized to develop or operate low-rent housing; usually an independent corporate body authorized by local government pursuant to state or territorial law.

local public agency (LPA). An official body contracted by the federal government to assist in urban renewal projects; may be one or more state, county, municipal, or other government entities authorized to undertake a project for which federal assistance is sought.

location. The time-distance relationships, or linkages, between a property or neighborhood and all other possible origins and destinations of people going to or coming from the property or neighborhood.

locational obsolescence. *See* external obsolescence.

location quotient (*LQ*). The ratio between two other ratios, i.e., the ratio of local employment in a specific industry to total employment in the local economy (*e*) and the ratio of national employment in a specific industry to total employment in the national economy (*E*). ($LQ = e/E$.)

location survey. The establishment of the position of points and lines of an area of ground, based on information taken from deeds, maps, and documents of record, as well as from computation and graphic processes. (R.S. Means)

lock-in period. A period during which a lender prohibits the borrower from prepaying any or all of the balance and from selling or assigning the note. Once a borrower accepts the terms of a loan offered by a lender, the terms are locked in for a specified period.

lodging
1. Pertaining to the lodging industry. *See also* average daily room rate (ADR); bed and breakfast; boarding house; hostel; hotel; motel; revpar; rooming house.
2. The falling down of crops, particularly small grains and hay, due to excessive vegetative growth, rain, or wind.

loess. Windblown material that is uniformly silty, as distinguished from till and water sediment.

loft. An attic-like space below the roof of a house or barn; any upper story of a warehouse or factory; may also refer to a loft building. *See also* loft building.

loft building. A multistory building with an open floor design that is used for small, light manufacturing businesses, warehousing, and sometimes office or residential units.

log
1. To cut and deliver logs.
2. Tree segment suitable for lumber, e.g., butt log, peeler log, saw log.

logarithm. The power, or exponent, to which a fixed number, or base, is raised to produce a given number; e.g., $2^3 = 8$, thus the logarithm of 8 in base 2 is 3.

log boom. A boom used to transport logs over water.

log deck. A storage area for logs.

log price conversion return. An indication of the stumpage value of timber made by deducting all costs necessary to fell a tree and deliver the logs to a mill from the market price of the logs.

log rules. Tables showing the calculated amount of lumber that can be sawed from logs of a given length and diameter; provide a means of measuring the actual board foot volume in logs by allowing for waste in slabs and sawdust. *See also* Humboldt rule; Scribner rule; Spaulding rule.

log scale. The measurement of felled trees, i.e., the length of a tree or log at a top, fixed diameter in relation to the diameter at the larger end, which is reflected in volume tables.

London interbank offered rate (LIBOR). The average of interbank-offered rates for dollar deposits in the London market on quotations at five major banks.

longitude. The distance of a particular point east or west on the earth's surface expressed in degrees; measured as the angle between the meridian of the point and the prime meridian in Greenwich, England.

longitudinal. Of or pertaining to longitude or length; running lengthwise.

long-lived item. A building component with an expected remaining economic life that is the same as the remaining economic life of the entire structure.

long-term lease. Generally a lease agreement extending for 10 years or more. The terms and provisions of a long-term lease are customarily set forth in detail in legally correct and complete form. Under such leases the tenant may desire, or be required, to do extensive remodeling or, if the property leased is land, to construct a building or other improvements.

long ton. A unit of weight equal to 2,240 pounds (1,016 kilograms). (R.S. Means)

loop. A group of instructions repeated one or more times in a calculation until a prescribed condition is satisfied. *See also* iterative routine.

loose estimate. One allowing for contingencies, a "safe" or high estimate. (R.S. Means)

loose-fill insulation. Any of several thermal insulation materials in the form of granules, fibers, or other types of pieces that can be poured, pumped, or placed by hand. (R.S. Means)

loss of access. Depriving an abutting owner of the inherent rights of ingress to and egress from the highway or street.

loss payable clause. A clause in insurance policies protecting the financial institution that holds the mortgage on the insured property. Any payment that the insurance company makes will be made payable to both the policyholder and the lender. (R.S. Means)

lot

1. A distinct piece of land; a piece of land that forms a part of a district, community, city block, etc.
2. A smaller portion into which a city block or subdivision is divided; described by reference to a recorded plat or by definite boundaries; a piece of land in one ownership, whether platted or unplatted.

lot and block description. *See* lot and block system; recorded map.

lot and block system. A system for the legal description of land that refers to parcels' lot and block numbers, which appear on recorded maps and plats of subdivided land; may also be used for assessment maps.

lot line. The boundary line of a plot of ground as legally described in the title to the property.

louver. A slat or fin over an opening that is pitched to keep out rain and snow; a finned sunshade on a building; the diffusion grill on a fluorescent light fixture.

low bid. In bidding for construction work, the lowest price submitted for performance of the work in accordance with the plans and specifications. (R.S. Means)

lower low water. The lower of the two low waters on any tidal day; the mean value of the lower low waters over a considerable period of time is used as a plane of reference for hydrographic work on the coasts of the United States.

lowest responsible bidder (lowest qualified bidder). The bidder who has submitted the lowest legitimate bid. The owner and architect must agree that this person (or firm) is capable of performing the work covered by the bid proposal. (R.S. Means)

lowest responsive bid. The lowest bid that meets the requirements set forth in the bid proposal. (R.S. Means)

low frequency. Describes an electric current with a small number of cycles per second.

low water line. The point on the shore where the tide ebbs; varies with season, time, wind, and other changes. *See also* mean low water line.

LPA. *See* local public agency.

lumber. Wood that has been processed in saw and planing mills and receives no further processing by sawing, resawing, passing lengthwise through a standard planing mill, or crosscutting to length; classified as veneer when it is no thicker than ¼ inch and is to be used for veneering; e.g., boards, clear lumber, dimension lumber, factory and shop lumber, green lumber, joist, plank, scantling lumber, strip lumber, structural lumber, timber, and yard lumber.

luminous ceiling. A suspended ceiling of translucent material installed below a system of fluorescent tubes, making the entire ceiling a source of light; used to reduce glare and shadows; a daylight ceiling.

LUMS. *See* land utilization and marketability study.

LUST. Leaking underground storage tank(s).

M

macadam. A paving consisting of compacted crushed stone or gravel bound by a covering of asphaltic material.

machine room. The room in an elevator system that is designed to house an elevator-hoisting machine and control equipment. (R.S. Means)

machine shed. A farm building used to store farm machinery; usually open on one side.

macroeconomics. Study of the economy as an aggregate system, focusing on national/domestic production, national/domestic income, the supply of money, the rate of inflation, the national budget, the balance of trade, and the interrelationships among constituent sectors. *See also* microeconomics.

made land. Ground which is formed by filling in natural or artificial pits with rubbish or other material; the creation of additional land along a shore by extending the shoreline farther into the water, usually with dredged sand as the fill material.

magnesite flooring. Flooring made of calcined magnesite and a magnesium chloride solution with a filler of sawdust, wood flour, ground silica, or quartz; floated in a 1½-in. layer over a concrete floor.

main. A pipe, conduit, or circuit leading to or from the branches of a utility system; carries the combined flow of all the branches.

main circuit. Circuit that carries a heavy electrical load to the branch circuits of a distribution system.

mainframe. A large, stationary computer.

main office expense. A contractor's main office expense consists of the expense of doing business that is not charged directly to the job. Depending on the accounting system used, and the total volume, this can vary from 2 to 20 percent, with the median about 7.2 percent of the total volume. (R.S. Means)

maintenance. Keeping a property in condition to perform its function efficiently; expenditures made for this purpose. Maintenance does not extend the useful life of the property or increase its book value. *See also* deferred maintenance; repairs.

maintenance bond. A contractor's bond in which a surety guarantees to the owner that defects of workmanship and materials will be rectified for a given period of time. A one-year bond is commonly included in the performance bond. (R.S. Means)

mall

1. Originally, a shaded walk.
2. An area designed for pedestrian use only.
3. A large enclosed shopping center, usually a regional shopping center.

management. Directing or conducting affairs; one of the elements of overhead or undistributed construction costs. *See also* asset management; facilities management; management program; property management; resident management.

management contract. An agreement between a management company and a property owner/investor in which the company assumes complete or partial responsibility for management of the property.

management fee. An expense item representing the sum paid or the value of management service; a variable operating expense, usually expressed as a percentage of effective gross income.

management program. A program of defined goals established to direct or conduct the management of a property and the manner or means by which these goals can be achieved.

man hole. A vertical access shaft from the ground surface to a sewer or underground utilities, usually at a junction, to allow cleaning, inspection, connections, and repairs. (R.S. Means)

manifold. Consisting of many different parts, elements, or features, e.g., the juncture of many small pipes with a larger pipe or main.

mansard roof. A roof with two slopes or pitches on each of the four sides, with the lower slopes steeper than the upper slopes; provides a good base when another story is added to a building.

mantel. The decorative facing placed around a fireplace; usually made of ornamental wood and topped with a shelf.

mantissa. The numbers to the right of the decimal point in a logarithm; e.g., the natural logarithm of 70 is 4.248495, so 0.248495 is the mantissa. *See also* characteristic.

manufactured homes (mobile homes). Manufactured homes are factory-finished inside and out, and usually have wheeled chassis. (R.S. Means)

marginal

1. In economics, describes the supplying of goods at a rate that barely covers the cost of production.

2. In real estate, describes a property with an earned income that covers only operating costs.

marginal demand. The additional demand that exists, based on an inventory of current supply, or is forecast to develop, based on an inventory of anticipated supply; also called *incremental demand.*

marginal land. Land that has limited usefulness because the costs of labor, coordination, and capital required to work or use it are approximately equal to the land's gross income. *See also* agents in production.

marginal probability. The probability that a single event will occur; determined as the sum of the joint probabilities involving that event.

marginal revenue. The additional gross revenue produced by selling one additional unit of production.

marginal tax rate. The income tax rate charged on the last dollar of income, which is the relevant tax rate for making investment decisions.

marginal utility. The increment of total utility added by the last unit of a good at any given point of consumption. In general, the greater the number of items, the lower the marginal utility, i.e., a greater supply of an item or product lowers the value of each item.

marginal utility school. A school of economic thought developed primarily through the writings of Karl Menger, W.S. Jevons, and Leon Walras, who explained the relationship between desirability and price by reference to the concept of marginal utility, i.e., the amount of satisfaction realized from an additional unit of a good.

margin of security. The difference between a loan and the market value of the mortgaged property.

marina. A boat basin that provides dockage and other services to pleasure craft.

marine soil. A soil that is formed from materials deposited by oceans and seas and later exposed by upward movement, e.g., the coastal plain soils of Maryland and Virginia. *See also* accretion.

market

1. A set of arrangements in which buyers and sellers are brought together through the price mechanism. *See also* real estate market.
2. A gathering of people for the buying and selling of things; by extension, the people gathered for this purpose.

marketability. The state of being salable.

marketability study

1. A process that investigates how a particular piece of property will be absorbed, sold, or leased under current or anticipated market conditions; includes a market study or analysis of the general class of property being studied.

2. A microeconomic study that examines the marketability of a given property or class of properties, usually focusing on the market segment(s) in which the property is likely to generate demand. Marketability studies are useful in determining a specific highest and best use, testing development proposals, and projecting an appropriate tenant mix.

marketable title. A title not subject to reasonable doubt or suspicion of invalidity in the mind of a reasonable, intelligent person; one which a prudent person guided by competent legal advice would be willing to accept and purchase at market value.

market analysis

1. The identification and study of the market for a particular economic good or service.

2. A study of real estate market conditions for a specific type of property. (USPAP, 1992 edition)

market area. The geographic or locational delineation of the market for a specific category of real estate, i.e., the area in which alternative, similar properties effectively compete with the subject property in the minds of probable, potential purchasers and users. *See also* trade area.

market data approach. *See* sales comparison approach.

market data grid. A tabular representation of market data organized into useful, measurable categories.

market disequilibrium. A general characteristic of real estate markets over the short term in which the supply and demand for real estate are out of balance.

market equilibrium

1. The theoretical balance toward which the supply of and demand for real estate move over the long run—a balance which is seldom achieved.

2. The balance created at any given point by the interaction of market participants, i.e., sellers representing the supply of properties and buyers representing the demand for properties.

marketing period

1. The time it takes an interest in real property to sell on the market subsequent to the date of an appraisal.

2. Reasonable marketing time is an estimate of the amount of time it might take to sell an interest in real property at its estimated market value during the period immediately after the effective date of the appraisal; the anticipated time required to expose the property to a pool of prospective purchasers and to allow appropriate time for negotiation, the exercise of due diligence, and the consummation of a sale at a price supportable by concurrent market conditions. Marketing time differs from exposure time, which is always presumed to precede the effective date of the appraisal. *(Advisory Opinion G-7* of the Appraisal Standards Board of The Appraisal Foundation and *Statement on Appraisal Standards No. 6,* "Reasonable Exposure Time in Market Value Estimates" address the determination of reasonable exposure and marketing time.)

Market value estimates imply that an adequate marketing effort and reasonable time for exposure occurred prior to the effective date of the appraisal. In the case of disposition value, the time frame allowed for marketing the property rights is somewhat limited, but the marketing effort is orderly and adequate. With liquidation value, the time frame for marketing the property rights is so severely limited that an adequate marketing program cannot be implemented. *(The Report of the Appraisal Institute Special Task Force on Value Definitions* qualifies marketing time in terms of the three above-mentioned values.) *See also* exposure.

marketing time. *See* marketing period.

market participants. Individuals actively engaged in real estate transactions. Primary market participants are those who invest equity in real property or use real estate, e.g., buyers, sellers, owners, lenders, tenants. Secondary market participants include those who advise primary participants, e.g., advisors, counselors, underwriters, appraisers.

market rent. The rental income that a property would most probably command in the open market; indicated by the current rents paid and asked for comparable space as of the date of the appraisal.

market segmentation. The process by which submarkets within a larger market are identified and analyzed. *See also* disaggregation.

market share. The portion of a trade area's potential, e.g., retail sales to be generated, office space to be absorbed, that can be attributed to a proposed facility; based on known market strength and the property's position relative to comparable, competitive facilities.

market study. A macroeconomic analysis that examines the general market conditions of supply, demand, and pricing or the demographics of demand for a specific area or property type. A market study may also include analyses of construction and absorption trends.

market support. Sufficient demand to ensure the viability of a real estate enterprise.

market survey. *See* market study.

market value. The major focus of most real property appraisal assignments. Both economic and legal definitions of market value have been developed and refined. Continual refinement is essential to the growth of the appraisal profession. A current economic definition of market value is stated as follows:

The most probable price, as of a specified date, in cash, or in terms equivalent to cash, or in other precisely revealed terms for which the specified property rights should sell after reasonable exposure in a competitive market under all conditions requisite to a fair

sale, with the buyer and seller each acting prudently, knowledgeably, and for self-interest, and assuming that neither is under undue duress. (*The Appraisal of Real Estate,* 10th ed., published in 1992 by the Appraisal Institute.)

The following definition has been agreed upon by agencies that regulate federal financial institutions in the United States including the Resolution Trust Corporation (RTC).

The most probable price which a property should bring in a competitive and open market under all conditions requisite to a fair sale, the buyer and seller each acting prudently and knowledgeably, and assuming the price is not affected by undue stimulus. Implicit in this definition is the consummation of a sale as of a specified date and the passing of title from seller to buyer under conditions whereby:

1. *buyer and seller are typically motivated;*
2. *both parties are well informed or well advised, and acting in what they consider their best interests;*
3. *a reasonable time is allowed for exposure in the open market;*
4. *payment is made in terms of cash in United States dollars or in terms of financial arrangements comparable thereto; and*
5. *the price represents the normal consideration for the property sold unaffected by special or creative fi-*

nancing or sales concessions granted by anyone associated with the sale. (USPAP, 1992 edition)

A suggested clarification of the definition appears below. This recommendation, made by the Appraisal Institute Special Task Force on Value Definitions, was adopted by the Appraisal Institute Board of Directors, July 1993.

The most probable price which a specified interest in real property is likely to bring under all of the following conditions:

1. *Consummation of a sale occurs as of a specified date.*
2. *An open and competitive market exists for the property interest appraised.*
3. *The buyer and seller are each acting prudently and knowledgeably.*
4. *The price is not affected by undue stimulus.*
5. *The buyer and seller are typically motivated.*
6. *Both parties are acting in what they consider their best interest.*
7. *Marketing efforts were adequate and a reasonable time was allowed for exposure in the open market.*
8. *Payment was made in cash in U.S. dollars or in terms of financial arrangements comparable thereto.*
9. *The price represents the normal consideration for the property sold, unaffected by special or creative fi-*

nancing or sales concessions granted by anyone associated with the sale.

This definition can also be modified to provide for valuation with specified financing terms.

Persons performing appraisal services that may be subject to litigation are cautioned to seek the exact definition of market value applicable in the jurisdiction where the services are being performed. For further discussion of this important term, see *The Appraisal of Real Estate,* 10th ed., pages 18-22. *See also* business value; disposition value; fair value; going-concern value; goodwill; insurable value; investment value; liquidation value; prospective value estimates; retrospective value estimates; use value; value as is.

market value as is. *See* value as is.

markup. A percentage of other sums that may be added to the total of all direct costs to determine a final price or contract sum. In construction practice, the markup usually represents two factors important to the contractor. The first factor may be the estimated cost of indirect expense often referred to as general overhead. The second factor is an amount for the anticipated profit for the contractor. (R.S. Means)

marquee. A permanent hood that projects over the entrance to a building and is not supported by posts or columns; sometimes used as a sign.

masonry. Anything constructed of stone, brick, tile, cement, concrete, or similar materials; work done by a mason.

masonry wall. A wall of stone, brick, tile, cement block, concrete, etc.

Massachusetts trust. A form of business organization, distinct from a corporation or partnership, that conducts its business through a trustee or trustees who hold legal title to the property of the business. Capital contributions are made to the trustees by beneficiaries, whose equitable title and interests in the property of the trust are evidenced by trust certificates. The beneficiaries receive the earnings of the trust and may enjoy limited liability, but control and management of the trust rest solely with the trustees.

mass appraisal. The process of valuing a universe of properties as of a given date utilizing standard methodology, employing common data, and allowing for statistical testing. (USPAP, 1992 edition)

mass appraisal model. A mathematical expression of how supply and demand factors interact in a market. (USPAP, 1992 edition)

master. A term applied to the third and highest level of achievement for a tradesman or mechanic, who by supervision, experience, and examination has earned a master's license attesting that he is a master of the trade and no longer requires supervision of his work, as is the case with the journeyman and apprentice levels. (R.S. Means)

master builder. A term applied to one who performs the functions of both design and construction. The master builder approach to building construction has been a practice commonplace in much of the world for many centuries. In the United States, design and construction are traditionally seen as two separate and distinct functions. (R.S. Means)

master-keyed lock. A locking system intended for use in a series, each lock of which may be actuated by two different keys, one capable of operating every lock of the series, and the other capable of operating only one or a few of the locks. (R.S. Means)

master lease. A lease controlling subsequent leases.

master plan. A comprehensive, long-range official plan that guides the physical growth and development of a community, combined with the basic regulatory and administrative controls needed to attain the physical objectives; includes land use plan, thoroughfare plan, community facilities plan, and public improvements program; also called *city plan, general plan,* or *comprehensive community plan.*

master switch. An electrical switch that controls two or more circuits. (R.S. Means)

mastic. An adhesive material used to cement two surfaces together; an elastic caulking compound.

matched boards. *See* tongue and groove.

material bond. A bond that assures the contractor that the material supplier will provide the materials necessary to complete the job.

materialman. A term applied to a person through whom the contractor may obtain the materials of construction. The materialman may be a manufacturer's representative or he may be a distributor or salesman of the tools, products, materials, assemblies, and equipment vital to the process of construction. (R.S. Means)

mat foundation. *See* floating foundation.

mature forest. A forest that has reached the age of maximum utilization; varies with the objectives of forest management.

maturity. The date when an obligation comes due.

MBAA. Mortgage Bankers Association of America.

MBM. In forestry, an abbreviation for 1,000 board feet.

meadow. A type of range vegetation that includes areas where sedges, rushes, and mesic grasses predominate; usually remains wet or moist throughout the summer.

mean. A measure of central tendency. The sum of the values of a set divided by the number of values. *See also* arithmetic mean; geometric average; median; mode; moving average; weighted average.

meander. A winding course.

meander line. A line that points out the curves and lines of a bank or shore; a survey line that establishes the bank or shoreline of a stream or lake.

mean deviation. *See* average deviation.

mean high water line. The point on the shore that is the mean distance between the points to which the tide rises; determined through long observation of the rise and fall of tides; often used as the seaward boundary line of privately owned uplands. *See also* mean low water line; ordinary high water mark.

mean low water line. The point on the shore that is the mean distance between the points to which the tide ebbs; determined through long observation of the rise and fall of tides.

measures of investment performance. Analytical techniques used to evaluate real estate investments.

mechanic's lien. A lien provided by statute for those who perform labor or services or who furnish materials in the improvement of real property.

median. A measure of central tendency; the value of the middle item in an uneven number of items arranged or arrayed according to size or the arithmetic average of the two central items in an even number of items similarly arranged; a positional average that is not affected by the size of extreme values.

median strip. In highway construction, a strip in the center of the highway that divides opposing lanes of traffic; may be a narrow, concrete buffer or a wide, landscaped area.

medium-textured soil. Loams, fine sandy loams, and clay loams.

meeting rail. *See* check rail.

megabyte. In computer usage, one million bytes. *See also* byte.

megalopolis. A large, urbanized area resulting from the gradual merging of many cities and metropolitan areas into one great urban agglomeration.

mellow. Describes a soil that can be easily worked due to its friable and loamy characteristics.

membrane. A thin sheet or film of waterproof material used to prevent moisture from penetrating a floor or wall.

membrane roofing. A term that most commonly refers to a roof covering employing flexible elastomeric plastic materials from 35 to 60 mils thick, that is applied from rolls and has vulcanized joints. The initial cost of an elastomeric-membrane roof covering system is higher than a built-up roof, but the life cycle cost is lower. (R.S. Means)

memory. The storage space of a computer, where instructions and data are kept during program execution.

merchant builder. A company primarily involved in constructing residential and commercial buildings for sale.

merchants' association. An organization that advances the common interests of shopping center or retail property tenants by planning advertisements, promotions, decorations, etc.

mercury vapor lamp. An electric discharge lamp that produces a blue-white light by creating an arc in mercury vapor enclosed in a globe or tube. These lamps are classified as low-pressure or high-pressure. (R.S. Means)

merge line. A line that divides into two parts a parcel that extends from one street to another street in the rear; designated so that the highest total value of the two parts will be developed, considering each part as a separate lot valued on the basis of its front foot value modified by the depth factor to the depth of the merge line.

merger
1. The absorption of two or more corporations into a single corporation by issuing stock in the controlling corporation to replace a majority of stock in the others; usually accomplished without dissolving the individual companies.
2. The creation of a common land ownership for adjacent properties that were formerly owned separately. *See also* assemblage.

meridian
1. A great circle on the earth's surface passing through the poles and any given point.
2. In the government survey system, the true north and south lines that run from a base line

where they are 24 miles apart; also called *guide meridians*. *See also* base line; range line; standard parallels.

mesquite. A type of range vegetation that includes areas where various species of mesquite (*prosopic*) predominate.

metal clad building. A building sheathed in metal.

metal lath. A sheet of metal that is slit at intervals; when expanded, the grillwork forms a base for plaster.

metal valley. *See* flashing.

metamorphic rock. Rock that has undergone pronounced alteration from the combined effects of pressure, heat, and water; frequently is compact and crystalline.

metes and bounds system. A system for the legal description of land that refers to the parcel's boundaries, which are formed by the point of beginning (POB) and all intermediate points (bounds) and the courses or angular direction of each point (metes).

metropolitan area plan. The extension and adaptation of general community planning to embrace an entire metropolitan area or a group of municipalities and suburban neighborhoods.

metropolitan statistical area (MSA). A city of at least 50,000 people; an urbanized area of at least 50,000 with a total metropolitan population of at least 100,000; designated under standards set in 1980 by the Federal Committee on MSAs. This term replaces the term *standard metropolitan statistical area (SMSA). See also* consolidated metropolitan statistical area (CMSA); primary metropolitan statistical area (PMSA).

mezzanine. An intermediate floor with less area than the standard full floors; in a theater, a shallow balcony between the main floor and the first balcony.

MGIC. *See* Mortgage Guarantee Insurance Corporation.

microeconomics. The study of the economics of individual spheres of activity or patterns and behaviors, e.g., a firm, an industry, a retail market, a consumer segment, pricing, local employment. *See also* macroeconomics.

microprocessor. In computer usage, a central processing unit, or CPU, that consists of only one semiconductor chip.

microrelief. Surface irregularity; used by farm appraisers to describe slight land surface irregularities, e.g., smooth channels, hogwallows, low hummocks, high hummocks, dunes.

microtel. A contemporary version of the budget hotel, taking the budget

concept back to the basics. As a result of amenity creep, i.e, the provision of additional amenities for free (morning newspapers, continental breakfasts, coffeemakers in guestrooms, shampoo, fitness centers, turndown service, etc.), many budget hotels have gradually turned into mid-rate hotels. In a microtel, guestrooms are downsized to only 192 square feet and amenities such as restaurants, lounges, meeting spaces, and swimming pools are absent. A microtel is 10% to 20% less expensive to construct, requires less land, and can undercut the room rates of comparable budget hotels by as much as 25%. With no amenities, microtels are easier to operate and maintain. *See also* budget hotel; hotel.

middle rail. In construction, the central, horizontal structural member.

milk house. A dairy building used exclusively for the storage of milk.

milk parlor. A dairy building used exclusively for milking cows.

mill. One-tenth of one cent; often used to express real estate taxes.

millage rate. A tax rate expressed in tenths of a cent; e.g., a tax rate of one mill per thousand means $1 of taxes per $1,000 of assessed value.

mill construction. A type of construction in which substantial, self-supporting masonry walls carry the wood roof and thicker floor decks are supported by heavy timber framing. In mill construction, corners, projections, and small section members that ignite easily are avoided, stories are separated by incombustible fire stops and elevator hatches, and stairways are encased in incombustible partitions. *See also* slow-burning construction.

mill-cut estimate. *See* will-cut cruise.

millwork. All building materials made of finished wood and manufactured in millwork plants and planing mills, e.g., doors, window frames, door frames, sashes, blinds, porch work, mantels, panel work, stairways, special woodwork; does not include yard lumber such as dimensional lumber or siding.

mineral deposit. An existing quantity of recoverable metallic or nonmetallic natural resources, usually subject to commercial exploitation.

mineral rights. *See* subsurface rights.

mineral wool. Insulating material made by blasting molten slag or rock with steam, e.g., rock wool, glass wool.

miner's inch. A flow of water equal to ⅕₀th or ¼₀th of a cubic foot per second.

mini-bay warehouse. A self-storage facility, typically leased on a monthly basis; consists of small units ranging in size from 20 to 500 square feet, some of which may be air-conditioned.

minimum lot. The minimum acceptable size of lots that can be developed in an area or community under current zoning regulations.

minimum rental. The base or fixed payment in a lease.

MIRR. *See* modified internal rate of return.

MIS. Management Information Systems. *See also* Geographic Information Systems (GIS).

mission style architecture. An architectural style based on the characteristics of early California missions. These churches of stone or adobe had small window openings, one or more towers, and sometimes vaulted interiors; ornamentation varied from primitive to refined and roofs of wood or thatch were later replaced with the red tile roofs so prevalent in the Southwest.

miter. The angular shape produced by cutting the ends of two boards at an angle and fitting them together.

mitigation of damages. A duty that the law imposes on an injured party to make a reasonable effort to minimize his or her damages after an injury. (R.S. Means)

mixed fund. An investment fund in which capital is subscribed before all of the property to be purchased is selected.

mixed occupancy. Two or more classes of occupancy in a single structure. (R.S. Means)

mixed-use development. An income-producing property that comprises multiple significant uses within a single site such as retail, office, residential, or lodging facilities. (R.S. Means)

mixed-use zoning. Zoning that allows multiple land uses to be developed within a single site.

mobile home. A complete, livable dwelling unit capable of being moved from place to place by a truck or automobile.

mobile home park. *See* trailer park.

mobility. In real estate, the ease with which people can move from one location to another.

mockup. A model, either full size or to scale, of a construction system or assembly used to analyze construction details, strength, and appearance. Mockups are commonly used for masonry and exposed concrete construction projects. (R.S. Means)

mode. A measure of central tendency; the most frequent, or typical, value in an array of numbers; a positional average that is not affected by extreme values. It is the most descriptive average and easily identified when the number of items is small; if the sample is too small, however, none of the values may be repeated and no mode exists.

model
1. A scale representation of an object, system, or building used for structural, mechanical, or aesthetic analysis.
2. A compilation of parameters used in developing a system. (R.S. Means)

model house. A house used for exhibition to sell other houses.

modem (*modulator/demodulator*). A device that converts signals from one kind of computer equipment into a form that is compatible with another kind of computer equipment, usually over telephone lines.

modern architecture. Contemporary, functional design intended to combine aesthetic quality and utility in a building.

modern colonial architecture. A residential architectural style characterized by windows divided into small panes and a simple, two-story design to which third-floor dormer windows may be added. *See also* New England colonial architecture.

modernization. A type of renovation in which worn or outdated elements are replaced with their current counterparts. *See also* curable physical deterioration; curable functional obsolescence.

modified economic age-life method. A method of estimating accrued depreciation in which the ratio between the effective age of a building and its total economic life is applied to the current cost of the improvements after the costs to cure curable physical and functional items are deducted. *See also* economic age-life method.

modified internal rate of return (*MIRR*). A measure of investment performance; similar to the internal rate of return except that negative cash flows, if any, are discounted to present value at a specified safe rate and positive cash flows are presumed to be reinvested to grow with compound interest at either the same specified safe rate or at a specified market rate until the termination of the investment; also called *adjusted internal rate of return*. *See also* financial management rate of return (*FMRR*); internal rate of return (*IRR*).

modular construction
1. Construction in which similar units or subcomponents are combined repeatedly to create a total system.

2. A construction system in which large prefabricated units are combined to create a finished structure.
3. A structural design which uses dimensions consistent with those of the uncut materials supplied. Common modular measurements are 4 inches to 4 feet. (R.S. Means)

module. A standard measure of any size used in construction and design; allows repetition in design and use and saves material and labor costs.

module width. The distance between window mullions, which determines the size of partitioned offices in a building.

moist room. An enclosure maintained at a given temperature and relative humidity and used for curing test cylinders of concrete or mortar. (R.S. Means)

moisture barrier. Insulating material placed in walls, floors, or other parts of a structure to block the passage of vapor or moisture and prevent condensation.

moisture equivalent. The percentage of water retained by a soil against a force 1,000 times stronger than gravity; an arbitrarily determined percentage that is correlated with other soil properties, e.g., moisture-holding capacity, wilting percentage, texture.

molded base. A base consisting of two members, a common base with molding above; a base consisting of three members, a common base with a base mold above and a shoe mold below. *See also* sanitary base.

molding. A finishing piece used to cover a joint, e.g., one formed by a ceiling and a wall; usually a long, narrow strip of plain or curved wood; may be ornamented.

monetary policy. The Federal Reserve's efforts to influence the level of economic activity by regulating the availability of money and the rate of interest.

money

1. Currency, i.e., minted coins and paper money, in the hands of the public plus demand deposits at commercial banks (M_1).

2. Currency plus demand and time deposits at commercial banks (M_2).

3. Currency plus demand and time deposits plus the liabilities of nonbank financial intermediaries (M_3).

4. The five components into which economists and statisticians desegregate the money supply, i.e., transactions money (M_1), broad money (M_2), additional near-monies (M_3), liquid assets (L), and total credit (D).

money market. The interaction of buyers and sellers who trade short-term money instruments.

money market certificates. Certificates issued by financial institutions, which sometimes pay interest based on the average yield recorded in the weekly auction of six-month Treasury bills and usually require that a minimum amount be deposited for six months.

monitor. A raised structure on a roof with windows or louvers that ventilate or light the building; usually found on a factory or warehouse.

monitor roof. A type of framing that includes an elevated central section and provides better lighting and ventilation; generally found on industrial buildings.

monolithic concrete. Concrete that is poured continuously so that it has no separations or joints due to different setting times.

monopoly. A market in which one person or group controls the supply of a good and, therefore, its price. *See also* oligopoly.

monopoly property. A property used by an enterprise that, through franchise, license, zoning regulation, etc., has the exclusive right to conduct that enterprise.

Monte Carlo simulation. A gaming studies model for risk analysis in which specific investment elements are assigned probabilities and integrated into a larger theoretical population; repeated sampling from this larger group provides a range of possible outcomes.

Monterey architecture. A residential, two-story style adapted from the architecture prevalent in California in the early Spanish era; usually characterized by a balcony that runs across the entire face of the building.

monthly payment. *See* debt service (I_M).

monument. A stone or other fixed object used to establish real estate boundaries.

monuments description. A method in which property is described by reference to natural or man-made objects in the field.

Moody's. An investor services agency that rates bonds, common stocks, preferred stocks, and commercial paper.

mop board. *See* baseboard.

moraine. A mass of material deposited by a glacier; e.g., terminal moraine is deposited at the front of a glacier and lateral moraine is deposited along the sides of a glacier; usually consists of an irregular ridge deposited by ice melting along the rim of the glacier at a rate equal to its forward flow.

moratorium
1. A temporary prohibition of new development.
2. A temporary suspension in the enforcement of liability for a financial obligation; often required by statute.

mortar. A pasty substance of lime and/or cement mixed with sand and water that hardens when exposed to air; used as a bonding material in brick and stone work.

mortgage. A pledge of a described property interest as collateral or security for the repayment of a loan under certain terms and conditions. *See also* adjustable-rate mortgage (ARM); contract sale; convertible mortgage; direct reduction mortgage; equity participation mortgage; graduated-payment mortgage (GPM); interest-only mortgage; mortgage note; participation mortgage; shared appreciation mortgage (SAM); variable-rate mortgage (VRM); wraparound mortgage; zero-coupon mortgage.

mortgage-backed securities. Bond-type securities generally backed by a pool of mortgages or trust deeds. *See also* collateralized mortgage obligations (CMOs); real estate mortgage investment conduits (REMICs).

mortgage banker. A person or company that makes mortgage loans with its own funds on its own behalf, usually in expectation of re-selling the loans to lenders at a profit and then servicing the loans.

mortgage broker. One who places mortgages, i.e., finds appropriate borrowers or willing lenders for a fee, which is usually a percentage of the loan amount.

mortgage capitalization rate. *See* mortgage constant (R_M).

mortgage coefficient (C). A multiplier used in the Ellwood formula to compute a capitalization rate. The mortgage coefficient is a function of the terms of the mortgage loan, the projected ownership period, and the equity yield rate.

mortgage company. A firm that brings mortgagors and mortgagees together for a fee, or one that ac-quires mortgages for resale.

mortgage constant (R_M). The capitali-zation rate for debt; the ratio of the annual debt service to the principal amount of the mortgage loan. A mortgage constant may be calcu-lated on the basis of the initial mort-gage amount or the outstanding mortgage amount; also called *mort-gage capitalization rate.* $(R_M = $ debt service/mortgage principal$)$

mortgage correspondent. One who acts as an agent for national lend-ers, making loan commitments for them using their standards of ac-

ceptability; may also service loans for the lender for an additional fee.

mortgage debt service (I_M). The peri-odic payment for interest on and retirement of the principal of a mortgage loan; also called *total mortgage debt service.*

mortgage deed. A deed that has the effect of a mortgage on the property conveyed and imposes a lien on the granted estate.

mortgagee. A party who advances funds for a mortgage loan and in whose favor the property is mort-gaged; the lender.

mortgage-equity analysis. Capitaliza-tion and investment analysis proce-dures that recognize how mortgage terms and equity requirements af-fect the value of income-producing property. *See also* Ellwood formula.

mortgage-equity formula. *See* Ellwood formula.

Mortgage Guarantee Insurance Cor-poration (MGIC). A privately held mortgage insurer; a secondary mar-ket for conventional, nonfederal mortgages.

mortgage insurance premium. A per-centage charged each year on the declining balance of the principal of a mortgage to insure the mortgagee against loss. Mortgage insurance is available on a private basis and is referred to as private mortgage insurance (PMI). *See also* private mortgage insurance (PMI).

mortgage lien. A filed charge using property as security. Often mortgage liens are obtained by contractors or material suppliers for a particular project. (R.S. Means)

mortgage note. A document or a clause in a document in which the borrower accepts responsibility for the repayment of a debt.

mortgage out. To finance a project without making a cash investment in it.

mortgage ratio (*M*). *See* loan-to-value ratio.

mortgage release price. A specified amount to be repaid to a lender to relinquish the lien on an individual parcel that collateralizes a portion of a mortgage loan secured by multiple parcels.

mortgage requirement. The periodic level payment, or installment, required for debt service, i.e., interest plus principal, on a direct reduction loan. *See also* mortgage constant (R_M).

mortgage residual technique. *See* residual techniques.

mortgage revenue bonds. Tax-exempt bonds sold by state and local governments or state housing finance agencies to pay for the acquisition, repair, or construction of real estate. Because the interest earned by bondholders is exempt from federal and possibly state and local taxation, the bonds are sold at a lower interest rate than taxable bonds; tax-exempt, lower-than-market interest rates are charged to borrowers because the interest savings on the bonds are passed on to the borrowers; also called *mortgage subsidy bonds.*

mortgage risk rating. A process in which the major risks undertaken in the making of a mortgage are thoroughly analyzed in accordance with the risk involved in the loan transaction or in connection with insurance of the mortgage; a basis for classifying mortgages as to their quality as investments.

mortgage term. The amount of time, specified in the mortgage contract, in which the mortgage loan must be paid off. *See also* amortization.

mortgagor. One who gives a mortgage as security for a loan; the borrower.

mortise. A notch or hole that is cut in a piece of wood or other material to receive the projecting part, or *tenon,* of another piece to join the two.

most appropriate use. In planning and zoning, the land use that is in the best interest of the community as a whole and will promote the greatest good for the greatest number; may or may not be the highest and best use; may be a present use or a future use.

most probable selling price. The price at which a property would most probably sell if exposed on the market for a reasonable time under the market conditions prevailing on the date of the appraisal. *See also* market value.

most probable use
1. The use to which a property will most likely be put based on market analysis and the highest and best use conclusion. The most probable use is the basis for the most probable selling price of the property. *See also* most probable selling price.
2. Highest and best use in the context of market value.

motel. A building or group of buildings located on or near a highway and designed to serve the needs of travelers by offering lodging and parking; may also provide other services and amenities, e.g., telephones, food and beverages, meeting and banquet rooms, recreational areas, swimming pool, shops.

mouse. An input device resembling an inverted track ball that allows a user to control a computer without using the keyboard.

movable form. A large prefabricated concrete form of a standard size which can be moved and reused on the same project. The form is moved either by crane or on rollers to the next location. (R.S. Means)

movable partition. A non-load-bearing demountable partition that can be relocated and can be either ceiling height or partial height. (R.S. Means)

move-up demand. In markets characterized by declining rents, office building tenants who "move up" from Class B to Class A space or from Class C to Class B space. *See also* fall-out demand; latent demand.

moving average. In statistics, successive arithmetic averages or arithmetic means developed by eliminating the first item in each averaged group and adding the next quantity in the series; used to reduce fluctuations in a graph or curve that reflects a pattern or trend. *See also* smoothing.

M roof. A type of roof consisting of two double-pitch roofs; has the advantages of using shorter material for rafters and reducing the elevation of the building.

MSA. *See* metropolitan statistical area.

muck. Organic soil material that is fairly well decomposed, relatively high in mineral content, and dark in color; accumulates in areas with poor drainage.

mud room. An entrance, particularly to a rural residence, where muddy footwear can be removed and stored. (R.S. Means)

mullion. A vertical member separating, and often supporting, windows, doors, or panels set in a series. (ULI) *See also* spandrel.

multicollinearity. The phenomenon of two or more variables being correlated in the sample data.

multifamily housing (FHA Section 207). A section of Title 11 of the National Housing Act under which the FHA insures mortgages, including advances made during construction, on multifamily rental housing projects of eight or more units. Amended in 1990 by the Cranston-Gonzalez Program.

multileg intersection. A road intersection with five or more travel routes.

multiple dwelling. A building composed of three or more dwelling units, usually with common access, service systems, and land use.

multiple listing. A listing that is not limited to one agent, but is offered by other agents who have agreed to cooperate in finding a purchaser for the property; also called *multiple listing service* (MLS).

multiple-nuclei theory. A theory of urban growth, developed by Chauncy Harris and Edward Ullman in 1945, as a synthesis of the concentric zone and sector theories; holds that an urban area develops around several distinct centers of development or nuclei, the number of which increases as the urban area grows. Major transportation arteries connect these nuclei to a central economic core. *See also* urban growth theories.

multiple ownership. A form of ownership whereby two or more people or entities own interests in the same real property at the same time. There are three basic forms of multiple ownership of real property. (R.S. Means)

multiple regression analysis. A type of analysis that measures the simultaneous influence of a number of independent variables on one dependent variable.

multiple use

1. A combination of compatible land uses in an area.
2. A combination of compatible uses in a single building.

multiplier. A figure that is multiplied by income to produce an estimate of value; called a *gross income multiplier* when gross income is used, a *gross rent multiplier* when gross rent is used, and a *net income multi-*

plier when net income is used; may be monthly or annual.

multistory. A term commonly applied to buildings with five or more stories. (R.S. Means)

multiunit housing. *See* apartment building; condominium; cooperative apartment unit.

multizone system
1. An air-conditioning system that is capable of handling several individual zones simultaneously.
2. A heating or HVAC system having individual controls in two or more zones in a building. (R.S. Means)

multizone units. Air-handling units with parallel heating and cooling air paths providing individual mixing of air-distribution circuits into a single duct for each zone. (R.S. Means)

municipal bonds. Long-term, federally tax-exempt obligations of local governments, e.g., villages, cities, counties, that are used to raise capital for long-term operations and development.

municipal lien. A claim or lien filed by a municipality against a property owner for collection of the property owner's proportionate share of a public improvement made by the municipality that also improves the property owner's land. (R.S. Means)

municipal notes. Short-term, federally tax-exempt obligations of local governments, e.g., villages, cities, counties, that are used to finance current operations until satisfactory long-term funds are obtained.

muntin. A slender, vertical or horizontal bar of wood or metal that divides panes in a window or panels in a door.

mutual assent. The agreement of two or more parties to be bound to the terms of a contract. A contract is not legally enforceable without mutual assent. (R.S. Means)

mutual insurance companies. An insurance company cooperatively owned by its policyholders, who usually receive dividends or reductions in premiums.

mutual saving bank. A financial institution owned by its depositors; a major source of home mortgage funds.

N

NAA. National Apartment Association.

NABM. National Association of Building Manufacturers.

NACORE. Nacore International; acronym derived from former name—i.e., National Association of Corporate Real Estate.

NACS. *See* National Association of Convenience Stores.

NAIOP. National Association of Industrial and Office Parks.

NAM. National Association of Manufacturers.

NAR. *See* National Association of Realtors.

NARC. National Association of Regional Councils.

NAREB. National Association of Real Estate Brokers.

NAREIT. *See* National Association of Real Estate Investment Trusts.

NARELLO. *See* National Association of Real Estate License Law Officials.

narrative report. The most complete type of appraisal report; includes an introduction, the premises of the appraisal, the presentation of data, an analysis of data and conclusions, and often addenda. In a narrative report, the appraiser supports and explains the opinions and conclusions presented and demonstrates the soundness of the final value estimate. The reporting requirements for narrative reports, which are the same as those applied to other types of reports, are set forth in the Standards Rules relating to Standards 2 and 5 of the Uniform Standards of Professional Appraisal Practice.

National Association of Convenience Stores (NACS). Trade association for the convenience store industry; involved in educational, legislative, and informational activities.

National Association of Real Estate Investment Trusts (NAREIT). An organization whose members include REITs, corporations, partnerships, and individuals involved in the management of multiple-owned real estate and those with business or professional interests in REITs. NAREIT compiles statistics and maintains government relations and public relations committees.

National Association of Real Estate License Law Officials (NARELLO). A national association for commissioners of state real estate licensing agencies.

National Association of Realtors (NAR). A trade and professional organization that serves the real estate industry and includes the following organizations: Commercial Investment Real Estate Institute, Counselors of Real Estate (American Society of Real Estate Counselors), Institute of Real Estate Management, Realtors Land Institute, Realtors National Marketing Institute, Society of Industrial and Office Realtors, and Womens Council of Realtors.

National Council of Real Estate Investment Fiduciaries (NCREIF). A professional organization of pension fund managers that promotes real estate as an investment vehicle for institutional investors. The NCREIF Research Institute maintains the Russell-NCREIF Property Index, which measures the performance of institutional real estate.

National Flood Insurance Program (NFIP). Program established under the Flood Disaster Protection Act (FDPA) of 1973, which requires mortgagors of floodplain properties to carry flood insurance.

national historic landmarks and national historic sites. *See* National Register of Historic Places.

national income. The total net earnings attributable to the various factors employed in the production of goods and services in a nation over a particular period. *See also* gross domestic product (GDP); gross national product (GNP).

National Institute of Building Science (NIBS). An organization created by Congress whose membership includes architects, builders, contractors, engineers, real estate agents, and civil servants interested in the housing industry. NIBS advocates a coherent building regulatory policy, establishes guidelines on the treatment of hazardous materials, and promotes new technology in the building industry.

National Register of Historic Places. An official listing of historic and cultural resources in the United States that are considered worthy of preservation under the National Historic Preservation Act of 1966. Prior to 1966 properties listed in the register were mainly national historic landmarks and national historic sites. Since that time the scope of the register has expanded to include sites of local, state, and regional significance as well. *See also* historic district.

native plants. Plants that are native to an area and have not been introduced by humans.

natural breakpoint. *See* breakpoint.

natural land classification. A classification of soils into groups that have common features in terms of landscape, texture, drainage, slope, and erosion, and a narrow range in rating; includes the two rural factors of soil type and topography. *See* great soil group.

natural resource property. A property with recoverable or adaptable natural resources that could be exploited commercially; contains natural deposits of valuable material, e.g., rock, sand, gravel, clay, oil, gas, coal, metals. An enterprise using these resources is called an *extractive industry*.

natural seasoning. The drying of lumber by stacking, which permits free circulation of air around each timber.

navigable waters. Fresh or salt waters that, alone or with other waters, form a continuous waterway over which commerce may be conducted.

navigable waters of the United States. Waters of the United States that are subject to the ebb and flow of the tide shoreward to the mean high water mark; waters that are, have been, or can be used in conducting interstate or foreign commerce.

NBS. National Bureau of Standards.

NCDH. National Council Against Discrimination in Housing.

NCHP. National Corporation for Housing Partnerships.

NCREIF. *See* National Council of Real Estate Investment Fiduciaries.

negative amortization. The difference between the required service and the actual debt service paid; unpaid interest is added to the outstanding loan balance so that the balance increases instead of decreases over time. Mortgage instruments in which negative amortization occurs are generally indexed loans for which the interest rate may change without affecting the monthly payment. Sometimes the interest shortfall is made payable at maturity. *See also* amortization.

negative easement. Property that is burdened by an easement; also called the *servient estate*. *See also* affirmative easement; secondary easement.

negative leverage

1. The increasing financial losses that result from borrowing when the cost of capital exceeds the return on capital; reverse leverage in which the total yield on the investment is less than the interest rate on borrowed funds. Negative leverage mag-

nifies losses; positive leverage magnifies profits.

2. A situation that occurs when the equity capitalization rate or yield rate is lower with financing than without financing.

negligence. The failure of a party to conform its conduct to the standard of care required by law. The law requires that a person exercise that degree of care which a reasonable person would exercise under the same or similar circumstances. (R.S. Means)

negotiable order of withdrawal (NOW) accounts. Interest-bearing accounts with checking privileges; a type of demand deposit.

negotiated procurement. A procedure used by the U.S. Government for contracting whereby the government and the potential contractor negotiate on both price and technical requirements after submission of proposals. Award is made to the contractor whose final proposal is most advantageous to the government. (R.S. Means)

negotiation. A process used to determine a mutually satisfactory contract sum, and terms to be included in the contract for construction. In negotiations, the owner directly selects the constructor and the two, often with assistance of the design professional, derive by compromise

and a meeting of the minds the scope of the project and its cost. (R.S. Means)

neighborhood. A group of complementary land uses; a congruous grouping of inhabitants, buildings, or business enterprises.

neighborhood analysis. The objective analysis of observable and/or quantifiable data indicating discernible patterns of urban growth, structure, and change that may detract from or enhance property values; focuses on four sets of considerations that influence value: social, economic, governmental, and environmental factors.

neighborhood and district life cycle. The typical, but not necessarily universal, four-stage cycle that describes the life pattern of neighborhoods and districts; the stages include growth, stability, decline, and revitalization.

neighborhood shopping center. The smallest type of shopping center, generally with a gross leasable area of less than 100,000 square feet. Typical anchors include supermarkets and pharmacies. Neighborhood shopping centers offer convenience goods and personal services, and usually depend on the market support of more than 1,000 households.

neoprene. A synthetic rubber with high resistance to petroleum products and sunlight. Neoprene is used in many construction applications, such as roofing and flashing, vibration absorption, and sound absorption. (R.S. Means)

neoprene roof. A roof covering made of neoprene sheet material with heat-welded joints, that can be either ballasted or non-ballasted. This type of roof covering has good elastic and durability properties over a long time span. (R.S. Means)

net adjustment. The difference between the total positive and negative adjustments made to a comparable sale price. *See also* gross adjustment.

net cash proceeds of resale. *See* net reversionary interest.

net earnings. *See* net operating income (*NOI*).

net floor area. The occupied area of a building not including hallways, elevator shafts, stairways, toilets, and wall thicknesses. The net floor area is used for determining rental space and fire-code requirements. (R.S. Means)

net ground lease. A lease of unimproved land in which the lessee agrees to accept and pay the owner's expenses, e.g., the ad valorem taxes, assessments, as well as all expenses for any improvements created by the lessee.

net income before depreciation. *See* net operating income (*NOI*).

net income before recapture. *See* net operating income (*NOI*).

net income multiplier. The relationship between price or value and net operating income expressed as a factor; the reciprocal of the overall rate.

net income ratio (*NIR*). The ratio of net operating income to effective gross income (*NOI/EGI*); the complement of the operating expense ratio, i.e., 1 - *OER*.

net lease. A lease in which the tenant pays all property operating expenses in addition to the stipulated rent.

net listing. A listing in which the broker is entitled to any proceeds of sale in excess of a specified selling price. In some states, this practice is illegal.

net operating income (*NOI*). The actual or anticipated net income that remains after all operating expenses are deducted from effective gross income, but before mortgage debt service and book depreciation are deducted; may be calculated before or after deducting replacement reserves.

net present value (*NPV*). The difference between the present value of all expected investment benefits, or positive cash flows, and the present value of capital outlays, or negative cash flows. For purposes of real property valuation, negative cash flows include the initial cash outlay required to purchase the property. Generally, when *NPV* is positive, the investment is acceptable; if *NPV* is zero, the investment is marginally acceptable; and when *NPV* is negative, the investment is unacceptable. Also called *dollar reward.*

net price. The lowest price, after all deductions, discounts, etc. (R.S. Means)

net realizable value (*NRV*)
1. Market value minus the cost of disposition.
2. The estimated selling price in the ordinary course of business less estimated costs of completion (to the stage of completion assumed in determining the selling price), holding, and disposal. (FASB)

net rental basis. Refers to a lease in which the tenant pays all operating expenses for the real estate.

net reversionary interest. The lump-sum benefit that an investor receives at the termination of an investment after the deduction of sales commissions and outstanding mortgage debt. *See also* reversionary benefit.

net sales. Gross sales less returns and allowances, e.g., freight, trade discounts.

net sales area. The floor area in a department or retail store that is available for the sale of merchandise, excluding storage and equipment areas, rest rooms, etc.; the actual floor area used for merchandising.

net site area. The area of a building site less streets and roadways. (R.S. Means)

net spendable income. *See* after-tax cash flow.

network. In computer usage, an interconnected group of computers or terminals that are linked together for a specific purpose, e.g., to share data files.

network analysis. A method of diagramming the investment decision-making process and the critical timing aspects involved.

net worth. The difference between total assets and total liabilities.

neutral soil. A soil that is not significantly acid or alkaline; has a pH between 6.6 and 7.3. *See also* pH.

new construction. A building project that has been completed recently, i.e., within the past three years. *See also* class of building; proposed construction.

newel post. A vertical post that supports the handrail at the top or bottom of a stairway or at a landing; the post around which a circular stairway winds.

New England colonial architecture. A residential architectural style developed to incorporate in wooden houses the classic features of brick and stone Georgian houses; characterized by white clapboard exteriors, shingle roofs, and openings embellished with detailed moldings. *See also* Cape Cod house; modern colonial architecture; salt box architecture.

NFIP. *See* National Flood Insurance Program.

NFPA. National Forest Products Association.

NHC. National Housing Corporation.

NHOF. National Homeowners Foundation.

NIBS. *See* National Institute of Building Science.

node. A cluster of properties with the same or complementary uses, generally a nucleus of office buildings and retail stores. Downtown central business districts (CBDs), the primary sites of office building nodes, usually house financial institutions, corporate headquarters, and government offices. Other office building nodes include uptown areas, which develop along the axis between the CBD and the suburbs; office parks, which accommodate the needs of research and development and manufacturing industries; and shopping centers, which provide office space for tenants serving residents of the trade area. Specialized legal, medical, and research activities may be housed in office nodes near courthouses, public record repositories, hospitals, and universities.

nogging

1. Brick that fills the spaces in a frame wall.
2. Pieces of wood inserted in a masonry wall to receive nails.

noise insulation. Sound-absorbing materials installed in partitions, doors, windows, ceilings, and floors. (R.S. Means)

noise reduction

1. The difference, expressed in decibels, between the noise energy in two rooms when a noise is produced in one of the rooms.
2. The difference in noise energy from one side of a partition to another when a noise is produced on one side. (R. S. Means)

nominal interest rate (I). A stated or contract rate; an interest rate, usually annual, that does not necessarily correspond to the true or effective rate of growth at compound interest; e.g., a true or effective 1% monthly interest rate may be called a nominal annual interest rate of 12%, although true growth with monthly compounding amounts to slightly more than 12.68% per year. *See also* effective interest rate (*i*).

nominal price. A price at its face value. *See also* real price.

nomogram. A diagram, chart, or arrangement of scales used in the graphic solution of problems with fixed numerical relationships.

nonapparent easement. An easement that is not obvious or ascertainable by a cursory inspection of the premises.

nonassumption clause. A conventional mortgage clause that states that the property of an owner-borrower cannot be sold or the mortgage assumed by a third party without the consent of the lender. *See also* due-on-sale clause.

nonbasic activities. In economic base analysis, activities producing outputs that are primarily consumed within the subject area or community. *See also* basic activities; economic base analysis.

nonbasic crops. Agricultural products that are entitled to government support but are not basic to the areas in which they are grown; e.g., oats, barley, rye, some dairy prod-

ucts, honey, wool. *See also* basic crops.

nonbasic income. Income that comes from within the community. *See also* economic base analysis.

nonbearing partition. A partition wall that divides space but does not carry overhead partitions or joists.

nonbearing wall. A self-supporting wall that carries no vertical load; also called *nonload-bearing wall.*

nonconforming building. A building or portion of a building that was lawfully erected or altered, but no longer conforms to the use, height, or area regulations of the zone where it is located because of a subsequent change in a zoning ordinance. *See also* legally nonconforming use.

nonconforming use. *See* legally nonconforming use.

nonconforming work. Work that does not fulfill the contractually agreed upon requirements. (R.S. Means)

nonconventional mortgage. Mortgages that are insured or guaranteed by an agency of the federal government, e.g., Federal Housing Administration, Veterans Administration, or by a private insuring company.

nondurable goods. Short-lived consumer goods such as food and clothing.

nonexcusable delay. A delay which is the fault of the contractor for which the contractor will receive neither a time extension or compensation. (R.S. Means)

nonexclusive zoning. An ordinance that clearly defines and permits exceptions to a particular type of zoning.

nonfee timesharing. A limited interest in real property in which the purchaser receives only those rights specifically granted by the developer, usually the right to use a timeshare unit and the related premises; does not impart legal title to the property.

nonload-bearing wall. *See* nonbearing wall.

nonoperating income. The income that a business concern receives from sources other than the business operation, e.g., from earnings on investments or capital gains.

nonrealty interests. *See* business value; personal property.

nonrecourse loan. Debt agreement secured by real estate which provides that the lender has no claim against the debtor in the event of default, but can only recover the property.

nonrecurring expense. An expense attributed to a condition that is not regularly repeated in the ordinary course of business operations, e.g., a loss due to fire or theft.

nonrestrictive specification. A type of specification which is written so as not to restrict the product to a particular manufacturer or material supplier. (R.S. Means)

nonskid floor. A concrete floor surface treated with carborundum powder, iron filings, or other material to improve its traction qualities, especially when wet. (R.S. Means)

normal curve. In statistics, a symmetrical, bell-shaped curve that represents the distribution of a population of certain types of measurements or the frequency distribution of all possible means in large samples that may be drawn from almost any kind of population.

normal distribution. *See* normal probability distribution.

normal probability distribution. In statistics, a continuous distribution that is usually represented by a normal curve; a probability function that produces a symmetrical, bell-shaped curve.

normal vacancy. *See* frictional vacancy.

nosing. The rounded, projecting edge of a stair tread or landing.

notary public. A public officer who is authorized to take acknowledgments and witness sworn affidavits.

notice of default. A document filed with the county concerning the lien(s) on property that is in default; states that notice of default must be given to the person named in the document to validate subsequent foreclosure proceedings and give the person an opportunity to reinstate.

notice to bidders. A notice included in the bidding documents that informs prospective bidders of the bidding procedures and the opportunity to submit a bid. (R.S. Means)

notice to creditors. During bankruptcy proceedings, the formal notification to creditors of a meeting, or the granting of an order for relief. (R.S. Means)

NOW accounts. *See* negotiable order of withdrawal accounts.

noxious weeds. Unwanted plants that are considered agricultural hazards due to their vigorous growth or propagation.

NTO. National Tenants Organization.

nuisance. Something that interferes with the use and enjoyment of property or is a source of discomfort and annoyance to others; legally divided into two classes: public, or common, nuisances which touch the public interest and pri-

vate nuisances, which destroy or injure an individual's property, interfere with its lawful use and enjoyment, or deny an individual common rights.

nuisance value. The price that probably would be paid to avoid or relieve an objectionable condition.

null hypothesis. In statistics, a statement that there is no difference between two comparable and calculated statistics; tested against evidence found in samples.

nurse crop. A crop planted primarily to shelter less vigorous seedlings; e.g., when barley and alfalfa are planted to establish an alfalfa stand, barley is the nurse crop.

nursing home. A facility designed, staffed, and equipped to accommodate individuals who are not in need of hospital care, but require skilled nursing care and other medical services. Skilled nursing facilities (SNF) are state-licensed nursing homes which provide around-the-clock care for convalescent patients (a level of care just below acute hospital care). *See also* elderly housing.

nutrients. Elements essential to plant growth and soil development; a factor in soil analysis.

O

oakum. Loose fiber obtained from hemp or rope; used to caulk joints.

O and D survey. *See* origin-destination survey.

OAR. *See* overall capitalization rate (R_O).

observed condition. The condition of a property ascertained from a detailed inspection; physical condition.

obsolescence. One cause of depreciation; an impairment of desirability and usefulness caused by new inventions, changes in design, improved processes for production, or other external factors that make a property less desirable and valuable for a continued use; may be either functional or external. *See also* curable functional obsolescence; depreciation; external obsolescence; incurable functional obsolescence.

O.C. *See* on center.

OCC. *See* Office of the Comptroller of the Currency

occupancy. The state of being in possession.

occupancy cost. The periodic expenditure of money necessary to occupy a property, excluding expenses directly attributable to the operation of a business. For a tenant, occupancy costs constitute the rent plus items such as heat, utilities, janitor service, taxes not included in the rent, and amortization of the tenant's costs of alterations over the term of the lease. For an owner-occupant, occupancy costs include all tenant costs plus a charge equivalent to market rent.

occupancy load. The maximum number of persons in an area at a given peak period. (R.S. Means)

occupancy permit. Public acknowledgment that a building meets applicable requirements for use. *See also* certificate of occupancy (C of O).

occupancy rate. The relationship or ratio between the income received from the rented units in a property and the income that would be received if all the units were occupied.

Occupational Safety and Health Act (OSHA) of 1970. Legislation imposing federal safety and health standards on employers. *See also* Occupational Safety and Health Administration.

Occupational Safety and Health Administration. An agency of the Department of Labor created by the Occupational Safety and Health Act (OSHA) of 1970 to establish and enforce safety and health standards in the workplace.

OCZM. Office of Coastal Zone Management.

offer. A set of terms presented by the bidder, a prospective buyer or tenant, that are subject to negotiation. If the other party, a seller or landlord, accepts these terms, the offer will result in a contract.

offering circular (prospectus). For an offering that must be qualified, a written description of the proposed offering that has been submitted and cleared by the proper agency; for an exempt offering, a brochure that describes the terms and conditions of the purchase in detail; called an *offering circular,* for state qualification, and a *prospectus,* for federal registration.

office occupancy. The use of a building or space for business, as opposed to manufacturing, warehousing, or other uses. (R.S. Means)

Office of the Comptroller of the Currency (OCC). A section within the Treasury Department which oversees the chartering of banks and may call on banks to submit reports of their operations for audit.

Office of Management and Budget (OMB). An executive agency of the U.S. Government which analyzes departmental requests for allocations, assists the president in preparing budget proposals attuned to anticipated revenue and executive policy, and supervises the administration of the budget. The OMB oversees statistical services and tracks the activities of government agencies to ensure that Congressional appropriations are spent economically. Appraisals performed for federal credit agencies under OMB supervision are subject to Circular A-129 of 1988.

Office of Thrift Supervision (OTS). *See* Financial Institutions Reform, Recovery and Enforcement Act (FIRREA).

off line. In computer usage, refers to peripheral equipment or devices not subject to the direct control of the central processing unit.

off-price shopping center. A retail mall with stores that sell brand-name goods at 20% to 70% below department store prices and appeal to middle-income and upper-middle-income consumers.

offset
  1. A ledge formed by a difference in the thickness of a wall. *See also* setback; set-off.

2. A deduction, usually from rent; e.g., an agreement in which a tenant is allowed to deduct a portion of the rent or escalation payments from the stipulated percentage or base rent. *See also* set-off provision.

offsite costs. Costs incurred in the development of a project, excluding actual building construction costs, e.g., the costs of streets, sidewalks, curbing, traffic signals, water and sewer mains; also called *common costs* or *offsite improvement costs.*

offsite improvements. Improvements such as streets, sidewalks, curbing, traffic signals, and water and sewer mains.

old growth. Mature timber stands that remain in their natural condition; generally yield the highest volume of timber and the best quality.

oligopoly. A market in which a few large producers dominate. *See also* monopoly.

OMB. *See* Office of Management and Budget.

on center (O.C.). The distance from the center of one structural member to the center of a similar member, e.g., spacing studs, joists, girders.

one-hour rating. A measure of fire resistance, indicating that an object can be exposed to flame for an hour without losing structural integrity or transmitting excessive heat. (R.S. Means)

one-on-two. A slope in which the elevation rises one foot in two horizontal feet. (R.S. Means)

on grade. A concrete floor slab resting directly on the ground. (R.S. Means)

on line. In computer usage, refers to equipment or devices under the direct control of the central processing unit.

onsite costs. Costs incurred for the actual construction of buildings and improvements on a particular parcel of land. *See also* construction costs; direct costs.

open-beam construction. Frame construction in which the ceiling and ceiling joists are eliminated, exposing the beams and deck of the roof and treating them as elements of interior finish; usually structural members of the roof are heavier and on wider centers.

open bid. An offer to perform a contract in which the bidder reserves the right to reduce his bid to compete with a lower bid. (R.S. Means)

open bidding. A bidding procedure wherein bids or tenders are submitted by and received from all interested contractors, rather than from a select list of bidders privately invited to compete. (R.S. Means)

open-end mortgage. A mortgage in which the mortgagor is permitted to borrow additional sums provided that a stated ratio of assets to debt is maintained or other specified terms are met.

open listing. A listing contract that provides that the agent will receive a commission if the property is sold through his or her efforts or if the agent produces a buyer under the terms of the contract before the property is sold.

open planning. House design in which few partitions divide different activity areas, e.g., living room, dining room, kitchen, family room.

open roof (open timbered roof). A style of roof with exposed rafters, sheathing, and supporting timbers visible from beneath, with no ceiling. (R.S. Means)

open space. Land designated for nonbuilding uses; typically of three ownership types: private open space adjacent to dwellings owned by individual residents, public open space owned by government, and common open space owned by a community association and set aside for the use of residents. (ULI)

open space ratio. The ratio of open space to the total site or to the land area improved with buildings.

open stairway. A stairway with one side or both sides open to the room in which it is located. (R.S. Means)

open steel construction. A type of construction in which a rigidly connected steel frame that is unwrapped, or without fireproofing, carries all loads directly to the foundation and footings. In a multistory structure, the exterior walls are carried on this framework, usually at each level.

open web joist. Lightweight, parallel trusses of prefabricated metal.

operating expense ratio (*OER*). The ratio of total operating expenses to effective gross income (*TOE/EGI*); the complement of the net income ratio, i.e., $1 - NIR$.

operating expenses. The periodic expenditures necessary to maintain the real property and continue production of the effective gross income, assuming prudent and competent management. *See also* total operating expenses.

operating income. Income derived from the operation of a business or real property; indicates a stage in the profit-and-loss account where all direct costs and income from the operation have been taken into account; as distinguished from net profit or cash flow.

operating profit. Profit that arises from the regular operation of an enterprise that performs services, excluding income from other sources and expenses not directly related to the operation. The term is used interchangeably with *operating income* and *net operating income,* but is distinguished from *net profit or cash flow.*

operating standards. Standards of performance; derived by analyzing the operating expenses of comparable properties; also called *comparative standards.*

operating statement. A financial statement that reflects the gross revenues, expenses, and net operating profit or loss of an investment over a fixed period. *See also* reconstructed operating statement.

operating system. The system required to run a computer program; controls the operation of computer activities and manages the flow of software instructions and data within the computer. *See also* applications software.

opinion of title. A certificate pertaining to the status of a recorded title to real property; usually issued by an attorney or title insurance company.

opportunity cost. The cost of options foregone or opportunities not chosen.

optimum use. *See* highest and best use.

option. A legal contract, typically purchased for a stated consideration, that permits but does not require one to buy, sell, or lease real property for a stipulated period of time in accordance with specified terms; a unilateral right to exercise a privilege.

option term. A stipulated time during which the holder of an option can exercise his or her rights under the option agreement.

oral report. An unwritten appraisal report that includes a property description as well as all facts, assumptions, conditions, and reasoning on which the value conclusion is based. The reporting requirements for oral reports, which are the same as those applied to written reports, are set forth in the Standards Rules relating to Standards 2 and 5 of the Uniform Standards of Professional Appraisal Practice.

orchard. A planting of uniformly spaced fruit- or nut-bearing trees; normally spaced for easy equipment operation and maximum production from a specific variety of tree. Some crops require plantings of more than one variety to ensure proper pollination.

ordinance. A public regulation, e.g., a law, usually local.

ordinary annuity. A common type of level annuity in which income payments are received at the end of each period. *See also* annuity; annuity payable in advance.

ordinary hazard contents. Building contents that burn at moderate speed and give off smoke, but release no poisonous fumes or gases that would cause an explosion under fire conditions. (R.S. Means)

ordinary high water mark. On nontidal rivers, the line on the shore established by the fluctuations of water and indicated by physical characteristics, e.g., a clear, natural line impressed on the bank, shelving, changes in the character of the soil, the destruction of terrestrial vegetation, the presence of litter and debris. *See also* mean high water line.

ordinary income. Income that is subject to income taxes at the taxpayer's regular rate, as distinguished from capital gains income which may be taxable at a lower rate.

ordinate. In the rectangular coordinate system, the distance from a point to the horizontal x-axis; denoted by the second number in an ordered pair; e.g., in the expression (3,7), 7 is the ordinate.

organic matter. The relatively decomposed material of the soil that is derived from organic sources, usually plant remains.

organic soil. Any soil that is predominantly organic matter.

organization cost. The cost incurred in the formation of a functioning enterprise, excluding costs for promotion, obtaining capital, constructing improvements, and acquiring the business.

organization fee. A one-time fee received by the promoter or general partner for organizing a syndicate.

oriel window. A window that projects from the outer face of a wall, especially from an upper story, and is supported by brackets or a cantilever; as distinguished from a bay window, which is at first-floor level and usually supported by a foundation.

orientation. The positioning of a structure on a lot with regard to its exposure to the sun and prevailing winds, privacy, and protection from noise.

original cost. In accounting, the acquisition cost of a property to its present owner; the net invoice price of an asset.

origin-destination survey. A traffic study technique in which the movement of people, vehicles, and goods in a given area is systematically sampled to determine where journeys begin and end, the purpose of journeys, the modes of travel, the time elapsed, and the land uses at the origin and the destination; also called an *O and D survey*.

OSHA. *See* Occupational Safety and Health Act of 1970.

other limiting conditions. Statement that defines the parameters of the appraisal assignment; included within the definition of the appraisal problem in an appraisal report for the appraiser's protection as well as the information and protection of the client and others using the report.

OTS. Office of Thrift Supervision. *See* Financial Institutions Reform, Recovery and Enforcement Act (FIRREA).

outbuilding. A building that is separate from a main building but attendant on it or collateral to it in its functions, such as a stable, a garage, or an outside lavatory. (R.S. Means)

outcrop. A segment of an underground rock stratum or a formation that breaks through the surface of the earth and forms a visible protuberance. (R.S. Means)

outer court. An outdoor space that is bounded on three sides by property lines or building walls, but maintains a view of the sky and is open

on one side to an adjacent street or public area. (R.S. Means)

outlet shopping center. An aggregation of factory outlet stores. (ULI)

out-of-plumb. Deviating from a true vertical line of descent, as determined by a plumb line. (R.S. Means)

outstanding balance (B). The present value of the debt service on a level-payment loan over the remaining amortization period discounted at the interest rate; also called *balance outstanding*.

out-to-out. In measurements, a term meaning that the dimensions are overall. (R.S. Means)

overage income. *See* overage rent.

overage rent. The percentage rent paid over and above the guaranteed minimum rent or base rent; calculated as a percentage of sales in excess of a specified breakeven sales volume. *See also* percentage rent.

overall. The total external dimension of any building material, including all projections. (R.S. Means)

overall capitalization rate (R$_o$). An income rate for a total real property interest that reflects the relationship between a single year's net operating income expectancy and the total property price or value; used to convert net operating income into an indication of overall property value ($R_o = I_o/V_o$).

overall yield rate (Y$_o$). The rate of return on the total capital invested, including both debt and equity. The Y_o takes into consideration changes in net income over the investment period and net reversion at the end of the holding period; it is applied to cash flow before debt service. Also called *property yield rate*.

overbuilding. Building more structures of a particular type than can be absorbed by the market at prevailing prices.

overburden

1. A mantle of soil, rock, gravel, or other earth material covering a given rock layer or bearing stratum.
2. An unwanted top layer of soil that must be stripped away to open access to useful construction materials buried beneath it. (R.S. Means)

overflight. The airspace over a property through which aircraft may pass so long as the property's occupants suffer no inconvenience beyond established standards.

overgrazing. The overstocking or overuse of a range, which causes better forage to disappear, secondary species to decline in vigor until they too are gone, and a change in the type and quality of forage.

overhang. A type of roof in which the rafters and roofing extend beyond the exterior walls of the structure; used to protect against precipitation and direct sunlight.

overhead. Expenses incurred for direction and administration which are necessary to the development and management of real estate and the operation of a business enterprise.

overhead door. A door, constructed of a single leaf or of multiple leaves, that is swung up or rolls open from the ground level and assumes a horizontal position above the entrance way it serves when opened. Commonly used as a garage door. (R.S. Means)

overhead easement. The right to use space at a designated distance above the surface of the land, e.g., for power lines, avigation, air rights.

overhead irrigation. Sprinkler irrigation installed with tall rises that deliver water above crops; frequently installed in orchards, groves, and vineyards.

overhead traveling crane. A lifting machine generally power-operated at least in its hoisting operation. The crane is carried on a horizontal girder, reaching between rails above window level at each side of a workshop, and consists of a hoisting cab that can travel from end to end on the girder. The whole area between the rails can thus be traversed by the cab. (R.S. Means)

overimprovement. An improvement that does not represent the most profitable use for the site on which it is placed because it is too large or costly and cannot develop the highest possible land value; may be temporary or permanent.

overpass. A grade separation where a highway passes over another highway or a railroad; constructed to avoid surface intersections and traffic congestion.

overriding royalty. An interest in unsevered oil and gas that the lessee retains when executing a sublease or assignment.

overrun
1. Cost or expense in excess of budgeted cost, e.g., in the budget for a real estate development.
2. The amount by which the lumber actually sawed from logs exceeds the estimated volume; usually expressed as a percentage.

overstocking. Placing too many animals in a given area, which results in overuse at the end of a planned grazing period; distinguished from overgrazing because an area can be overstocked for a short period, if the animals are removed before the area is overutilized; continued overstocking will lead to overgrazing.

overstory. The portion of a forest that contains the tallest trees, or the top canopy.

oversupply. An excess of supply over demand; indicated by high vacancy rates, sluggish absorption rates, and declining rents.

owned real estate. *See* real estate owned (REO).

owner-contractor agreement. The contract formed between owner and contractor describing performance of the construction work for a project (or a portion thereof). (R.S. Means)

owner-occupied. Describes real estate physically occupied by the owner as opposed to property owned by an investor or absentee landlord and rented to tenants. An owner-occupant can usually obtain better mortgage rates and preferred tax treatment.

owner of record. The owner of title to a property as indicated by public records.

owner's equity. The owner's or owners' claims against the assets of a business. Owner's equity implies

that the business is a single proprietorship and, therefore, represents
the proprietor's claims against assets of the single proprietorship.
(R.S. Means)

ownership of real property. The holding of rights or interests in real estate. *See also* estate in possession; fee
simple estate; fee simple title;
leased fee estate; legal owner; partial interest.

ownership rate. The ratio between the
number of household heads in a

given subgroup who own their
homes either free and clear or under mortgage and all the persons in
that subgroup, e.g., 40% of household heads between 25 and 34 own
their own homes.

owner's representative. The designated official representative of the
owner (may be an architect, engineer, or contractor) to oversee a
project. (R.S. Means)

P

packaged boiler. A factory-assembled
water or steam heating unit ready
for installation. All components, including the boiler, burner, controls,
and auxiliary equipment, are
shipped as a unit. (R.S. Means)

packaged air conditioner. A factory-
assembled air-conditioning unit
ready for installation. The unit may
be mounted in a window, an opening through a wall, or on the building roof. These units may serve an
individual room, a zone, or multiple zones. (R.S. Means)

package mortgage. A mortgage that
covers personalty as well as realty.

pad

1. An area in a mobile home park
   that is reserved for the exclusive
   use of a mobile home owner, as
   distinguished from commonly
   used areas.
2. The land underlying a condominium unit or a store in a shopping center.

paired data analysis. A quantitative
technique used to identify and
measure adjustments to the sale
prices or rents of comparable properties; to apply this technique, sales
or rental data on nearly identical
properties are analyzed to isolate a

single characteristic's effect on value or rent.

PAM. *See* pledged account mortgage.

P and L statement. Profit and loss statement. *See also* operating statement.

panel
1. A section of a surface, e.g., a wall, a ceiling, that is raised or recessed and usually enclosed in a frame-like border.
2. Prefabricated construction materials, e.g., gypsum board, plywood, fiberboard, plasterboard.

panel board. A panel to which electrical meters and control equipment are attached for electrical service distribution.

panel heating. A radiant heating system in which pipes or coils are embedded in walls or ceilings to serve as heating panels.

panel wall. A prefabricated section of wall that is erected in one piece. *See also* curtain wall; tilt-up construction.

panic hardware. A door-locking assembly that can be released quickly by pressure on a horizontal bar. Panic hardware is required by building codes on certain exits. (R.S. Means)

par. Denotes equality, or 100%, without a premium or discount, e.g., the par value of a mortgage is its face,

or nominal, amount; more commonly used to describe the value imprinted on stock certificates or the principal amount at which bonds can be redeemed at maturity.

parameter
1. A variable that can assume any of a given set of values.
2. A statistic that characterizes a population; usually unknown and must be inferred.

parapet. A low wall or railing along the edge of a roof, balcony, bridge, or terrace; constructed for protection, to control water resulting from rain or artificial flooding, or to insulate against the sun's rays.

parcel. A piece of land of any size in one ownership.

parcel identifier. A code number that serves as an abbreviation of, or replacement for, a parcel's legal description; used to facilitate the storage and use of land data in an information system; may be based on geocodes, government surveys, or tax maps. *See also* lot and block system.

parent material. The unconsolidated mass from which the soil profile develops.

parent rock. The rock from which the parent material of soils is formed.

parging. A thin coating of mortar that is applied to a masonry wall; used on the exterior face of below-grade walls for waterproofing or to smooth rough masonry.

parity. The state of being equivalent; used to refer to federal price policies for agricultural products. Such policies are designed to bring farm income into parity with the incomes of other sectors of the national economy.

parking area. The area of a facility, e.g., a shopping area, an industrial plant, a supermarket, designated for the parking of customer and employee automobiles.

parking garage. A commercial facility where automobiles may be parked for a fee; may be either public or private.

parking ratio. The number of available parking spaces per rentable unit of area, residential unit, hotel room, restaurant seat, etc.; also, the ratio of total parking area to gross leasable area. The parking ratio is a standard comparison that indicates the relationship between parking spaces or parking area and an economic or physical unit of comparison.

parkway. An arterial highway for non-commercial traffic with full or partial control of access; usually located in a park or park-like development.

parquet floor. A floor that is laid in rectangular or square patterns, rather than long strips; often made of prefinished, thin, fabricated wood blocks.

partial interest. Divided or undivided rights in real estate that represent less than the whole. *See also* partition; undivided partial interest.

partially amortizing mortgage loan. A loan that is not fully amortized at maturity; the outstanding principal must be repaid in one lump sum; often created by writing a loan for one maturity and calculating debt service payments based on a longer amortization period. *See also* balloon mortgage.

partial payment factor (1/a_n). The compound interest factor that represents the installment needed to repay \$1 with interest at a specified rate for a specific number of periods; the reciprocal of the level annuity, or Inwood, factor. Expressed annually, it is the mortgage constant or annual constant. The partial payment factor is one of the six functions of a dollar found in standard financial tables.

partial taking. The taking of part of any real property interest for public use under the power of eminent domain; requires the payment of compensation.

participation. *See* equity participation; income participation.

participation mortgage

1. A debt secured by real estate in which the lender receives a share of the income and sometimes the reversion from a property on which the lender has made a loan. Such a mortgage permits the lender to share in income and/or the proceeds of resale. *See also* equity participation mortgage; income participation.
2. A mortgage held by more than one lender.

partition

1. The legal separation of undivided partial interests such as co-ownership in real estate. This division of real property into separately owned parcels according to the owners' proportionate shares, which is usually pursuant to a judicial decree, severs the unity of possession, but does not create or transfer a new title or interest in property.
2. An interior wall that divides a building, e.g., a permanent, inside wall that divides a house into various rooms.

partnership. A business arrangement in which two or more persons jointly own a business and share in its profits and losses. *See also* general partnership; limited partnership.

party wall. A common wall erected along the boundary between adjoining properties; the respective owners have a common right of use.

passive activity loss. A loss incurred by an individual who would, in other circumstances, have received income from an enterprise, but has no regular, continuous, or substantial involvement in the business operation. According to the Tax Reform Act of 1986, the passive activity loss deducted may not exceed the amount invested.

pass-through. A form of rent escalation in which the tenant pays a direct share of the operating expenses.

pasture. Land devoted to the production of domesticated or native forage used for grazing.

patented land. Governmental land that has been conveyed or transferred to private parties.

patio. A courtyard; an open, paved area used for outdoor living; may or may not be partially or entirely surrounded by other parts of a building.

patio house. A type of single-family, attached house that is typically one-story, L- or U-shaped, and without a basement. The entire lot area is used; the design is based on the lot line construction of a house with living area in the enclosure or garden court; also called *court garden*. (ULI)

payback period. The length of time required for the stream of cash flows produced by the investment to equal the original cash outlay.

PCC. Production Credit Corporation.

peat soil. Unconsolidated soil material that consists mainly of undercomposed or slightly decomposed organic matter that has accumulated under excessively moist conditions.

pedalfers soil. A soil in which alumina and iron oxide have shifted downward in the soil profile, but with no horizon or carbonate accumulation.

pedestrian overpass. A structural grade separation, e.g., a bridge, that permits pedestrian traffic to pass over a highway.

pedestrian underpass. A structural grade separation, e.g., a tunnel, that permits pedestrian traffic to pass under a highway.

pedocal soil. A soil with a horizon of accumulated carbonates in the soil profile.

peeler log. A log that can be used for the manufacture of rotary-cut veneer.

penetration ratio. The rate at which stores obtain sales from within a trade area or sector relative to the number of potential sales generated; usually applied to existing facilities.

Pennsylvania colonial architecture. An informal, residential architectural style characterized by a high roof line on the main section of the house, whitewashed or plastered exterior stone walls, simple details, and a roof of slate or wood shingles; a regional variation of colonial architecture adapted for flat ground.

pension fund. Contributions from employers and employees that are placed with a trustee, who must invest and reinvest them prudently, accumulate funds, and pay plan benefits to retirees.

penstock. A conduit that conveys water to a power plant; a sluice-like device used to control the flow of water.

penthouse
1. A building on the roof of a structure that contains elevator machinery, ventilating equipment, etc.
2. A separate dwelling or apartment on the roof of an apartment house or other building.
3. Any roof-like shelter or overhanging part, e.g., a part that shelters a doorway.

pent-up demand. Demand characterizing a market in which there is a scarcity of supply and vacancy rates are below typical levels. *See also* demand.

per capita. By the head; according to the number of individuals.

per capita income. The total personal income of area residents divided by the number of residents.

per capita retail sales. Total sales for defined retail categories; e.g., total sales in a metropolitan area, divided by the population of that area, and corrected for export and import.

percentage adjustments. Adjustments for differences between the subject and comparable properties expressed in percentages; percentage adjustments are often used to reflect changes in market conditions and differences in location.

percentage agreement. A contractual agreement for which compensation will be based on a certain percentage of the total cost of construction. (R.S. Means)

percentage fee. A fee paid to the contractor or the architect that is a percentage of the total construction cost. (R.S. Means)

percentage lease. A lease in which the rent or some portion of the rent represents a specified percentage of the volume of business, productivity, or use achieved by the tenant.

percentage-of-completion method. A method of recording income from construction contracts in which income is based on the percentage of construction completed. Performance is often measured on a cost-incurred basis.

percentage of the loan paid off (*P*). The percentage of the principal amount of a loan paid off prior to full amortization over the projection period; the complement of the balance outstanding ($P = 1 - B$). P and B are loosely defined as percentages.

percentage rent. Rental income received in accordance with the terms of a percentage lease; typically derived from retail store tenants on the basis of a certain percentage of their retail sales.

perch. A unit of measure found in old deeds, usually accepted as being equivalent to 16½ feet.

percolation. The seepage of water through soil; the soil's ability to absorb water or other liquid, e.g., effluent from a septic system.

percolation test. A test conducted by hydraulic engineers and others to determine the percolation rate of soil; used by health departments to determine the amount of land area needed for an operational septic system.

perennial forb. A type of range vegetation in which perennial forbs predominate. True perennial forb vegetation is rare because forb cover is usually temporary and replaced by more permanent vegetation when the disturbing factor is removed.

performance bond. A bond that guarantees completion of an undertaking in accordance with an agreement, e.g, a bond supplied by a contractor who guarantees to complete a building or road, a bond given to a municipality by a subdivider who guarantees proper completion, road construction, and utility installations.

performance standards. Tests performed to determine whether a prospective land use will harmonize with the goals of applicable zoning requirements; e.g., in an industrial area, performance standards would include tests of smoke control, noise levels, off-street parking and loading, expansion room for future utilization, and similar factors.

perimeter. The total length of the periphery of a given area, e.g., the distance around the outside of a building.

perimeter heating. Any heating system in which registers are located along the outside dimensions of a room, especially under windows.

periodic growth. Growth that occurs in periodic increments, e.g., financial growth at compound interest; as distinguished from continuous growth, as observed in nature.

periodic payment factor. The direct reduction loan factor for a loan, given the interest rate and amortization term; can be monthly, quarterly, semiannual, or annual.

peripheral. Any external device that communicates with a computer, e.g., a printer, a disk drive.

permanent loan. A long-term loan used to finance the purchase and operation of a completed structure; as distinguished from temporary loans, e.g., land and construction loans.

permanent monument. In surveying, a boundary line marker in a fixed location that is not perishable.

permeability. Describes the behavior of water in soil. A soil permeated by water is friable, deep, and without dense or compact horizons that would restrict the free movement of water.

perpetual easement. An easement that lasts forever.

perpetuity. The state of being everlasting, e.g., an ordinary annuity that extends into the future without termination.

personal liability. The possibility of incurring a loss due to a legal claim.

personal property. Identifiable portable and tangible objects that are considered by the general public to be "personal," e.g., furnishings, artwork, antiques, gems and jewelry, collectibles, machinery and equipment; all property that is not classified as real estate. (USPAP, 1992 edition) Personal property includes movable items that are not permanently affixed to, and part of, the real estate.

personalty. *See* personal property.

pH. A measurement that describes the acidity or alkalinity of a substance; technically, the common logarithm of the reciprocal of the hydrogen ion concentration of a system expressed in grams per liter.

PHA. Public Health Administration.

phase one audit. *See* environmental property assessment (EPRA).

phase soil. The part of a soil unit or soil type that exhibits minor variations from the characteristics normal for the soil type; variations are mainly in external characteristics, e.g., relief, stoniness, accelerated erosion, and may be of great importance.

photogrammetry. The science, art, and technological skill involved in obtaining reliable measurements and quantitative information from photographs.

physical age-life method. A method of estimating incurable physical deterioration in which the ratio between the actual age of a building component and its estimated total physical life is applied to the current reproduction or replacement cost of each incurable component after the cost to cure curable physical items has been estimated. Items of incurable physical deterioration are classified as either short- or long-lived, and the physical age-life ratio is applied separately to each category. The physical age-life method should be used with short-lived items and can be used with long-lived items. Total physical age estimates of long-lived components may be difficult to derive from the market. The physical age-life method assumes that deterioration occurs at a constant, average, annual rate over the estimated physical life of the improvements.

physical deterioration. An element of accrued depreciation. *See also* curable physical deterioration; incurable physical deterioration.

physical life. The total period a building lasts or is expected to last as opposed to its economic life.

physical possession. The state or condition of being in occupancy.

picture window. A large window, usually a fixed pane of plate or insulating glass; sometimes divided into small panes; designed to command an interesting view or to allow more light into the interior of the building.

pier

1. A quay or wharf that extends seaward at an angle from the shore; provides a landing place on each side for vessels to receive and discharge passengers and cargo.
2. A square column.
3. A support placed where two abutting bridge spans meet.

pierhead line. *See* structure limit line.

piggy back

1. A method of transportation whereby truck trailers are carried on trains or cars are carried on trucks.
2. In staple application to gypsum wallboard, a second staple is driven directly on top of the first. The staple will spread to create a firm bond between the wallboard and the tile. (R.S. Means)

pig parlor. A farm building designed and used for the breeding and raising of hogs and swine.

pilaster. A rectangular, upright, architectural member; serves as a pier, but architecturally treated as a column.

pile. A wood timber; a round or square tube of solid or hollow steel that is filled with concrete and driven into the ground to support the foundation of a building, pier, or other structure.

pilings. Columns that extend below ground to bear the weight of a structure when the surface soil cannot; may extend down to bearing soil or support the load by skin friction; e.g., sheet piling is used to form bulkheads or retaining walls and to support docks or piers.

pinon-juniper. A type of range vegetation that includes pinon, juniper, and digger pine.

pipe chase. A vertical space in a building reserved for vertical runs of pipe. (R.S. Means)

pipeline. A conduit of connecting pipes used to transmit liquids or gases.

pipeline easement. The right to construct, operate, and maintain a pipeline over the lands of others within prescribed geographical limits. The language of the easement determines the extent of the rights granted.

piping. A system of pipes that carry water and occasionally other fluids under pressure and waste pipes that depend on the flow of gravity.

piscary. The right to fish in another person's waters; one of the burdens, or servitudes, that may be attached to land as a result of this right.

pitch. The slope or incline of a roof, expressed in inches of rise per foot of length or as the ratio of the rise to the span.

pits, ponds, or lagoons. Man-made or natural depressions in a ground surface that are likely to hold liquids or sludge containing hazardous substances or petroleum products. The likelihood of such liquids or sludge being present is determined by evidence of factors associated with the pit, pond or lagoon, including, but not limited to, discolored water, distressed vegetation or the presence of an obvious waste water discharge. (ASTM)

pivot sprinkler. An automatic irrigation system in which a mechanically moved main line rotates around a pivot point.

plaintiff. The party that initiates a claim or action against another party. (R.S. Means)

PLAM. *See* price level-adjusted mortgage.

plan. A horizontal cross section of any level of a structure that shows room arrangement and the location of doors, windows, etc.; may also show the site and objects surrounding the building.

plank. A piece of unfinished lumber two to four inches thick and at least eight inches wide.

plank-and-beam framing. A type of frame construction in which heavier structural members are spaced farther apart than in other framing systems, and supporting posts, roof beams, and the roof deck are left exposed as part of the interior decor.

planned unit development (PUD). A type of residential, commercial, and/or industrial land development in which buildings are clustered or set on lots that are smaller than usual, and large, open, park-like areas are included within the development. Individual properties are owned in fee with joint ownership of open areas or, if local law requires, open areas are deeded to the city.

planning district. A geographical area that is planned using a system of zones in which each district is delineated according to population density or other criteria.

planning grid. A graph-like paper with the lines at right angles or other selected angles to each other, used by architects or engineers in modular planning. (R.S. Means)

plan room. A service provided by construction industry organizations or service companies, sometimes available to interested constructors, materialmen, vendors and manufacturers. Plan rooms provide access to contract documents for projects currently in the process of receiving competitive or negotiated bids. (R.S. Means)

plans and specifications. Working papers used in construction. Plans include all drawings pertaining to the property under consideration, e.g., building drawings, mechanical drawings, electrical drawings. Specifications are written instructions to the builder that contain information pertaining to dimensions, materials, workmanship, style, fabrication, colors, and finishes; they supplement the working drawings.

plant. In real estate, land, buildings, machinery, equipment, furniture, etc.; a portion of an assembled property, e.g., a power plant; the fixed property of an enterprise, e.g., an educational plant.

plantation. In forestry, an area planted to forest seedlings or seeded by broadcast methods; also called *tree farm*.

planting easement. The right to use and control an area of land to establish and maintain plant growth for safety and beautification.

plaster. A mixture of lime, sand, and water that is used to finish walls and ceilings.

plaster ground. A narrow strip of wood or metal placed around openings and the perimeter of a room; may be at the base, at chair rail height, or at picture mold height; used as a nailing strip for trim and as a plane for plastering.

plaster of paris. Calcined gypsum, i.e., gypsum that has been converted into a fine, white powder by heat.

plat
1. A plan, map, or chart of a city, town, section, or subdivision indicating the location and boundaries of individual properties.
2. A map or sketch of an individual property that shows property lines and may include features such as soils, building locations, vegetation, and topography.

plat book. A record showing the location, size, and owner of each plot of land in a stated area.

plate. A horizontal structural member that is laid across the top of a row of studs to serve as a frame for interior partitions and exterior walls;

provides lateral rigidity for the wall by tying the studs together; serves as support for upper-story floor joists and as lower support for rafters; also called *top plate*.

plate glass. A high-quality glass that has been ground and polished on both sides.

pledged account mortgage (PAM). A mortgage arrangement in which the borrower deposits a sum of money into a special savings account to cover any interest on the mortgage that is not covered by the monthly payment; a special type of adjustable-rate mortgage or graduated-payment mortgage in which no negative amortization occurs.

plenum
1. The space between the finished or suspended ceiling and the unfinished ceiling.
2. The chamber in a warm-air furnace where air is heated before the ducts carry it to the registers.

plex. A dwelling that is similar to a townhouse, but has many characteristics of single-family detached housing; may or may not occupy its own structure from ground to roof. A plex has an outside entrance, is separated from other structures by open space, and is designed for occupancy by one or more families. A structure designed for occupancy by two families is a duplex; for three, a triplex; for four, a fourplex; and so on. The prefix identifies the number of dwelling units per building. (ULI)

plinth. A square block of trim material placed upright at the floor line on either side of the bottom of a door opening, or at the base of a column; meets the lower end of the door casing and the end of the baseboard; also called *plinth box*.

plot plan. A plan showing the layout of improvements on a property site or plot; usually includes location, dimensions, parking areas, landscaping, and other features.

plottage. The increment of value created when two or more sites are combined to produce greater utility. *See also* assemblage.

plumb bob. A cone-shaped metal weight, hung from a string, used to establish a vertical line or as a sighting reference to a surveyor's transit. (R.S. Means)

plumbing fixture. A receptacle in a plumbing system, other than a trap, in which water or wastes are collected or retained for use and ultimately discharged to drainage. (R.S. Means)

plumbing system. Arrangements of pipes, fixtures, fittings, valves, and traps in a building which supply water and remove liquid-borne wastes, including storm water. (R.S. Means)

plumb level. A level that is set in a horizontal position by placing it at a right angle to a plumb line. (R.S. Means)

ply. Denotes the number of thicknesses or layers in a material, e.g., three-ply; used for roofing felt, veneers, etc.

plywood. An assembled wood product constructed of three or more layers of veneer laid with the grain of adjoining plies at right angles and joined with glue; usually an odd number of plies is used for balanced construction.

PMA. Production and Marketing Administration.

PMI. *See* private mortgage insurance.

PMM. *See* purchase-money mortgage.

PMSA. *See* primary metropolitan statistical area.

pneumatic structure. A fabric envelope supported by an internal air pressure slightly above atmospheric pressure. The pressure is provided by a series of fans. (R.S. Means)

POB. *See* point of beginning.

podzol. A zonal group of soils with an organic mat and a thin layer of organic mineral over a gray leached layer that rests on an alluvial dark

brown horizon; developed under a coniferous or mixed forest, or under vegetation in a temperate-to-cold, moist climate.

point
1. A tooth for a saw.
2. A mason's tool. (R.S. Means)
3. *See also* points.

point estimate. A final value indication reported as a single dollar amount. A point estimate is typically regarded as the most probable number, not the only possible number, and is often required for revenue and compensation purposes.

pointing. The process of removing deteriorated mortar from masonry and replacing it with new mortar; also, the final patching, filling, or finishing of mortar joints in new masonry work.

point of beginning (POB). A survey reference point that is tied into adjoining surveys. In a metes and bounds description, courses that connect monuments or points are generally described from this point.

point of decreasing returns. The point at which additional expenditures of the agents in production no longer yield a return commensurate with the original expenditure.

points. A percentage of the loan amount that a lender charges a borrower for making a loan; may represent a payment for services rendered in issuing a loan or additional interest to the lender payable in advance; also called *loan fee.*

pole construction. A construction method in which poles or timbers are installed at intervals for structural support and no continuous foundations are used; frequently used in farm outbuildings.

pole line easement. An easement for the construction, maintenance, and operation of a pole line, usually for the transmission of electric power.

police power. The right of government under which property is regulated to protect public safety, health, morals, and general welfare.

pollution. The fouling of air, water, or soil by the introduction of injurious or corrupting elements.

ponding
1. The process of flooding the surface of a concrete slab by using temporary dams around the perimeter in order to satisfactorily cure the concrete.
2. The accumulation of water at low points in a roof. The low points may be produced or increased by structural deflection. (R.S. Means)

porosity. The ratio, usually expressed as a percentage, of the volume of voids in a material to the total volume of the material, including the voids. (R.S. Means)

port authority. A commission or other agency with the power to coordinate land, air, and water traffic in and around a port.

porte cochere. A roof that extends from a building's entrance over an adjacent driveway to shelter people getting in or out of vehicles.

portico. A roof supported by columns; either part of a building or standing alone.

possessory interest. The right to the occupancy and use of any benefit in a transferred property, granted under lease, permit, license, concession, or another contract.

possible capacity. The maximum number of vehicles that can pass a given point on a lane or roadway in one hour under prevailing roadway and traffic conditions.

post. A vertical, structural member that carries stresses in compression; used where strength in bending is not required.

post-and-beam framing. A type of framing in which beams are spaced up to eight feet apart and supported on posts and exterior walls; framing members are much larger and heavier than those used in other framing systems.

posterior distribution. In Bayesian analysis, a decision-making distribution that represents the decision maker's uncertainty concerning the unknown value of the population mean after considering sample evidence. *See also* prior distribution.

posts and timbers. Lumber of square or approximately square cross section, five by five inches and larger; graded primarily for use as posts or columns carrying longitudinal load, but adapted for other uses where strength in bending is not important; also called *posts and pier.*

poststressed concrete. Concrete that has been strengthened by placing reinforcing cables in metal sheaths in the wet concrete. The cables are stressed after the concrete sets and the sheathing is filled with grout. After the grout sets, the cables are released and the stress is transmitted to the concrete.

posttensioned concrete. Concrete that has the reinforcing tendons tensioned after the concrete has set. (R.S. Means)

potential gross income (*PGI*). The total income attributable to real property at full occupancy before vacancy and operating expenses are deducted.

potential gross income multiplier (*PGIM*). The ratio between the sale price of a property and its potential gross income $(PGIM = V/PGI)$.

power center. A large community shopping center with more than 250,000 square feet of space anchored by three or more tenants that occupy 60% to 90% of the space; the number of specialty stores is kept to a minimum. *See also* shopping center

power feed wiring. The main electric power line that enters a building from a utility or a private source; supplies electric power to machinery and equipment through main bus ducts or heavy wiring enclosed in conduits; does not include branch feed lines or controls from the main line to machinery.

power of attorney. A legal instrument in which a person authorizes another to act as his or her attorney or agent.

power plant. A plant within a structure or building that generates power from coal, gas, oil, or water for its own use or for commercial distribution to others; includes engines, dynamos, etc. *See also* hydroelectric plant; water power plant.

powers of government. The four powers of government to which all estates in real property are subject, i.e., taxation, eminent domain, police power, escheat. The government also controls overflight.

PPS. Personal Property Specialist, a designation conferred by the International Association of Assessing Officers (IAAO).

practical capacity. The maximum number of vehicles that can pass a given point on a roadway in one hour without creating undue traffic density and unreasonable delay, hazards, or driving restrictions.

prairie. An extensive tract of level or rolling land that is originally treeless, grass-covered, and characterized by a deep, fertile soil.

Prairie School. A style of architecture prominent in the late 19th and early 20th centuries that emphasized strong horizontal and rectangular elements, unity between the exterior structure and interior design, and simplicity; employed natural materials to create harmony between structures and their surroundings. Among the leaders of the Prairie School were Frank Lloyd Wright, George Grant Elmslie, and George Washington Maher.

prairie soils. A zonal group of soils with a dark brown or grayish brown surface horizon that grades through brown soil to lighter-colored parent material at two to five feet; develops under tall grasses in a temperate, relatively humid climate; does not include all dark-colored soils of treeless plains, only

those in which carbonates are not concentrated in any part of the profile.

preaction sprinkling system. A dry pipe sprinkler system in which water is supplied to the piping when a smoke or heat detector is activated. (R.S. Means)

precast
1. A concrete member that is cast and cured in other than its final position.
2. The process of placing and finishing precast concrete. (R.S. Means)

precast concrete. Concrete structural components that are not poured in place, but are cast separately on site or at another location.

precise level. An instrument similar to an ordinary surveyor's level but capable of finer readings and including a prism arrangement that permits simultaneous observation of the rod and leveling bubble. (R.S. Means)

pre-engineered building. A building constructed of predesigned, manufactured, and assembled units, e.g., wall, framing, floor, and roof panels that are erected at the construction site.

prefabricated construction. A construction method that uses standard prefabricated units that are assembled at a site along with site fabrication of some minor parts. (R.S. Means)

prefabricated house. A dwelling that is partially constructed in a factory and transported to the site for installation and final assembly.

prefabricated masonry panel. A wall panel of masonry units constructed at an assembly site and moved to a job site for erection. (R.S. Means)

prefabrication. The manufacture and assemblage of construction materials and parts into component structural units, e.g., wall, floor, and roof panels, which are later erected at the construction site.

preferential assessment. An assessment system in which farmland is taxed at the value of its productive capacity rather than its market value; the land must meet certain conditions to get reduced taxes, e.g., it must be in agricultural use for a specified number of years.

preferred stock. A share of ownership that has prior claim on a company's earnings, before dividends on the common stock may be paid, as well as prior claim on the company's assets in the event of liquidation.

prefinished. Lumber, plywood, molding, or other wood products with a finish coating of paint, stain, vinyl, or other material applied before it is taken to the job site. (R.S. Means)

preframed. A construction term for wall, floor, or roof components assembled at a factory. (R.S. Means)

preliminary review. An appraisal review that considers the thoroughness of the appraisal and the report's adherence to performance requirements relating to format, methodology, consistency, and reasonableness.

prepaid interest. Interest that is paid in one period but not due until a future period under the terms of the debt obligation; in accrual accounting, prepaid interest is expended as incurred.

prepayment meter. A coin-operated water or gas meter that passes a fixed amount of fluid for each coin. (R.S. Means)

prepayment penalty. An extra charge incurred by a borrower who pays a mortgage or other debt instrument before its due date; provided for in the debt instrument and usually expressed as a percentage of the loan; may be limited or prohibited in some states.

prepayment privilege. A clause in a mortgage that allows the mortgagor to pay part or all of the mortgage debt before it becomes due.

preposttensioning. A method of fabricating prestressed concrete in which some of the tendons are pretensioned and a portion of the tendons are posttensioned. (R.S. Means)

prequalification of bidders. The investigation and subsequent approval of prospective bidders' qualifications, experience, availability, and capability regarding a project. (R.S. Means)

prescription. Legal title obtained by long possession. Occupancy for a period prescribed by the code of civil procedure bars any action for the recovery of the property and gives title by prescription.

prescriptive easement. *See* easement by prescription.

present operator. Refers to individual cropping the land, either through direct operation or tenant farming.

present value (*PV*). The value of a future payment or series of future payments discounted to the current date or to time period zero.

present worth (*PW*). *See* present value (*PV*).

present worth of $1 (1/*S*ⁿ). A compound interest factor that indicates how much $1 due in the future is worth today. The present worth of $1 factor is one of the six functions of a dollar found in standard financial tables; also called *present value of $1*.

present worth of $1 per period (*aₙ*). A compound interest factor that in-

dicates how much $1 paid periodically is worth today. The present worth of $1 per period factor is one of the six functions of a dollar found in standard financial tables; also called *present value of $1 per period* or *ordinary level annuity factor*.

preservation easement. A restriction that prohibits certain physical changes in an historic property; usually based on the property's condition at the time the easement was acquired or immediately after proposed restoration of the property.

prestressed concrete. Concrete that has been strengthened by stressing the reinforcements in the concrete before it sets and releasing them after the concrete has hardened.

prestressing
1. To place a hardened concrete member or an assembly of units in a state of compression prior to application of service loads.
2. The stress developed by prestressing, such as by pretensioning or posttensioning. (R.S. Means)

pre-tax cash flow (*PTCF*). The portion of net operating income that remains after total mortgage debt service is paid but before ordinary income tax on operations is deducted; also called *before-tax cash flow* or *equity dividend*.

pretensioned concrete. Concrete which has its reinforcing tendons stressed before the concrete is placed. Tension on the tendons is then released to provide load transfer where concrete has achieved strength. (R.S. Means)

price. The amount a particular purchaser agrees to pay and a particular seller agrees to accept under the circumstances surrounding their transaction.

price level. The average of the prices, usually wholesale prices, of selected, representative commodities at a stated time; usually expressed as an index number. *See also* Consumer Price Index.

price level-adjusted mortgage (PLAM). A mortgage in which the interest rate remains fixed, but the outstanding balance is adjusted according to price level changes. The interest rate on a PLAM is a real interest rate with no inflation premium. On each annual anniversary of the loan, the outstanding balance is adjusted for inflation and monthly payments are recomputed based on the new balance.

price supports. Various governmental programs designed to keep market prices from falling below a certain minimum level; e.g., agriculture is supported by outright subsidies or the purchase of crops at prices higher than market prices.

pricing and rent projection study. An analysis conducted to determine sales and marketing strategies for real estate projects.

primary easement. An easement to which a secondary easement is attached, e.g., an easement in a sewer pipe to which a secondary easement of access is attached for the purpose of cleaning out and repairing the sewer pipe. *See also* secondary easement.

primary metropolitan statistical area (PMSA). An area of more than one million people that consists of a large, urbanized county or a cluster of counties with very strong internal economic and social links; designated under standards established in 1980 by the Federal Committee of MSAs. *See also* consolidated metropolitan statistical area (CMSA); metropolitan statistical area (MSA).

primary soil. A soil formed in place by the weathering of underlying rock and minerals.

primary subcontractor. Subcontractors who may perform major portions of the work in a construction project, such as installation of plumbing, mechanical, or electrical systems. They may have a contract directly with the owner. (R.S. Means)

primary trade area. The geographic area around a retail facility from which approximately 60% to 70% of the facility's customers are drawn; the geographic radius and driving time identified with the primary trading area vary with the type of facility. *See also* trade area.

prime bid. A bid presented directly to the owner or his agent, rather than a subcontractor's bid to a general contractor. (R.S. Means)

prime contract. An agreement formed between the owner and the contractor for a major portion of the work on a construction contract. (R.S. Means)

prime cost. The direct cost of labor and materials in any project.

prime rate. The interest rate that a commercial bank charges for short-term loans to borrowers with high credit ratings.

principal. A capital sum invested; a payment that represents partial or full repayment of the capital loaned or invested, as distinguished from the payment of interest; the unrecovered capital remaining in a loan or investment.

principal meridians. In land surveying, major north-south lines established as general reference points. There are about 25 principal meridians in the 48 contiguous states of the United States.

principal risk. The risk that principal or a capital investment will be worth less (especially as a reversion) than anticipated or forecast.

principle of diminishing marginal productivity. *See* law of decreasing returns.

prior appropriation. A doctrine under which water is owned by the state and granted for beneficial use through appropriation; appropriative surface water rights are acquired by use and the performance of certain legal requirements as directed by the state, the county, or an irrigation district. The owner of a water right may be entitled to surface water not contiguous to the land on which it is used.

prior distribution. In Bayesian analysis, a decision-making distribution that represents the decision maker's uncertainty about the unknown value of the population mean before a sample of the population is taken. *See also* posterior distribution.

private alley. A narrow path that is not open to public use; its use is legally confined to a certain property owner or owners.

private mortgage insurance (PMI). Insurance provided by a private mortgage lender to protect against loss caused by a borrower's default on a residential or commercial mortgage loan.

private offering. An offering that is assumed to be exempt from securities registration. Those seeking a private offering exemption under federal securities law may follow Regulation D of the Securities Act of 1933 or may continue to claim the private offering exemption under judicial and administrative interpretations of Section 4(2) of the same act.

private placement. An exempt placement of securities with an investor, usually an institution, under circumstances that do not constitute a private offering. *See also* private offering.

private road. A road on private property that is maintained and kept open for use by the owner, the tenant(s), or their licensees, invitees, or guests; not open to the general public.

private sector. The portion of the economy that produces goods and services and is distinguished from the governmental sector.

private stairway. A stairway intended to serve only one tenant. (R.S. Means)

private waters. Waters on land that is privately owned; subject to private control only; a stream that runs in a bed to which a riparian owner holds title.

private way of necessity. An appurtenant easement that is granted to meet practical needs, e.g., to allow ingress and egress from a parcel of land that is legally landlocked.

probability (*P*). The relative likelihood that a specified event will occur. *See also* risk; uncertainty.

probability analysis. The assessment of probability using quantitative methods. *See also* risk analysis; utility functions.

probability range. The confidence level associated with a specific value estimate or set of value estimates.

proceeds of resale. The net difference between the transaction price and the selling expenses of a property; refers to the property's reversion.

processor. The hardware that performs the actual arithmetic and logical operations of the computer system using programs and data stored in the memory.

process-related equipment and mechanical systems. Fixed building equipment and mechanical systems needed to carry out an industrial process, e.g., air hoses, process piping, craneways, bus ducts, industrial wiring, heavy electrical cables, freezer equipment.

producer. Provider of building materials or equipment such as a processor, manufacturer, or equipment rental/sales firm. (R.S. Means)

product disaggregation. *See* disaggregation.

production. *See* agents in production.

productivity
1. The capacity of a soil to produce crops in the existing environment under a specified system of management.
2. The amount of goods produced by labor, or other agents in production, per unit of time.
3. The net value of the services provided per unit of space. *See also* econometrics.
4. The income or benefits a property is capable of providing, which depend on the physical and locational attributes of the site and improvements as well as the legal entitlements and regulatory constraints imposed by local, state, and federal governments. *See also* attributes.

productivity rating. The effect of surface soil texture, subsoil characteristics, topography, climate, drainage, soil, organic matter, and fertility on the productive capacity of a soil; used to determine the most suitable land use and cropping patterns for a property and to estimate yields and potential income.

profile
1. A drawing showing a vertical section of ground, usually taken along the center line of a highway or other construction project.
2. A template used for shaping plaster.
3. A guide used in masonry work.
4. A British term for batter board. (R.S. Means)

profit
1. The amount by which the proceeds of a transaction exceed its cost.
2. In theoretical economics, the residual share of the product of an enterprise that accrues to the entrepreneur after paying interest for capital, rent for land, and wages for labor and management. *See also* entrepreneurial profit.
3. In accounting, an increase in wealth that results from the operation of an enterprise. Gross profit usually is the selling price minus cost; items such as selling and operating expenses are deducted from gross profit to indicate net profit. *See also* operating profit.

profitability index (*PI*). The present value of anticipated investment returns (benefits) divided by the present value of the capital outlay (cost); also called *benefit/cost ratio*.

profit and loss statement. *See* operating statement.

profit sharing. Provisions in special agreements or contracts for construction where the contractor, as an incentive to save money for the owner, is paid, in addition to the final contract sum, some percentage of any net savings he may achieve if he is able to deliver the finished project to the owner's satisfaction at a total cost below a specified limiting amount. (R.S. Means)

pro forma. A financial balance sheet or income statement for a business prepared by an accountant; in appraisal, a reconstructed operating statement used to project gross income, operating expenses, and net operating income for a future period based on specified assumptions; also called *pro forma statement*. *See also* reconstructed operating statement.

pro forma invoice. An invoice sent before the order has been shipped in order to obtain payment before shipment. (R.S. Means)

progress billing. A billing system in which a contractor sends bills generally based on stages of completion, as specified in the contract.

progression. In appraisal, the concept that the value of an inferior property is enhanced by its association with better properties of the same type. *See also* regression.

progressive tax. A tax that increases according to the income or wealth of the taxpayer. *See also* regressive tax.

project certificate for payment. A statement to the owner confirming the amounts due individual contractors. Issued by the design professional where multiple contractors have separate direct agreements with the owner. (R.S. Means)

project cost(s)
1. The total cost of a project, including professional compensation, land costs, construction costs, costs for furnishings and equipment, financing, and other charges.
2. Costs clearly associated with the acquisition, development, and construction of a real estate project. (FASB)

project enhancement. The increase in a property's market value in anticipation of a public project requiring condemnation action.

projection. A process in which past and contemporaneous experience is extrapolated into the future using a mechanical formula; may be a simple, straight-line projection or one based on a complex formula; presumes that the conditions and rates of change of the past and present will continue in the future.

projection period. A presumed period of ownership; a period of time over which expected net operating income is projected for purposes of analysis and valuation.

project profit. The difference between the total cost of a project and its sale price or market value. As used by some appraisers, the term *project profit* includes both entrepreneurial profit and developer's fee. *See also* developer's fee; entrepreneurial profit.

promissory note. A legal instrument, agreement or contract made between a lender and a borrower by which the lender conveys to the borrower a sum or other consideration known as principal for which the borrower promises repayment of the principal plus interest under conditions set forth in the agreement. (R.S. Means)

proper stocking. Placing a number of animals in a specific area to make appropriate use of the forage over a planned grazing period; will lead to proper grazing.

property. *See* personal property; real property.

property brief. A description of a property for sale complete with details and pictures in a form suitable for presentation to a prospective buyer.

property line. The boundary between two parcels of land or between a property and a traveled way, e.g., a street or alley.

property management. The process of maintaining and creating value in real property consistent with the owner's objectives through the efficient balance of tenant and owner relations, financial budgeting and expense control, risk management and all other operational aspects of the property in compliance with the highest standards of professional ethics. (BOMA)

property model. A formula developed to project the benefit pattern of a given property by considering the periodic income stream and the reversion in one operation. Property models describe properties with level income and no change in value, properties with level income and changing value, properties with income and value changing by fixed amounts per period (straight-line), properties with income and value changing at a constant ratio (exponential-curve), and properties with income and value changing in a variable or irregular pattern.

property residual technique. A capitalization technique in which the net operating income is attributed to the property as a whole, not to separate land and building components. In yield capitalization, the present value of the income stream is computed and added to the present value of the reversion at the assumed termination of the investment.

property tax. A tax levied on real or personal property.

property tax base. The assessed value of all property within a designated area, e.g., an assessment or tax district.

property yield. The dollar return on the entire real property from all sources, i.e., the annual net operating income including any gain or loss in the original property investment at termination.

property yield rate (Y_o). *See* overall yield rate (Y_o).

proposed construction. A building project of proven feasibility which has not yet been initiated. *See also* new construction.

proprietary lease. A type of lease given to tenant-shareholders in a cooperative apartment corporation. In such a venture, the tenant purchases a specific number of shares of stock to obtain possession of an apartment and makes monthly payments to the corporation to cover his or her pro rata share of operating expenses and debt service.

proprietary specification. A specification that describes a product, material, assembly, or piece of equipment by trade name and/or by naming the manufacturer or manufacturers who may produce products acceptable to the owner or design professional. (R.S. Means)

pro rata share

1. A share of a fund or deposit that is divided or distributed proportionately.

2. A share of a burden or obligation that is divided proportionately; e.g., a tenant in a multitenant building or development may be required to pay a pro rata share of the building's operating expenses based on the number of square feet the tenant occupies. In a shopping center, the tenant's share of operating costs is often stated as a fraction, with the gross leasable area of the tenant's premises as the numerator and the gross leasable area or gross leased area of the entire shopping center as the denominator.

3. The share of a trade area that a retail facility is likely to capture; assumes that capture is a function of property size as a proportion of the overall inventory of competitive space in the trade area, i.e., that the facility cap-

tures a "fair share" of the trade area.

prorates. Expenses that are prorated in escrow between the buyer and the seller based on the closing date, e.g., property taxes, interest.

proscenium. The portion of a stage that is in front of the curtain; sometimes includes the curtain and the framework that supports it; an arch or opening that separates the stage from the auditorium.

prospective value estimate. A forecast of the value expected at a specified future date. A prospective value estimate is most frequently sought in connection with real estate projects that are proposed, under construction, or under conversion to a new use, or those that have not achieved sellout or a stabilized level of long-term occupancy at the time the appraisal report is written. *See also* date of value estimate; value as is.

prospectus. *See* offering circular.

provider. *See* course provider.

provisional licensure. Authorization to engage in the practice of a profession to a specified or limited extent, usually for a specified or limited duration of time. *See also* transitional licensure.

proximate cause. The cause of an injury or of damages which, in natural and continuous sequence, unbroken by any legally recognized intervening cause, produces the injury, and without which the result would not have occurred. Existence of proximate cause involves both 1) causation in fact, i.e., that the wrongdoer actually produced an injury or damages, and 2) a public policy determination that the wrongdoer should be held responsible. (R.S. Means)

proximity damage. An element of severance damages that is caused by the remainder's proximity to the improvement being constructed, e.g., a highway; may also arise from proximity to an objectionable characteristic of a site or improvement, e.g., dirt, dust, noise, vibration.

pruning. The selective cutting or removal of branches or twigs from a tree, shrub, or vine.

public accommodation. Under the Americans with Disabilities Act (ADA) of 1990 [Section 301 (7)], any of twelve categories of private facilities whose operations may affect commerce. The intent of the ADA legislation is to afford people with disabilities equal access to an array of establishments that are readily available to people without disabilities. *See also* Americans with Disabilities Act (ADA) of 1990.

public domain land. Land owned by the federal government.

public facilities. Facilities that are owned by the public or a municipality and are operated for the public's benefit. (ULI)

public good. An economic good that is used or enjoyed collectively and is often furnished by government, e.g., public education, parks, museums; as distinguished from a free good.

public housing. Rental projects that are owned and managed by state or local government agencies and made available to low- and middle-income tenants at reduced rates. *See also* Section 8 housing.

Public Housing Administration. A unit of the Department of Housing and Urban Development that administers legislation providing loans and subsidies to local housing authorities to encourage the creation of low-rental dwelling units.

public lands. Land owned by the government; public domain. In the United States, the federal government holds title to vast tracts, including Indian reservations, national parks and forests, and grazing lands.

public land system. A system in which a parcel of land is described by reference to its position in the public land survey, e.g., the NE1/4 of the SW1/4 of Section 4, in Township 5 South, Range 7 West, Mt. Diablo

Base and Meridian. *See also* government survey system.

public record. *See* recording.

public sewer. A common sewer controlled completely by a public authority. (R.S. Means)

public space
1. An area within a building to which the public has free access, such as a foyer or lobby.
2. An area or piece of land legally designated for public use. (R.S. Means)

public system. A water or sewer system owned and operated by a governmental authority or by a utility company that is controlled by a government authority. (R.S. Means)

public utility property. A property that produces commodities or services for general community consumption; usually a monopoly or quasi-monopoly with or without benefit of franchise; ordinarily subject to some form of government regulation and control.

public way. A street, alley, or other parcel of land open to the outside air and leading to a public street. A public way is deeded or otherwise permanently appropriated for public use. A minimum width is usually specified by code. (R.S. Means)

PUD. *See* planned unit development.

pulpwood. A forest product used in the pulp and paper industry.

punch list. A list of items within a project, prepared by the owner or his representative, and confirmed by the contractor, which remain to be replaced or completed in accordance with the requirements of the contract for construction at the time of substantial completion. (R.S. Means)

punitive damages. Damages awarded by a judge to a plaintiff not merely to compensate the plaintiff for losses incurred, but to punish the defendant for wrongful conduct and to use the plight of the defendant as an example to potential wrongdoers. (R.S. Means)

purchase and leaseback. *See* sale-leaseback.

purchase and sale agreement. The written contract for the sale of real property. The statute of frauds requires that a contract for the sale of real property must be in writing. (R.S. Means)

purchase money. Money that is paid for property.

purchase-money mortgage (PMM). A mortgage that is given by a purchaser to a seller in lieu of cash as partial payment for the purchase of real property; if the purchaser defaults on a payment, the seller may foreclose. A PMM is an alternative to an institutional loan.

purchase option. *See* option.

purchasing power. The ability and willingness to pay for an economic good; contingent upon disposable income. *See also* effective demand; effective purchasing power.

purchasing power risk. The risk that future dollars received will have less purchasing power than present dollars as a result of inflation. This risk is rarely accounted for in specific terms in appraisal analysis because it is assumed that income receipts and expenses will generally change proportionately and in the same direction.

purlins. Horizontal structural members that support roof rafters or a roof deck.

purpose of an appraisal. The stated reason for an appraisal assignment, i.e., to estimate the defined value of any real property interest or to conduct an evaluation study (consulting assignment) pertaining to real property decisions.

pylon. A gateway; a marking post or tower in an airport; a post or marker that guides pilots over a prescribed course of flight.

pyramid roof. A roof with four sides and four ridges that resembles a pyramid; usually comes to a point in the center.

pyramid zoning. A system of zoning in which the uses permitted in more restrictive zones are permitted in less restrictive zones as well.

Q

quadratic mean. *See* standard deviation.

qualitative techniques. Techniques used to derive qualitative adjustments to comparable sale prices in the sales comparison approach. *See also* ranking analysis; relative comparison analysis.

quality assurance. A system of procedures for selecting the levels of quality required for a project or portion thereof in order to perform the functions intended, and for assuring that these levels are obtained. (R.S. Means)

quality and condition survey. An analysis of the quality and condition of building components which distinguishes among deferred maintenance items (those in need of immediate repair), short-lived items (those that must be repaired or replaced in the future), and items that are expected to last for the remaining economic life of the building.

quality control. A system of procedures and standards by which a constructor, product manufacturer, material processor, or the like monitors the properties of the finished work. (R.S. Means)

quantitative techniques. Techniques used to derive quantitative adjustments to comparable sale prices in the sales comparison approach. *See also* graphic analysis; paired data analysis; statistical analysis; trend analysis.

quantity overrun/underrun. The difference between estimated quantities and the actual quantities in the completed work. (R.S. Means)

quantity survey method. A cost-estimating method in which the quantity and quality of all materials used and all categories of labor required are estimated and unit cost figures are applied to arrive at a total cost estimate for labor and materials.

quarry tile. A hard-burned, unglazed ceramic tile.

quarter. In the government survey system, one-fourth of a section of land containing 640 acres, or 160 acres of land.

quarter round. A molding in the shape of a quarter of a circle.

quartile. One of the items that divide a frequency distribution into four equal groups; there are three quartile points and the second is the median.

quay. A landing place that is built parallel to navigable water and used in loading and unloading vessels.

queen post. One of two vertical members in a triangular truss, which are equidistant from the apex.

question of fact. Questions arising from evidence given in court that involve contention or dispute and must be decided by jury; based on absolute reality, i.e., events, actions, or conditions that actually occurred or physical objects or appearances that actually existed, not on mere supposition or opinion.

question of law. Questions arising from evidence given in court that deal with the letter of the law and must be determined by the court; based on interpretation of legal principles, conceived law, and established rules of duty.

quiet title. A legal action that establishes title to real property.

quilt insulation. A thermal barrier with paper faces that are stitched or woven. (R.S. Means)

quitclaim deed. A form of conveyance in which any interest the grantor possesses in the property described in the deed is conveyed to the grantee without warranty of title. *See also* deed.

quotient. The answer or result obtained by dividing one number by another.

R

rabbet. A groove cut on the edge or end of a board or other timber to receive the edge of another board with a similar cut.

raceway. A slim, metal conduit that carries electric or telephone wires with convenience outlets at frequent intervals; a plug-in strip.

radial corridor theory. *See* axial theory; radial plan.

radial highway. A traffic artery that runs from an urban center to less densely developed suburban or rural areas.

radial plan. A system of roads radiating from a city center with urban accretions along the way; results from natural, uncontrolled growth; may lead to good planning if combined with concentric, or ring, roads to form a spider-web plan or a star-shaped plan with green wedges between urban areas. *See also* axial theory.

radiant heating. A type of steam, electric, or hot water heat that uses pipes concealed in floors, ceilings, or walls; also called *concealed heating.*

radiant heating system. A system in which floors or other surfaces are warmed by hot air or, more commonly, hot water; pipes are embedded in the floor slab or in the side walls, and the air or water is distributed by forced circulation. Heating temperatures are generally lower.

radiation. The emission of heat or light rays; applied in heating systems through the use of radiators, convectors, etc.

radiator. An exposed fixture that heats by a combination of radiation and convection, e.g., the common, cast-iron radiator; distinguished from convectors, which are finned heating elements concealed in walls or cabinets, e.g., baseboard heating.

radon. A colorless, odorless, naturally occurring, inert gaseous element formed by the decay of radium atoms in the ground. Although seepage of radioactive radon into the atmosphere is harmless, the build-up of radon in an enclosed area such as a drain or basement may be hazardous. Brokers are obligated to disclose whether a property has radon seepage and advise clients to contact state environmental agencies to determine whether existing radon levels are safe.

rafter. Structural members, e.g., joists, beams, that shape and support the roof deck or sheathing and the roof covering.

raft foundation. *See* floating foundation.

rail. The horizontal piece in a door, window sash, or panel; the top, horizontal member of a balustrade. *See also* stile.

railroad grade crossing. The intersection of a traffic artery and a railroad at the same grade elevation.

railroad siding agreement. A contract between a railroad and another, usually adjacent, industrial facility for the construction and maintenance of a sidetrack on either party's land. *See also* industrial siding.

raised ranch. A bilevel house with the lower level at or partly below grade and the front entrance between grades.

rake. In construction, a board or molding placed along the sloping sides of a frame gable to cover the ends of the siding.

RAM
1. In appraising, *see* reverse annuity mortgage.
2. In computer usage, random access memory; high-speed, volatile memory where data and programs reside during pro-

gram execution. The user can enter and retrieve data from RAM, but when power is cut off, this memory is lost.

ramp. An inclined walk or roadway; in highway construction, the roadway used to enter or leave a controlled-access highway.

ranch
1. A facility for raising livestock under range conditions where forage grasses are the main source of feed.
2. Sometimes used synonymously with *farm* or *homestead* to describe a rural property.

ranch improvements. All buildings, fences, water developments, and corrals associated with a ranch.

ranch-style house. A rambling, one-story house that is low to the ground and has a low-pitched gable roof or roofs, an open interior design, and sometimes a basement.

ranch unit. In public domain states, an entire operating ranch unit; a combination of fee-owned land, Taylor Grazing Act permit land, and/or Forest Service permit land.

random. Without uniformity of dimension or design, e.g., describes a masonry wall with stones placed irregularly, not in a straight course.

random access. In computer usage, direct or immediate access to any memory location, regardless of the location last accessed.

random sample

1. In statistics, the chance selection of a number of observations from a universe, i.e., the random selection of items from an entire aggregate of items.
2. In forestry, a sample chosen so that each individual tree or stem in the population has an equal, or independent, chance of being included.

random shingles. Shingles of different widths.

range

1. An extensive stretch of grazing land or land that produces native forage plants.
2. The region or area over which something is found, is distributed, or occurs.
3. The difference between the smallest and largest sample observation in a statistical distribution.
4. *See* range line.

range capacity. The grazing capacity of grassland that typically maintains a satisfactory grass cover; expressed as the number of acres of grass needed to carry one animal unit through one grazing season or other specified period.

range capacity formula

Range capacity = density x use factor

x surface acres / forage acre requirement

range hood. A hood for collecting smoke from an oven or range. Some range hoods are ventless; others are equipped with circulating devices for ventilating cooking smoke.

range inventory. An itemized list of all the resources of a management area, e.g., range sites, range condition classes, range condition trends, range use, estimated proper stocking rates, physical developments, natural conditions.

range line. In the government survey system, one of a series of government survey lines which extend due north and south at six-mile intervals and are numbered east or west from the principal meridian. Range lines form the east and west boundaries of townships.

range management. The planning and directing of range use to obtain maximum, sustained animal production and the perpetuation of natural resources.

range of value. The range, or confidence interval, in which the final market value estimate of a property may fall; usually stated as a variable amount between a high and low value limit.

range site. An area of land with a combination of soil, climatic, topographic, and natural characteristics that is significantly different from adjacent areas; considered as a unit for purposes of discussion, investigation, and management, and present significant differences in potential forage production and management requirements for proper land use.

range states. The 17 western states in the United States, where most of the land is used to sustain livestock.

range survey. The science of range reconnaissance in which data are assembled to estimate grazing capacity; consists of two phases: 1) the mapping of grazing types and any cultural and topographic features that may influence grazing value; and 2) an analysis of the density and species composition of the vegetation to determine its livestock grazing capacity.

range utilization. The extent to which animals have consumed the total, current herbage production of a range area; expressed in percentage by weight.

range vegetation types. *See* Types of Range Vegetation in the addenda.

ranking analysis. A qualitative technique for analyzing comparable sales; a variant of relative comparison analysis in which comparable sales are ranked in descending or ascending order of desirability and

each is analyzed to determine its position relative to the subject.

rate. The ratio of one quantity to another; e.g., the ratio of net operating income to sale price or value is the overall capitalization rate; the reciprocal of a factor. *See also* factor.

rate base. The total amount of value on which a public utility is permitted by law to earn a fair return.

rate of interest. The amount of annual interest paid on borrowed money.

rate of return. The ratio of income or yield to the original investment; the ratio of the current annual net income generated from the operation of an enterprise to the capital investment, the net yield over the duration of the investment, or the appraised value of the property, considering temporal limitations (e.g., the term to maturity on bond issues) or a finite economic life (e.g., of buildings).

rate surcharge. The difference between the capitalization rate and the discount rate; the increment added to a basic return on capital to provide for recapture or to compensate for the risk of future loss in capital value. *See also* risk rate.

ratification. Confirmation of an act performed on behalf of another but without that person's authorization. For example, a real estate broker may make a decision that is beyond his or her authority and must be approved by the owner of the agency to be binding.

rating grid. A decision-making method in which arbitrary weights are assigned to the various factors involved in a decision that is to be made by several individuals.

ratio. The relationship between two similar magnitudes with respect to the number of times the first contains the second, either integrally or fractionally; e.g., the ratio of three to four may be written 3:4 or ¾.

raw land. Land on which no improvements have been made; land in its natural state before grading, construction, subdivision, or the installation of utilities.

raw material. Nonfabricated material that is used in processing or manufacturing and thereby changed in nature or form; e.g., iron is a raw material used in the production of steel, steel is a raw material used in the manufacture of automobiles.

raw water

1. Water that requires treatment before it can be used, such as water for steam generation.
2. Any water used in ice making except distilled water.
3. Water used strictly for cooling such as river water or sea water at a nuclear generating plant. (R.S. Means)

RCN. Replacement cost new.

RDB. Research and Development Board.

REA. Rural Electrification Administration.

readily achievable. The term used in the Americans with Disabilities Act (ADA) of 1990 to refer to a modification that is easy to install and does not require much expense. The Americans with Disabilities Act (ADA) of 1990 specifies the considerations that enter into determination of a readily achievable modification.

ready-mixed concrete. Concrete manufactured for delivery to a purchaser in a plastic and unhardened state. (R.S. Means)

real estate. Physical land and appurtenances attached to the land, e.g., structures. An identified parcel or tract of land, including improvements, if any. *See also* real property.

real estate analysis. *See* analysis.

real estate consulting. *See* consulting.

real estate counseling. *See* counseling.

real estate cycle. The successive periods of expansion, peak, contraction, and trough that characterize the activity of the real estate market. Business and real estate cycles do not generally move in tandem. Since real estate development and sales activity are especially responsive to the downward movement in interest rates, increased activity in real estate markets often heralds an economic recovery. *See also* business cycle.

real estate investment trust (REIT). A corporation or trust that combines the capital of many investors to acquire or provide financing for all forms of real estate. A REIT serves much like a mutual fund for real estate. Its shares are freely traded, often on a major stock exchange. To qualify for the favorable tax treatment currently (1993) accorded such trusts, 95% of the taxable income of a REIT must be distributed among its shareholders, who must number at least 100 investors; no fewer than five investors can own more than 50% of the value of the REIT. The Federal Securities and Exchange Commission stipulates that REITs with over 300 investors have to make their financial statements public. (NAREIT)

real estate market. The interaction of individuals who exchange real property rights for other assets such as money; a group of individuals or firms that are in contact with one another for the purpose of conducting real estate transactions.

real estate mortgage investment conduits (REMICs). Equity instruments issued by an investment bank that are similar to collateralized mortgage obligations; in this arrangement, the certificate represents a proportionate share of ownership in a pool of mortgages. Investors in REMICs enjoy a tax pass-through similar to that of a REIT. Introduced as technical provisions of the Tax Reform Act of 1986, REMICs were created to facilitate broad participation in the mortgage-backed securities market.

real estate owned (REO). Denotes real estate that has been acquired by a lending institution for investment or through foreclosure of mortgage loans; also called *owned real estate (ORE).*

real estate-related transaction. Under Title XI of the Financial Institutions Reform, Recovery and Enforcement Act of 1989 (FIRREA), any transaction involving 1) the sale, lease, purchase, investment in, or exchange of real property or interests in property, and the financing thereof; 2) the refinancing of real property or interests in property; and 3) the use of real property or interests in property as security for a loan or investment, including mortgage-backed securities. *See also* federally related transactions (FRT).

real estate syndicate. A general partnership, limited partnership, joint venture, unincorporated association, or similar organization that is formed or operated solely as an investment in real property; its activities include, but are not limited to, sale, exchange, trade, and development; offers investors the tax, legal, and practical advantages of real property investment.

real estate taxation appraisal. *See* ad valorem tax.

realignment. A change in the horizontal layout of a highway, may also affect vertical alignment. (R.S. Means)

Realist. A member of the National Association of Real Estate Brokers.

realized gain. Profit realized from the sale of a capital asset, but not necessarily taxed. *See also* boot; recognized gain.

real price. A nominal price that has been adjusted for changes in the price level. *See also* nominal price.

real property. All interests, benefits, and rights inherent in the ownership of physical real estate; the bundle of rights with which the ownership of the real estate is endowed. In some states, real property is defined by statute and is synonymous with *real estate*. *See also* personal property; real estate.

real rate of return. The return on an investment adjusted for inflation.

Realtor. A registered trademark that identifies a member of the National Association of Realtors (NAR); an active member of a local real estate board that is a member of NAR.

Realtors Land Institute (RLI). An organization of real estate professionals active in land brokerage and agribusiness.

Realtors National Marketing Institute (RNMI). An organization that offers education and training to individuals engaged in real estate brokerage and sales.

realty. *See* real property.

reappraisal lease. *See* revaluation lease.

reasonable accommodation. Under the Americans with Disabilities Act (ADA) of 1990, a term that refers to making an existing employment facility readily accessible to and usable by people with disabilities. *See also* Americans with Disabilities Act (ADA) of 1990.

reassessment. The process in which all property within a taxing jurisdiction is revalued to assign new assessed values. *See also* revaluation.

rebuttal testimony. Testimony that is produced to refute the testimony presented by the other side in a court case.

recapture of depreciation. *See* depreciation recapture.

recapture rate. The annual rate at which invested capital is returned to the investor over a specified period; the annual amount, in addition to interest or return on interest (compound interest), which can be recaptured from an investment, divided by the original amount invested. When the term was coined, investors assumed that property was a wasting asset and its value could only decline due to depreciation. Today appraisers use the term when some income provision must be made to compensate for the loss of invested capital.

recasting. The process of restructuring an existing loan, generally when the risk of default is evident. A loan is generally recast by extending its term and reducing the annual interest rate.

receiver. A person who is appointed by a court to exercise control over and administer a property or business when it appears necessary, in the interest of justice, that a qualified and impartial person assume such authority.

recent soil. A secondary soil that has been so recently deposited that weathering and aging have produced little or no change in the soil profile.

recession. A mild form of depression; a period of reduced economic activity; a slackening in economic activity not sufficient to precipitate a major change in the business cycle.

reciprocal. The quantity resulting from the division of 1 by a given number; e.g., the reciprocal of 4 is ¼. The product of reciprocal numbers is always 1, e.g., 4 x ¼ = 1.

reciprocal easements. Easements and restrictive covenants granted to limit the use of the land in a subdivision tract for the benefit of all the homeowners. *See also* easement; restrictive covenant.

reciprocity. A relationship between two entities whereby favors or privileges granted by one are returned by the other, e.g., if state A certifies appraisers and brokers already certified by state B to work in state A, reciprocity exists when state B similarly certifies appraisers and brokers previously certified by state A. *See also* temporary practice.

reclamation. Any method that brings wasted natural resources into productive use; e.g., desert land may be reclaimed through irrigation, forest may be restored by artificial planting and seeding, and fields that are not too badly eroded may be reclaimed through proper cultivation.

Reclamation, Bureau of. A principal bureau of the U.S. Department of the Interior engaged in irrigation projects, which supply water to arid sections of 17 western states, and in related activities such as the construction of dams and reservoirs, power plants, transmission lines, canals, tunnels, and aqueducts.

recognized gain. The taxable portion of profit, generally made on the sale or exchange of property. *See also* boot; realized gain.

reconciliation

1. The last phase of any valuation assignment in which two or more value indications derived from market data are resolved into a final value estimate, which may be either a final range of value or a single point estimate. *See also* point estimate; range of value.

2. In the sales comparison approach, reconciliation may involve two levels of analysis: derivation of a value indication from the adjusted prices of two or more comparable sales expressed in the same unit of comparison and derivation of a value indication from the adjusted prices of two or more comparables expressed in different units of comparison.

reconciliation criteria. The criteria that enable an appraiser to form a meaningful, defensible conclusion about the final value estimate.

Value indications are tested for the appropriateness of the approaches and adjustments applied, the accuracy of the data, and the quantity of evidence analyzed.

reconditioning. *See* renovation.

reconstructed operating statement. A statement prepared by an appraiser that represents his or her opinion of the probable future net operating income of an investment property. In preparing reconstructed operating statements, appraisers may consult accountants' financial balance sheets and auditors' statements. *See also* pro forma.

reconveyance. A written instrument that passes title to real property back to the original owner; e.g., in a deed of trust arrangement, upon liquidation of the debt, the property is reconveyed from a third-party trustee to the trustor (borrower).

record drawings. Construction drawings updated to show the progress of the work, usually based on data furnished by the contractor to the designer. (R.S. Means)

recorded map. A map of a parcel of land that has been filed in the office of the county recorder; e.g. "as per map recorded in book 56 at page 20 of *Maps, Records of Blank County, California.*"

recorded plat. *See* plat.

recording. The filing of a copy of a legal instrument or document, e.g., a deed, in a government office provided for this purpose; creates a public record of the document for the protection of all concerned and gives constructive notice to the public at large.

recording act. A state law governing the recording of documents such as deeds, mortgages, and liens.

record owner. *See* owner of record.

recourse. A lender's right to seek from a borrower in default on a loan compensation beyond the property pledged as collateral. *See also* recourse debt.

recourse debt. A debt agreement secured by real property that gives the lender legal rights against the debtor beyond the right to property value; equivalent to a general obligation of the debtor.

recreational lease. A lease on recreational facilities granted a tenant in a condominium or townhouse development by a developer-lessor for a stipulated time and rent; typically long-term with increases in rent tied to an index.

rectangular survey system. A system for the legal description of land that refers to the parcel's location in a township, an area approximately six miles square that is formed by the intersection of principal merid-

ians and base lines. Each township contains 36, one-square-mile sections of 640 acres. Also called *federal rectangular survey system* and *government survey system.*

redemption. The process of canceling a defeasible (revocable) title to property, such as one created by a mortgage foreclosure or tax sale. The terms *equity of redemption* and *equitable right of redemption* refer to the right of a mortgagor in default to recover title by paying off the entire mortgage prior to the foreclosure sale. After the property has been sold, the mortgagor has no right to redemption unless a statutory redemption period applies according to state law.

redevelopment. The development or improvement of cleared or undeveloped land in an urban renewal area; technically includes the erection of buildings and other development and improvement of the land by private or public redevelopers to whom the land has been made available; does not include site or project improvements that are installed by a local public agency to prepare the land for sale or lease. *See also* redevelopment agency; urban renewal.

redevelopment agency. A quasi-governmental agency charged with the improvement of housing in an urban renewal area and the relocation of residents displaced by demolitions. Redevelopment agencies may exercise the power of eminent domain to condemn properties and contract developers to develop projects. *See also* redevelopment; urban renewal.

reentry. The right of a fee owner to repossess real property pending a breach in the conditions under which the real property was transferred, e.g., a landlord may repossess leased property if rent is not paid or other terms of the lease are broken. *See also* repossession.

reference standards. Professionally prepared generic specifications and technical data compiled and published by competent organizations generally recognized and accepted by the construction industry. These standards are sometimes used as criteria by which the acceptability and/or performance of a product, material, assembly, or piece of equipment can be judged. (R.S. Means)

reference standard specification. A type of nonproprietary specification that relies on accepted reference standards to describe a product, material, assembly, or piece of equipment to be incorporated into a project. (R.S. Means)

refinance. To obtain a new loan, the proceeds of which are used to pay off an existing loan. Generally, properties are refinanced to obtain better terms and lower interest rates than those established at the time of the original loan.

regional analysis. *See* economic base analysis; market analysis.

regional resort. A resort that is popular in a particular season and is usually located within a three-hour traveling radius of a metropolitan area; most of its patrons travel by automobile from a nearby metropolitan area.

regional shopping center. A shopping center that offers a variety of general merchandise, apparel, furniture, home furnishings, services, and recreational facilities and is built around one or more full department stores of at least 100,000 square feet each. Regional shopping centers generally have between 400,000 and 750,000 square feet of gross leasable area.

registrar. The official responsible for maintaining records of deeds, mortgages, and other recorded documents.

registration
1. The process of enrolling or recording formally on a list.
2. An application to the Securities and Exchange Commission (SEC) for an interstate sale.

regression. In appraisal, the concept that the value of a superior property is adversely affected by its association with an inferior property of the same type. *See also* progression.

regression analysis. A method that examines the relationship between one or more independent variables and a dependent variable by plotting points on a graph; used to identify and weight analytical factors and to make forecasts.

regressive tax. A tax levied on all taxpayers at flat rate regardless of differences in their income or wealth. *See also* progressive tax.

regrowth. The younger, smaller trees in a timber stand that have not yet reached minimum diameter at breast-height and are still growing; also called *reproduction.*

rehabilitation. *See* renovation.

reimbursement expenses. Amounts expended for, or on account of, a project that are to be reimbursed by the owner in accordance with the terms of the appropriate agreement. (R.S. Means)

reimbursement rate. A rate, usually set by the state Department of Health, that represents reimbursement to an owner-operator for the care provided in a skilled nursing home or health-related facility; usually refers to the rate paid for public assistance patients who qualify under Medicare/Medicaid programs.

reinforced concrete. Concrete that is strengthened by embedding iron or steel bars, rods, or mesh in it.

reinforced concrete construction. Construction in which reinforced concrete is used for foundations, frames, floors, roofs, or other structural members.

reinforcement. A system of steel rods or mesh that absorbs tensile and shearing stresses in concrete work; complements the inherent compressive qualities of concrete.

reinforcing. The process of strengthening. Steel rods or mesh are imbedded in concrete to increase its strength under tension. Frequently asbestos and glass fibers are used as reinforcement for plaster. *See also* reinforced concrete.

reinstatement. The restoration of a mortgage or deed of trust to good standing after payments are made to remedy the default.

reinsurance. The reassignment of all or part of the insurance carried from one company to another.

reinvestment presumption. An implausible assumption that all money received from an investment before its termination is actually reinvested. Some analysts fix the rate at which income is reinvested to equal the *IRR,* a popular, albeit misleading, presumption.

reinvestment rate. The rate of return that is presumed to be obtainable on reinvested income; an obtainable rate of return on capital recaptured from a prior investment.

REIT. *See* real estate investment trust.

rejection. Refusal of the terms on which an offer or bid is presented.

relative comparison analysis. A qualitative technique for analyzing comparable sales; used to determine whether the characteristics of a comparable property are inferior, superior, or equal to those of the subject property. Relative comparison analysis is similar to paired data analysis, but quantitative adjustments are not derived.

release clause. A clause stipulating that, upon payment of a specific amount of money to the holder of a trust deed or mortgage, the lien on a particular described lot or area shall be removed, i.e., from the blanket lien on the whole property.

release of lien. The act of releasing a person's or entity's mechanic's lien against a property. (R.S. Means)

reliction. The increase in land along a body of water caused by the gradual subsidence of the water. The uncovered land usually belongs to the owner of the riparian rights. *See also* accretion.

relief. The configuration or irregularities of a land surface; the topography of land.

relief map. A map showing the topographical relief of an area, usually with generalized contour lines.

relinquishment. The conveyance of a portion of a transportation facility from a state transportation agency to another government agency for transportation use.

relocation
1. The moving of individuals or businesses from one location to another.
2. A process in which a federal, state, or local public agency provides relocation services, paying moving costs and related expenses to individuals, families, and businesses displaced by urban renewal projects or other federal or federally assisted programs; required by statute.

relocation company. A company that helps corporations move employees from one location to another. The corporation will usually cover the costs of the relocation company's services, which include the purchase, marketing, and sale of the present home of the employee being transferred. *See also* Employee Relocation Council.

relocation payment. A cash amount paid by a federal, state, or local public agency to reimburse individuals, families, and businesses for reasonable moving costs and other expenses resulting from their displacement by urban renewal projects or other federal or federally assisted programs.

relocation plan. A program devised by government agencies to relocate residents of an urban renewal area who will be displaced by project activities or other government actions.

remainder

1. A future possessory interest in real estate that is given to a third party and matures upon the termination of a limited or determinable fee; e.g., A gives B a life estate in A's farm for B's lifetime. A also gives C an interest in the farm to take effect upon B's demise. C has a remainder interest.
2. In eminent domain condemnation, the property remaining in possession of the owner after a partial taking.

remainderman. A person who is entitled to an estate after a prior estate or interest has expired. *See also* remainder.

remaining economic life. The estimated period during which improvements will continue to contribute to property value; an estimate of the number of years re-

maining in the economic life of the structure or structural components as of the date of the appraisal.

remedies. The manner in which a breach of contract is settled by a court or arbitrators. (R.S. Means)

REMIC. *See* real estate mortgage investment conduits.

remnant. A remainder that has negligible economic utility or value due to its size, shape, or other detrimental characteristics; also called *uneconomic remnant. See also* remainder.

remodeling. A type of renovation that changes property use or configuration by changing property design.

rendering. In perspective drawing, to finish with ink or color to bring out the effect of the design, e.g., an architect's rendering of a proposed project.

renegotiable rate mortgage (RRM). A rollover mortgage formerly sponsored by the Federal Home Loan Bank Board; called an *adjustable mortgage loan (AML)* under current regulations.

renegotiation of a lease. To arrive at a new set of lease terms upon termination of an existing lease, generally for the purpose of revising the annual rent. Lease provisions often stipulate that the revision of rent should be based on mutual agreement. Index leases provide for rent revision at specific intervals based on changes in the cost of living index; revaluation leases call for rent adjustments based on a set rate of return on the appraised value of the property under market rental conditions at the time of the revaluation. *See also* lease; rent.

renewal option. The right, but not the obligation, of a tenant to continue a lease at a specified term and rent.

renovation. The process in which older structures or historic buildings are modernized, remodeled, or restored. Generally, the objective of renovation is to maintain or restore the basic plan and style of a building rather than to modify the original design by accretions or alterations, though new construction often accompanies restoration. Renovation is closely associated with urban renewal and may encompass the development of facilities to serve the community; also called *rehabilitation*. *See also* modernization; remodeling; restoration; urban renewal.

rent. An amount paid for the use of land, improvements, or a capital good. *See also* assart rent; breakpoint; contract rent; crop share rent; dead rent; ground rent; livestock share rent; market rent; overage rent; percentage rent.

rentable area
1. The amount of space on which the rent is based; calculated according to local practice.
2. The tenant's pro rata portion of the entire office floor, excluding elements of the building that penetrate through the floor to areas below. The rentable area of a floor is fixed for the life of a building and is not affected by changes in corridor sizes or configuration. Rentable area is recommended for measuring the total income-producing area of a building and for computing a tenant's pro rata share of a building for purposes of rent escalation. Lenders, architects, and appraisers use rentable area in analyzing the economic potential of a building. On multi-tenant floors, both the rentable and usable area for any specific office suite should be computed. The rentable area of a floor is computed by measuring to the inside finished surface of the dominant portion of the permanent building walls, excluding any major vertical penetrations of the floor. No deductions should be made for columns and projections necessary to the building. (BOMA)

rental requirement. A condition in a commitment letter that stipulates that a certain amount of space must be rented at a minimum rental rate if the entire loan amount is to be funded.

rental value. *See* market rent.

rent concession. A discount or other benefit offered by a landlord to induce a prospective tenant to enter into a lease; usually in the form of one or more months of free rent, but it may be expressed in extra services to the tenant or some other consideration; also called *rent offset*.

rent control. A legal regulation that specifies the maximum rental payment for the use of property.

rent escalation. *See* escalation clause.

rent multiplier. *See* gross rent multiplier; multiplier.

rent offset. *See* rent concession.

rent roll. A report that is prepared regularly, usually each month, and indicates the rent-paying status of each tenant.

rent subsidy. Supplementary money granted by a government agency or charitable organization to indigent people who cannot meet rental payments.

rent-up period. A period of time during which a rental property is in the process of initial leasing; may begin before or after construction and lasts until stabilized occupancy is achieved.

REO. *See* real estate owned.

repairs. Current expenditures for general upkeep to preserve a property's condition and efficiency; may include renewal of small parts of any property component; does not include replacement, i.e., the renewal of any substantial part of the property or a change in the form or material of the building. *See also* cost of repairs; maintenance.

replacement allowance. An allowance that provides for the periodic replacement of building components that wear out more rapidly than the building itself and must be replaced during the building's economic life.

replacement cost. The estimated cost to construct, at current prices as of the effective appraisal date, a building with utility equivalent to the building being appraised, using modern materials and current standards, design, and layout.

replacement cost coverage. Type of insurance that guarantees that the insurance company will pay to replace the damaged property with new property (depreciation will not be deducted). (R.S. Means)

replacement cost new (*RCN*). *See* replacement cost.

replacement reserves. *See* replacement allowance.

report. Any communication, written or oral, of an appraisal, review, or analysis; the document that is transmitted to the client upon completion of an assignment. (USPAP, 1992 edition). Reporting requirements are set forth in the Standards Rules relating to Standards 2 and 5 of the Uniform Standards of Professional Appraisal Practice.

report of defined value. The documented statement provided at the conclusion of an appraisal.

repossession. The retaking of possession of a property. A landlord may repossess a property after a tenant fails to meet rental payments or breaks other terms of the lease; a mortgagor repossesses after the mortgagee falls behind on mortgage payments. *See also* reentry.

reproduction cost. The estimated cost to construct, at current prices as of the effective date of the appraisal, an exact duplicate or replica of the building being appraised, using the same materials, construction standards, design, layout, and quality of workmanship and embodying all the deficiencies, superadequacies, and obsolescence of the subject building.

repurchase agreements and reverse repurchase agreements. Short-term financing arrangements made by securities dealers, banks, and the Federal Reserve System in which a person who needs funds for a short period uses his or her portfolio of money market investments as collateral and sells an interest in the portfolio with the obligation to repurchase it, with interest, at a specified future time. A reverse repurchase agreement refers to the obligation of the security dealer, bank, or Federal Reserve System to relinquish control over the portfolio upon fulfillment of the terms by the borrower; also called *repos.*

RES. Residential Evaluation Specialist. A designation conferred by the International Association of Assessing Officers (IAAO) upon residential real property assessors.

rescission. The cancellation of a contract and restoration of the parties to their original positions. Contracts may be rescinded by mutual consent of the parties involved or by court decree for fraud or misrepresentation. If a seller rescinds a contract with a buyer who has defaulted, the seller must return to the buyer all payments less the rent for the occupancy period. In contract sales and land contracts, forfeiture clauses may preclude such restitution.

research and development building. A type of industrial building popular in high technology industries such as computers, electronics, and biotechnology; generally a hybrid of office, manufacturing, and warehouse space housed in appealing, higher-quality buildings; often characterized by a location in a campus-like industrial park with extensive landscaping, harmonious architecture, and ample open space; also called *R&D building.*

research and development space. Space that is designed and equipped to meet the specific research and development needs of a high technology industry. *See also* flex space.

reservation. A clause found in legal instruments and conveyances that creates a new right or interest on behalf of the grantor. While title passes to the grantee, some use or income is reserved for the grantor. Reservations may include mineral rights, rental income, or easements.

reserve

1. An appropriation from surplus funds that is allocated to deferred or anticipated contingencies. In business, a credit account created to accumulate funds to retire debt or cover losses that are payable or expected to accrue in the future.

2. In association with natural resource property, the extent of commercially available resources, proven or unproven, that are not required or involved in current operations.

reserve for depletion. In accounting, an amount set aside before determining net worth to offset the depletion of an asset, e.g., a mineral deposit that is carried on the accounts at a value assigned before the depletion occurred.

reserve for depreciation. In accounting, an amount set aside before determining net worth to offset the depreciation of fixed assets that are carried on the accounts at values assigned before they suffered depreciation; also called *provision for depreciation* or *allowance for depreciation. See also* book value.

reserve for replacements. *See* replacement allowance.

reserve requirement. A requirement of the Federal Reserve System that member banks keep part of their deposit liabilities frozen in reserve accounts.

reservoir. A natural or artificial place, e.g., a lake, a pond, a tank, where water is collected and stored to supply a community, an irrigation system, or a power plant; the water above a dam that is used to control the flow of the stream.

residence. Any property used as a dwelling; in law, the legal domicile; used for owner occupancy, not investment income.

residential building rate. The rate of housing starts per 1,000 population; used to determine the level of residential construction in a community.

residential occupancy. Occupancy of a building in which sleeping accommodations are provided for normal residential purposes. The term excludes institutional occupancy. (R.S. Means)

residential property. A vacant or improved parcel of land devoted to or available for use as an abode, e.g., single-family homes, apartments, rooming houses.

residential restriction. A covenant or zoning ordinance that permits the construction of only residential buildings in a subdivision or district.

residential square. A park-like city square; usually owned cooperatively by the occupants of row houses or townhouses that abut the square.

resident management. An additional project expense incurred by employing a salaried, live-in-manager; over and above the off-premises management expense; also called *on-premises management.*

residual. The quantity left over; used to describe capitalization procedures that develop the value of a property component based on its

residual income. *See also* residual techniques.

residual capitalization rate. An overall capitalization rate used to estimate the resale price of a property; usually based on the anticipated stabilized income for the year beyond the holding period; also called *terminal capitalization rate.*

residual demand. Total anticipated demand less that portion absorbable by existing vacant properties or planned supply. *See also* demand.

residual soil. Soil formed in place by the weathering of mineral material or by the disintegration and decomposition of rock.

residual stands. Timber stands that have been partially logged, leaving some of the original old growth trees; tend to develop a young growth understory if not relogged.

residual techniques. Procedures used to capitalize the income allocated to an investment component of unknown value after all investment components of known values have been satisfied; may be applied to a property's physical components (land and building), financial interests (mortgage and equity), or legal estates (leased fee and leasehold).

Resolution Trust Corporation (RTC). *See* Financial Institutions Reform, Recovery and Enforcement Act (FIRREA).

resort hotel. A hotel, typically situated in a scenic area, that either provides or is near activities that attract leisure travelers, e.g., swimming, tennis, golf, boating, skiing, ice skating, riding, hiking, sightseeing. Resort hotels generally offer restaurant, lounge, and entertainment outlets; a fitness center; concierge and valet services; transportation and tour services; and a limited amount of meeting and banquet space. Seasonality often affects the level of occupancy. *See also* hotel.

resort property. Property located in resort areas or devoted to public or private recreational use, e.g., summer homes, lodging facilities, tennis courts, golf courses, ski resorts.

restaurant. A facility that prepares and serves food. *See also* fast-food restaurant.

restaurant activity index. The ratio between an area's restaurant sales, expressed as a percentage of total U.S. restaurant sales, and the area's food store sales, expressed as a percentage of total U.S. food store sales; reflects the current level of restaurant activity, but does not indicate the cause of changes in activity.

restaurant growth index. The ratio between an area's daytime and nighttime population, expressed as a percentage of the total U.S. population, and the area's restaurant sales, expressed as a percentage of total restaurant sales.

restitution. A court-ordered money award that is intended to restore the parties to their financial position as it existed before the contract was formed. (R.S. Means)

restoration. A type of renovation in which a property is returned to its original appearance and condition.

restriction. *See* deed restriction; restrictive covenant; zoning ordinance.

restrictive covenant. A private agreement that restricts the use and occupancy of real estate that is part of a conveyance and is binding on all subsequent purchasers; may involve control of lot size, setback, placement of buildings, number and size of improvements, architecture, cost of improvements, or use. Generally associated with the conditions, covenants, and restrictions written into deeds and leases. By specifying the permissible uses in a neigborhood, restrictive covenants help stabilize property values. *See also* deed restrictions; covenants and restrictions; reciprocal easement.

resubdivision. To replan the grid or further divide the lots in an existing subdivision.

resurfacing. The placing of a new surface on an existing pavement to improve its conformation or increase its strength. (R.S. Means)

resurvey. The surveying of a tract of land according to a former plat or survey; using the best evidence obtainable, the surveyor locates the courses and lines in the same places they were located by the first surveyor.

retail land developer. A person engaged in development for retail lot sales.

retail lot sales. The sale of lots to ultimate owners on a volume basis; as distinguished from the sale of individual lots to an intermediate owner, e.g., a merchant builder.

retaining wall. A sloping or vertical structural support that confines or restricts the movement of adjoining earth or water.

retention
1. A percentage, usually 10%, withheld from a periodic payment to a contractor, in accordance with the owner-contractor agreement, for work completed. The retention is held until all terms of the contract have been fulfilled; also called *retainage*.
2. The amount of preservative, fire-retardant treatment, or resin retained by treated or impregnated wood. (R.S. Means)

retention basin. *See* retention pond.

retention pond. A man-made impoundment with a permanent pool of water that is used to reduce storm water runoff.

retirement community. A large, privately built development designed to attract young retirees by emphasizing outdoor recreational activities (e.g., golf, swimming, tennis). The housing options are usually offered for purchase and may include condominiums, duplexes, or townhouses; amenities are geared to retired seniors. *See also* elderly housing.

retrofit. A modification in the design, construction, materials, or equipment of an existing building to reduce energy use.

retrospective value estimate. An estimate of value that is likely to have applied as of a specified historic date. A retrospective value estimate is most frequently sought in connection with appraisals for estate tax, condemnation, inheritance tax, and similar purposes.

return of capital. The recovery of invested capital, usually through income and/or reversion.

return on capital. The additional amount received as compensation (profit or reward) for use of an investor's capital until it is recaptured. The rate of return on capital is analogous to the yield rate or the interest rate earned or expected.

reuse appraisal. An appraisal performed to estimate the value of vacant land or improved property in an urban renewal project area; conducted under the provisions of the National Housing Act of 1949, as amended, and subject to the restrictions and controls set forth in the urban renewal plan for the project area.

revaluation. The mass appraisal of all property within an assessment jurisdiction to equalize assessed values; the reappraisal of a property.

revaluation lease. A lease that provides for periodic rent adjustments based on a revaluation of the real estate under prevailing market rental conditions.

revenue stamps. Stamps purchased from the state government and affixed, in amounts provided by law, to documents or instruments that represent original issues, sales, or transfers of stocks and bonds and deeds of conveyances; may provide an indication of sale price; also called *documentary stamps*.

reverse annuity mortgage (RAM). A type of mortgage designed for retirees and other fixed-income home owners who owe little or nothing on their homes; typically permits owners to use some or all of the equity in their homes as supplemental income while retaining ownership. These owners are borrowing against the value of their homes on a monthly basis; the longer they borrow, the less equity they retain. The loan becomes due on a specific date or when a certain event occurs, e.g., the sale of the property or death of the borrower.

reverse leverage. *See* negative leverage.

reversion. A lump-sum benefit that an investor receives or expects to receive at the termination of an investment; also called *reversionary benefit. See also* net reversionary interest.

reversionary right. The right to repossess and resume full and sole use and ownership of real property that has been temporarily alienated by a lease, an easement, etc.; may become effective at a stated time or under certain conditions, e.g., the termination of a leasehold, the abandonment of a right-of-way, the end of the estimated economic life of the improvements.

reversion factor. A compound interest factor that is used to discount a single future payment to its present worth, given the appropriate discount rate and discount period. *See also* present worth of \$1 ($1/S^n$).

reverter clause. A clause that provides that title reverts to the grantor when a restriction set forth in the deed is violated; affects the marketability of the title and thus the value of the property.

review. The act or process of critically studying a report prepared by another. (USPAP, 1992 edition) *See also* desk review; field review.

review appraiser. An appraiser who examines the reports of other appraisers to determine whether their conclusions are consistent with the data reported and with other generally known information.

revitalization. A stage in a neighborhood life cycle characterized by renewal, modernization, and increasing demand.

revpar. Revenue per available room; a unit of comparison applied in the appraisal of lodging facilities; calculated by multiplying a hotel's percentage of occupancy by the average room rate. Revpar is used throughout the lodging industry to compare the income of competing facilities.

RFC. Reconstruction Finance Corporation.

ribbon board. A horizontal structural member that is let into outside wall studs to support upper-story floor joists that are being spiked to the studs in a balloon frame; also called *ledger* or *ledger board.*

ribbon development. *See* roadside development.

ridge. The top, horizontal edge or peak of a roof.

ridge board. The horizontal structural member at the top of a roof against which the upper ends of the rafters are butted.

ridge regression. An alternative to multiple regression, introduced to overcome the problem of multicollinearity, i.e., highly correlated property characteristics that produce inflated and unstable regression coefficients.

right of access. *See* access rights.

right of drainage. An easement that gives the owner of land the right to drain water through or from the land of another, from its source or from any other place.

right of entry. The right to enter and begin construction on land that is in the process of being acquired.

right of first refusal. An option that gives the holder, who is usually the lessee, the right to purchase a property before any offer to purchase can be made by a third party.

right of immediate possession. The right to occupy property after preliminary steps for acquisition have been taken, but before a final settlement has been reached.

right of redemption. A property owner's right to reacquire foreclosed property by paying the mortgage debt or real estate taxes within a limited time after the final payment due date.

right of reentry. *See* reentry.

right of survivorship. Right of the surviving joint tenant to acquire the interest of the deceased joint tenant in joint tenancies and tenancies by the entirety without any probate proceedings.

right of way. A privilege to pass over the land of another in some particular path; usually an easement over the land of another; a strip of land used in this way for railroad and highway purposes, for pipelines or pole lines, and for private or public passage.

rights. An enforceable, legal claim to title of or interest in real property.

right, title, and interest. A phrase appearing in deeds, leases, and other instruments that effect a transfer of property title which indicates that the grantor is conveying all that he or she held claim to.

right-to-farm legislation. Laws that protect agricultural owners from private nuisance lawsuits and new ordinances that would restrict normal farming practices, e.g., environmental or land protection laws; exist in different forms in several states.

right-to-know. A right granted to workers by the Occupational Safety and Health Act (OSHA), by which they must be informed of the risks and hazards associated with the chemicals and substances that they are required to use in the workplace. (R.S. Means)

right to use. *See* leasehold estate; timesharing.

right to work law. State law providing, in general, that employees are not required to join a union as a condition of retaining or receiving a job. (R.S. Means]

rigid conduit. A rigid pipe used as a protective enclosure for electrical wiring.

rigid foundation. *See* floating foundation.

rigid insulation. A type of sheet insulation available in four forms: structural wall insulation, fiberboard, structural deck insulation, and rigid board insulation.

rill erosion. The loss of soil by heavy rains after fields are tilled. Small channels are cut into the soft, loose earth as the water races down a slope.

riparian. Pertaining to the bank of a river or another body of water.

riparian lease. A lease on land situated between the high water mark and the low water mark.

riparian owner. The owner of riparian land, who is ordinarily entitled to the benefits of riparian rights.

riparian rights

1. The incidental right of the owners of land bordering a lake or stream to the use and enjoyment of the water that flows across their land or is contiguous to it; entitles the user to reasonable use that does not materially diminish the quality or quantity of the water for other owners. The owners' rights are equal, regardless of their location along the stream or the time when each property was purchased.

2. The incidental right of an owner of land abutting a body of water to use the water area for piers, boat houses, fishing, boating, navigation, and the right of access for such purposes, limited by public need if on a navigable stream. Riparian rights may also involve use of the water for irrigation and the alluvium deposited by the water. In some states, the common law doctrine of riparian rights has been superseded by the doctrine of beneficial use. *See also* accretion; beneficial use; prior appropriation; reliction; water rights

riprap

1. A foundation or wall of stones or rocks that are loosely placed together without order; usually constructed adjacent to deep water to prevent scour on the sides of bulkheads, or at river bends to prevent erosion from fast flowing water; may also be made of wood or concrete beams laid in regular patterns.

2. Irregularly broken, large pieces of rock, used along stream banks and ocean fronts as protection against erosion. (R.S. Means)

rise

1. The vertical distance from the top of a tread to the top of the next higher tread.

2. The height of an arch from springing to the crown.

3. The vertical height from the supports to the ridge of a roof. (R.S. Means)

rise and run. The angle of inclination or slope of a member or structure, expressed as the ratio of the vertical rise to the horizontal run. (R.S. Means)

riser

1. The vertical part of a stair step that is in back of the tread.

2. A vertical pipe or vent that services other fixtures.

riser height. The vertical distance between the tops of two successive treads. (R.S. Means)

risk. The probability that foreseen events will not occur. Risk may be incurred as a result of the impact of general economic and market conditions upon the performance of the specific property, the interaction of a group of real estate investments in a portfolio, or the operation of the real estate enterprise as an independent venture. *See also* probability (*P*); uncertainty.

risk-adjusted discount rate. In risk analysis, a discount rate that is adjusted to offset one or more risk factors—e.g., when a future downswing in the business cycle is likely, the risk associated with a project may increase near the end of its term, necessitating a special adjustment to the discount rate. Such discount rates include all of the elements of risk associated with an income stream for a specified period adjusted to offset additional term risk. *See also* risk rate.

risk analysis. Quantitative methods used to assess risk by measuring the probability of various occurrences. Risk analysis examines the potential for change in market conditions and property performance, which can affect *NOI* forecasts and value. *See also* probability analysis; utility functions.

risk factor. The portion of a given return or rate of return from capital invested in an enterprise that is assumed to cover the risks associated with the particular investment; as

distinguished from, and in excess of, the return or rate obtainable from funds in an investment in which the safety of principal is virtually assured.

risk management. An approach to management and procedure designed to prevent occurrence of culpability, potential liability, contravention of law, or other potential risk that could bring about loss in the process of building construction. (R.S. Means)

risk premium. In risk or security analysis, the return over and above the risk-free rate.

risk rate. The annual rate of return on capital that is commensurate with the risk assumed by the investor; the rate of interest or yield necessary to attract capital. *See also* risk-adjusted discount rate; safe rate.

river bed. The land between a river's banks that is worn away by the regular flow of water.

rivulet. A small stream.

RNMI. *See* Realtors National Marketing Institute.

road. A rural collector road without curbs.

roadside development. A residential, commercial, or industrial strip development that occupies the frontage properties abutting a highway leading from an urban community.

roadway. The area of a highway including the surface over which vehicles travel as well as the land along the edges, such as slopes, ditches, channels, or other gradations necessary to ensure proper drainage and safe use. (R.S. Means)

rock. Natural, consolidated or unconsolidated mineral matter of various compositions. *See also* igneous rock; metamorphic rock; sedimentary rock.

rock wool. *See* mineral wool.

rod. A unit of length that measures 5½ yards or 16½ feet.

ROI. Return on investment.

roll. *See* tax roll.

rolling grille door. A device similar to a roll-up door, but with an open grille rather than slats; used as security protection. (R.S. Means)

rollover mortgage. A mortgage in which the terms, or interest rate, are reviewed and adjusted periodically according to contract. Technically the outstanding principal balance is due on the renewal date, but lenders may extend the mortgage for a second renewal period or even renew the entire amount of the mortgage at the going market rate. Usually only the interest rate is adjusted, and monthly payments are based on the remaining term for the following renewal period. Also called *renewable mortgage.*

roll roofing. A roofing material that is made of compressed fibers saturated with asphalt and is supplied in rolls.

roll-up door. A device consisting of horizontal interlocking metal slats that ride along wall guides. When the door is opened the slats coil around a barrel assembly located above the door. (R.S. Means)

ROM. Read only memory; in computer usage, permanent, high-speed memory that usually contains a manufacturer's program; not used to record data; retained when power to the computer is shut off.

roof. The top portion of a structure. Types include butterfly roof, double-pitch roof, flat roof, gable roof, gambrel roof, hip roof, lean-to roof, M roof, mansard roof, pyramid roof, sawtooth roof, semicircular roof, single-pitch roof.

roof decking. Prefabricated sections of lightweight insulated waterproof panels. This type of roof deck is quickly completed and consequently inexpensive. Roof decking is made of different roofing materials, such as plywood, aluminum, steel, or timber. (R.S. Means)

roofer. A piece of lumber, usually one inch thick, that is fastened to the rafters; used to enclose the top of a building frame and to support the roof covering; also called *roof sheathing.*

roofing. Any material that acts as a roof covering, making it impervious to the weather, such as shingles, tile, or slate. (R.S. Means)

roofing felt. Sheets of felt or some other close-woven, heavy material that are placed on top of the roof boards for insulation and waterproofing; treated with bitumen or another tar derivative to increase its water resistance; applied with a sealing compound or with intense heat, which softens the tar so it adheres to the roof.

roofing shingles. *See* shingles.

roofing square
1. A steel square used by carpenters.
2. A measure of roofing material. (R.S. Means)

roofing tile. A preformed slab of baked clay, concrete, cement, or plastic laid in rows as a roofing cover. Tiles have a variety of patterns, but fall into two classifications: roll and flat. (R.S. Means)

roof insulation. Lightweight concrete used primarily as insulating material over structural roof systems. (R.S. Means)

roof pitch. The slope or inclination of a roof, usually expressed in inches; e.g., a 5-inch pitch, a 5-in-12 pitch, and a 5-to-12 pitch all mean that the roof slope rises five inches for every 12 inches of horizontal distance.

roof sheathing. Any sheet or board material, such as plywood or particle board, connected to the roof rafters to act as a base for shingles or other roof coverings. (R.S. Means)

roof structure. Any structure on or above the roof of a building. (R.S. Means)

roof truss. A truss used in the structural system of a roof. (R.S. Means)

room count. The number of rooms in a building; a unit of comparison used primarily in residential appraisal. No national standard exists on what constitutes a room. The Federal Housing Administration counts an alcove opening off the living room as one-half room, but does not count dining space within a kitchen. The generally accepted method is to consider as separate rooms only those rooms that are effectively divided and to exclude bathrooms.

room finish schedule. Information provided on design drawings specifying types of finishes to be applied to floors, walls, and ceilings for each location. (R.S. Means)

rooming house. A house where lodging is provided to paying guests. *See also* bed and breakfast; boarding house.

room night. In the lodging industry, a unit of demand that denotes one room occupied for one night by one or more individuals.

root-mean-square average. *See* standard deviation.

root stock. The part of a tree or vine that includes the root system; may differ in type from the crown and trunk of the plant. A plant is budded or grafted to a different root stock to provide a root system that is more resistant to disease or nematodes or to encourage rapid growth. The life span of the tree or vine depends upon the type of root stock.

rotary interchange. An intersection of multiple highways in which traffic interchange for entrance and exit is controlled in a circular traffic flow.

rotunda. A circular building or room that is covered by a dome.

roughage. Plant materials that contain a small proportion of nutrients per unit of weight and are usually bulky, coarse, high in fiber, and low in total digestible nutrients; may be classified as dry or green.

rough hardware. Metalware, e.g., nails, screws, bolts, that is buried in construction and rarely exposed to view.

rough in
1. The base coat in three-coat plasterwork.
2. Any unfinished work in a construction job. (R.S. Means)

rough opening. An opening in a wall or framework into which a door frame, window frame, subframe, or rough buck is fitted. (R.S. Means)

rough work. The framing, boxing, and sheeting for a wood-framed building. (R.S. Means)

rounding. Expressing an amount as an approximate number—i.e., exact only to a specific decimal place. An appraisal conclusion may be rounded to reflect the lack of precision associated with the value opinion.

round timber. Timber used in its original round form, e.g., poles, pilings, mine timbers. *See also* lumber; timber.

row crop. Farm crops planted in rows to permit cultivation during growth; generally vegetables or produce for human consumption, but some seed crops are planted in rows.

row house. An attached house in a row of architecturally uniform houses separated by party walls and covered by a continuous roof.

row stores. *See* strip development.

royalty. In real estate, the money paid to an owner of realty for the right to deplete the property of a natural resource, e.g., oil, gas, minerals, stone, builders' sand and gravel, timber; usually expressed as a stated part or price per unit of the amount extracted; a combination of rent and a depreciation, or depletion, charge. *See also* landowner's royalty; overriding royalty.

RRM. *See* renegotiable rate mortgage.

RTC. *See* Resolution Trust Corporation.

rubber tile. A resilient, durable tile containing either natural or synthetic rubber that is burn resistant and sound absorbent.

rubble. Field stone.

rubblework. Masonry built of rubble or roughly dressed stones that are laid in irregular courses.

rule of joinder. A consideration in highest and best use analysis that the combination of two parcels into one will produce a higher use, resulting in a higher value, than the aggregate of the values of the two parcels appraised separately.

rule of 72. A rule of thumb for calculating the number of years it will take for a deposit in a fixed interest-bearing account to double, i.e., divide 72 by the rate of interest being paid on the deposit; thus, if a time deposit is earning 8% annual interest, it will take 9 years for the deposit to double.

running lines. Set boundary lines; refer to the calls (natural objects that mark the boundary of the land conveyed) in the grant and field notes carried into the grant, or to the map

or plan referred to in the conveyance.

runway. Decking over an area of concrete placement, usually of movable panels and supports, on which buggies of concrete travel to points of placement. (R.S. Means)

rural. Pertaining to the country as opposed to urban or suburban; land under an agricultural use; signifies areas that exhibit relatively slow growth with less than 25% development.

rural-urban boundary or fringe. Transitional land on the periphery of an urban or suburban area.

rurban. An area in transition from agricultural use to suburban residential and commercial development; an area with both rural and suburban characteristics that is within commuting distance of a city.

rustic siding. Siding designed to resemble the exterior of a rough-hewn cabin.

_R_ value. A standard for measuring the ability of an insulation material to resist the flow of heat. *R* value is derived by measuring the British thermal units (Btus) transmitted in one hour through the thickness of the insulation. The higher the *R* value, the more effective the insulation.

S

safe rate. The minimum rate of return on invested capital. Theoretically the difference between the total rate of return and the safe rate is considered a premium to compensate the investor for risk, the burden of management, and the illiquidity of the capital invested; also called *riskless rate. See also* risk rate.

sagebrush. A type of range where species of sagebrush predominate.

sale barn. A livestock shed in an auction sale yard where livestock are exhibited as they are sold.

sale contract. A written document signed by a buyer and a seller who agree to the transfer of ownership interests in real estate; also called *agreement of sale* or *earnest money contract. See also* contract date.

sale-leaseback. A financing arrangement in which real property is sold by its owner-user, who simultaneously leases the property from the buyer for continued use. Under this arrangement, the seller receives cash from the transaction and the buyer is assured a tenant and thus a fixed return on the investment.

sale price. *See* price.

sales-assessment ratio. A ratio derived by dividing the sale price of a property by its assessed value.

sales commission. A fee paid to a salesperson or broker who arranges for the sale of property; generally expressed as a percentage of the sale price.

sales comparison approach. A set of procedures in which a value indication is derived by comparing the property being appraised to similar properties that have been sold recently, applying appropriate units of comparison, and making adjustments to the sale prices of the comparables based on the elements of comparison. The sales comparison approach may be used to value improved properties, vacant land, or land being considered as though vacant; it is the most common and preferred method of land valuation when comparable sales data are available.

sales-ratio analysis. A study of the relationship between assessed values and sale prices and the deviations that result from differences between the two; used to determine the efficiency and fairness of the assessment process in a particular jurisdiction.

sales value. A value determined by 1) adding to the stated sale price the proceeds from the issuance of a real estate option that is exercised and other payments that are in substance additional sales proceeds—these nominally may be management fees, points, or prepaid interest or fees that are required to be maintained in an advance status and applied against the amounts due to the seller at a later date and 2) subtracting from the sale price a discount to reduce the receivable to its present value and by the net present value of the services that the seller commits to perform without compensation or by the net present value of the services in excess of the compensation that will be received. (FASB)

saline soil. A soil that contains enough common alkali salts to harm plant growth.

salt box architecture. *See* New England colonial architecture.

saltbush. A type of range vegetation that includes areas predominated by various salt desert shrubs such as *atriplex*.

salvage value. The price expected for a whole property, e.g., a house, or a part of a property, e.g., a plumbing fixture, that is removed from the premises usually for use elsewhere.

SAM. *See* shared appreciation mortgage.

sample. In statistics, a limited or finite number of observations selected from a universe and studied to draw qualified, quantitative generalizations with respect to the universe.

sampling. The selection of representative statistical data from which inferences are drawn about the characteristics of an entire statistical population; is especially useful in forecasting market demand.

sampling error. The difference between a sample statistic and the characteristic that would have been found if the entire population had been tested.

sand. Small rock or mineral fragments ranging in diameter from 1 to 0.005 millimeters and classified as follows: coarse sand, 1 to 0.50 millimeters; sand, 0.50 to 0.25 millimeters; fine sand, 0.25 to 0.10 millimeters; very fine sand, 0.100 to 0.005 millimeters; soils that contain 90% or more of all grades of sand combined.

sandwich beam. *See* flitch beam.

sandwich building. A structure that does not have freestanding side walls, but shares party walls with the adjoining buildings.

sandwich construction. Composite construction usually incorporating thin layers of a strong material bonded to a thicker, weaker, and lighter core material, such as rigid foam or paper honeycomb, to create a product which has high strength-to-weight and stiffness-to-weight ratios.

sandwich lease. A lease in which an intermediate, or sandwich, leaseholder is the lessee of one party and the lessor of another. The owner of the sandwich lease is neither the fee owner nor the user of the property; he or she may be a leaseholder in a chain of leases, excluding the ultimate sublessee.

sandwich leaseholder. The lessor under a sandwich lease.

sandwich lot. A vacant lot situated between buildings in a built-up area which awaits development.

sandwich panel

1. A panel formed by bonding two thin facings to a thick, and usually lightweight, core. Typical facing materials include plywood, single veneers, hardboard, plastics, laminates, and various metals such as aluminum or stainless steel. Typical core materials include plastic foam sheets, rubber, and formed honeycombs of paper, metal, or cloth.

2. A prefabricated panel, which is layered composite, formed by attaching two thin facings to a thicker core. An example is precast concrete panels, which consist of two layers of concrete separated by a nonstructural insulating core. (R.S. Means)

sandy loam. A soil that contains much sand and enough silt and clay to make it somewhat coherent; will form a weak cast when dry and squeezed in the hand.

sanitary base. A three-member base consisting of a common baseboard, a base mold above, and a shoe mold that is let up behind the common base. The shoe mold is fastened to the floor and the common base is nailed to the studs above it; in common and molded bases, the common baseboard rests directly on the floor.

sanitary code. Municipal regulations established to control sanitary conditions of establishments that produce and/or distribute food, serve food, or provide medical services. (R.S. Means)

sanitary district. An assessment district established with particular reference to improvements, e.g., sewers and sewage disposal plants, that are constructed in the interest of sanitation and health; a municipal corporation organized to secure, preserve, and promote the public health.

sanitary engineering. The part of civil engineering related to public health and the environment, such as water supply, sewage, and industrial waste. (R.S. Means)

sanitary landfilling. A waste disposal method in which solid waste is spread on land in thin layers, compacted to the smallest practical volume, and covered with soil periodically; used to protect the environment.

sanitary sewer. A sewer that carries only sewage, not storm water runoff.

SARA. *See* Superfund Amendment and Liability Act of 1986.

sash. The framework that holds the glass in a window or door.

satellite cities. Subordinate communities in a metropolitan area which have vital economic ties with the central city.

satellite tenant. An independent merchant or an affiliate of a national chain who leases a store in a shopping center, as distinguished from a major department store operator; attracted to the shopping center by the presence of a major tenant and the traffic that the major tenant will generate.

satisfaction. The payment or discharge of a debt or obligation.

satisfaction of mortgage. A certificate issued by the mortgagee when the mortgage is paid off, certifying completion of payment on the mortgage and authorizing its discharge from the record.

satisfaction piece. The document which records and acknowledges the payment of an indebtedness secured by a mortgage. (R.S. Means)

saturation zone. The lower ground water zone; the area below the aeration zone that serves as a reservoir for ground water which supplies wells, streams, and springs.

savings and loan association (S & L). A financial intermediary that receives savings deposits, lends money at interest, and distributes dividends to depositors after paying operating expenses and establishing appropriate reserves. *See also* Financial Institutions Reform, Recovery and Enforcement Act (FIRREA).

saw log. A log that is large enough to be used for sawed lumber or other sawed products; its size and quality vary with regional use practices.

sawtooth roof. A roof consisting of a series of single-pitch roofs; allows abundant light and ventilation; usually found on factory buildings, garages, and similar structures.

scale
1. The estimated sound contents of a log or group of logs in terms of a given log rule; to estimate the sound contents of a log or group of logs.
2. A measured length on maps and engineering plans that is used to convert map measurements into actual measurements; e.g., one inch on a map may equal one foot in actual length.

scantling lumber. Yard lumber two inches thick and less than eight inches wide.

scarcity. The present or anticipated undersupply of an item relative to the demand for it. Conditions of scarcity contribute to value.

scatter diagram. A chart that shows data points plotted according to coordinates that represent two variables.

scenic easement. A restriction that is imposed on the use of the grantor's property to preserve the natural, scenic, or historic attractiveness of adjacent lands owned by the grantee, usually a city, a county, a state, or the federal government.

scheduled rent. Income due under existing leases.

schedule number. Schedule numbers are American Standards Association designations for classifying the strength of pipe. Schedule 40 is the most common form of steel pipe used in the mechanical trades. (R.S. Means)

schedule of values (cost breakdown). A listing of elements, systems, items, or other subdivisions of the work, establishing a value for each, the total of which equals the contract sum. The schedule of values is used for establishing the cash flow of a project. (R.S. Means)

schematic design phase (schematic drawing). The phase of design services in which the design professional consults with an owner to clarify the project requirements. The design professional prepares schematic design studies with drawings and other documents illustrating the scale and the relationship of the project's components to the owner. A statement of estimated construction cost is often submitted at this phase. (R.S. Means)

scope of the appraisal. Extent of the process in which data are collected, confirmed, and reported.

S corporation. A corporation that has elected to be taxed like a partnership, in accordance with the provisions of subchapter S of the tax code of the Internal Revenue Service. (R.S. Means)

scrap value. The price expected for a part of a property that is sold and removed from the premises to reclaim the value of the material of which it is made, e.g., plumbing fixtures sold for their metal content.

scratch coat. The first coat of plaster, which is scratched or scored to provide a proper base for the second coat.

SCR brick. A larger-than-average brick designed for use in a one-story wall where a single layer of such bricks is sufficient.

scribing. The fitting of woodwork along an irregular surface.

Scribner rule. A diagram rule for measuring logs into 1-in. boards at least 4 inches wide, assuming a ¼-in. saw kerf; does not consider the taper of logs and gives a large overrun for small logs and logs longer than 16 feet; not recommended for logs less than 12 inches in diameter; generally used on fir and pine timber; also called *Scribner scale.*

SCS. Soil Conservation Service.

scuttle. A framed opening in a ceiling or roof that is fitted with a lid or cover.

seal. A legal term used to describe the signature or other representation of an individual agreeing to the terms and conditions of an agreement or contract. (R.S. Means)

sealed bid. A bid, based on contract documents, that is submitted sealed for opening at a designated time and place. (R.S. Means)

sealed bidding. A basic method of procurement that involves the solicitation of bids and the award of a contract to the responsible bidder submitting the lowest responsive bid. This type of bidding is commonly used on public works projects. (R.S. Means)

sea level. The level of the surface of the sea between mean high and low tides. Land elevation is measured in feet above sea level.

seamless flooring. Fluid or trowel-applied floor surfaces that do not contain aggregates. (R.S. Means)

seasonal dwelling. A dwelling not intended for year-round use, e.g., a leisure home such as a beach house or ski lodge.

seasonal stream. A stream that flows only during the rainy part of the year.

seat. Membership in a national securities exchange.

SEC. *See* Securities and Exchange Commission.

second and third liens. Encumbrances that are subordinate to the first lien; also called *junior liens.*

second and third mortgages. Mortgages that are subordinate to the first mortgage; also called *junior mortgages.*

secondary easement. The right of the owner of an easement to keep the easement in repair; includes the right to enter the servient estate at all reasonable hours to perform necessary repairs and maintenance or to make original constructions necessary for the enjoyment of the easement; as distinguished from an ancillary easement, which is the right to go on another's land to carry off a profit *(profit à prendre).*

secondary financing. A loan that is junior or subordinate to one or more loans or encumbrances, which have priority to the property as security for the amounts owed.

secondary location. A location that is near or adjacent to the prime location; a second-best location; enhanced by its proximity to the prime location.

secondary mortgage market. A market created by government and private agencies for the purchase and sale of existing mortgages; provides greater liquidity for mortgages. Fannie Mae, Freddie Mac, and Ginnie Mae are the principal operators in the secondary mortgage market.

secondary soil. A soil that has been transported and redeposited by water or wind.

secondary trade area. The portion of a trade area that supplies additional support to a shopping center beyond that provided by the primary trade area. A shopping center may obtain 20% to 30% of its total customers from its secondary trade area, which is adjacent to the perimeter of the primary trade area. *See also* trade area.

second bottom. The first terrace level of a stream valley; lies above the floodplain and rarely, if ever, floods. *See also* first bottom; floodplain.

second deed of trust. A deed of trust that is subordinate to the first deed of trust.

second foot. A measure that equals a flow of one cubic foot of water per second, or 449 gallons per minute.

second growth. Forest growth that comes up after the old stand is removed by cutting, fire, or other causes; smaller trees left after lumbering, or trees available for a second logging operation.

section
1. In the government survey system of land description, one of the 36 sections, each one mile square, into which each township is divided.
2. In architecture, a detailed drawing that depicts a cross section of a building.

Section 8 housing. A federal program that provides assistance for lower-income households. The difference between the HUD-established allowable rent for each unit and the household's contribution is paid by HUD to the project owner or manager. *See also* limited-equity housing; public housing.

sectional insulation. Insulation that is manufactured to be assembled in the field, such as pipe insulation molded in two parts to fit around a pipe in the field. (R.S. Means)

sectional overhead doors. Doors made of horizontally hinged panels that roll into an overhead position on tracks, usually spring-assisted. (R.S. Means)

sector theory. A theory of urban growth developed by Homer Hoyt in 1934 which holds that urban development around a central economic core can be broken down into distinct sectors differentiated by the social and economic status of the residents. These sectors are connected to the central core by thoroughfares, characterized as bands of retail businesses and industrial plants. Also called *wedge theory*. *See also* urban growth theories.

secular cycle. A long-term cycle of real estate market activity that reflects changes in the characteristics of the existing population and its income.

secular trend. In statistics, a long-term growth or decline established within the data; should not cover a period of less than 10 years.

securities. A class of investments represented by engraved, printed, or written documents that show ownership or creditorship in a corporation or other form of business organization; includes creditorship in public bodies, e.g., bonds, stocks, mortgages, notes, coupons, scrip, warrants, rights, options.

Securities and Exchange Commission (SEC). A federal agency created by the Securities Exchange Act of 1934 to carry out the provisions of that act and to take over, from the Federal Trade Commission, the administration of the Securities Act of 1933.

securitization. Business investment that is represented by securities rather than by direct sole ownership.

security. An asset that is deposited or pledged as a guarantee of the payment or fulfillment of an obligation or debt. *See also* private offering; registration; subscription agreement.

security agreement. An agreement between a secured party and a debtor that creates a security interest.

security deposit. A cash payment to a landlord that is held during the term of a lease to ensure against failure to pay rent, theft of property, or damages to property by the tenant.

sedimentary peat. A soil made up of finely divided plant, and sometimes animal, remains. *See also* peat soil.

sedimentary rock. A rock composed of particles deposited after suspension in water; chief groups are: conglomerates, from gravel; sandstones, from sands; shales, from clays; and limestones, from calcium carbonate deposits.

seed money. The money needed to initiate a project, e.g., funds needed to acquire or control a site, to obtain zoning, to perform feasibility studies.

seepage. The loss of water from a natural or artificial watercourse or body of water by slow percolation or movement through the ground or the walls of a reservoir.

segmentation. *See* market segmentation.

segregated cost method. *See* unit-in-place method.

seisin. Possession of real property by one who claims ownership of a freehold interest therein (fee simple or life estate).

seismic load (earthquake load). The assumed lateral load an earthquake might cause to act upon a structural system in any horizontal direction. (R.S. Means)

selected bidding. A process of competitive bidding for award of the contract for construction whereby the owner selects the constructors who are invited to bid to the exclusion of others, as in the process of open bidding. (R.S. Means)

select lumber. Lumber, e.g., flooring, that is selected for length, color, grain, and the relative absence of imperfections; very similar to clear grade, usually containing a substantial quantity of it.

self-contained appraisal report. A report that, in compliance with Standards Rule 2 of the Uniform Standards of Professional Appraisal Practice, sets forth the data considered, the appraisal procedures followed, and the reasoning employed in the appraisal. A self-contained report addresses each item in the depth and detail required by its significance to the appraisal and provides sufficient information so that the client, the users of the report, and the public will understand the appraisal and not be misled or confused.

self-liquidating mortgage. A mortgage loan that will be completely repaid at maturity by amortization payments. If the installment payments are constant, it is a constant-payment loan; otherwise, it is a variable-payment loan.

self-supporting walls. Walls that support their own weight, but do not carry the weight of the floors above or below, the roof, or the live load.

seller's market. An active market in which the sellers of available properties can obtain higher prices than those obtainable in the immediately preceding period; a market in which a few available properties are demanded at prevailing prices by many users and potential users.

semiarid land. Land that receives little precipitation—i.e., from 10 to 20 inches of rainfall annually.

semibasement. A basement that is only partly below ground level. (R.S. Means)

semicircular roof. A type of curved roof that is often used on barns.

semi-detached dwelling. One of a pair of dwellings with a party wall between them. (R.S. Means)

semi-detached house. One of a pair of houses with a party wall between them. (R.S. Means)

semi-housed stair. A stair which has a wall on one side only. (R.S. Means)

senior mortgage. A mortgage that has preference over another mortgage.

sensitivity analysis. A method for isolating how change in one or more variables may affect investment risk. *See also* risk analysis.

septic system. A private sewage system that usually consists of a septic tank, a distribution box, a septic field, and connecting pipes and laterals.

septic tank. A tank in which sewage is held until the organic matter decomposes by natural bacterial action and most of the solid matter dissolves into liquids and gases that flow into the septic field. *See also* cesspool.

sequence of adjustments. The order in which quantitative adjustments are applied to the sale prices of comparable properties. The sequence of adjustments is determined by the market and through analysis of the data. Percentage adjustments must be applied in a specific sequence whenever they are added and subtracted—i.e., property rights conveyed, financing (cash equivalency), conditions of sale (motivation), and market conditions (time).

service drop. The overhead conductors that connect the electrical supply or communication line to the building being served. (R.S. Means)

service industry. An industry based on the sale of a service, e.g., insurance, banking, accounting, rather than a product.

service line. A pipeline that connects a public water or gas main with a property.

service road. *See* frontage road.

services

1. In economics, the contributions of business organizations or persons who render a service, e.g., teacher, accountant, rather than produce goods.
2. The facilities that are provided to a community by local government, e.g., police and fire protection, water and sewer systems.

service station. A commercial enterprise specifically designed to provide services and products for automobiles and trucks; also called *filling station, gasoline station,* or *gasoline service station.*

servient estate. *See* negative easement.

setback

1. Zoning regulations that designate the distance a building must be set back from the front property line.
2. The height at which the upper floors of a building are recessed, or set back, from the face of the lower structure.

setback line. A line outside a right-of-way, established by public authority or private restriction; between this line and the roadway, the construction of improvements is controlled.

set-off. A reduction in the thickness of a wall; a flat or sloping ledge or projection below the thinner part of a wall; also a sunken panel or a recess of any kind in a wall.

set-off provision. A lease provision that allows for a reduction in rent. *See also* offset.

set-off rule. In eminent domain, a rule governing the setting off of special benefits. Federal courts and some state courts allow benefits to be set off against both the value of the land taken and the damages to the remainder; in other jurisdictions, benefits are set off against damages to the remainder only.

settlement

1. Sinking of solid particles in grout, mortar, or fresh concrete, after placement and before initial set.
2. An agreement by which the parties consent to settle a dispute between them.
3. The total amount of money that both the insurance company and the policy holder agree on to close the claim. (R.S. Means)

settling. The lowering in elevation of sections of pavement or structures due to their mass, the loads imposed on them, or shinkage or displacement of the support. (R.S. Means)

set up

1. The stationing of a surveying instrument, such as a transit.
2. Descriptive of concrete or similar firm material.
3. In plumbing, to bend up the edge of a sheet of lead lining material.
4. To caulk a pipe joint with lead by driving it in with a blunt chisel. (R.S. Means)

severance

1. The act of removing anything attached or affixed to land, or a part of the land itself, that causes a change of its character from real property to personal property.
2. The separation of mineral ownership from land ownership; a conveyance of land in which mineral rights are excepted or reserved.
3. The termination of a joint tenancy or a tenancy in common. *See also* severance damages.

severance damages. In a partial taking, a decline in the market value of the remainder that arises as a result of the taking and/or the construction of the proposed improvement. *See also* just compensation; severance.

sewage. Any liquid-borne waste containing animal or vegetable matter in suspension or solution. Sewage may include chemicals in solution; ground, surface, or storm water may be added as it is admitted to or passes through the sewers. (R.S. Means)

sewage ejector. A plumbing device used to raise sewage to a higher elevation. (R.S. Means)

sewage gas. The mixture of gases, odors, and vapors, sometimes including poisonous and combustible gases, found in a sewer. (R.S. Means)

sewage treatment plant. Structures and appurtenances that receive raw sewage and bring about a reduction in organic and bacterial content of the waste so as to render it less dangerous and less odorous. (R.S. Means)

sewer. An underground system of pipes or conduits that carries sewage and/or rainwater from a point of reception to a point of disposal. *See also* combination sewer; sanitary sewer; septic system; storm sewer.

sewer appurtenances. Manholes, sewer inlets, and other devices, constructions, or accessories related to a sewer system but exclusive of the actual pipe or conduit. (R.S. Means)

sewer line easement. An easement for the construction, maintenance, and operation of a sewage disposal line.

SFD. Single-family dwelling.

SFR. Single-family residence.

shack. A primitively built wooden structure; a hut or shanty.

shake. A hand-split shingle that is usually edge-grained.

sharecropper. A tenant farmer who receives land, living quarters, seed, stock, and implements from the owner and, in return, shares the crops produced.

share cropping rent. A compromise between renting and wage payments in which the tenant usually contributes labor only and is managed and financed by the owner.

shared appreciation mortgage (SAM). A debt secured by real estate in which the borrower receives assistance in the form of capital when buying the real property in return for giving the lender a portion of the property's future appreciation in value; also called *shared equity mortgage.*

shared business. A retail enterprise that, together with other complementary retail establishments, ex-

erts a cumulative attraction upon shoppers in a given area. While the attraction of a shared business is not as strong as that of a generative business, the gravitational pull of a combination of retail operations is sufficient to draw customers to the area. *See also* generative business; suscipient business.

sheathing. The first, tight covering applied to the outside of a building.

sheathing line. The outside vertical plane of exterior wall sheathing.

shed roof. *See* lean-to roof.

sheet erosion. The loss of surface soil by water, usually in even amounts over a given area.

sheet piling. Planking or steel shafts placed vertically and close together to form a temporary wall around an excavation.

Sheetrock. A trade name for drywall or gypsum wallboard.

shell. The structural portion, common areas, common systems, demising walls, and other elements of a building. For occupancy by a tenant, a shell building requires tenant improvements.

shell construction

1. A type of reinforced concrete construction in which thin curved slabs are primary elements.

2. Construction in which a curved exterior surface has been obtained by using shaped steel and hardboard or curved plywood panels. (R.S. Means)

shelter belt. A band or row of trees or large shrubs planted to protect farm buildings in open plains country from blizzards, snowstorms, and prevailing winds.

shingles. A surfacing material used on roofs or walls and composed of thin, small sheets of waterproof material, e.g., asphalt, fiberglass, wood, slate, tile, laid in an overlapping pattern.

shoe. A structural member that is laid horizontally on rough flooring to serve as a base for interior partition framing; common in platform construction; also used as a base for bearing partitions on top of an I-beam or steel beam where studs are let down to support the partitions.

shop drawings. Drawings created by a contractor, subcontractor, vendor, manufacturer, or other entity that illustrate construction, materials, dimensions, installation, and other pertinent information for the incorporation of an element or item into the construction. (R.S. Means)

shopping center. A tract of land, under individual or joint real estate ownership or control, improved with a coordinated group of retail buildings with a variety of stores and free parking. *See also* anchor tenant; community shopping center; fashion shopping center; festival shopping center; neighborhood shopping center; off-price shopping center; outlet shopping center; power shopping center; regional shopping center; satellite tenant; specialty shopping center; super–mall; superregional shopping center.

shopping goods. Goods from variety, department, and general merchandise stores, e.g., clothing, furniture, appliances.

shoreline. The land between high and low tide; the strip of land along the shore.

shoring. Temporary structural columns, beams, and braces that are used to support loads during building construction.

short-lived item. A building component with an expected remaining economic life that is shorter than the remaining economic life of the entire structure.

short-term cycle. A temporary cycle of real estate market activity that occurs in response to the availability of credit.

short-term lease. An indefinite term, but usually implies a contract with a term of less than 10 years.

short-term mortgage trust. A trust that is primarily engaged in making construction and development loans; its revenue is derived from interest and fees.

short ton. A unit of weight in the English system equal to 2,000 pounds. (R.S. Means)

shoulder. The outer edge of a paved highway that is used to accommodate stopped vehicles; may or may not be paved.

shower pan. A pan of concrete, terrazzo, concrete and tile, or metal used as a floor in a shower bath. (R.S. Means)

SIC. *See* Standard Industrial Classification.

side. The longitudinal wall of a structure.

side ditch. An open watercourse for the control and removal of storm water from the paved surface of an adjacent highway; may be paved.

side jamb. A piece of finish material that is laid vertically on the interior sides of a door or window to shape the opening.

sidewalk door. A cellar door opening directly onto a sidewalk. The door is flush with the sidewalk when closed. (R.S. Means)

sidewalk elevator
1. An elevator opening onto a sidewalk.

2. An elevator platform without a cab that rises to a level flush with a sidewalk. (R.S. Means)

siding
1. Finish or exterior lumber used on outside walls, e.g., bevel siding, boards and battens, shingles.
2. An auxiliary railroad track used for meeting and passing trains, storing cars, loading and unloading, and other designated purposes; connects at both ends with the main track.

sight line. A line or area of unobstructed visibility; usually indicates the distance from which a business property or commercial site is visible to approaching vehicular traffic.

sight line easement. An easement granted to protect a sight line; usually prohibits construction or natural growth that might obstruct a property's visibility to approaching vehicular traffic.

silage. *See* ensilage.

sill
1. Framing lumber placed atop and around a foundation to serve as a level base for exterior wall studs and the ends of floor joists.
2. The lowest piece on which a window or exterior door rests; usually slanted downward

slightly to provide for rainwater runoff.

silo. A structure of wood, concrete, or steel that is used to store fodder for conversion into silage; a storage bin for grain; a grain elevator.

silt. Small mineral soil grains with particles that range in diameter from 0.050 to 0.020 millimeters.

silt clay loam. A soil composed of moderate amounts of fine grades of sand and clay, but more than 50% silt and clay, with more clay than silt loam; cloddy when dry; tends to ribbon when wet soil is squeezed between finger and thumb.

silt loam. A soil made up of moderate amounts of fine grades of sand, small amounts of clay, and at least 50% silt; appears cloddy when dry; is smooth when wet and will not ribbon when squeezed.

simple interest. Interest that is paid only on the original principal, not on any interest accrued.

simulation. The use of an experimental model that is designed to approximate actual conditions.

single contract. A construction contract arrangement under which a prime contractor is accountable for all of the work. (R.S. Means)

single-family house. A dwelling that is designed for occupancy by one family.

single floor. A floor of joists and flooring only, without intermediate support. (R.S. Means)

single-hung window. A window with a movable and fixed sash that is vertically hung. (R.S. Means)

single-pitch roof. A single-plane roof with a pitch of more than 20 degrees.

single room occupancy (SRO). Residential apartment units without private baths and cooking facilities; often rented on a weekly basis.

sinking fund. A fund in which periodic deposits of equal amounts are accumulated to pay a debt or replace assets; usually designed to receive equal annual or monthly deposits that will accumulate, with compound interest, to a predetermined sum at the end of a stated period of time.

sinking fund factor ($1/S_n$). The compound interest factor that indicates the amount per period that will grow, with compound interest, to $1. The sinking fund factor is one of the six functions of a dollar found in standard financial tables.

sinking fund table. A table indicating the amounts that will accumulate to a desired sum by a specified date in the future if invested annually in a compound interest-bearing account at a stated rate.

SIOR. *See* Society of Industrial and Office Realtors.

siphon. A bent tube that carries water from an irrigation ditch to a field.

site. Land that is improved so that it is ready to be used for a specific purpose.

site development costs. Direct and indirect costs incurred in preparing a site for use, e.g., costs for clearing, grading, installing public utilities.

site drainage
1. An underground system of piping carrying rainwater or other wastes to a public sewer.
2. The water so drained. (R.S. Means)

site improvements. Improvements on and off a site that make it suitable for its intended use or development. Onsite improvements include grading, landscaping, paving, and utility hookups; offsite improvements include streets, curbs, sidewalks, drains, and connecting utility lines.

site investigation. A complete examination, investigation, and testing of surface and subsurface soil conditions. The report resulting from the investigation is used in design of the structure. (R.S. Means)

site orientation. The relationship between a structure and its surroundings.

site plan. A plan showing the layout of site improvements on a plot. The site plan usually includes the location of site improvements, e.g., curbs, sidewalks, sewers, drains, fills, and easements. (R.S. Means)

siting factor. The origin of settlement in a city, which generally influences subsequent land use and growth patterns.

situs. In real estate, the physical location of a property; in personal property, the taxable location because personal property may be moved from one place to another.

six functions of $1. The six related compound interest functions used in the mathematics of finance and shown in standard compound interest tables. They are: the amount of $1 ($S^n$), the amount of $1 per period ($S_n$), the sinking fund factor ($1/S_n$), the present worth of $1 ($1/S^n$), the present worth of $1 per period ($a_n$), and the partial payment factor ($1/a_n$).

skeleton steel construction. *See* steel construction.

skewness. In statistics, the degree of deviation from symmetry in a distribution.

skin. A covering, outer coating, or surface layer; in construction, the covering of a structure.

skin wall. External wall covering of aluminum, porcelain enamel, steel, or other material.

skylight. A glass opening in a roof.

slab. Any broad, flat, relatively thin piece of wood, stone, or other solid material; often used to describe a floor or foundation of concrete, either on the ground or supported above it.

slab floor. A floor of reinforced concrete. (R.S. Means)

slab on grade construction. A type of construction in which the floor is a concrete slab poured after plumbing and other equipment is installed. (R.S. Means)

slash. Debris left on the ground after logging, e.g., branches, bark, tops, chunks, cull logs, uprooted stumps, broken or uprooted trees; also a large accumulation of debris left by wind or fire. *See also* slashing.

slashing. Forest area where logging has left tree limbs and tops; an area that is deep in debris from fire or wind.

sleeper. A timber that is laid horizontally, e.g., on the ground to support something above it; a strip of wood that is anchored to a concrete floor or nailed to subflooring and to which the finished floor is nailed.

sliding window. *See* traverse window.

slip. Navigable water space between two piers; generally used for small boat storage.

slip form. A form that is pulled or raised as concrete is placed. The form may move in a generally horizontal direction to lay concrete evenly for highway paving or on slopes and inverts of canals, tunnels, and siphons; or vertically to form walls, bins, or silos. (R.S. Means)

slope. The degree of inclination or deviation of a surface from the horizontal; the grade, usually expressed as a percentage. In highway usage, the graded area beyond the shoulder that extends to natural, undisturbed ground. Slopes are classified as follows: 0%–2%, nearly level and/or gently undulating; 3%–8%, gently sloping and/or undulating; 9%–15%, moderately sloping and/or rolling; 16%–30%, strongly sloping and/or hilly; 31%–45%, steep; and over 45%, very steep.

slope easement. An easement acquired to permit the cuts and fills of highway construction.

slope ratio. Relation of the horizontal projection of a surface to its rise. For example, 2 feet horizontal to 1 foot rise is shown as 2:1 or 2 to 1. (R.S. Means)

slow-burning construction. Mill construction in which structural members will char for some time under ordinary fire temperatures before they fail.

SMSA. *See* standard metropolitan statistical area.

sludge
1. The semi-liquid, settled solids from treated sewage.
2. Waste material composed of wet fines produced from grinding a terrazzo floor.
3. Accumulated solids in the wash water reservoir of paint spray booths. (R.S. Means)

Small Business Administration (SBA). Federal agency that promotes small businesses.

smart buildings. *See* integrated buildings.

smog. Fog mixed with smoke and air pollutants.

smoke and fire vent. A vent cover, installed on a roof, that opens automatically when activated by a heat-sensitive device, such as a fusible link. (R.S. Means)

smoke detector. A fire detector that indicates the presence of smoke based on a light-obscuring principle using photoelectric cells. (R.S. Means)

smoothing. The removal of irregularities from a graph by ignoring random variations. *See also* exponential smoothing; moving average.

snow fence. A portable, slat fence that is placed at strategic points along a highway or road to control drifting snow.

snow load. The live load allowed by local code, used to design roofs in areas subjecct to snowfall. (R.S. Means)

Society of Industrial and Office Realtors (SIOR). A real estate organization that serves industrial property owners, users, and investors; confers the SIOR designation.

sod. Vegetation that grows to form a mat; also called *turf.*

soffit. The underside of a building member, e.g., an arch, a cornice, an overhang, a stairway.

soft costs. *See* indirect costs.

soft goods. Nondurable merchandise such as wearing apparel.

software. A set of instructions that directs a computer to perform a function, e.g., a cost-analysis procedure.

softwood. Wood from conifers, e.g., redwood, cedar, pine, fir; does not refer to the hardness of the wood.

soil. The natural medium for plant growth on the surface of the earth; a natural body in which plants grow; composed of organic and mineral materials.

soil absorption system. A disposal system, such as an absorption trench, seepage bog, or seepage pit, that utilizes the soil for subsequent absorption of treated sewage. (R.S. Means)

soil aggregate. A single mass or duster of soil that consists of many soil particles held together e.g., a clod, a prism, a crumb, a granule. *See also* granular structure.

Soil Bank. A program administered by the U.S. Department of Agriculture in which farmers contract to divert land from the production of unneeded crops to conservation uses, for which they receive an annual rent payment.

Soil Bank Act. A federal statute designed to help farmers divert a portion of their cropland from production, thereby avoiding the accumulation of excessive agricultural commodities, and to promote soil conservation by paying farmers to put cropland in the Soil Bank, i.e., take it out of production entirely or out of the production of certain crops.

soil capability. The relative suitability of soils for crops, grazing, and other purposes. All of the soils in each of the eight capability classes have limitations and present management problems of the same relative degree, but of different kinds. Productivity may vary widely among the soils in each capability class. *See*

also Land Capability Classification System; Storie Index.

soil class. A classification of soil by particle size, used by the U.S. Department of Agriculture: 1) gravel, 2) sand, 3) clay, 4) loam, 5) loam with some sand, 6) silt-loam, and 7) clay-loam. (R.S. Means)

soil classification test. A series of tests combined with sensory observations used to classify a soil. The tests may include such aspects as grain size, distribution, plasticity index, liquid limit, and density. (R.S. Means)

soil conservation. Methods and techniques used to prevent soil depletion and to restore soil productivity; includes the use of chemical or organic fertilizers to replace elements lost through usage or leaching, the adoption of proper tillage methods and crop rotation to prevent the breakdown of soil structure, and the use of terracing or contour cultivation to reduce the erosion of topsoil.

Soil Conservation Service. A division of the U.S. Department of Agriculture concerned with obtaining a better balance of agriculture through physical adjustments in the use of land, conserving natural resources, and reducing flood hazards; provides technical assistance for local soil conservation districts.

soil erosion. The wearing or carrying away of topsoil by running water or wind. *See also* erosion.

soil fertility. The quality that enables a soil to provide the proper quantity and balance of compounds for the growth of specific plants when other factors, e.g., light, temperature, the physical condition of soil, are favorable; reflects the relative quantities of available soil nutrients.

soil fumigation. The practice of chemically treating the soil, usually before planting, to destroy diseases, fungus, nematodes, or noxious grasses and weeds. Chemicals may be sprayed or drilled into the soil; if chemical gas is used, retention is usually accomplished by covering the ground with plastic sheets.

soil genesis. The origin of the soil, particularly the processes responsible for developing the solum from unconsolidated parent material.

soil horizons. Layers or three-dimensional areas of soil with characteristics produced by soil-forming processes; approximately parallel to the soil surface, but of varying thicknesses and irregular boundaries. In agricultural appraisal, the top six feet of soil, containing the surface soil, subsoil, and substratum horizons, are most significant.

soil map. A map that illustrates the distribution and location of soil types, phases, and complexes, as well as other cultural and physical features.

soil mechanics. The application of the laws and principles of mechanics and hydraulics to engineering problems dealing with soil as a building material. (R.S. Means)

soil phase. A subdivision of soil type that denotes atypical characteristics, e.g., deep phase, shallow phase, poorly drained phase.

soil porosity. The degree to which the soil mass is permeated with pores or cavities; expressed as the percentage of the total soil volume that is unoccupied by solid particles.

soil profile. A vertical cross section of a soil showing its horizons and extending into the parent material.

soil profile group. A grouping of soils based on their profile characteristics. Alluvial soil profile groups are characterized by progressive increases in compaction and fine clay accumulations in the subsoils. Primary soil profile groups are differentiated based on the nature and composition of the underlying parent material.

soil rights. The right a landowner holds to the ground on and beneath the surface of the land.

soil sample. A vertical cross section of the soil profile that is usually taken from the top six to 18 inches of the soil.

soil series. A group of soils with the same type of profile: the same general range of color, structure, consistency, and sequence of horizons; the same conditions of relief and drainage; and common or similar origin, or parent material, and mode of formation.

soil stabilizer

1. A machine that mixes in place soil and an added stabilizer, such as cement or lime, in order to stiffen the soil.
2. A chemical added to soil to stiffen it and increase the stability of a soil mass. (R.S. Means)

soil structure. The arrangement of individual particles in a soil and the size and shape of soil aggregates; principal types are columnar, adobe, granular, buckshot, crumb, lumpy, cloddy, puddled, nut-like, and massive.

soil survey report. A written report that is accompanied by a soil map and describes the areas surveyed, the characteristics and use capabilities of the soil types and phases shown on the map, and the principal factors responsible for soil development.

soil texture. The relative proportion of the various size groups of individual soil grains.

soil type. A soil that has a relatively uniform texture throughout, in addition to the soil series characteristics.

solar design. A building design that makes use of the sun's energy; either active, using solar collectors outside the building envelope to gather energy for space or water heating, or passive, allowing the position and intensity of the sun to provide interior heating.

solar easement. A limitation on the use of property that prohibits any construction or activity that might obstruct or interfere with the reception of sunlight by an adjacent property of solar design.

solar orientation. The position of a structure in relation to the sun.

solar storage. Fluid and/or rocks used to hold some of the heat energy collected by a solar heat collector. (R.S. Means)

sole. A piece of wood, usually a two-by-four, on which wall and partition studs rest; also called *sole plate*.

solid set. A sprinkler irrigation system with permanently installed laterals and sprinklers.

solum. The upper part of the soil profile, above the parent material, where soil-forming processes are taking place. In mature soil, this includes the A and B horizons where the character of the material may be, and usually is, very different from the parent material beneath. Living roots and life processes are mostly confined to the solum.

sound absorption
1. The process of dissipating sound energy.
2. The measure of the absorptive ability of a material or object, expressed in sabins or metric sabins. (R.S. Means)

sound deadening board. A board with good sound absorption qualities; used in sound-control. (R.S. Means)

sound insulation
1. The use of materials and assemblies to reduce sound transmission from one area to another or within an area.
2. The degree to which sound transmission is reduced. (R.S. Means)

soundness. The freedom of a solid from cracks, flaws, fissures, or variations from an accepted standard. In the case of a cement, soundness is freedom from excessive volume change after setting. In the case of aggregate, soundness is the ability to withstand the aggressive action to which concrete con-taining it might be exposed, particularly that action due to weather. (R.S. Means)

soundproofing
1. The design and construction of a building or unit to reduce sound transmission.
2. The materials and assemblies used in a building or unit to reduce sound transmission. (R.S. Means)

sound-rated door. A door constructed to provide greater sound attenuation than that provided by a normal door; usually carrying a rating in terms of its sound transmission class (STC). (R.S. Means)

sound transmission class (STC). A single number indicating the sound insulation value of a partition, floor-ceiling assembly, door, or window, as derived from a curve of insulation value as a function of frequency. The higher the number is, the greater the insulation value. (R.S. Means).

sound value. For fire insurance purposes, a term synonymous with *depreciated cost.*

Southern colonial architecture. A style of architecture similar to Georgian and modern colonial, but distinguished by the use of two-story columns that form a porch across a long facade or on a side.

space heater. A small heating unit, usually equipped with a fan, intended to supply heat to a room or portion of a room. The source of heat energy may be electricity or a fluid fuel. (R.S. Means)

Spackle. A trade name for a paste used to fill in cracks in a surface before painting.

span. The horizontal, clear distance between supports. e.g., of a bridge, between columns in a structure.

spandrel. A triangular space formed by an arch, with a horizontal construction member above it and a vertical member or arch beside it; also any horizontal space between two structural features of a building, e.g., between the top of first-floor windows and the windows on the second floor.

spandrel beam. A beam that lies in the same vertical plane as the exterior wall.

Spanish architecture. A residential architectural style designed for outdoor living and characterized by a heavy tile roof, adobe or stucco walls, and an enclosed patio.

Spaulding rule. The statute rule of log measurement in California; employs a table to measure logs from 12 to 24 feet long, with longer logs scaled by doubling the values shown in the table; ignores the taper in logs and gives an overrun for large logs; produces considerable overrun when the modern band saw is used because it assumes a large saw kerf; used throughout the redwood region in its original form or as the Humboldt rule; also called *Spaulding scale.*

spec data sheet. A copyrighted name, owned by the Construction Specifications Institute (CSI). For a document written or approved and published by CSI, the sheet presents all pertinent properties and technical data related to a particular product. Useful to contractors and specifiers in the preparation of specifications for the construction process. (R.S. Means)

special assessment. An assessment against real estate levied by a public authority to pay for public improvements, e.g., sidewalks, street improvements, sewers; an amount levied against individual owners in a condominium or cooperative to cover their proportionate shares of a common expense.

special benefits. Specific, i.e., not general, benefits that accrue to the property remaining after a partial taking. *See also* benefits; general benefits; set-off rule.

special districts. Special service governments created to provide a particular service, e.g., economic development districts, water resource management districts. (ULI)

special exceptions. Uses that do not conform to the zoning code, but may be permitted under specific, tightly controlled circumstances.

special-purpose property. A limited-market property with a unique physical design, special construction materials, or a layout that restricts its utility to the use for which it was built; also called *special-design property.*

specialty shopping center. Nontraditional shopping center that has no anchor tenant and is characterized by a unique feature, mix of tenants, or theme.

special use permit. Permission granted by a local zoning agency that authorizes a use as a special exception to the applicable zoning. A special use permit in a residentially zoned area might allow for construction of a church or hospital. Such uses are considered conditional uses, only permitted upon the approval of the zoning authority. *See also* legally nonconforming use; zoning variance.

special warranty deed. A warranty clause inserted in a deed of lands in which the grantor covenants that he and his heirs will defend title to the lands against legal claims created by the actions or omissions of the grantor or his heirs. If the warranty is against the claims of all persons, it is a general warranty. *See also* bargain and sale deed; quitclaim deed.

specifications. Written instructions to the builder that contain all necessary information pertaining to dimensions, materials, workmanship, style, fabrication, colors, and finishes; supplement the details shown on the working drawings.

specific data. Details about the property being appraised, comparable sale and rental properties, and relevant local market characteristics.

specific heat. The quantity of heat required to raise the temperature of one pound of any substance by 1° Fahrenheit; expressed in Btus.

specific lien. A lien levied against a specified property, unlike a general lien which binds all the assets of the individual subject to the lien; also called a *particular lien.*

specific performance. An action that compels the performance of an agreement for the sale of real property.

speculation. The purchase or sale of property motivated by the expectation of realizing a profit from a rise or fall in its price.

speculative building. A structure that is built with the expectation that it will be sold or rented when completed.

speculative land. Land that is held primarily for future sale.

speculator. One who speculates, i.e., one who buys a commodity such as real estate expecting to sell it at a higher price.

speed-change lane. An auxiliary travel lane designed to facilitate the acceleration and deceleration of vehicles entering and leaving the road.

spendable income. *See* after-tax cash flow (*ATCF*).

split face. An exposed, rough face of a masonry unit or stone created by splitting rather than forming or sawing the face. (R.S. Means)

split-level house. A house with living areas on two or more levels with one level positioned approximately midway between the other levels.

split rate capitalization. A capitalization procedure in which different discount rates are applied to different portions of the income flows earned by real property, e.g., one rate is applied to annual equity dividends and another is applied to the equity reversion; also called *fractional rate capitalization*.

spot clearance. Demolition activities in which single structures or comparatively small groups of struc-

tures are removed from an area, but a substantial number of existing structures are retained.

spotter

1. The person who directs a truck driver into a loading or unloading position.
2. The horizontal framework between the machinery deck of a pile driver and the leads. (R.S. Means)

spot zoning. An exception to the general zoning regulations; permits specific, usually small, parcels of land to be zoned for a use that is not permitted in the surrounding area. *See also* zoning variance.

spray booth. An enclosed or partly enclosed area used for the spray painting of objects, usually equipped with a waterfall system to catch overspray and/or a filtered air supply and exhaust system. (R.S. Means.)

sprayed acoustical plaster. An acoustical plaster applied with a special spray gun. The plaster usually has a rough surface and may be perforated with hand tools before hardening. (R.S. Means)

sprayed asbestos. A fire-resistive and sound-absorbing coating of asbestos fibers and an adhesive applied to surfaces with a spray gun. Sprayed asbestos is no longer used in the U.S.A. (R.S. Means)

sprayed fireproofing. An insulating material sprayed directly onto structural members with or without wire mesh reinforcing to provide a fire-endurance rating. (R.S. Means)

spray-on insulation. Any of a number of lightweight concretes or mineral fibers and adhesives applied to surfaces and/or structural members for fire resistance, thermal insulation, or acoustic absorption. (R.S. Means)

spreader dam. A dam built across a gully so that accumulated runoff is diverted onto the flats on either side.

spreadsheet. A tabular representation of data organized into useful, measurable categories.

sprinkler system
1. A fire protection system installed in buildings that consists of an overhead system of pipes that contain pressurized water and are fitted with valves or sprinkler heads that open automatically at certain temperatures.
2. An irrigation system for landscaping.

spur track. A segment of railroad track that serves an industrial site or plant with no regular train service; generally connected to the main track at only one end; may be ap-

plied to railroad company tracks used for siding purposes.

square
1. In roofing, a finished roof area of 100 square feet.
2. In mathematics, any number multiplied by itself.

square foot cost. The cost of one square foot of an improvement; obtained by dividing the actual, or estimated, cost of a building by its gross floor area or by dividing the actual, or estimated, cost of a land improvement by its square foot area; can be multiplied by the number of square feet in a building or land improvement to produce the actual or estimated cost.

square foot method. *See* comparative-unit method; quantity survey method; unit-in-place method.

squatter's rights. Rights to the occupancy of land that are created by long, undisturbed use, but held without legal title or arrangement; similar to a right at common law.

stability. A stage in a neighborhood life cycle in which the neighborhood experiences equilibrium without marked gains or losses.

stabilized expense. A projected expense that is subject to change, but has been adjusted to reflect an equivalent, stable annual expense.

stabilized income. Income at that point in time when abnormalities in supply and demand or any additional transitory conditions cease to exist and the existing conditions are those expected to continue over the economic life of the property; projected income that is subject to change, but has been adjusted to reflect an equivalent, stable annual income. *See also* stabilized occupancy.

stabilized occupancy. Occupancy at that point in time when abnormalities in supply and demand or any additional transitory conditions cease to exist and the existing conditions are those expected to continue over the economic life of the property; the optimum range of long-term occupancy which an income-producing real estate project is expected to achieve under competent management after exposure for leasing in the open market for a reasonable period of time at terms and conditions comparable to competitive offerings. *See also* stabilized income.

stabilized value

1. A value estimate that excludes from consideration any abnormal relationship between supply and demand such as is experienced in boom periods, when cost and sale price may exceed the long-term value, or during periods of depression, when cost and sale price may

fall short of long-term value.

2. A value estimate that excludes from consideration any transitory condition which may cause excessive construction costs, e.g., a bonus or premium for material, the abnormal inefficiency of labor, the cost of delay or an excessive sale price, e.g., a premium paid due to a temporary shortage of supply.

stack. A vertical waste or vent pipe.

staff appraiser. An appraiser employed by another, usually a thrift institution or government agency. *See also* fee appraiser; institutionally employed appraiser.

staging. Temporary scaffolding used to support workers and materials during construction.

stainless steel. An alloy of steel that contains a large percentage of chromium combined with nickel, copper, or other alloys; a hard, corrosion-resistant steel that retains a polish.

staircase

1. A single flight or multiple flights of stairs including supports, frameworks, and handrails.
2. The structure containing one or more flights of stairs. (R.S. Means)

stairhead. The first stair at the top of a flight of stairs. (R.S. Means)

stair headroom. The least clear vertical distance measured from a nosing of a tread to an overhead obstruction. (R.S. Means)

stair turret. A structure containing only a winding stair. (R.S. Means)

stairway. The flights of stairs and landings in a building that form a continuous passage from one floor to another.

stairwell. A vertical shaft enclosing a stair. (R.S. Means)

Standard and Poor's. A subsidiary of McGraw-Hill, Inc., that provides numerous investor services, including ratings of bonds, common stocks, preferred stocks, and commercial paper.

standard area measures. *See* Measures in the addenda.

standard cubic content. *See* cubic content.

standard depth
1. The depth of the typical neighborhood or community lot, usually applied to lots in particular use categories such as central business district lots, outlying commercial lots, and lots in different-priced residential neighborhoods.
2. In mass appraising, the assumed depth of a typical neighborhood or community lot. These assumed standard depths may bear little relation to actual community conditions.

standard deviation. In statistics, a measure of the extent of absolute dispersion, variability, or scatter in a frequency distribution; obtained by extracting the square root of the arithmetic mean of the squares of the deviations from the arithmetic mean of the frequency distribution.

standard error. In statistics, a measure of the distribution of an estimate of a parameter.

standard error of forecast. In statistics, an estimate of the variation likely to be encountered in making forecasts based on a regression equation.

standard error of the estimate. In statistics, an estimate of the variation likely to be encountered in making predictions based on a regression equation.

standard fixed-rate mortgage. A mortgage that is fully amortizing, with a fixed interest rate and constant monthly payments; usually for a term ranging from 10 to 30 years.

Standard Industrial Classification (SIC). A system of classification developed and used by the Bureau of the Census which identifies various types of industrial activity using numerical codes of one to four digits.

standard metropolitan statistical area (SMSA). A term formerly applied to a single city with a population of at least 50,000 or a city of at least 25,000 that is combined with contiguous areas with densities of at least 1,000 people per square mile to produce a population of at least 50,000. The city and contiguous areas must be located in a county or counties with a population of at least 75,000. In 1980, SMSA was replaced by the term *metropolitan statistical area* (MSA). *See also* consolidated metropolitan statistical area (CMSA); primary metropolitan statistical area (PMSA).

standard of suitability. A description of the investor's background which an agency may require to ensure that a real estate offering is fair, just, and equitable; may include the investor's educational background, business experience and sophistication, profession, place of residence, annual income, net worth, or a combination of these facts.

standard parallels. In the government survey system of land description, the east and west lines that establish the north and south boundary lines of townships; run parallel to a baseline at 24-mile intervals.

standby commitment. A lender's promise to make a temporary loan to the borrower if he or she is un-able to get other financing; requires payment, usually based on a percentage of the desired loan. A standby commitment usually serves as a basis for securing a construction loan because the construction lender must be sure that the loan will be paid off when construction is completed.

stand cruise. An estimate of the amount of lumber in a standing forest based on a particular log rule or volume table; no deduction is made for breakage or other waste.

standing seam. A seam in sheet metal and roofing, made by turning up two adjacent edges and folding the upstanding parts over on themselves. (R.S. Means)

standing stock. Existing stock. *See also* stock.

standing timber. Timber that is still on the stump, i.e., in the tree.

starter course. The base on which and from which wall or roof shingles are laid; used to provide watertight joints at the first, or lowest, shingle course.

starting income. The level of income on the date of valuation; as distinguished from stabilized or projected income, which may or may not equal starting income.

starts. Units on which construction has begun; used as a statistical factor in evaluating the real estate market, e.g., housing starts.

state licensure and certification. *See* course provider; federally related transaction (FRT); Financial Institutions Reform, Recovery and Enforcement Act (FIRREA); provisional licensure; real estate-related transaction; temporary practice; transitional licensure.

state rule. In condemnation, the process of determining just compensation by estimating the value of the portion to be acquired as part of the whole property plus the net severance damages. *See also* before-and-after rule.

station
1. A point on the earth's surface that can be determined by surveying.
2. On a survey traverse, particularly a roadway, every 100 foot interval is called a station. (R.S. Means)

statistical analysis. Quantitative techniques used to identify and measure adjustments to the sale prices of comparable properties; techniques include statistical inference and linear and multiple regression analysis.

statistical inference. The process of reasoning from the specific to the general. *See also* inferential statistics.

statistical table. A systematic arrangement of numerical data, presented in columns or rows for comparison.

statistics
1. Quantities that have been calculated from sample data.
2. The branch of mathematics that deals with masses of numerical data; has its own terminology, methodology, and body of knowledge. *See also* descriptive statistics; inferential statistics.

statute of frauds. A statute specifying that certain kinds of contracts, such as for the sale or lease of real property, are unenforceable unless signed and in writing, or unless there is a written memorandum of terms signed by the party to be charged. Statute varies by state. (R.S. Means)

statute of repose. A legislative enactment that bars a claim against a party unless the claim is brought within a specified period of time following an event described in the statute, regardless of whether or not the statute of limitations period for that claim has expired. (R.S. Means)

statutory law. Law created by legislative enactment.

statutory redemption period. *See* redemption.

steel. Any number of alloys of iron and carbon, with small amounts of other metals added to achieve special properties. The alloys are generally hard, strong, durable, and malleable. (R.S. Means)

steel construction. A rigidly connected frame of steel or reinforced concrete that carries all external and internal loads and stresses to the foundations; enclosing walls are supported by this frame, usually at floor levels. If the steel frame has no fireproofing, it is known as *unprotected metal construction.*

steep land. Describes land with slopes ranging from 30% to 45%. *See also* slope.

step down transformer. An electric transformer with a lower voltage at the secondary winding terminals than at the primary winding terminals. (R.S. Means)

stepped floor. A floor on a stage or platform that rises in steps, as opposed to a ramped floor. (R.S. Means)

step-up or step-down annuity. A type of increasing or decreasing annuity, usually created by a lease contract that calls for a succession of level annuities of different amounts to be paid in different periods of the lease term.

step-up or step-down lease. A lease that provides for a certain rent for an initial period, followed by an increase or decrease in rent over stated periods.

step-wise regression analysis. *See* multiple regression analysis.

stick built. A term describing frame houses assembled piece-by-piece from lumber delivered to the site with little or no previous assembly into components. The more typical type of residential construction is stick built. (R.S. Means)

stile

1. A structural member of a parallel or glazed door.
2. An exterior or perimeter member of a window, other than the meeting, or check, rail in a double-hung window.

stock

1. All goods kept on hand by a commercial firm or merchant.
2. Livestock, e.g., cattle, sheep, horses; animals kept or raised on a farm or ranch.
3. The ownership shares of a company or corporation.
4. The standing supply of dwelling units available in a market. *See also* housing stock.

stock, IRS Code Section 1244. In the event that a corporation's stock becomes worthless, it may offset up to $50,000 of loss against ordinary income in each taxable year, provided the corporation meets the requirements of Section 1244 of the Internal Revenue Code. (R.S. Means)

stock corporation. A common legal entity in which investors provide organizational capital by subscribing to shares that represent ownership and a right to all proprietary benefits, but are subject to the prior claims of operating expenses and debt service on capital raised by selling bonds, debentures, and other money market instruments.

stock driveway. A corridor of government-owned land that is used by local stock raisers to move herds between seasonal pastures or from the range to a shipping point.

stocking rate. The actual number of animals on a certain area at a specific time; expressed in animal units or cows.

stock trail. A trail through grazing land that permits greater use of the range in rough, steep, or heavily wooded areas.

stool. The wooden base or support at the bottom of a window, e.g., the shelf-like interior piece that extends across the bottom of a window opening.

store area. The ground floor rentable area of an office building to be occupied as store space; square footage of store area is computed by measuring from the building line in the case of street frontages, and from the inner surface of other outer building walls and from the inner surface of corridor and other permanent partitions and to the center of partitions that separate the premises from adjoining rentable areas. No deduction is made for vestibules inside the building line or for columns or projections necessary to the building. No addition is made for bay windows extending outside the building line. (BOMA)

stores. Raw materials held for use in manufacturing, as distinguished from manufactured stock; various supplies for repairs, maintenance, etc., that are required in operations; the contents of a storeroom that is stocked to provide for current consumption; as distinguished from merchandise stock.

Storie Index. A rating system in which a soil's relative suitability for general, intensive agriculture is expressed numerically by assigning factors that represent the characteristics of the soil profile: the depth of soil, the texture of the surface, the dominant slope of the area, and other factors that are subject to management or modification, e.g., drainage, flooding, nutrient level.

storm sewer. A sewer that carries rainwater and sometimes industrial waters.

story. A horizontal division of a building; the portion between one floor and the floor above or below it.

story-and-a-half. The designation of a building in which the second story rooms have low headroom at the eaves. (R.S. Means)

straight-line change per period. Refers to a type of annuity or income/property model that increases by a fixed amount per period; also called *constant amount change per period.*

straight-line depreciation. A depreciation method in which depreciable assets, estimated at cost or on some other basis, are written off in equal, annual amounts over the estimated useful life of the assets. *See also* accelerated depreciation.

straight-line method. A method in which the periodic amount of capital recapture or depreciation is estimated by dividing the total capital to be recovered by the number of periods over which it is to be recaptured; assumes an equal amount of capital is recaptured in each period.

straight-line recapture. The recovery of capital in equal, periodic increments over the remaining economic life of an asset.

stratification. Division of the urban real estate market into many submarkets.

stratified. Composed of, or arranged in, strata or layers, e.g., stratified alluvium; describes layers in soils that are inherited from the parent material, as distinguished from horizons, which are layers produced by the process of soil formation.

stratified random sample. A statistical sample in which the population is divided into fairly uniform groups, or strata, and a random sample is drawn from each selected stratum.

straw man. An individual who buys property in another's behalf to conceal the identity of the real buyer; one who holds title for another and appears as the owner of record.

stream
1. A body of water that flows in a channel or bed; a river or brook; any flow of water, e.g., from a faucet.
2. The flow of income from a property, i.e., the income stream.

street floor. The floor of a building nearest to street level. According to some building codes, the street floor is a floor level not more than 21 inches above or 12 inches below grade level at the main entrance. (R.S. Means)

street improvements. Facilities that are provided and usually maintained by local government, e.g., paving, curbs, sidewalks, sewers.

strength in compression. The ability of a construction component to withstand an external force that tends to shorten it to the point of deformation.

stress. The action in a structural member caused by an outside force acting against it; any or all forces that act on a structural member at the same time.

stressed skin. A building design in which the frame and skin, or sheathing, are joined so that the skin helps resist strain.

stretcher. A brick or other masonry unit that is laid lengthwise in a wall.

stringer. A long, heavy, horizontal timber that supports a floor; an inclined member that supports the treads and risers of a stairway.

strip center. A strip shopping center or strip retail center. *See also* shopping center; strip development.

strip development. Commercial development in which the main thoroughfares of a city are bordered by an almost continuous row, or strip, of retail stores and allied service establishments; also any shopping area that consists of a row of stores.

strip lumber. Yard lumber that is less than two inches thick and less than eight inches wide.

strip map. A map that shows the location of existing buildings, the land uses, the ownership of surrounding properties, and various physical features of the land, e.g., roads, waterways, fences, pavements; covers a limited geographic area.

STRIP(S). Separate Trading of Registered Interest and Principal of Securities.
1. A fund separated into its corpus (principal) and coupons (interest), which are sold separately as zero-coupon securities; also refers to the zero-coupon securities sold by the U.S. Treasury.
2. A real estate investment separated into components that represent the income and the residual value. Cash flow is paid to one group of investors while proceeds of resale are paid to another.

strong market. A market that reflects either high demand and increasing price levels or a large volume of transactions.

structural analysis. The determination of stresses in members in a structure due to imposed loads from gravity, wind, earthquake, thermal effects, etc. (R.S. Means)

structural frame. All the members of a building or other structure used to transfer imposed loads to the ground. (R.S. Means)

structural height. The vertical distance from grade to the top of the structure. (R.S. Means)

structural lumber. Lumber that is at least two inches thick and at least four inches wide.

structural steel. Steel rolled in a variety of shapes and manufactured for use as load-bearing structural members. (R.S. Means)

structural timber. Structural lumber with a nominal dimension of five inches or more on each side, used mainly as posts or columns. (R.S. Means)

structure. An edifice or building; an improvement.

structure limit line. A line in navigable waters, established by the federal government through the Army Corps of Engineers, that marks the boundary beyond which no structure is permitted.

strut. A piece of wood fixed between two other pieces or members and designed to distribute pressure or weight along its length.

stubble. The basal portion of herbaceous plants that remains after the top portion has been harvested mechanically or by grazing animals.

stucco. A cement plaster that is used as a finish for exterior wall surfaces; usually applied over a metal or wood lath base.

stud grade. A grade of framing lumber under the National Grading Rule established by the American Lumber Standards Committee. Lumber of this grade has strength and stiffness values that make it suitable for use as a vertical member of a wall, including use in load-bearing walls. (R.S. Means)

studio apartment. A dwelling unit of one room that serves as an eating, sleeping, and living area; also called an *efficiency apartment.*

studs. Vertical framing members.

stumpage. Standing timber; usually applied with reference to its value. *See also* stumpage value.

stumpage value. In timber cruising, the contributory value of economically merchantable timber as it stands in the forest; the contribution of timber to the total property value of the real estate.

subbase
1. The lower part of a structural base that consists of two or more horizontal members, e.g., the base of a column; a baseboard.
2. A bed of crushed rock or gravel that is used as a stable base under a slab or roadway.

subbasement
1. A level, or levels, of a building below the basement.

2. A story immediately below a basement. (R.S. Means)

subcontractor. A person or company that performs contractual work for a developer or general contractor; one who performs some phase of the work on a project, e.g., plumbing, electrical work; may or may not have a contract with the ultimate buyer.

subdivision. A tract of land that has been divided into blocks or plots with streets, roadways, open areas, and other facilities appropriate to its development as residential, commercial, or industrial sites.

subdivision development method. A method of estimating land value when subdivision and development are the highest and best use of the parcel of land being appraised. All direct and indirect costs and entrepreneurial profit are deducted from an estimate of the anticipated gross sales price of the finished lots; the resultant net sales proceeds are then discounted to present value at a market-derived rate over the development and absorption period to indicate the value of the raw land.

subdivision regulations. Laws that regulate the design and engineering standards for public improvements in a subdivision, e.g., streets, drainage, sewers, water, electricity, telephone, street landscaping; establish an application and review process that the prospective subdivider or developer must follow.

subfloor. A floor that is laid on top of the floor joists and underneath the finish floor.

subflooring. Plywood sheets or construction grade lumber used to construct a subfloor. (R.S. Means)

subframe (rough buck, subbuck)
1. A structural frame of wood members or channel-shaped metal members that support the finish frame of a door or window.
2. A framework supporting wall siding or panels. (R.S. Means)

subjective probability. A decision maker's evaluation of the relative likelihood of unknown events.

subject to mortgage. A legal subjection of a property to an existing mortgage if the purchaser has actual or constructive notice of the mortgage, for example, if a mortgage of real property has been recorded. The new owner is not liable for mortgage payments unless he has agreed to that liability. However, the mortgagee may foreclose if there is a default in payments. (R.S. Means)

sublease. An agreement in which the lessee in a prior lease conveys the right of use and occupancy of a property to another, the sublessee.

sublessee. One who enjoys the benefits, rights, and obligations of a sublease.

sublet. *See* sublease.

submarginal land. Land that does not have enough income to cover the cost of production, even if the land were free; may refer to the average, physical quality of the land, with reference to the area's average quality.

submarket. A division of a total market that reflects the preferences of a particular set of buyers and sellers.

subordinate lien. Any mortgage lien subsequent to the first. In event of foreclosure, holders of such liens may resort to the property for payment only if there is any surplus after prior liens have been paid, with priority usually determined by the chronological sequence in which the mortgages were initiated. (R.S. Means)

subordination. A contractual arrangement in which a party with a claim to certain assets agrees to make his or her claim junior, or subordinate, to the claims of another party.

subrogation. The assumption by a third party of the legal rights of another to collect debts and damage.

An insurance carrier may, for example, step into the shoes of the insured and file a claim or lawsuit against any party when the insured could have sued. (R.S. Means)

subscription agreement. A contract or other agreement that binds the subscriber to purchase an interest in a syndicate security.

subsidence. The sinking of the upper part of the ground due to a number of causes, e.g., the lowering of the water table during a long period of drought, the removal of a mineral such as coal; when severe, can cause structural damage to buildings.

subsidy. A government grant that enables the sponsor to reduce the cost of one or more housing components, e.g., land, labor, material, financing, and thus lower the cost to the occupant.

subsoil. Usually the B horizon of soils, but its identification depends on the type of soil profile; commonly the part of the soil that lies below plow depth or below the solum.

substantial completion. The condition of the work when the project is substantially complete, and ready for owner acceptance and occupancy. Any items remaining to be completed should, at this point, be duly noted or stipulated in writing. (R.S. Means)

substantial destruction. Destruction of a building that is so complete that the structure is untenantable and cannot be restored without constructing a new building; relieves a tenant of liability for rent.

substantial performance. A party's performance of most of its contractual obligations, which entitles it to payment of at least a portion of the contract price and precludes a termination for default. (R.S. Means)

substituted partner. The transferee of an initial partner, who purchased after the close of the original syndication.

substitute facilities. The doctrine applied to the taking of a property already devoted to a public use by which just compensation is estimated by the condemnor furnishing an adequate, substantially equivalent substitute property.

substitute properties. Equally desirable properties that compete with the subject in its market area.

substitution. The appraisal principle that states that when several similar or commensurate commodities, goods, or services are available, the one with the lowest price will attract the greatest demand and widest distribution. This is the primary principle upon which the cost and sales comparison approaches are based.

substructure. A building's entire foundational structure, which is below grade, or ground, and provides a support base or footings on which the superstructure rests.

subsurface easement. The right to use land at a designated distance below its surface, e.g., for pipelines, electric and telephone circuits and cables, storage facilities.

subsurface investigation. The sampling and laboratory testing process (including soil borings) to establish subsurface profiles, relative strengths, compressibility, and other characteristics of strata deep enough to affect project design. (R.S. Means)

subsurface rights

1. The rights to the use and profits of the underground portion of a designated property; usually refers to the right to extract coal, minerals, oil, gas, or other hydrocarbon substances as designated in the grant; may include a right-of-way over designated portions of the surface.
2. The right to construct and maintain tunnels, subways, subcellars, pipelines, sewers, etc.

subsurface water sources. Sources of water below the earth's surface, e.g., underground streams running in defined underground channels, underground percolating waters channeling into surface or underground streams, diffused underground percolating waters, underground basins, wells, springs drawing from underground percolating waters.

suburban. Describes a neighborhood that contains complementary properties with less concentrated population than is typically found in an urban neighborhood.

succession. The legal right or act of acquiring property by descent; obtaining an asset by will or inheritance.

summation approach. *See* cost approach.

summation method. *See* built-up method.

sum-of-the-years' digits. A variation of the declining-balance method of depreciation in which successive numbers representing the life of the asset in years are added together. The first year's depreciation fraction is calculated using the asset's life in years as the numerator and the sum of the digits as the denominator. In the second year the process is repeated, using the second highest digit as the numerator, and so on. At the end of the last year, there is no remaining cost after writing off that year's depreciation.

sump pump. An automatic, electric pump that is installed in a base-

ment or other low area to empty the sump or cesspool.

superadequacy. An excess in the capacity or quality of a structure or structural component; determined by market standards.

Superfund Amendment and Liability Act of 1986 (SARA). Federal legislation exempting third parties who acquired real property after the disposal or placement of hazardous materials on the site, provided at the time of acquisition such defendants made "all appropriate inquiry into the previous ownership and uses of the property consistent with good commercial or customary practice in an effort to minimize liability." SARA created a fund to pay for clean-up or damages caused by hazardous material spills or waste disposal sites.

superhighway. Any type of limited-access highway that is designed for high-speed through traffic, e.g., an expressway, a freeway.

supermall. A type of shopping center with national discount and factory outlet stores as tenants; may approach or exceed an area of one million square feet. *See also* shopping center.

supermarket. A large, retail store built on one level and stocked with goods that are conveniently and conspicuously displayed so that customers may make their selections without the help of a clerk; usually sells food products and household supplies which are paid for at a checkout counter.

superregional shopping center. A shopping center that offers an extensive variety of general merchandise, apparel, furniture, home furnishings, services, and recreational facilities built around at least three major department stores of at least 100,000 square feet each; typically has 800,000 to one million square feet of gross leasable area.

superstructure. The portion of a building that is above grade. The part of a bridge above the beam seats or the spring line of an arch. (R.S. Means)

supplemental agreement. A change to an existing contract accomplished by the mutual action of the parties. (R.S. Means)

supplemental feeding. Supplying concentrates or harvested feed to livestock to correct deficiencies in the range diet.

supplemental pasture. An artificial pasture used quantitatively or qualitatively to augment range forage, particularly in emergency situations; may consist of annual grasses and legumes or the aftermath of meadows, grainfields, etc.

supplemental recreational use. A recreational use, e.g., hunting, fishing, that is incidental to the primary use of the land, e.g., for farming or ranching; may provide additional income to the property owner or lessee.

supplemental services. [In construction] services described in the schedule of designated services which are outside the normal range of services, including renderings, energy studies, value analyses, project promotion, and expert testimony. (R.S. Means)

supply. In real estate, the amount of a type of real estate available for sale or lease at various prices in a given market at a given time.

supply analysis. *See* competitive supply analysis.

supply and demand. In economic theory, the principle that states that the price of a commodity, good, or service varies directly, but not necessarily proportionately, with demand, and inversely, but not necessarily proportionately, with supply. In a real estate appraisal context, the principle of supply and demand states that the price of real property varies directly, but not necessarily proportionately, with demand and inversely, but not necessarily proportionately, with supply.

support

1. Adequacy of documentation for an appraisal.
2. *See* market support.

surety. One who accepts liability for any future debt, default, absence, or miscarriage of another, under the presumption that no loss is anticipated. Surety bonds are commonly required by municipal and county ordinances regarding licensing and contracting.

surface easement. The right to use the surface of the land only, e.g., for access, flowage, right-of-way; also called *surface right*.

surface soil. An area of soil about five to eight inches thick that is disturbed by plowing; an equivalent area of uncultivated land.

surface stream. A surface watercourse that flows, more or less permanently, in a well-defined, natural channel.

surface water. Water that spreads over the surface of the ground, stands in swamps, or percolates through the soil.

surface well. A hole or shaft that is dug or drilled into the earth to obtain underground water, which is pumped or raised to the surface by another method.

surplus income. *See* excess rent.

surplus land. Additional land that allows for future expansion of the existing improvement(s); cannot be developed separately and does not have a separate highest and best use. Surplus land is associated with an improved site that has not been developed to its maximum productivity according to its highest and best use as though vacant. *See also* excess land.

surplus productivity. The net income that remains after the costs of various agents of production have been paid.

surplus profits. The amount by which the net income of a business exceeds a reasonable return upon its capital requirements.

survey

1. The process in which the quantity and/or location of a piece of land is scientifically ascertained; may reflect the physical features of land, e.g., grades, contours, structures.
2. A map or plot that describes the courses, distances, and quantity of land and shows the lines of possession.
3. A market analysis procedure used to identify consumer preferences.

survey plat. *See* survey.

suscipient business. A retail enterprise that depends on an external source to draw shoppers to the area where it is located, e.g., a newspaper stand near a major transportation facility. *See also* generative business; shared business.

suspended ceiling. A ceiling system that is supported by overhead, structural framing.

swale
1. A shallow depression, in a flat area of land, that may be artificial and used in a storm water drainage system.
2. A low tract of land, usually marshy. (R.S. Means)

swamplands. Lands that require drainage to dispose of needless water or moisture before they are suitable for cultivation.

sweat equity. The value of labor contributed by the owner to improve real property.

switching. *See* free switching.

syndicate. *See* syndication.

syndication. A private or public partnership that pools funds for the acquisition and development of real estate projects or other business ventures. *See also* partnership.

synergism. A situation that results when the total effect produced is greater than the sum of the independent actions combined to create the effect; in real estate, usually applied to multiuse properties in which the value of the total development is greater than the sum of the individual parts.

systems. A process of combining prefabricated assemblies, components, and parts into single integrated units utilizing industrialized production, assembly and other methods. (R.S. Means)

systems maintenance administration. The process of coordinating the technical aspects of building systems and the management of human and energy resources to achieve maximum operational efficiency. (BOMA)

systems maintenance technician. The hands-on specialist responsible for the efficient operation of a building's systems which results in increased operating profits for the building owner and the comfort and safety of the occupants. (BOMA)

T

takeoff (quantity takeoff)
1. The process in which detailed lists are compiled, based on drawings and specifications, of all the material and equipment necessary to construct a project. The cost estimator uses this list to calculate how much it will cost to build the project.
2. The activity of determining quantities from drawings and specifications.
3. The actual quantity lists. (R.S. Means)

takeout commitment. A lender's commitment to provide long-term financing when a building or other improvement on real estate is completed.

taking
1. The acquisition of a parcel of land through condemnation.
2. In land use law, application of police power restrictions to a parcel of land that are so restrictive as to preclude any reasonable use.

talus. A slope; a sloping mass of rocky fragments at the foot of a cliff.

tangible property. Property that can be perceived with the senses; in-cludes land, fixed improvements, furnishings, merchandise, cash, and other items of working capital used in an enterprise.

tank farm. An area for housing storage tanks.

tar and gravel roofing. Built-up roofing made up of gravel or sand poured over a heavy coating of coal-tar pitch applied to an underlayer of felt. (R.S. Means)

tax. A compulsory contribution legally exacted from persons, corporations, and other organizations by a government, for the support of government and the maintenance of public services.

tax abatement. A reduction in the local taxes levied on a project for a specific period of time.

taxable income
1. Income subject to income tax.
2. For income-producing property, net operating income before replacement reserves minus depreciation and interest on debt.

taxable value. *See* assessed value.

taxation. The right of government to raise revenue through assessments on valuable goods, products, and rights.

tax base. The unit of value to which the tax rate is applied to determine the tax due; for property taxes, the assessed valuation; for income taxes, the net taxable income.

tax book. *See* tax roll.

tax deed. A deed that conveys title to a property purchased at a tax sale; may or may not convey absolute title, free of all prior claims and liens, depending on state law.

tax district. A political subdivision of one or more assessment districts where a governmental unit has the authority to levy taxes.

tax exemption. Total exemption or freedom from tax; granted to educational, charitable, religious, and other nonprofit organizations. Partial exemptions from ad valorem tax are granted to homesteads in some states.

tax-free cash. A specific property's annual depreciation charges minus annual mortgage amortization, or principal repayment.

tax-free exchange. The exchange, but not sale, of a real property held for investment or used in a trade or business for a similar property; allows the property holders to defer capital gains.

tax-free income. Income that is free from taxation due to provisions in the federal income tax laws. Net spendable income that is sheltered by excess losses is not tax-free.

tax levy. In property taxation, the total revenue that will be realized by a tax.

tax lien. A lien that is automatically attached to property in the amount of its unpaid property taxes.

tax map. A map, drawn to scale, that shows the boundaries and locations of individual lots and parcels in an assessment jurisdiction; also called *assessment map* or *cadastral map*.

tax parcel. A variation of the lot and block system of land description used by assessors; tax parcels are numbered and referenced to coded map books by section, block, and lot.

tax participation. A provision in a lease that obligates the lessee to assume all or part of the property taxes.

taxpayer. Describes an interim improvement that allegedly does not represent the ultimate, most profitable use of the land. The term derives from the improvement's marginal income, which covers the property taxes.

tax preference items. Certain types of income on which both individuals and corporations must pay some tax under the minimum tax schedule.

tax rate. The ratio between the tax and the tax base; applied to the assessed value to determine the amount of tax; obtained by dividing the amount of the tax levy by the total assessed value of all properties in the tax district; usually expressed in dollars per $100 or $1,000 (mills) of assessed value.

tax roll. The official list of all taxpayers subject to property tax, the amounts of their assessments, and the taxes due.

tax sale. The sale of a taxpayer's property to collect delinquent taxes from the proceeds of sale; conducted when the taxpayer has failed to redeem the property within the statutory period.

tax shelter. Investment features that provide relief from income taxes or allow the investor to claim deductions from taxable income.

tax stop. A clause in a lease that limits the landlord's tax obligation because the lessee assumes any taxes above an established level.

tax title. *See* tax deed.

Taylor permit. A permit that allows a private party to use the public domain for grazing purposes; issued to a stock raiser under the terms of the federal Taylor Grazing Act.

TAZ. *See* traffic analysis zone.

t-distribution. In statistics, a symmetrical, but abnormal, distribution; used in small samples, with fewer than 30 degrees of freedom, when the standard deviation may produce an inaccurate estimate. A t-distribution is flatter than the normal curve and therefore assigns a lower probability to any given interval. Values computed to reflect this flattening of the normal curve are called *t-values.* A statistical test to determine the confidence intervals of t-values is called a *t-test. See also* f-distribution.

TDN. Total digestible nutrients; the portion of livestock feed that is digested and used by the animal for maintenance, growth, and production.

TDR. *See* transferable development right.

team track. A track on which a railroad spots cars for loading and unloading by shippers; open to public use, as distinguished from private industrial siding. In a team yard, tracks are spaced to allow for driveways in between to accommodate vehicles.

technical analysis. Investment analysis that studies the functioning of the market as a discrete mechanism unaffected by external economic factors. *See also* fundamental analysis.

tempera. The process of painting transparent colors on plastered walls or panels using powdered pigment and parchment size mixed with water and gum arabic or egg white or yolk; applied to a hard surface of fine, thin plaster called *gesso*.

temporary easement. An easement granted for a specific purpose and applicable for a specific time period. A construction easement, for example, is terminated after the construction of the improvement and the unencumbered fee interest in the land reverts to the owner.

temporary practice. Under Title XI of the Financial Institutions Reform, Recovery and Enforcement Act of 1989 (FIRREA), one state shall recognize, on a temporary basis, the license or certification of an appraiser issued by another state provided: 1) the assignment entails property that is part of a federally related transaction, 2) the appraiser's business is of a temporary nature, and 3) the appraiser registers with the appraiser licensing or certifying agency in the state of temporary practice. *See also* federally related transaction (FRT); reciprocity.

temporary practice permit. *See* temporary practice.

tenancy
1. The holding of property by any form of title.
2. The right to use and occupy property as conveyed in a lease.

tenancy at sufferance. An estate in real estate in which a person, who formerly had an estate in land, wrongfully continues in possession of the real estate after the estate is terminated.

tenancy at will. An estate in real estate that has no fixed term and may be cancelled at will by the landlord or the tenant.

tenancy by the entirety. An estate held by a husband and wife in which neither has a disposable interest in the property during the lifetime of the other, except through joint action.

tenancy for years. One of two legally recognized ways to describe the length of the relationship between a landlord and a tenant. In tenancy for years, the beginning and end of the estate are clearly specified; provided the tenant does not default, the estate is automatically renewed each year until the specified expiration date. *See also* tenancy from period to period.

tenancy from period to period. One of two legally recognized ways to describe the length of the relationship between a landlord and a tenant. In this arrangement, the ultimate length of the leasehold interest is not stated; the leasehold interest owner pays rent periodically, with each payment renewing the interest for an additional period. *See also* tenancy for years.

tenancy in common. An estate held by two or more persons, each of whom has an undivided interest.

tenancy in severalty. An estate in real estate held by one owner.

tenant. One who holds or possesses real property; commonly a person who occupies and uses the property of another under a lease, although such a person is technically a lessee, not a tenant.

tenant changes. *See* tenant improvements.

tenant contributions. All costs that are the responsibility of the tenant(s), over and above the contract rent specified in the lease.

tenant farmer. The lessee of a farm, whose rental is usually in crops, cash, or a combination of the two.

tenant finish allowance. *See* tenant improvement allowance.

tenant improvement allowance. A dollar amount provided to the tenant by the landlord for the construction of tenant improvements, which may or may not equal the cost of construction or remodeling.

tenant improvements
1. Fixed improvements to the land or structures installed and paid for by a tenant or lessee.
2. The original installation of finished tenant space in a construction project; subject to periodic change for succeeding tenants; also called *TIs*.

tenant workletter. Written agreement between a landlord and a tenant specifying the tenant improvement work to be performed by each.

tender
1. An offer showing willingness to buy or sell at a specific price and under specific conditions.
2. In futures, the act on the part of a seller of a contract of giving notice to the clearinghouse that he intends to deliver the physical commodity in satisfaction of a futures contract.
3. A formal bid or offer. (R.S. Means)

tendon. The wires and cables used to reinforce prestressed and post-stressed concrete.

tenement
1. Real property and the rights of ownership to real property; real property rights of a permanent nature that relate to, and pass

with, the land; includes both corporeal and incorporeal rights.

2. A type of dwelling house or unit.

tenement house. A multistory dwelling that consists of occupancy units that do not have private baths and/or private kitchens.

tenure. The holding or possession of anything; the right to possess and use property; the period of possession and use.

terminal. In transportation, the point at which people and goods can enter or leave the system.

terminal capitalization rate. The rate used to convert income, e.g., *NOI*, cash flow, into an indication of the anticipated value of the subject real property at the end of the holding period. The terminal capitalization rate is used to estimate the resale value of the property. Also called *residual capitalization rate*.

terminal value. *See* reversion.

termites. Insects that destroy wood by eating the wood fiber. Termites are social insects that exist in most parts of the U.S., but they are most destructive in the coastal states and in the Southwest. Termites can enter wood through the ground or above the ground, although the subterranean type is most common in the U.S. They eat the softer springwood first and prefer sap-

wood over heartwood. (R.S. Means)

termite shield. A metal sheet that is placed in the exterior walls of a structure near ground level, usually under the sill, to prevent termites from entering.

terms of sale. Conditions and agreements in a contract of sale.

terneplate. A plate of inferior quality in which tin is alloyed with a large percentage of lead; used as a roofing material.

terrace

1. A broad surface channel or embankment constructed across sloping lands on or near contour lines at specific intervals; used to control runoff or soil erosion.

2. A flat or undulating plain, usually rather narrow and with a steep front, that borders a river, lake, or sea. Many streams are bordered by a series of terraces at different levels, indicating floodplains in successive periods. Older terraces may be dissected by streams and become more or less hilly, but they are still considered terraces.

3. An elevated, level surface of earth with a vertical or sloping front and/or sides faced by masonry or turf; a series of such surfaces rising one above the other.

4. A finished, but unroofed, outdoor area adjacent to, and accessible from, a house or other structure; usually at grade or slightly elevated.

terra-cotta. Hard, usually unglazed, earthenware of fine quality that has been hard-burned and molded; used for architectural decoration, e.g., facing material.

terrazzo. A floor material made of small fragments of colored stone or marble that are embedded in cement and polished to a high glaze.

tertiary trade area. An outlying segment of the trade area that contributes a recognizable share of a shopping center's sales volume and accounts for up to 10% of its total customers; designated when a tributary area appears to extend beyond the normal limits of the secondary trade area, usually in a specific direction.

testate. One who dies leaving a valid will; the condition of dying with a valid will.

theory. A statement that sets forth an apparent relationship among observed facts and has been substantiated to a degree.

therm. A measure of heat equal to 100,000 Btus. *See also* Btu.

thermal. Of or pertaining to heat or temperature.

thermal conduction. The transmission of heat through or within a solid object.

thermal insulation. Material that is highly resistant to the passage of heat; used to block the passage of heat from a warm building to the exterior when outdoor temperatures are low, and to block the entrance of heat into a cooled interior when outside temperatures are high.

thermostat. A device that automatically establishes and maintains a desired temperature; electrically operated and actuated by thermal conduction or convection.

thoroughfare. A street or path that is open at both ends and free from any obstruction; a highway.

thread of the stream. The center line between the banks of a stream.

threshold. A strip of wood, stone, or metal that is placed beneath a door.

tidal basin. A dock or basin without water gates in which the water level changes. *See also* bottom land.

tidal waters. Waters in which the tide ebbs and flows.

tide. The alternate rise and fall of the surface of a body of water. The inflow of the water is called the *flood tide,* or *high tide;* the reflux is called the *ebb tide.* Slack tide is the period between changes in the tide movement.

tie. A device that joins two or more structural members, e.g., timber, rod, chain, clip, wire.

tie beam. A structural member used to hold two separated members together.

tier. A row of townships, running east and west, that lies between any two consecutive township lines; comprises an area six miles wide.

TIGER files. *See* Topographically Integrated Geographic Encoding and Referencing data files.

tile. Originally a molded and burned clay or cement used for flooring, facing walls, and trim; now includes tiles made of many different materials, e.g., asphalt, plastic, vinyl, fiberglass, and used for a number of purposes, e.g., field tile, sewer tile, ceiling tile, acoustical tile.

till. An unstratified deposit of earth, sand, gravel, and boulders that have been transported by glaciers.

tillable land. Land suitable for growing annual crops that require plowing, harrowing, planting, cultivating, and harvesting; as distinguished from farmland that is not so suited, e.g., marshland, swampland, woodlots.

till plain. A level or undulating land surface that is covered by glacial till.

tilth. The physical condition of a soil with respect to its suitability for the cultivation of a specific plant.

tilt-up construction. A method of construction in which concrete wall sections are cast horizontally and lifted or tilted into position.

timber. Forest stands and their products; wood in forms that are suitable for heavy construction; specifically, sawed lumber four by four inches or more in breadth and thickness.

timber cruising. *See* cruise.

timberland. Agricultural property from which merchantable timber is harvested periodically, usually every 20, 50, or 80 years depending on the species and growing conditions.

time deposits. Funds deposited at a bank that can be withdrawn only after proper notification, e.g., money in certificates of deposit.

time period zero. The starting date of an investment.

time series. A statistical technique for presenting data graphically. The analysis of a time series consists of describing and measuring the cyclical movements, random variations, seasonal variations, and secular trends observed over a period of time.

time-series chart. In statistics, graphic representation of data in which the independent variable, plotted along the horizontal axis, is time, and the values of the dependent variable, plotted along the vertical axis, are shown at various time intervals. These values are connected by straight lines to form a continuous curve that extends over the entire period covered by the chart.

timesharing. Limited ownership interests in, or the rights of use and occupancy of, residential apartments or hotel rooms. There are two forms of timesharing—fee timeshares and nonfee timeshares. Fee timeshares may be based on timeshare ownership or interval ownership. There are three types of nonfee time-shares: a prepaid lease arrangement, a vacation license, and a club membership.

time value of money. The concept underlying compound interest which holds that $1 received today is worth more than $1 received in the future due to opportunity cost, inflation, and the certainty of payment.

time-weighted rate. The average of all actual, instantaneous rates over a period of time; also called *unit-method rate* or *share-accounting rate*.

title. The combination of all elements that constitute proof of ownership. *See also* abstract of title.

Title I. The portion of the Housing Act of 1949, as amended, that contains most of the basic legislative provisions pertaining to urban renewal programs; authorizes most of the federal financial and technical aid for communities participating in such programs. Through the amending Housing Act of 1954, Title I sets out workable program prerequisites and adds provisions for rehabilitating blighted areas as well as redeveloping slum areas.

Title XI. *See* Appraisal Subcommittee; Financial Institutions Reform, Recovery and Enforcement Act (FIRREA).

title company. A corporation that issues or insures title to real property.

title defect. A legal right held by another to claim property or make demands on the property owner. *See also* easement; encumbrance.

title insurance. Insurance against financial loss resulting from claims that arise out of defects in the title to real property that were not disclosed at the time the policy was issued. *See also* Torrens system.

title opinion. An analysis and interpretation of a title search that concerns present ownership, encumbrances, clouds on the title, and other infirmities.

title search. An investigation of public records to abstract the nature of any instruments that relate to the status of the title to a specific piece of real estate; may include the study of liens, encumbrances, easements, and other conditions that affect the quality of the title of ownership.

tobacco barn. A farm building for the curing of tobacco; usually of simple frame construction and design with hinged side panels that open to provide ventilation; may also be used for grading and packing the tobacco for market.

tolerance
1. The permitted variation from a given dimension or quantity.
2. The range of variation permitted in maintaining a specified dimension.
3. A permitted variation from location or alignment. (R.S. Means)

toll road. A highway for which users must pay a toll charge.

tombstone ad. A simple notice announcing that a security issue is being offered for sale or has been sold; states the name of the underwriter, the issue, and the date sold; may also indicate whether the security issue is original or secondary.

ton
1. A measure of weight equal to 2,000 pounds or 907.2 kg.
2. In cooling systems, a measurement of chiller size equal to 12,000 Btus of heat removal per hour. (R.S. Means)

tongue and groove. A method of joining two pieces of board in which a tongue is cut in the edge of one board and a groove is cut in the other board to receive the tongue; describes any material prepared for joining in this fashion, e.g., tongue-and-groove lumber.

Topographically Integrated Geographic Encoding and Referencing (TIGER) data files. Geographically referenced data files that are commercially available to GIS users.

topographic map. A map that shows the topography of an area of the earth's surface using contour lines, tinting, or shading.

topography. The relief features or surface configurations of an area, e.g., hills, valleys, slopes, lakes, rivers. Surface gradations are classified as compound slope, gently sloping land, hilly land, hogwallows, hummocks, rolling land, steep land, undulating land, and very steep land.

top out. To install the highest structural member or complete the highest course in a construction. (R.S. Means)

top rail. The horizontal member that forms the top of a paneled door or a window; also called *top stile*.

topsoil. The surface portion of the soil usually containing organic matter, a mixture of particle sizes, and some animal life. (R.S. Means); includes the average plow depth of the A horizon when the horizon is deeper than plow depth. *See also* horizon.

Torrens system. A system of land registration used in some jurisdictions in which the sovereign governmental authority issues title certificates covering the ownership of land, which often serve as title insurance.

total load. Dead load plus live load; the total weight that must be compensated for in building design.

total operating expenses. The sum of all fixed and variable operating expenses and the replacement allowance cited in the appraiser's operating expense estimate.

total personal income. Monetary income plus noncash income, e.g., food stamps, imputed income.

town. Technically a territorial quasi-corporation, e.g., a New England town, or a political subdivision of the state or county, e.g., townships; commonly an urban community; sometimes applied to any form of municipal corporation.

townhouse. A single-family, attached dwelling unit with party walls; usually an individual unit in a series of five to 10 houses, with common walls between the units and side yards on the end units only; may have one to three stories and all necessary facilities and amenities.

township. In the government survey system of land description, the area between two township lines and two range lines; normally contains 36 sections of approximately 640 acres each.

township lines. In the government survey system of land description, survey lines that run east and west at six-mile intervals north and south of a baseline and form the north and south boundaries of townships.

township road. A rural road that is outside the primary state highway system and the county road system; under the jurisdiction of a township.

TPL. *See* Trust for Public Land.

tract. A parcel of land; an area of real estate that is frequently subdivided into smaller parcels.

tract house. A house in a large, residential development where the houses are mass-produced and very similar in style, material, and price.

trade area. The geographic area from which the steady, sustaining patronage for a shopping center is obtained; its extent is governed by many factors, e.g., the shopping center itself, its accessibility, the extent of physical barriers, the location of competing facilities, the limitations of driving time and distance. *See also* market area; primary trade area; secondary trade area; tertiary trade area.

trade fixture. An item owned and attached to a rented space or building by a tenant and used in conducting a business; also called *chattel fixture. See also* fixture.

trading on equity. The use of borrowed funds in an effort to increase the rate of return on the equity investment. *See also* leverage.

traffic. The movement of people and vehicles along a path or past a specific point; the people and vehicles that move along a path or past a point.

traffic analysis zone (TAZ). A microlocational referent for which data have been compiled in the TIGER files of the 1990 census; used to identify the pattern and volume of traffic.

traffic count. A count of the number of people and/or vehicles that move past a location over a period of time; a significant criterion used in rating the competitiveness of a site.

traffic density. The number of vehicles that occupy a particular length of a roadway's moving lanes at a given time; usually expressed in vehicles per mile.

traffic survey. A survey conducted to obtain traffic information, e.g., data on traffic quantity and composition, travelers' origins and destinations, the purpose of trips, means of transportation; usually related to a specific time on a certain day of the week.

trailer. A mobile home; a house trailer.

trailer park. Any site with facilities suitable for parking two or more mobile homes somewhat permanently.

transactional audit. *See* environmental property assessment (EPRA).

transaction price. The amount a particular buyer agrees to pay and a particular seller agrees to accept under the circumstances surrounding their transaction.

transferable development right (TDR). A development right that cannot be used by the landowner but can be sold to landowners in another location; generally used to preserve agricultural land; may also be used to preserve historic sites or buildings and open space or to protect scenic features.

transient housing study. A supply and demand analysis of transient housing needs and potentials in a community or specific area on both a qualitative and quantitative basis.

transition. Changes in district or neighborhood use, e.g., agricultural to residential, residential to commercial.

transitional. *See* transitional licensure.

transitional licensure. A category of state licensure authorized by the Appraisal Subcommittee. Transitionally state-licensed appraisers will meet either the experience or education requirements set by the state, and must meet the missing experience or education requirement within two years of being tested and transitionally licensed by the state. The Appraisal Subcommittee recommends that transitional licenses be issued only during the first two years of a state's new appraiser licensing program. *See also* Appraisal Subcommittee.

transported soil. Secondary soils; soils that have been moved and redeposited by water or wind.

traveled way. The portion of a roadway that is designed for the movement of vehicles; excludes shoulders, acceleration and deceleration lanes, and other auxiliary lanes.

traverse window. A type of window with two movable sashes set in separate grooves, permitting the windows to slide past each other horizontally.

tread. The horizontal width of a step; the area between risers in a stairway.

Treasury bills. Short-term, direct debt obligations of the U.S. Government, usually with a maturity of three months, six months, or one year, and issued at a discount from face value.

Treasury bonds. Long-term debt instruments with maturities of 10 years or more.

Treasury Department. *See* Department of the Treasury.

Treasury notes. Intermediate securities with maturities of one to 10 years.

trellising. A support system for grapes or other vine crops; usually consists of wires or thin ropes that extend above the vine between anchor posts.

trend. A series of related changes brought about by a chain of causes and effects. Trends are forecast through economic base analysis, market analysis, and analysis of economic indicators and surveys.

trend analysis

1. A quantitative technique used to identify and measure adjustments to the sale prices of com-

parable properties; useful when sales data on highly comparable properties are lacking, but a broad database on properties with less similar characteristics is available. Market sensitivity is investigated by testing various factors that influence sale prices.

2. The Office of the Comptroller of the Currency requires that an appraisal inform the reader of any market trends, regardless of whether the trend reflects rising or declining values. The OCC stresses the importance of identifying negative trends so that a regulated institution can avoid extending credit on insufficient collateral. The OCC cites the following examples of negative trends: increasing vacancy rates, greater use of rent concessions, and declining sales prices. The effect of market activity on the subject property may be reflected in listings, options, or sales agreements, which indicate such trends. (*Federal Register*)

triangular scale. A drafting instrument that is triangular in cross section and has a different scale on each edge. Some edges have two opposing scales, one two times the other, such as ⅛ inch and ¼ inch equals 1 foot. (R.S. Means)

triangulation. A method of surveying over long distances by establishing a network of triangles. Most sides in the network are computed from a known side that may be calculated, and two measured angles. Lengths are measured periodically as a check. (R.S. Means)

trim. The visible finishing work on the interior of a building; includes all wood, metal, or plastic ornamental parts used to cover joints between jambs and plaster around windows and doors; may also include hardware.

trimmer. A beam or floor joist that supports the end of a header in floor framing.

trip. In locational analysis, refers to the use of an automobile, i.e., automobile trips to and from a particular property.

triple-net lease. A net lease under which the lessee assumes all expenses of operating the property, including both fixed and variable expenses.

triplex. A house containing three separate dwelling units, each on a different level; also describes an apartment that occupies three levels.

true bearing. The clockwise angle between a direction line and a meridian line that is referenced to the geographic North Pole. (R.S. Means)

trunk

1. The main wood shaft of a tree.
2. The shaft portion of a column.
3. Descriptive of the main body of a system, as a sewer trunk line.
4. Transmission channel that runs between two central office or switching devices, connecting exchanges to the main telephone network. (R.S. Means)

truss. One of various structural frames based on the geometric rigidity of a triangle and composed of members that are subject to longitudinal compression and tension only; rigid under anticipated loads and able to span a large area without interior support. *See also* bowstring truss; camber; flat roof; sawtooth roof.

trust. A temporary, conditional, or permanent fiduciary relationship in which the legal title to, and control of, property are placed in the hands of a trustee for the benefit of another person.

trust agreement. A written agreement between a grantor and a trustee that establishes the terms of a trust.

trust deed. A deed that establishes a trust, an instrument that conveys legal title to a property to a trustee, stating the trustee's authority and the conditions that bind the trustee in dealing with the property. *See also* deed of trust; mortgage.

trustee. A person who controls legal title to a property under a trust agreement.

Trust for Public Land (TPL). A nonprofit, charitable organization established in 1973 and concerned with the open space needs of urban dwellers as well as the preservation of wilderness; almost completely self-supporting, with 80% of its yearly income obtained from land transactions and the remainder from foundations and contracts.

trust instrument. Any written instrument under which a trust is created, e.g., a will, a trust agreement, a declaration of trust, a deed of trust, an order of court.

t-test. *See* t-distribution.

tuck-pointing. Finishing joints along their center lines with a narrow, parallel ridge of fine putty or fine lime mortar; in existing brick or masonry work, raking out deteriorated mortar joints and refilling them with new mortar. *See also* grout.

Tudor architecture. A formal, residential architectural style characterized by exterior walls of stone or brick laid in a formal pattern, window and door trim of dressed or cut stone, casement-type windows, and roofs of slate spaced to resemble stone.

turf. The uppermost layer of soil containing roots of propagated grass. (R.S. Means)

turnkey contract. A construction contract similar to a design/construction contract except the contractor is responsible for all financing and owns the work until the project is complete and turned over to the owner. (R.S. Means)

turnkey project. A construction project in which the builder is responsible for all aspects of construction and must deliver a completed facility, including all items necessary for occupancy; the occupant or user of the property need only "turn the key" and commence operation.

turnpike. A controlled-access highway for which users pay a toll.

TVA. Tennessee Valley Authority.

t-value. *See* t-distribution

two step sealed bidding. A procurement procedure whereby contractors submit technical proposals in response to government performance specifications. Each contractor whose technical proposal is acceptable then submits a sealed bid in accordance with normal bidding procedures. (R.S. Means)

type soils. A group of soils, developed from a particular type of parent material, that have similar genetic horizons, including similar texture and arrangement in the soil profile.

typical operator concept. In measuring the productive capacity of a farm or ranch, the assumption that operations will be managed by a typical local operator using standard management practices.

U

UCIAR. *See* Uniform Commercial and Industrial Appraisal Report.

ULI. *See* Urban Land Institute.

UL label. A seal of certification attached by Underwriters Laboratories, Inc., to building materials, electrical wiring and components, storage vessels, and other devices, attesting that the item has been rated according to performance tests on such products, is from a production lot that made use of materials and processes identical to those of comparable items that have passed fire, electrical hazard, and other safety tests, and is subject to the UL reexamination service. (R.S. Means)

unaccommodated demand. A component of latent demand attributable to cyclical or seasonal factors. Such demand may seek comparable alternative facilities outside the market area or less desirable facilities within the market area. *See also* latent demand.

unbalanced improvement. An improvement that does not represent the highest and best use of the site on which it is placed; may be an overimprovement or an underimprovement.

uncertainty. The probability that unforeseen events will occur. *See also* probability; risk.

underfloor wiring system. A system in which ducts or raceways are built into a floor to house electrical wiring.

underground stream. Water that flows underground in a defined channel.

underground waters. Waters that include underground streams, basins, or lakes; reservoirs; artesian waters; percolations contributing to underground and surface streams or watercourses; diffuse percolations; and the underflow of watercourses.

underimprovement. An improvement that is inadequate to develop the highest and best use of its site; usually a structure that is of lesser cost, quality, and size than typical neighborhood properties.

underlying loan. The loan or loans that are covered by a wraparound mortgage, all-inclusive deed of trust, or contract of sale.

underpass. A passageway under a street, highway, or railroad right-of-way; in rural areas, a passageway under a highway for the passage of animals and farm equipment; also a grade separation where one traveled way passes underneath an intersecting traveled way or a railroad right-of-way.

underpinning. Timbers, steel beams, or other temporary props used to support a foundation during construction; also permanent supports installed to increase the load-bearing capacity of a foundation or wall.

understocking. Placing a number of animals on a given area so that the area is underused at the end of the planned grazing period.

understory

1. The portion of a forest that is under, or below, the overstory, or top canopy.
2. The plants growing beneath the canopy of another plant; e.g., grasses, forbs, and low shrubs growing under a tree or brush canopy.

underwriter

1. An individual or organization that assumes a risk for a fee.
2. In investment, a party who agrees to guarantee payment for a securities issue with the intention of selling it to individual investors.
3. In real estate, a party who evaluates the risk involved in making a mortgage and approves or denies the mortgage.

Underwriters Laboratories, Inc. A private, nonprofit organization that tests, inspects, classifies, and rates devices and components to ensure that manufacturers comply with various UL standards. (R.S. Means)

underwriter's method. Calculation of an R_O using a debt coverage ratio $(R_O = DCR \times R_M \times M)$.

undisturbed sample. A sample taken from soil in such a manner that the soil structure is deformed as little as possible. (R.S. Means)

undivided fee rule. In condemnation appraisal, a rule that states that property is to be valued as if the title were held by a single entity, even if the real estate is divided into more than one estate owned by more than one individual or entity. *See also* unit rule.

undivided interest. Fractional ownership without physical division into shares.

undivided partial interest. An interest in a specific property that is shared by the co-owners; no co-owner may unilaterally convey or encumber any specific part thereof.

undulating land. Land on compound slopes of 3% to 8%.

unearned increment. An increase in the value of property that is not anticipated by the owner and is due primarily to the operation of social or economic forces rather than to the personal efforts, intelligence, skill, or initiative of the owner; usually, but not necessarily, applied to land. This concept was developed by Henry George, who believed that increases in the value of property ought not to accrue to the owners since they were due to social forces and hence "unearned." By contrast, however, he did not agree that losses were also due to social forces and that owners ought then to be compensated. *Unearned increment,* therefore, may be said to be a misnomer because the increment usually is a reward for the risk taken in such ventures.

Uniform Commercial and Industrial Appraisal Report (UCIAR). A standardized, 13-page appraisal report form which is especially appropriate for appraisals of smaller commercial and industrial properties; principally used by small and medium-sized thrift institutions to process the sale of loans; includes a checklist and four optional addenda.

Uniform Construction Index. The forerunner of the MASTERFORMAT adopted by the Construction Specifications Institute in 1978. This system divides technical data and all related accounting, specifying and tracking functions into 16 divisions. (R.S. Means)

uniformity. In assessment, denotes assessed values that bear the same relationship to market value, or another value standard, as all other assessments in the tax district; implies equalization of the tax burden.

Uniform Residential Appraisal Report (URAR). A standardized appraisal form developed jointly by the Federal National Mortgage Association, the Federal Home Loan Mortgage Corporation, the Federal Housing Administration, the Veterans Administration, and the Farmers' Home Administration and used to communicate valuations of one- to four-family residential properties.

Uniform Standards of Professional Appraisal Practice (USPAP). Current standards of the appraisal profession, developed for appraisers and the users of appraisal services by the Appraisal Standards Board of The Appraisal Foundation. The Uniform Standards set forth the procedures to be followed in developing an appraisal, analysis, or opinion and the manner in which an appraisal, analysis, or opinion is communicated. They are endorsed by the Appraisal Institute and by other professional appraisal organizations.

unimproved land. Vacant land or land that lacks the essential, appurtenant improvements required to make it useful.

union. A pipe fitting used to join two pipes without turning either pipe, consisting of a collar piece which is slipped on one pipe, and a shoulder which is threaded or soldered on that pipe and against which the collar piece bears. (R.S. Means)

unit. A single thing; any standard by which quantities of the same type may be measured.

unit cost. The price or cost of one of a number of similar items or units of property which, when multiplied by the total number, will determine the price or cost of the whole; usually expressed as cost per square foot or cubic foot; also called *unit price.*

United States Public Land Descriptions. *See* government survey system.

unit-in-place method. A cost-estimating method in which total building cost is estimated by adding together the unit costs for the various building components as installed; also called *segregated cost method.*

unit rule. The rule that determines what constitutes the larger parcel, the complete unit affected by a partial taking; used to estimate severance damages and/or special ben-efits to the remainder. The test of unity involves three factors: physical location, use, and ownership. *See also* undivided fee rule; unity of title; unity of use.

units of comparison. The components into which a property may be divided for purposes of comparison, e.g., price per square foot, front foot, cubic foot, room, bed, seat, apartment unit.

unit value. The market value of the whole reduced to a value per unit of measurement.

unity of title. The rule that states that, to be considered part of the remainder property, a parcel must be held by the condemnee under the same quality of ownership as the parcel from which the taking occurs; applied in both federal and state courts. *See also* undivided fee rule.

unity of use. The rule that states that, to be considered part of the remainder, a parcel must be devoted to the same use as the parcel from which the taking occurs.

universe. In statistics, the entire body of possible data; used to distinguish between all the data and a sample obtained from the data.

update of an appraisal. An extension of an original, complete appraisal and report on which a client has relied for a prior business decision.

The practice of requiring updates is a reasonable portfolio management technique for financial institutions to apply in monitoring asset quality. Before accepting an update appraisal, an institution must ascertain that three conditions have been met: 1) the original appraiser/firm and client are involved; 2) the real estate has undergone no significant change since the original appraisal; and 3) the time period between the effective date of the original appraisal (or most recent update) and the effective date of the pending update is not unreasonably long for the type of real estate involved. (USPAP)

upland

1. A parcel that abuts a parcel with riparian rights; describes an owner once removed from a water right by a riparian owner.
2. Land above the surface of a body of water or above a mean high water line.

upland soil. Soil developed from the disintegration and decomposition of rocks in place and the weathering of the resulting debris; a primary soil; usually found on hilly to mountainous terrain.

upset price. In law, an amount representing the minimum bid at which a property may be sold.

upside/downside potential. A method of risk analysis in which numerical values are assigned to the best and worst anticipations for an investment and general conclusions are formed about the risks associated with each.

uptown. A business district developed to relieve congestion in the central business district, generally along a major arterial providing access to the suburbs. *See also* central business district; node.

URAR. *See* Uniform Residential Appraisal Report.

urban. Describes a mature neighborhood with a concentration of population typically found within city limits or a neighborhood commonly identified with a city.

urban growth theories. *See* axial theory; central place theory; concentric zone theory; multiple-nuclei theory; sector theory.

urban land economics. The study of the allocation of urban space among alternative uses.

Urban Land Institute (ULI). A not-for-profit organization that conducts research on land use and development; publishes periodicals and guides to the development of specific property types.

urban renewal. The controlled process of redevelopment in urban areas;

often used to refer to public projects, but also includes private redevelopment efforts. *See also* redevelopment; redevelopment agency; Title I.

urban renewal area. A blighted, deteriorated, or deteriorating area, or an area of open land, that is approved by the U.S. Department of Housing and Urban Development as appropriate for an urban renewal project.

urban renewal plan. A plan, developed by a locality and approved by its governing body, that guides and controls a special urban renewal project area.

urban renewal project. Specific activities conducted by a local public agency in an urban renewal area to prevent or eliminate slums and blight; may involve slum clearance, redevelopment, rehabilitation, conservation, or a combination of these activities.

urea-formaldehyde foam insulation. A type of foamed-in-place insulation that releases formaldehyde gas. It was banned by the Consumer Public Safety Commission in 1982 from use in residences and schools. Holding that the risks had not been proven, a federal court lifted the ban in 1983.

usable area. The actual occupiable area of a floor or an office; computed by measuring the finished surface of the office side of corridor and other permanent walls, to the center of partitions that separate the office from adjoining usable areas, and to the inside finished surface of the dominant portion of the permanent outer building walls. The usable area of a floor is equal to the sum of all usable areas of that floor. No deductions are made for columns and projections necessary to the building. (BOMA) *See also* architect's standard net assignable area.

USDA. United States Department of Agriculture. *See also* Department of Agriculture.

use classification. Categories into which real estate can be divided according to its use: residential, commercial, industrial, agricultural, and special purpose.

use density. The number of buildings of a particular use classification per unit of area; sometimes expressed as a percentage of land coverage or density of coverage.

use factor. An index of the grazing use made of a particular forage species; based on a system of range management that will maintain more economically important forage species for an indefinite time; expressed as a percentage of the current year's weight production located within reach of stock that is consumed. *See also* weighted-use factor.

useful life. The period of time over which a structure may reasonably be expected to perform the function for which it was designed.

use of an appraisal. The manner in which a client employs the information contained in an appraisal report.

use value. The value a specific property has for a specific use.

use value assessment. An assessment based on the value of property as it is currently used, not on its market value considering alternative uses; may be used where legislation has been enacted to preserve farmland, timberland, or other open space land on urban fringes.

use variance. A privilege that allows a property owner to develop or use his or her property in a manner that violates the strict terms of the applicable zoning authority or board of adjustment; granted on a property-by-property basis.

USGS. United States Geological Survey.

USPAP. *See* Uniform Standards of Professional Appraisal Practice.

USTC. United States Trade Commission.

usufruct. The right to use and enjoy the fruits or profits of something belonging to another.

utilities. Services rendered by public utility companies, e.g., telephone, electricity, gas, water.

utility. The ability of a product to satisfy a human want, need, or desire.

utility functions. Subjective weights that are assigned to possible investment outcomes to reflect a particular investor's relative preference for each. *See also* probability analysis; risk analysis.

utility-probability analysis. The assessment of risk using quantitative methods.

utility room. A room that is designed or used for laundry, heating equipment, or related purposes.

V

VA. *See* Department of Veterans Affairs.

vacancy. Unrented space.

vacancy allowance. *See* vacancy and collection loss.

vacancy and collection loss. An allowance for reductions in potential income attributable to vacancies, tenant turnover, and nonpayment of rent; also called *vacancy and credit loss* or *vacancy and contingency loss.*

vacancy rate
1. The relationship between the amount of vacant space and total space in a building.
2. The relationship between the rent estimated for vacant building space and the total rent estimated for all the space in the building. *See also* frictional vacancy.

vacant land. *See* unimproved land.

valance
1. A board at the top of a window, used to conceal the hanging mechanism for draperies.
2. A short drapery hung across the top of a window. (R.S. Means)

valley
1. The line where two sloping roofs intersect.

2. The lowland that lies between two hills.

valley flashing. Pieces of lead, tin, or sheet metal that are placed along the valley of a roof to make the roof intersection waterproof.

valuation. The process of estimating the market value, insurable value, investment value, or some other properly defined value of an identified interest or interests in a specific parcel or parcels of real estate as of a given date. *Valuation* is a term used interchangeably with appraisal.

valuation accounts. In accounting, reserves for depreciation or amortization; in appraisal, a reduction in the cost of the assets to which they apply.

valuation process. A systematic procedure employed to provide the answer to a client's question about the value of real property.

valuator. *See* appraiser.

value
1. The monetary worth of a property, good, or service to buyers and sellers at a given time.
2. The present worth of the future benefits that accrue to real prop-

erty ownership. *See also* aggregate of retail values (*ARV*); business value; disposition value; fair value; going-concern value; goodwill value; insurance value; investment value; liquidation value; market value; use value; value as is.

value after the taking. In condemnation, the market value of the remainder parcel in a partial taking.

value as is. The value of specific ownership rights to an identified parcel of real estate as of the effective date of the appraisal; relates to what physically exists and is legally permissible and excludes all assumptions concerning hypothetical market conditions or possible rezoning. *See also* date of value estimate; prospective value estimate.

value before the taking. In condemnation, the market value of the whole property affected by the taking.

valued policy laws. State laws governing the amount insurance companies must pay relative to the value of the loss. Practically all standard fire policies limit claim payments to the "actual cash value" of the property at the time of loss, even though the full amount of insurance might be more. (If a house is insured for $100,000 but is really worth only $80,000, the insurance company would only have to pay $80,000 if the house burned to the ground.) However, in some states there are valued policy laws which require the insurance company to pay the full amount of insurance. (In those states, the homeowner would get the full $100,000.) (R.S. Means)

value engineering. A science that studies the relative value of various materials and construction techniques. Value engineering considers the initial cost of construction, coupled with the estimated cost of maintenance, energy use, life expectancy and replacement cost. (R.S. Means)

value estimate. *See* estimate of value.

value for other use. A means of valuing a corridor of real estate; used particularly in valuing railroad corridors. *See also* across the fence method.

value indication. An estimate of value derived through application of the appraisal process.

value in exchange. *See* exchange value.

value in place. The amount a prudent purchaser would pay for an item, e.g., equipment, fixtures, in place; determined by the use the item contributes to the whole.

value in use. *See* use value.

valve. A device that regulates the flow of liquids or gases in a pipe.

vapor barrier. Material that is used to retard the passage of vapor or moisture into walls and floors and prevent condensation, e.g., foil-surfaced insulation placed in walls, paint applied to exterior foundation walls.

vara. A Spanish and Portuguese unit of linear and square measurement sometimes used in California, Florida, and New Mexico as well as Mexico and other countries once under Spanish rule; varies in length from 32.993 to 33.87 inches.

variability. In statistical analysis, the scattering of the values of a frequency distribution from the measure of central tendency. The three most common measures of dispersion or data variability encountered are the range, the average absolute deviation, and the standard deviation.

variable. A quantity that may take any one of a specified set of values.

variable air volume (VAV). An air distribution system capable of automatically delivering a reduced volume of constant temperature cool air to satisfy the reduced cooling load of individual zones. (R.S. Means)

variable-amortization loan. A mortgage loan in which amortization payments may not be required for an initial period, i.e., in a standing loan, or may be increased or decreased during the loan term. The rate of interest on the outstanding principal remains the same, but the amount of interest paid differs because the outstanding principal varies as the loan is amortized. *See also* variable-payment mortgage (VPM).

variable annuity. An income stream in which the payment amounts vary per period. A variable annuity is characteristic of one kind of income model and one kind of property model.

variable expenses. Operating expenses that generally vary with the level of occupancy or the extent of services provided.

variable-payment mortgage (VPM). A mortgage that calls for installment payments of varying amounts during its term; may or may not be fully amortized, or liquidated, at maturity. *See also* constant-payment mortgage; variable-amortization loan.

variable-rate mortgage (VRM). A mortgage with an interest rate that may move up or down following a specified schedule or the movements of a standard or index to which the interest rate is tied. *See also* adjustable-rate mortgage (ARM).

variable volume air system. An air-conditioning system that automatically regulates the quantity of air supplied to each controlled area according to the needs of the different zones, with preset minimum and maximum values based on the load in each area. (R.S. Means)

variance

1. A written authorization from the responsible agency permitting construction in a manner which is not allowed by a code or ordinance. (R.S. Means) *See* zoning variance.

2. In statistics, a measure of the degree of spread among a set of values; a measure of the tendency of individual values to vary from the mean value.

variate. The specific value of a variable; generally called a *variable*.

vault

1. A continuous length of arched ceiling.

2. A room specially designed for secure storage.

3. A below-street extension of the basement of an adjacent property.

vegetation. Plants collectively; the community of plants in a region, as distinguished from the kinds of plants that comprise the plant community.

vegetative density. The estimated percentage of ground cover in rangeland; the area that would be represented by projecting all herbaceous plants and all the current year's growth of shrubby plants onto the ground surface and viewing it from directly above. *See also* forage density.

veneer. An ornamental or protective layer of material that covers a base of another substance, e.g., walnut veneer on less valuable wood, a brick exterior finish over a structure of less expensive material.

veneer construction. Construction of wood, reinforced concrete, or steel, faced with a thin layer of another material such as structural glass or marble. (R.S. Means)

veneered construction. A method of construction in which a layer of facing material is applied to the external surface of steel, reinforced concrete, or frame walls, e.g., face brick veneer over a frame construction.

veneer wall. A wall with a facing which is attached to, but not bonded to, the wall. (R.S. Means)

vent

1. A pipe built into a drainage system to provide air circulation, thus preventing siphonage and back pressure from affecting the function of the trap seals.

2. A stack through which smoke, ashes, vapors, and other airborne impurities are discharged from an enclosed space to the outside atmosphere (R.S. Means)

3. A small opening that allows the passage of air through any space in a building, e.g., an attic, an unexcavated area under a first-floor construction, the soffits of an overhang.

ventilation. The circulation of air in a room or building; the process of changing the air of a room by natural or artificial means.

vent pipe. A small pipe that extends from plumbing fixtures to a vent stack in the roof and allows sewer gases to escape to the outside air.

venture capital. A common term for funds used for equity investment.

vernacular architecture. Architecture designed and built by individuals according to custom and for its adaptive response to the environment and contemporary life-styles, without reference to the aesthetic and functional criteria of architectural history. *See also* formal architecture.

vertical division. The division of real property into air, ground (surface), and subterranean rights.

vestibule. A small entrance hall to a building or room.

vest-pocket park. A park or playground that is built on a small plot; often located in built-up areas or on vacant or abandoned lots.

Veterans Administration (VA). *See* Department of Veterans Affairs.

vicinage. The vicinity, region, or area near or around a particular place.

view

1. A drawing that represents a particular viewpoint, e.g., front view, side view.
2. The scene or prospect viewed from a site or property.

virgin forest. A mature or overmature forest.

viscosity. The degree to which a fluid resists flow under an applied force. (R.S. Means)

visual rights. The right to clear vegetation and restrict structures at intersections; where enabling legislation has been enacted, the right to prohibit advertising media along highway rights-of-way.

vital statistics. Statistics pertaining to births, marriages, deaths, health, diseases, and other human events and conditions.

vitrified tile. Pipe made of clay that is hard-baked and glazed to make it impervious to water; used particularly for underground drainage.

volt. A unit of electromotive force. Residences are usually wired with

110-volt or 110- and 220-volt circuits. Factories and large commercial properties may have 440-volt power circuits in addition to 110 and 220 circuits.

W

wages. Pay given for labor, usually manual or mechanical, at short, stated intervals, as distinguished from a salary or fee. More broadly, the share of investment return paid out as a reward for labor, as distinguished from the renumeration received by capital in its various forms.

wainscot

1. A facing or paneling applied to the walls of a room.
2. The lower part of an interior wall that is finished with a material different from the upper part.

waiver of lien. An instrument by which a person or organization, who has or may have a right of mechanic's lien against the property of another, relinquishes such a right. (R. S. Means)

wall. A vertical structure of stone, brick, wood, or a similar material

that encloses, divides, supports, and protects, e.g., one of the vertical, enclosing sides of a building or room; also a solid masonry fence or retaining wall.

wall-bearing. *See* bearing wall.

wall-bearing construction. Construction in which the roof and floors are carried directly by exterior walls of plain brick, pilastered brick, or other masonry; posts and columns are used only when the length of the interior span requires intermediate support for a roof or floor.

wallboard. Any artificially prepared sheet materials or panels that are used to cover walls or ceilings as a substitute or base for plaster. *See also* drywall.

wall covering. Any material or assembly used as a wall finish and not an integral part of the wall. (R.S. Means)

wall furnace. A small, gas-fired, hot air furnace that fits between the studs of a wall; has no ducts; uses a small fan to circulate room air through the furnace and to distribute heated air.

wall height. The vertical distance from the top of a wall to its support, such as a foundation or support beam. (R.S. Means)

wall panel. A nonbearing or curtain wall between the columns or piers in a structure; supported by the girders or beams of the structural frame at each story level.

wall tile. Ceramic or plastic tile that is used as a finish material for interior walls or wainscot.

warehouse. A structure that is designed and used for the storage of wares, goods, and merchandise; usually classified as industrial.

warehousing of mortgages. An arrangement in which an originator-mortgagee obtains short-term, interim credit secured by mortgages to bridge the gap between the completion of construction and the eventual sale of the mortgages on the property to an investor-mortgagee; characterized by the lender/borrower relationship, an outright lending of funds, and an agreement in which the lender collects interest on the amount of the loan.

warm air heating system. A heating system in which warm air is distributed through a single register or series of ducts. Circulation may be by convection (gravity system) or by a fan in the ductwork (forced system). (R.S. Means)

warranted price. Amount justified in exchange. The fixing of a warranted price presupposes a prospective exchange of property, e.g., of real estate for money. *Warranted* refers to that which is justified or fair. Because the price that is warranted can vary according to the circumstances of either or both parties, there can be no determination of what is warranted except in connection with definite assumptions or limiting conditions. Thus the term *warranted price,* without a statement of the underlying assumptions or limiting conditions, has no meaning. A warranted price in view of the seller's peculiar circumstances might be different from the warranted price that a buyer should pay in view of the prospective benefits of the purchase.

warranty deed. A deed that conveys to the grantee title to the property free and clear of all encumbrances, except those specifically set forth in the document.

wash fountain. *See* Bradley fountain.

waste. A type of range vegetation that includes all vegetated areas that cannot be used economically due to inaccessibility, dense timber, or sparse forage growth. Large areas of sparse forage are classified as waste for grazing unless they are near a better type of range; it is impractical to run stock over large areas to get to a small amount of feed.

waste line. A pipe that carries waste from a bathtub, shower, lavatory, or any other fixture or appliance except a toilet.

waste pipe. *See* waste line.

wasting assets. *See* diminishing assets.

water. *See* ground water; irrigation; surface water.

water bottom land. *See* bottom land.

water closet (W.C.)
1. A plumbing fixture used to receive human wastes and flush them to a waste pipe.
2. A room that contains a water closet. (R.S. Means)

water cooling tower. An outdoor structure, frequently placed on a roof, over which warm water is circulated for cooling by evaporation and exposure to the air. A natural draft cooling tower is one in which the airflow through the tower is due to its natural chimney effect. A mechanical draft tower employs fans to force or induce a draft. (R.S. Means)

waterfront property. Land abutting a body of water; a part of a community abutting a body of water.

water-holding capacity. The amount of water that soil with free drainage will hold against the pull of gravity; expressed as a percentage of the dry weight of the soil.

water level. The level of the surface of any body of water. *See also* water table.

water line easement. Similar to a sewer line easement, except that water is to be supplied through the line.

water main. A main supply pipe in a water system providing water for public or community use. (R.S. Means)

water measures. *See* acre-foot; acre-inch; cubic foot per second; hour-inch; miner's inch; second foot.

water power. Power created by a quantity of water passing from a higher to a lower level; adaptable to commercial and industrial use.

water power plant. A plant or mill that uses water power to operate its equipment. *See also* hydroelectric plant; power plant.

waterproofing
1. To make impervious to water or dampness.

2. Any material used to waterproof, e.g., pitch or other bituminous materials.

water rights. A right to a definite or conditional flow or quantity of water, usually for use at stated times and in stated quantities, e.g., for irrigation or for hydroelectric power development. A water right may be a right acquired by prescription, e.g., arising from the open, notorious, and undisputed use of water for the statutory term of years; a right acquired by appropriation, e.g., a grant from an agency of government with the right to distribute the unappropriated surplus waters of the state; or a riparian right under the common law doctrine of riparian ownership of waters that wash land. *See also* riparian rights.

watershed. The drainage area that contributes water to a bordering stream; also called *drainage basin.*

water softener. A device to remove calcium and magnesium salts from a water supply, usually by ion exchange. (R.S. Means)

water table

1. The upper limit of the part of the soil, or underlying material, that is wholly saturated with water; the depth below the surface at which free water is found.

2. A projection at the bottom line of a building superstructure, outside the vertical plane of the foundation, that provides for the runoff of rainwater.

watt. A measure of electricity equal to the power created by a current of one ampere flowing at one volt pressure.

watt-hour. The standard measure of electrical energy; the power in watts times the number of hours that the power is maintained.

WCR. *See* Women's Council of Realtors.

weak market. A market characterized by low demand and declining price levels; also called a *soft market.*

wealth. All things that are owned; material objects themselves or the evidences of possession, e.g., securities; commonly includes money and anything of monetary value. Technically, money is not wealth, but a medium of exchange for acquiring wealth.

weathering. The chemical and physical disintegration and decomposition of rocks, minerals, and other organic materials or surfaces.

weatherstrip. A thin strip of metal, felt, wood, or other material that is used to cover the joint between a door or window sash and the jamb, casing, or sill; keeps out air, dust, rain, etc.

wedge theory. *See* sector theory.

weep holes. A series of small holes in a retaining wall or similar structure that permit the drainage of water through the wall, reducing the pressure against the wall.

weighted average. An average in which each component is adjusted by a factor that reflects its relative importance to the whole; obtained by multiplying each component by its assigned weight, adding the products, and dividing the sum of the products by the sum of the weights. *See also* band of investment.

weighted rate. A rate that has been adjusted to reflect its relative influence on a total result. *See also* band of investment; weighted average.

weighted use factor. The factor obtained by multiplying the use factor of each vegetative species on the range by its respective percentage in the composition and totaling these products.

weighting. A technique used to rate comparable sales data according to their reliability relative to the subject property or their similarity to the subject property. Applications include weighted mean analysis, band of investment, and compatibility matrixes.

weir. A device installed in an irrigation ditch or stream to measure the quantity of water passing a particular point.

well

1. Any enclosed space of considerable height, such as an air shaft or the space around which a stair winds.
2. A collection device for ground water.
3. A wall around a tree trunk to hold back soil.
4. A slot in a machine or device into which a part fits. (R.S. Means)
5. A hole drilled into the earth, usually by boring, to obtain water, petroleum, natural gas, etc.

Western framing. Framing in which the studding for each story rests on a sill; as distinguished from balloon framing.

wetlands. Areas that are frequently inundated or saturated by surface or ground water and support vegetation typically adapted for life in saturated soil conditions; generally include swamps, marshes, bogs, and similar areas, but classification may differ in various jurisdictions. Section 404 of the Clean Water Act define wetlands as "those areas that are inundated or saturated by surface or ground water at a frequency and duration sufficient to support, and that under normal circumstances do support, a prevalence of vegetation typically adapted for life in saturated soil conditions." *See also* bottom land.

wetting

1. The soaking of asbestos materials to diminish the level of air contamination they give off when distributed. The water is mixed with saturants and surfactants before it is applied to the asbestos.
2. Coating a base metal with filler metal prior to soldering or brazing. (R.S. Means)

wharf. A structure along which vessels can be held or docked for loading and unloading; usually constructed parallel to the shoreline. If the long side extends into the water from the shore, it is called a *pier*.

wheel leveler. A small elevator that raises the floor of a truck or trailer to a loading dock by lifting the truck's rear wheels.

white rot. A type of decay in wood caused by a fungus that leaves a white deposit. (R.S. Means)

whole property. *See* larger parcel.

wicket. A small door or gate, especially one that is mounted as part of a larger one. (R.S. Means)

widow's walk. A narrow walkway on the roof of a house. (R.S. Means)

wild land. Land that has been left natural, uninhabited, unoccupied, and uncultured, and is not used by the owner, an agent, or a lessee for any artificial purpose.

will-cut cruise. The estimated amount of lumber that can be sawed from the timber in a given area; calculated by deducting an allowance for breakage or other waste from the stand cruise.

windbreak. A physical feature that shelters a house from the wind, especially a tall hedge of trees or shrubs planted for this purpose.

windfall

1. An unexpected or sudden capital gain.
2. In forestry, *see* blowdown.

wind load. The amount of pressure that the wind exerts on the exposed surface of a wall or roof; usually expressed in pounds per square foot of surface area.

window. A glass opening in a wall or ceiling that provides natural light and ventilation; types include awning, casement, circlehead or fan, clerestory, double hung, fixed, and traverse or sliding. *See also* Window Types in the addenda.

window jamb trim. A thin, vertical strip of molding that covers the junction of the vertical members of the window frame and the jamb.

window of time analysis. A method measuring labor productivity losses on a specific project by comparing labor productivity achieved during a period of time when work activities are subject to disruptive events and conditions, versus productivity during a period of time without disruptions. (R.S. Means)

window sash. A movable frame that holds the window glass. Sash windows move vertically and may be single, in which only the lower half of the window opens, or double, in which both portions are movable.

window schedule. A tabulation, usually on a drawing, listing all windows on a project and indicating sizes, number of lights, type of sash and frame, and hardware required. (R.S. Means)

window sill. The lower, or base, framing of a window opening.

window stop. Component of a window frame directly under the head. *See also* Window Types in the addenda.

window well. *See* light well.

windrow

1. A ridge of loose soil, such as that produced by the spill off of a grader blade.
2. A row of leaves or snow heaped up by the wind. (R.S. Means)

wing

1. A building section or addition that projects from the main structure.

2. The offstage space at a side of a stage. (R.S. Means)
3. One of the four leaves of a revolving door. (R.S. Means)

winter fat. A type of range vegetation that includes areas where winter fat (*eurotia*) constitutes the predominant vegetation.

wire glass. Window glass in which fine wire mesh is embedded to prevent shattering or breaking when exposed to extreme heat.

witness corner. In the metes and bounds system, a monument that identifies a point on the land surface that corresponds to a point in the legal description of a site.

Wolmanized. A trade name for chemically treated lumber used in building outdoor structures such as porches and decks.

Women's Council of Realtors (WCR). An organization that provides members with a referral network, programs and systems for personal and career growth, and opportunities for increased productivity and financial security. WCR also promotes the development of leadership skills in professional women.

wood frame construction. Construction in which walls and partitions are formed by the wood framing of studs, or posts and girts, supporting a wooden roof and floor decks;

may be covered with wood, metal, stucco, composition siding, or shingles, or veneered with brick or stone facing.

woodland. Any land with trees; usually the wooded land of a farm as distinguished from cropland; wooded land with trees that are usable for timber or will grow to become timber.

workability. That property of freshly mixed concrete or mortar that determines the ease and homogeneity with which it can be mixed, placed, compacted, and finished. (R.S. Means)

work capacity. The greatest volume in number and/or size of construction projects that a contractor can manage efficiently without increasing the overhead costs. (R.S. Means)

working assets. Assets that are consumed in business activities but are not themselves integral parts of the product, e.g., supplies used in an operation.

working capital. The readily convertible capital that a business uses to conduct operations; in accounting, current assets minus current liabilities as of a certain date.

working drawing. A scale drawing, usually a blueprint, of all or part of a structure; contains detailed dimensions and instructions to guide

workers on a construction job.

workinghouse. A penthouse structure above the storage section of a grain elevator that houses the mechanical equipment necessary to the elevator's operation; also called *headhouse*.

work letter. An agreement, usually part of a lease, that specifies the level of interior finish and equipment that the landlord is to provide to the tenant, including lighting, partitioning, door allowance, and electrical capacity.

workout. A plan drawn up to address specific arrangements involving a loan, e.g., 1) restructuring, 2) locating additional sources of capital, 3) maximizing value by selling the property (development of which was financed by the loan), or 4) determining how the lender and developer can share in the value.

wraparound mortgage. A mortgage that is subordinate to, but inclusive of, any existing mortgage or mortgages on a property. Usually a third-party lender refinances the property, assuming the existing mortgage and its debt service and wrapping around a new, junior mortgage. The wraparound lender gives the borrower the difference between the outstanding balance of the existing mortgage or mortgages and the face amount of the new mortgage.

writ of certiorari. *See* certiorari.

writ of execution. A legal order that directs a proper agent of the court, often a sheriff, to carry out an order of the court.

wrought iron

1. A comparatively pure form of iron with practically no carbon, which is easily forged, welded, etc.

2. Steel that has been molded and worked into ornamental shapes and patterns; used for railings, gates, furniture, etc.

wye. A railroad juncture track, with one track joining the main track from one direction and another joining the main track from another direction.

wythe. A masonry partition wall between flues in the same chimney stack.

x-brace. Paired set of sway braces. (R.S. Means)

x-bracing. The cross-bracing of a partition or floor joist.

Y

yard
1. A unit of length in the English system equal to three feet.
2. A term applied to that part of a plot not occupied by the building or driveway. (R.S. Means)

yard lumber. Lumber of all sizes and shapes that is intended for general building purposes. The grading of yard lumber is based on the intended use of the particular grade; it is applied to each piece with reference to its size and length.

yearling. An animal approximately one year of age. A short yearling is from nine to 12 months old; a long yearling is from 12 to 18 months old.

year-long grazing. Continuous grazing for a 12-month period, or a calendar year.

y-highway. Expressway intersection at a grade that steers traffic in three directions. (R.S. Means)

yield
1. The volume of freshly mixed concrete produced from a known quantity of ingredients.
2. The total weight of ingredients divided by the unit weight of the freshly mixed concrete.
3. The number of product units, such as block, produced per bag of cement or per batch of concrete. (R.S. Means)
4. For appraisal usage, *see* current yield; yield to maturity.

yield and change formula. Method of deriving a capitalization rate by deducting the rate of stabilized change in property value and/or income from the yield rate ($R = Y - \Delta a$).

yield capitalization. The capitalization method used to convert future benefits into present value by discounting each future benefit at an appropriate yield rate or by developing an overall rate that explicitly reflects the investment's income pattern, value change, and yield rate.

yield rate (Y). A rate of return on capital, usually expressed as a compound annual percentage rate. A yield rate considers all expected property benefits, including the proceeds from sale at the termination of the investment. Yield rates include the interest rate, discount rate, internal rate of return (IRR), overall yield rate (Y_O), and equity yield rate (Y_E).

yield to maturity. In finance, the total rate of return that would be realized on an investment such as a bond if purchased at the current market price, held as an investment, and redeemed for the principal amount at maturity.

Z

zero-coupon mortgage. A debt secured by real estate with interest payments accruing rather than being paid by the borrower; in some circumstances, a rate of interest may be imputed, e.g., for income taxation.

zero lot line. In zoning, the location of a structure on a lot so that one or more sides rest directly on the boundary line of the lot, i.e., there is no setback of the building.

zonal soil. Any of the great groups of soils that has well-developed soil characteristics reflecting the influence of the active factors in soil genesis, e.g., climate and living organisms, vegetation.

zone control. A system that stabilizes the distribution of heat to match the various needs in different parts of a building.

zoning. The public regulation of the character and extent of real estate use through police power; accomplished by establishing districts or areas with uniform restrictions relating to improvements; structural height, area, and bulk; density of population; and other aspects of the use and development of private property.

zoning exception. *See* special exceptions; zoning variance.

zoning map. A map that depicts the various sections of a community, divides the sections into zones, and indicates the land uses permitted under the zoning ordinance.

zoning ordinance. A statute enacted by a legislative body, under the police powers of government, to regulate and control the use of real estate for the health, morals, safety, and general welfare of the public.

zoning permit. A permit issued by municipal or local government officials authorizing the use of a piece of land for a stated purpose. (R.S. Means)

zoning variance. A legally authorized modification in the use of property at a particular location that does not conform to the regulated use set forth in the zoning ordinance for the surrounding area; not an exception or change in the legally applicable zoning. *See also* legally non-conforming use; special use permit.

z-value. The standard normal deviate; represents the number of standard deviation units that the random variable, or observation, in a data set is above or below the mean. Tables for the area under a normal curve are constructed in terms of z values for a given z; the tables provide the basis for determining the probability of an outcome between two values or the probability of an outcome being greater or less than a specific value.

Table of Contents

Topical Index

The following lists divide the terms defined in this text into nine subject classifications: 1) agriculture, forestry, and soils; 2) computers; 3) construction, engineering, architecture, surveying, and city planning; 4) economics, investment analysis, and market analysis; 5) financial (accounting, banking, brokerage, insurance, and taxation); 6) general appraisal and property types; 7) government agencies and programs; 8) legal (litigation, certification, and regulation); and 9) mathematics and statistics.

AGRICULTURE, FORESTRY, AND SOILS

COMPUTERS

applications software
American Standard Code for Information Interchange (ASCII)
backup
batch processing
bidirectional
binary
bit
boot
boot strap program
buffer
bug
byte
central processing unit (CPU)
compiler

computer-assisted mass appraisal (CAMA)
computer program
cps (characters per second)
cursor
database
data mode
documentation
DOS (disk operated system)
hard copy
hard disk
hard drive
hardware
iterative routine
kilobyte
lease-by-lease analysis

mainframe
megabyte
memory
microprocessor
modem
monitor
mouse
network
off line
on line
operating system
peripheral
processor
programming language
RAM (random access memory)
ROM (read only memory)
software

CONSTRUCTION, ENGINEERING, ARCHITECTURE, SURVEYING, AND CITY PLANNING

ABC roads
above-grade living area (AGLA)
abut
abutment
acceleration lane
accessory building
acoustical material
acoustical tile
acre
acreage
addition
adobe construction
aerial photograph
after-completion costs
air-conditioning
air plenum
air quality standard

alcove
American bond
American standard
anchor bolt
anodized aluminum
approach nose
approach zone
apron
aqueduct
arcade
arch
architect's approval
architect's punch list
architect's standard net assignable area
architectural area of buildings
architectural concrete construction

architectural style
architectural volume of buildings
architecture
architrave
area
areaway
Art Deco
arterial highway
Art Nouveau
asbestos
ashlar
aspect
asphaltic concrete
asphalt tile
assisted housing
atrium
atrium house

ECONOMICS, INVESTMENT ANALYSIS, AND MARKET ANALYSIS

FINANCIAL (ACCOUNTING, BANKING, BROKERAGE, INSURANCE, AND TAXATION)

GENERAL APPRAISAL AND PROPERTY TYPES

GOVERNMENT AGENCIES AND PROGRAMS

Americans with Disabilities Act (ADA) of 1990

Americans with Disabilities Act Accessibility Guidelines on Buildings and Facilities (ADAAG)

Bureau of Public Roads

Bureau of Reclamation

capital improvement plan

Coastal Zone Management Act

Competitive Banking Act

Comprehensive Environmental Response, Compensation, and Liability Act (CERCLA)

Comptroller of the Currency

Community Reinvestment Act

Council of Government (COG)

Department of Agriculture

Department of Housing and Urban Development (HUD)

Department of Justice

Department of the Interior

Department of the Treasury

Department of Transportation

Department of Veterans Affairs

Employee Relocation Council (ERC)

environmental property assessment (EPRA)

Environmental Protection Agency (EPA)

Equal Credit Opportunity Act (effective 1992)

Farm Credit Administration (FCA)

Farmers Home Administration (FmHA)

Federal Advisory Council

Federal Aviation Administration (FAA)

Federal Communication Commission (FCC)

Federal Deposit Insurance Corporation (FDIC)

Federal Emergency Management Agency (FEMA)

Federal Energy Administration (FEA)

Federal Farm Loan Act

Federal Financial Institutions Examination Council (FFIEC)

Federal Financial Institutions Regulatory Agencies (FFIRA)

Federal Highway Administration

Federal Home Loan Bank

Federal Home Loan Bank Board (FHLBB)

Federal Home Loan Bank System

Federal Home Loan Mortgage Corporation (FHLMC)

Federal Housing Administration (FHA)

Federal Interagency Real Property Appraisal Committee (FIRPAC)

Federal Intermediate Credit Banks

Federal Loan Bank (FLB)

Federal National Mortgage Association (FNMA)

Federal Open Market Committee (FOMC)

Federal Power Commission (FPC)

Federal Reserve Bank

Federal Reserve Board

Federal Reserve System

Federal Savings and Loan Association

Federal Savings and Loan Insurance Corporation (FSLIC)

Financial Institutions Reform, Recovery and Enforcement Act (FIRREA)

Flood Disaster Protection Act (FDPA)

National Flood Insurance Program (NFIP)

National Institute of Building Science (NIBS)

National Register of Historic Places

Occupational Safety and Health Act (OSHA) of 1970

Office of Thrift Supervision (OTS)

port authority

Public Housing Administration

redevelopment agency

Resolution Trust Corporation (RTC)

Section 8 housing

Securities and Exchange Commission (SEC)

Small Business Adminis-
  tration
Soil Bank
Soil Bank Act
Soil Conservation Service

subsidy
Superfund Amendment
  and Liability Act of 1986
  (SARA)

Taylor permit
Title I
Trust for Public Land (TPL)

LEGAL (LITIGATION, CERTIFICATION, AND REGULATION)

abandonment
abatement
absentee landlord
absolute assignment
absolute conveyance
absolute owner
abstract of title
abutter's rights
acceleration clause
access
accession
access rights
accommodation
acknowledgment
acquisition fee
action in rem
administrator
administrator's deed
adverse possession
affidavit
affirmative easement
agency
agent
agreement of sale
airport zoning
air quality control region
air rights
alienation
all-inclusive deed of trust
allotment
alodial
alteration
Americans with Disabilities
  Act (ADA) of 1990

Americans with Disabilities
  Act Accessibility Guidelines on Buildings and
  Facilities (ADAAG)
appropriation
appurtenance
arbitrator
area controls
assignee
assignor
attachment
attorney-in-fact
authority
avigation easement
before-and-after rule
beneficial interests
beneficial use
beneficiary of trust deed
benefits
blue sky
blue sky law
bona fide sale
bond for deed
boundaries
bounded description
building code
building permit
building restrictions
bulk regulations
bundle of rights theory
capital improvement plan
caveat
caveat emptor
certificate

certificate of beneficial
  interest
certificate of limited
  partnership
certificate of occupancy
  (C of O)
certificate of title
certiorari
chain of title
chattel
chattels personal
chattels real
civil law
clearance easement
clear title
closed-end trust
closing
closure
cloud on title
cluster zoning
commercial facility
committee deed
common law
common property
community associations
community property
compensable damages
compensable interest
compensation
comprehensive plan
concession
concurrency
condemnation
condemnee

MATHEMATICS AND STATISTICS

FIRREA Guidelines for Review Appraisers

The minimum standards required by the Financial Institutions Reform, Recovery and Enforcement Act of 1989 (FIRREA) state that all appraisals shall

1. Conform to the Uniform Standards of Professional Appraisal Practice (USPAP) adopted by the Appraisal Standards Board of The Appraisal Foundation, except that the departure provision of the USPAP shall not apply to federally related transactions.

2. Disclose any steps taken that were necessary or appropriate to comply with the Competency Provision of the USPAP.

3. Be based upon the definition of market value as set forth in section 34.42 (f) [12 CFR Part 34].

4. Be written and presented in a narrative format or on forms that satisfy all the requirements of this section, be sufficiently descriptive to enable the reader to ascertain the estimated market value and the rationale for the estimate, and provide detail and depth of analysis that reflect the complexity of the real estate appraised.

5. Analyze and report in reasonable detail any prior sales of the property being appraised that occurred within the following time periods:

   - For one- to four-family residential property, one year preceding the date when the appraisal was prepared.
   - For all other property, three years preceding the date when the appraisal was prepared.

6. Analyze and report data on current revenues, expenses, and vacancies for the property if it is and will continue to be income-producing.

7. Analyze and report a reasonable marketing period for the subject property.

8. Analyze and report on current market conditions and trends that will affect projected income or the absorption period, to the extent they affect the value of the subject property.

9. Analyze and report appropriate deductions and discounts for any proposed construction, or any completed properties that are partially leased or leased at other than market rents as of the date of the appraisal, or any tract developments with any unsold units.

10. Include in the certification required by USPAP an additional statement that the appraisal assignment was not based on a requested minimum valuation, a specific valuation, or the approval of a loan.

11. Contain sufficient supporting documentation with all pertinent information reported so that the appraiser's logic, reasoning, judgment, and analysis in arriving at a conclusion indicate to the reader the reasonableness of the market value reported.

12. Include a legal description of the real estate being appraised, in addition to the description required by USPAP.

13. Identify and separately value any personal property, fixtures, or intangible items that are not real property but are included in the appraisal, and discuss the impact of their inclusion or exclusion on the estimate of market value.

14. Follow a reasonable valuation method that addresses the direct sales comparison, income, and cost approaches to market value; reconciles those approaches; and explains the elimination of each approach not used.

Courtesy of Robert L. Parson, MAI

Significant U.S. Supreme Court Decisions Affecting Property Rights and Real Estate Appraisal

Prepared by J.D. Eaton, MAI

1. *Kohl v. United States,* 91 U.S. 367 (1875).
   The right of eminent domain is held by the government of the United States.

2. *Boom Company v. Patterson,* 98 U.S. 403 (1878).
   Compensation for a taking of private property is based on the value of the property put to its highest and best use.

3. *Kerr v. South Park Commissioners,* 117 U.S. 379 (1886).
   Project enhancement must be disregarded when estimating value for eminent domain purposes.

4. *Monongahela Navigation Company v. United States,* 148 U.S. 312 (1893).
   The amount of compensation due for an eminent domain taking is a judicial decision, not a legislative one.

5. *Chicago, Burlington, and Quincy Railroad Company v. Chicago,* 166 U.S. 226 (1897).
   Under the Fourteenth Amendment to the U.S. Constitution, states are prohibited from taking private property for a public use without the payment of just compensation.

6. *Bauman v. Ross,* 167 U.S. 548 (1897).
   Special benefits may be offset against the value of the land taken and damages to the remainder property in an eminent domain partial taking. (*See* definition of special benefits.)

7. *Sharp v. United States,* 191 U.S. 341 (1903).
   Unity of use must exist between parcels of land before they will be considered

as a single larger parcel for eminent domain valuation purposes. (*See* definition of larger parcel.)

8. *Hairston* v. *Danville and Western Railway Company,* 208 U.S. 598 (1908).
   The quantity of land to be taken for a public use under the power of eminent domain is a legislative determination that is not judicially reviewable.

9. *United States* v. *Welch,* 217 U.S. 333 (1910).
   The destruction of an appurtenant easement by condemnation is a taking and compensation must be ascertained with reference to the dominant estate to which it is attached.

10. *United States* v. *Grizzard,* 219 U.S. 180 (1911).
    Just compensation for a partial taking must include damages to the remainder property to satisfy the requirements of the Fifth Amendment to the U.S. Constitution.

11. *Bothwell* v. *United States,* 254 U.S. 231 (1920).
    Business losses are not a compensable damage item when real estate is taken by condemnation.

12. *Pennsylvania Coal Company* v. *Mahon,* 260 U.S. 393 (1922).
    If a police power action "goes too far" it becomes a taking, requiring compensation pursuant to the Fifth Amendment to the U.S. Constitution.

13. *United States* v. *New River Collieries,* 262 U.S. 341 (1923).
    Where private property is taken for public use and there is a market prevailing at the time and place of the taking, the market price is just compensation.

14. *Brown* v. *United States,* 263 U.S. 78 (1923).
    The United States can condemn land for the construction of a substitute facility. (*See* definition of substitute facility.)

15. *A.W. Duckett & Company, Inc.* v. *United States,* 266 U.S. 149 (1924).
    Property is valued for condemnation purposes as a whole, rather than as the sum of the estates into which it may have been carved.

16. *Campbell* v. *United States,* 266 U.S. 368 (1924)
    In an eminent domain action, an owner is not entitled to damages to a remainder parcel caused by the use to which the government will put lands taken from others for the same project.

17. *Mitchell* v. *United States,* 267 U.S. 341 (1925).
    Damages to a business incidental to an eminent domain taking of land are not compensable.

18. *Village of Euclid* v. *Ambler Realty Company,* 272 U.S. 365 (1926).
    Generally, zoning is a proper police power function.

19. *Cincinnati* v. *Vester,* 281 U.S. 439 (1930).
    Defining what constitutes a Fifth Amendment "public use" is a judicial matter.

20. *Olson* v. *United States,* 292 U.S. 246 (1934).
    Just compensation is the market value of the property condemned at the time of the taking contemporaneously paid in money. Market value is based on all uses for which the land taken is suitable.

21. *McCandless* v. *United States,* 298 U.S. 342 (1936).
    The most profitable use to which land can be put may be considered relevant to its market value for eminent domain purposes.

22. *Danforth* v. *United States,* 308 U.S. 271 (1939).
    The mere enactment of legislation authorizing condemnation cannot constitute a taking.

23. *United States* v. *Miller,* 317 U.S. 369 (1943).
    Project enhancement cannot be considered in estimating value for eminent domain purposes, but if a taking occurs as part of the expansion of a public project not initially contemplated, enhancement from the first phase of the project may be considered. (*See* definition of project enhancement.)

24. *United States ex rel T.V.A.* v. *Powelson,* 319 U.S. 266 (1943).
    The burden of establishing the value of the lands taken is upon the owner. The probability of assembling the land condemned with lands owned by others may be considered in estimating market value.

25. *United States* v. *General Motor Corp.,* 323 U.S. 373 (1945).
    Compensation for a temporary taking of a leasehold interest, shorter in term than the remaining term of the leasehold, is the rental value for the period of temporary occupancy, giving consideration to the long-term tenant's costs of vacating and reoccupying the premises.

26. *United States* v. *Petty Motor Co.,* 327 U.S. 372 (1946).
    The measure of damage for the taking of the use and occupancy of a leasehold interest for the remainder of the lessee's term is the value of the use and occupancy less the rent that the lessee would pay for such use and occupancy.

27. *United States* v. *Causby,* 328 U.S. 256 (1946).
    Low and frequent flights of aircraft over private land can be as much a taking as a more conventional entry upon it, thus just compensation is due.

28. *United States* v. *Cors,* 337 U.S. 325 (1949).
    An enhancement in the value of a property taken by condemnation caused by the government project for which the taking is being effected must be disregarded in establishing just compensation. (*See* definition of project enhancement.)

29. *Kimball Laundry Co.* v. *United States,* 338 U.S. 1 (1949).
    Going-concern, or business, value is a compensable damage in a condemnation action when the government takes a business property with the intent of carrying on the business.

30. *United States* v. *Toronto, Hamilton & Buffalo Navigation Co.,* 338 U.S. 396 (1949).
    When the market value of property taken by eminent domain cannot be determined, other measures of value may be relevant in establishing just compensation.

31. *Berman* v. *Parker,* 348 U.S. 26 (1954).
    The taking by condemnation of an entire project area, including properties not suffering from blight, for urban renewal is constitutional. Once the public purpose has been established, the means of executing the project are for Congress and Congress alone to determine.

32. *United States* v. *Dow,* 357 U.S. 17 (1958).
    When the government enters into possession of property prior to acquisition of title, the date of possession becomes the date of taking and the date of value for eminent domain purposes.

33. *United States* v. *Virginia Electric & Power Company,* 365 U.S. 624 (1961).
    Condemnation blight is to be disregarded in estimating market value for the purpose of establishing just compensation in an eminent domain action. (*See* definition of condemnation blight.)

34. *Goldblatt* v. *Town of Hempstead,* 369 U.S. 590 (1962).
    Government action in the form of a regulation may be so onerous as to constitute a taking which constitutionally requires compensation; there is no set formula to determine where regulation ends and taking begins.

35. *United States* v. *Rands,* 389 U.S. 121 (1967).
    The interests of riparian owners are subject to the government's power to con-

trol navigable waters and the proper exercise of that power is not compensable under the Fifth Amendment to the U.S. Constitution.

36. *Almota Farmers Elevator & Warehouse Co. v. United States,* 409 U.S. 470 (1973).
In valuing leasehold improvements taken by condemnation, consideration may be given to the probability that the ground lease upon which the improvements are located could be renewed; the economic life of the leasehold improvements is not necessarily limited to the term of the current lease.

37. *United States* v. *Fuller,* 409 U.S. 488 (1973).
When fee lands are condemned, consideration is not given to any enhancement in the value of the fee lands created by revocable federal permits on abutting lands.

38. *Penn Central Transportation Co. v. New York City,* 438 U.S. 104 (1978).
A city may restrict development of privately owned historic landmarks without the payment of just compensation. Significant factors in determining whether a taking, requiring the payment of just compensation, has occurred are 1) the economic impact of the regulation on the owner, 2) the extent to which the regulation has interfered with distinct, investment-backed expectations, and 3) the character of the governmental action.

39. *United States* v. *Bodcaw Co.,* 440 U.S. 202 (1979).
An owner's cost of procuring a real estate appraisal in an eminent domain action is not part of just compensation as required by the Fifth Amendment to the U.S. Constitution.

40. *United States* v. *564.54 Acres of Land, More or Less,* 441 U.S. 506 (1979).
Condemnation of a private, nonprofit organization's property does not require application of the substitute facilities doctrine. (*See* definition of substitute facilities.)

41. *Kaiser Aetna v. United States,* 444 U.S. 164 (1979).
Private efforts converting nonnavigable waters into navigable waters do not result in the public gaining legal access thereto.

42. *Agins v. City of Triburon,* 447 U.S. 225 (1980).
The application of a general zoning law effects a taking requiring compensation if it denies an owner economically viable use of his or her land.

43. *San Diego Gas & Electric Co. v. City of San Diego,* 450 U.S. 621 (1981).
Dissenting opinion suggests that a regulation that results in a taking requires payment of just compensation; even if the regulation is subsequently rescinded,

just compensation would be required for the temporary taking from the date of enactment to the date the regulation is rescinded.

44. *Loretto* v. *Teleprompter Manhattan CATV Corp.*, 458 U.S. 419 (1982).
A permanent physical occupation of private property authorized by state law is a taking requiring compensation without regard to whether the state or a party authorized by the state is the occupant.

45. *Hawaii Housing Authority* v. *Midkiff*, 467 U.S. 229 (1984).
Taking the title to real property from lessors and transferring it to lessees to reduce the concentration of fees simple in the state meets the criteria of a "public use" required by the Fifth Amendment to the U.S. Constitution.

46. *United States* v. *50 Acres of Land*, 469 U.S. 24 (1984).
A public condemnee is not entitled to the cost of acquiring a substitute facility when the market value of the condemned property is ascertainable.

47. *United States* v. *Riverside Bayview Homes*, 474 U.S. 121 (1985).
Pursuant to § 404 of the Clean Water Act, the owner of wetlands must obtain a permit from the Army Corps of Engineers before filling them. Denial of such a permit, under certain circumstances, may constitute a taking requiring the payment of just compensation.

48. *MacDonald, Sommer & Frates* v. *County of Yolo*, 477 U.S. 340 (1986).
There is no set formula to determine when regulation ends and a taking of private property begins under the Fifth and Fourteenth Amendments to the U.S. Constitution; it is a question of degree and cannot be disposed of by general propositions.

49. *Keystone Coal Association* v. *DeBenedictus*, 480 U.S. 470 (1987).
A comparison of values before and after a regulatory action is relevant and even essential in determining whether there has been a taking of property requiring just compensation pursuant to the Fifth Amendment to the U.S. Constitution.

50. *First English Evangelical Lutheran Church* v. *Los Angeles County*, 482 U.S. 304 (1987).
Under the just compensation clause, a landowner may recover damages when government has taken property by land use regulation. If the regulation is rescinded after being found to be a taking, compensation is due for the temporary taking from the date the regulation was adopted to the date it was rescinded.

51. *Nollan* v. *California Coastal Commission,* 483 U.S. 825 (1987).

    An exaction by government in return for a land use permit will be found to be a taking requiring the payment of just compensation, unless the exaction can be shown to diminish the harm that will be caused by the land use. (*See* definition of exaction.)

52. *Lucas* v. *South Carolina Coastal Council,* No. 91-453 (1992).

    A land use regulation which eliminates the economically viable use of land will be found to be a taking requiring the payment of just compensation, unless such prohibition can be justified by principles of public nuisance laws.

Exam Content Outlines

The following Examination Content Outlines have been adopted by the Appraiser Qualifications Board of The Appraisal Foundation. The purpose of these outlines is to provide a basis for the Appraiser Qualifications Board's endorsement of examinations as required by Title XI, Section 1116 of FIRREA.

The Examination Content Outlines provide examination developers and examinees with the scope of knowledge to be covered by the examination and a weighting of the relative importance of each category.

The terminology used to indicate the level of difficulty has been interpreted as follows:

Conceptual

Questions designed to determine the candidates' ability to understand and interpret appraisal concepts, principles and analysis procedures. These questions may, in some instances, require calculation skills for the candidate to demonstrate comprehension skills.

Definitions

Questions which test the candidates' ability to recall basic concepts, principles, definitions of widely used terms and the appropriate application of these terms in a factual setting.

Analysis/Application

Questions which require integrated use of analysis skills with supporting calculations along with comprehension and definitional knowledge. The use of existing, accepted methodology for analyzing appraisal data to calculate the numeric value of generally accepted concepts will be emphasized.

It is recommended that the examination be in a multiple-choice format. It is the position of the Appraiser Qualifications Board that the use of calculators be permitted.

Questions regarding the Content Outlines should be addressed:

Appraiser Qualifications Board

The Appraisal Foundation

1029 Vermont Avenue, N.W., Suite 900

Washington, DC 20005

National Uniform Examination Content Outline
General Real Property Appraiser Classification

	% WEIGHT	LEVEL OF DIFFICULTY
I. Influences on Real Estate Value A. Physical B. Economic C. Governmental and legal D. Social	2-3%	Conceptual

II. Legal Considerations in Appraisal
A. Real estate vs. real property
B. Real property vs. personal property
   1. Fixtures
   2. Trade fixtures
   3. Machinery and equipment
C. Limitations on real estate ownership
   1. Private
     a. Deed restrictions
	7-8%	Conceptual, Definitions

	% WEIGHT	LEVEL OF DIFFICULTY

    b. Leases

    c. Mortgages

    d. Easements

    e. Liens

    f. Encroachments

  2. Public

    a. Police power

      (1) Zoning

      (2) Building and fire codes

      (3) Environmental regulations

    b. Taxation

      (1) Property tax

      (2) Special assessments

    c. Eminent domain

    d. Escheat

D. Legal rights and interests

  1. Fee simple estate

  2. Life estate

  3. Leasehold interest

  4. Leased fee interest

  5. Other legal interests

    a. Easement

    b. Encroachment

E. Forms of property ownership

  1. Individual

  2. Tenancies and undivided interests

  3. Special ownership forms

    a. Condominium

    b. Cooperative

F. Legal descriptions

  1. Metes and bounds

  2. Government survey

  3. Lot and block

G. Transfer of title

  1. Basic types of deeds

  2. Recordation

	% WEIGHT	LEVEL OF DIFFICULTY
III. Types of Value	2-3%	Conceptual, Definitions
A. Market value or value in exchange		
B. Price		
C. Cost		
D. Investment value		
E. Value in use		
F. Assessed value		
G. Insurable value		
H. Going concern value		

III. Types of Value   2-3%   Conceptual, Definitions

A. Market value or value in exchange
B. Price
C. Cost
D. Investment value
E. Value in use
F. Assessed value
G. Insurable value
H. Going concern value

IV. Economic Principles   3-5%   Conceptual, Definitions

A. Anticipation
B. Balance
C. Change
D. Competition
E. Conformity
F. Contribution
G. Increasing and decreasing returns
H. Opportunity cost
I. Substitution
J. Supply and demand
K. Surplus productivity

V. Real Estate Markets and Analysis   5-7%   Conceptual, Analysis/Application

A. Characteristics of real estate markets
  1. Availability of information
  2. Changes in supply vs. demand
  3. Immobility of real estate
  4. Segmented markets
  5. Regulations
B. Absorption analysis
  1. Demographic data
  2. Competition
  3. Absorption
  4. Forecasts
  5. Existing space inventory

	% WEIGHT	LEVEL OF DIFFICULTY

    6. Current and projected space surplus

    7. New space

  C. Role of money and capital markets

    1. Competing investments

    2. Sources of capital

  D. Real estate financing

    1. Mortgage terms and concepts

      a. Mortgagor

      b. Mortgagee

      c. Principal and interest

    2. Mortgage payment plans

      a. Fixed rate, level payment

      b. Adjustable rate

      c. Buydown

      d. Other

    3. Types of mortgages

      a. Conventional

      b. Insured

VI. Valuation Process   2-4%   Conceptual

  A. Definition of the problem

    1. Purpose and use of appraisal

    2. Interests to be appraised

    3. Type of value to be estimated

    4. Date of the value estimate

    5. Limiting conditions

  B. Collection and analysis of data

    1. National and regional trends

    2. Economic base

    3. Local area and neighborhood

      a. Employment

      b. Income

      c. Trends

      d. Access

	% WEIGHT	LEVEL OF DIFFICULTY

      e. Locational convenience

    4. Site and improvements

  C. Analysis of highest and best use

  D. Application and limitations of each approach to value

    1. Sales comparison

    2. Cost

    3. Income capitalization

  E. Reconciliation and final value estimate

  F. The appraisal report

VII. Property Description   2-4%   Conceptual, Definitions

  A. Site description

    1. Utilities

    2. Access

    3. Topography

    4. Size

  B. Improvement description

    1. Size

    2. Condition

    3. Utility

  C. Basic construction and design

    1. Techniques and materials

      a. Foundations

      b. Framing

      c. Finish (exterior and interior)

      d. Mechanical

    2. Functional utility

VIII. Highest and Best Use Analysis   5-7%   Conceptual, Definitions, Analysis/Application

  A. Four tests

    1. Physically possible

    2. Legally permitted

    3. Economically feasible

    4. Maximally productive

  B. Vacant site or as if vacant

  C. As improved

	% WEIGHT	LEVEL OF DIFFICULTY

D. Interim use

IX. Appraisal Math and Statistics   3-5%   Conceptual,
  A. Compound interest concepts   Definitions,
    1. Future value of $1   Analysis/Application
    2. Present value of $1
    3. Future value of an annuity of $1 per period
    4. Present value of an annuity of $1 per period
    5. Sinking fund factor
    6. Installment to amortize $1 (loan constant)
  B. Statistical concepts used in appraisal
    1. Mean
    2. Median
    3. Mode
    4. Range
    5. Standard deviation

X. Sales Comparison Approach   10-12%   Conceptual,
  A. Research and selection of comparables   Definitions,
    1. Data sources   Analysis/Application
    2. Verification
    3. Units of comparison
      a. Income
        (1) Potential gross income multiplier
        (2) Effective gross income multiplier
        (3) Overall rate
      b. Size
        (1) Square foot
        (2) Acres
        (3) Other
      c. Utility (examples only)
        (1) Motel and apartment units
        (2) Theater seats
        (3) Other
  B. Elements of comparison
    1. Property rights conveyed

	% WEIGHT	LEVEL OF DIFFICULTY

    a. Easements

    b. Leased fee/leasehold

    c. Mineral rights

    d. Others

  2. Financing terms and cash equivalency

    a. Loan payment

    b. Loan balance

  3. Conditions of sale

    a. Arm's-length sale

    b. Personalty

  4. Market conditions at time of contract and closing

  5. Location

  6. Physical characteristics

  7. Tenant improvements

C. Adjustment process

  1. Sequence of adjustments

  2. Dollar adjustments

  3. Percentage adjustments

  4. Paired sales analysis

D. Application of sales comparison approach

XI. Site Value   3-5%   Conceptual,

A. Sales comparison   Definitions

B. Land residual   Analysis/Application

C. Allocation

D. Extraction

E. Ground rent capitalization

F. Subdivision analysis

  1. Development cost: direct and indirect

  2. Contractor's overhead and profit

  3. Forecast absorption and gross sales

  4. Entrepreneurial profit

  5. Discounted value conclusion

G. Plottage and assemblage

	% WEIGHT	LEVEL OF DIFFICULTY
XII. **Cost Approach**	9-12%	Conceptual,
A. Steps in cost approach		Definitions,
1. Reproduction vs. replacement cost		Analysis/Application
a. Comparative unit method		
b. Unit-in-place method		
c. Quantity survey method		
d. Cost service index		
2. Accrued depreciation		
a. Types of depreciation		
(1) Physical deterioration		
(a) Curable		
(b) Incurable		
(c) Short-lived		
(d) Long-lived		
(2) Functional obsolescence		
(a) Curable		
(b) Incurable		
(3) External obsolescence		
(a) Locational		
(b) Economic		
b. Methods of estimating depreciation		
(1) Age-life method		
(2) Breakdown method and sequence of deductions		
(3) Market extraction of depreciation		
B. Application of the cost approach		
XIII. **Income Approach**	20-24%	Conceptual,
A. Estimation of income and expenses		Definitions,
1. Gross market income		Analysis/Application
2. Effective gross income		
a. Vacancy		
b. Collection loss		
3. Operating expenses		
a. Fixed expenses		

	% WEIGHT	LEVEL OF DIFFICULTY

1. Relevance and limitations
2. Potential gross income and expense estimate
   a. Market vs. contract rents
   b. Vacancy and lease commissions
   c. Tenant improvements and concessions
3. Discount rates and yield rates (definition and concept but no calculations of yield rate)
4. Discounting cash flows (from operations and reversion where all cash flows projected in dollar amounts and tables or calculators can be used)

	% WEIGHT	LEVEL OF DIFFICULTY
XIV. Valuation of Partial Interests	4-6%	Conceptual, Definitions, Analysis/Application

    A. Interests created by a lease
       1. Leased fee
       2. Leasehold
       3. Subleasehold
       4. Renewal options
       5. Tenant improvements
       6. Concessions
    B. Lease provisions
       1. Overage rent
       2. Expense stops
       3. Net leases
       4. Minimum rent
       5. Percentage rent
       6. CPI adjustments
       7. Excess rent
    C. Valuations considerations
       1. Identifying the cash flows to the different interests, including turnover ratios

	% WEIGHT	LEVEL OF DIFFICULTY
2. Discount rate selection for different interests		
3. Relationship between the values of the interests		
D. Other partial interests		
1. Life estates		
2. Undivided interests in commonly held property		
3. Easements		
4. Timeshares		
5. Cooperatives		
XV. Appraisal Standards and Ethics	7-11%	Conceptual, Definitions

Courtesy of The Appraisal Foundation

National Uniform Examination Content Outline
Residential Real Property Appraiser Classification
(1-4 Units)

	% WEIGHT	LEVEL OF DIFFICULTY
I. Influences on Real Estate Value	3-4%	Conceptual
A. Physical and environmental		
B. Economic		
C. Governmental and legal		
D. Social		
II. Legal Considerations in Appraisal	6-8%	Conceptual, Definitions
A. Real estate vs. real property		
B. Real property vs. personal property		
C. Limitations on real estate ownership		
1. Private		
a. Deed restrictions		
b. Leases		
c. Mortgages		
d. Easements		
e. Liens		
f. Encroachments		
2. Public		
a. Police power		
(1) Zoning		
(2) Building and fire codes		
(3) Environmental regulations		

	% WEIGHT	LEVEL OF DIFFICULTY

      b. Taxation
        (1) Property tax
        (2) Special assessments
      c. Eminent domain
      d. Escheat

D. Legal rights and interests
    1. Fee simple estate
    2. Life estate
    3. Leasehold interest
    4. Leased fee interest
    5. Other legal interests
      a. Easement
      b. Encroachment

E. Forms of property ownership
    1. Individual
    2. Tenancies and undivided interests
    3. Special ownership forms
      a. Condominiums
      b. Cooperative
      c. Timesharing

F. Legal descriptions
    1. Metes and bounds
    2. Government survey
    3. Lot and block

G. Transfer of title
    1. Basic types of deeds
    2. Recordation

III. Types of Value

	% WEIGHT	LEVEL OF DIFFICULTY
III. Types of Value	3-5%	Conceptual, Definitions

A. Market value or value in exchange
B. Price
C. Cost
D. Investment value
E. Value in use
F. Assessed value
G. Insurable value

	% WEIGHT	LEVEL OF DIFFICULTY
IV. Economic Principles	7-9%	Conceptual,
A. Anticipation		Definitions
B. Balance		
C. Change		
D. Competition		
E. Conformity		
F. Contribution		
G. Increasing and decreasing returns		
H. Substitution		
I. Supply and demand		
J. Surplus productivity		
V. Real Estate Markets and Analysis	5-7%	Conceptual

  A. Characteristics of real estate markets
    1. Availability of information
    2. Changes in supply vs. demand
    3. Immobility of real estate
    4. Segmented markets
    5. Regulations
  B. Absorption analysis
    1. Demographic data
    2. Competition
    3. Absorption
    4. Forecasts
  C. Role of money and capital markets
    1. Competing investments
    2. Sources of capital
  D. Real estate financing
    1. Mortgage terms and concepts
      a. Mortgagor
      b. Mortgagee
      c. Principal and interest
    2. Mortgage payment plans
      a. Fixed rate, level payment
      b. Adjustable rate
      c. Buydown
      d. Other

	% WEIGHT	LEVEL OF DIFFICULTY

3. Types of mortgages
    a. Conventional
    b. Insured

VI. Valuation Process   4-6%   Conceptual

A. Definition of the problem
    1. Purpose and use of appraisal
    2. Interests to be appraised
    3. Type of value to be estimated
    4. Date of the value estimate
    5. Limiting conditions
B. Collection and analysis of data
    1. National and regional trends
    2. Economic base
    3. Local area and neighborhood
        a. Employment
        b. Income
        c. Trends
        d. Access
        e. Locational convenience
    4. Site and improvements
C. Analysis of highest and best use
D. Application and limitations of each
    approach to value
    1. Sales comparison
    2. Cost
    3. Income capitalization
E. Reconciliation and final value estimate
F. The appraisal report

VII. Property Description   2-4%   Conceptual,
A. Site description   Definitions
    1. Utilities
    2. Access
    3. Topography
    4. Size

	% WEIGHT	LEVEL OF DIFFICULTY
B. Improvement description		
1. Size		
2. Condition		
3. Utility		
C. Basic construction and design		
1. Techniques and materials		
a. Foundations		
b. Framing		
c. Finish (exterior and interior)		
2. Functional utility		
VIII. Highest and Best Use Analysis	5-7%	Conceptual,
A. Four tests		Definitions,
1. Physically possible		Analysis/Application
2. Legally permitted		
3. Economically feasible		
4. Maximally productive		
B. Vacant site or as if vacant		
C. As improved		
D. Interim use		
IX. Appraisal Statistical Concepts	1-3%	Conceptual,
A. Mean		Analysis/Application
B. Median		
C. Mode		
D. Range		
E. Standard deviation		
X. Sales Comparison Approach	21-24%	Conceptual,
A. Research and selection of comparables		Definitions,
1. Data sources		Analysis/Application
2. Verification		
3. Units of comparison		
a. Data sources		
b. Size		
(1) Square foot		
(2) Acres		
(3) Other		

	% WEIGHT	LEVEL OF DIFFICULTY

      c. Utility (examples only)

        (1) Rooms

        (2) Beds

        (3) Other

  B. Elements of comparison

    1. Property rights conveyed

      a. Leased fee/leasehold

      b. Easements

      c. Others

    2. Financing terms and cash equivalency

      a. Loan payment

      b. Loan balance

    3. Conditions of sale

      a. Arm's-length sale

      b. Personalty

    4. Market conditions at time of contract and closing

    5. Location

    6. Physical characteristics

  C. Adjustment process

    1. Sequence of adjustments

    2. Dollar adjustments

    3. Percentage adjustments

    4. Paired sales analysis

  D. Application of sales comparison approach

XI. Site Value   4-6%   Conceptual,

  A. Sales comparison   Definitions,

  B. Land residual   Analysis/Application

  C. Allocation

  D. Extraction

  E. Plottage and assemblage

XII. Cost Approach   8-10%   Conceptual,

  A. Steps in cost approach   Definitions,

    1. Reproduction vs. replacement cost   Analysis/Application

      a. Comparative unit method

	% WEIGHT	LEVEL OF DIFFICULTY

      b. Unit-in-place method

      c. Quantity survey method

      d. Cost service index

   2. Accrued depreciation

      a. Types of depreciation

         (1) Physical deterioration

           (a) Curable

           (b) Incurable

           (c) Short-lived

           (d) Long-lived

         (2) Functional obsolescence

           (a) Curable

           (b) Incurable

         (3) External obsolescence

           (a) Locational

           (b) Economic

      b. Methods of estimating depreciation

         (1) Age-life method

         (2) Breakdown method and sequence of deductions

         (3) Market extraction of depreciation

  B. Application of the cost approach

	% WEIGHT	LEVEL OF DIFFICULTY
XIII. Income Approach	7-9%	Conceptual, Definitions, Analysis/Application

  A. Estimation of income and expenses

   1. Gross market income

   2. Effective gross income

      a. Vacancy

      b. Collection loss

   3. Operating expenses

      a. Fixed expenses

      b. Variable expenses

      c. Reserve for replacements

   4. Net operating income

  B. Operating expense ratios

  C. Gross rent multiplier

	% WEIGHT	LEVEL OF DIFFICULTY

XIV. Valuation of Partial Interests
  A. Life estates
  B. Undivided interest in commonly held property
  C. Easements
  D. Timeshares
  E. Cooperatives
  F. Leased fee estate
  G. Leasehold estate
	1-3%	Conceptual, Definitions

XV. Appraisal Standards and Ethics	7-11%	Conceptual, Definitions

Courtesy of The Appraisal Foundation

License Law Officials

Alabama
D. Phillip Lasater, Executive Director, and Ella Mae Moore, Asst. Executive Director, Alabama Real Estate Commission, c/o State Capitol, Montgomery 36130

Alaska
Grayce Oakley, Executive Secretary, Department of Commerce & Economic Development, Real Estate Commission, 3601 C St., Suite 722, Anchorage 99503 (907) 563-2169

Arizona
Jerry A. Holt, Commissioner, Department of Real Estate, 202 E. Earll Drive, 4th Floor, Phoenix 85012

Arkansas
Roy L. Billheimer, Executive Secretary, Arkansas Real Estate Commission, 612 Summit St., Little Rock 72201-4740

California
Commissioner & Director, Department of Real Estate, P.O. Box 187000, Sacramento 95818-7000

Colorado
Michael B. Gorham, Director, Colorado Real Estate Commission, 4th Floor, 1776 Logan St., Denver 80203

Connecticut

Laurence L. Hannafin, Director, Department of Consumer Protection, Real Estate Division, 165 Capital Avenue, Hartford 06106

Delaware

Delaware Real Estate Commission, Margaret O'Neill Bldg., P.O. Box 1401, Dover 19903

District of Columbia

Department of Consumer & Regulatory Affairs, Occupational & Professional Licensing Administration, P.O. Box 37200, Washington 20013-7200

Florida

Darlene Keller, Director, Division of Real Estate, 400 W. Robinson St., Orlando 32801

Georgia

Charles Clark, Real Estate Commissioner, Georgia Real Estate Commission, 148 International Blvd., Suite 500, Atlanta 30303-1734

Hawaii

Calvin Kimura, Executive Secretary, Hawaii Real Estate Commission, Department of Commerce & Consumer Affairs, 828 Fort St. Mall, Suite 600, Honolulu 96813

Idaho

Jeri Pyeatt, Executive Director, Idaho Real Estate Commission, Statehouse Mail, Boise 83720-6000

Illinois

Nikki M. Zollar, Director, Department of Professional Regulation, 100 W. Randolph, Suite 9-300, Chicago 60601

Indiana

Indiana Real Estate Commission, 6 E. Main St., P.O. Box 495, Greenfield 46140

Iowa

Roger L. Hansen, Executive Secretary, Professional Licensing Division, Iowa Real Estate Commission, 1918 S.E. Hulsizer Avenue, Ankeny 50021

Kansas

E.W. Yockers, Director, Kansas Real Estate Commission, 900 Jackson, Room 501, Topeka 66612-1220

Kentucky

Bob Roberts, Chairman, James P. Daniels, Executive Director, Kentucky Real Estate Commission, 10200 Linn Station Rd., Suite 201, Louisville 40223

Louisiana

Anna-Kathryn Williams, Executive Director, Louisiana Real Estate Commission, P.O. Box 14785, Baton Rouge 70898

Maine

Carol Leighton, Maine Real Estate Commission, State House Station-35, Augusta 04333

Maryland

Lloyd Seay, Chairman, Maryland Real Estate Commission, Room 804, 501 St. Paul Place, Baltimore 21202

Massachusetts

Charles Kostopoulos, Chairperson, Joseph R. Autilio, Executive Secretary, Board of Registration of Real Estate Brokers and Salesmen, 100 Cambridge St., Room 1518, Boston 02202

Michigan

Ann Millben, Licensing Administrator, Real Estate, Department of Commerce, P.O. Box 30243, Lansing 48909

Minnesota

Lenor A. Scheffler-Rice, Director of Licensing, Department of Commerce, 133 E. 7th St., St. Paul 55101

Mississippi

John W. Neelley, Administrator, Mississippi Real Estate Commission, 1920 Dunbarton St., Jackson 39216

Missouri

Janet Brandt Thomas, Executive Director, Missouri Real Estate Commission, 3605 Missouri Blvd., Jefferson City 65109

Montana

Jack Moore, Chairman, Board of Realty Regulation, 111 N. Jackson, Helena 59620

Nebraska

Les Tyrrell, Director, Nebraska Real Estate Commission, P.O. Box 94667, Lincoln 68509

Nevada

George Whitney, Acting Administrator, Real Estate Division, Department of Commerce, 1665 Hot Springs Rd., Carson City 89710

New Hampshire

John P. Cummings, Executive Director, New Hampshire Real Estate Commission, 95 Pleasant St., Spaulding Bldg., 4th Floor, State Office Park South, Concord 03301

New Jersey

Micki G. Shillito, Executive Director, New Jersey Real Estate Commission, The Commerce Bldg., 20 W. State St., Trenton 08625

New Mexico

William M. Tucker, Executive Secretary, New Mexico Real Estate Commission, 4125 Carlisle, Albuquerque 87107

New York

Gail Bates, Director, Division of Licensing Services, Department of State, 270 Broadway, New York 10017 (Phone: 417-5740); 84 Holland Ave., Albany 12208-3490 (Phone: 518-474-4429)

North Carolina

Phillip T. Fisher, Executive Director, North Carolina Real Estate Commission, P.O. Box 17100, Raleigh 27619

North Dakota

Dennis Schulz, Secretary-Treasurer, North Dakota Real Estate Commission, 314 E. Thayer Ave., P.O. Box 727, Bismarck 58502

Ohio

Dennis Tatum, Superintendent, Ohio Division of Real Estate, 77 High Street, 20th Floor, Columbus 43266-0547

Oklahoma

Norris Price, Executive Director, Secretary-Treasurer, Oklahoma Real Estate Commission, 4040 N. Lincoln Blvd., Suite 100, Oklahoma City 73105

Oregon

Morella Larsen, Commissioner, Oregon Real Estate Agency, Commerce Bldg., 158 12th St., N.E., Salem 97310-0240

Pennsylvania

George L. Shevlin, Commissioner, Professional & Occupational Affairs, Department of State, Box 2649, Harrisburg 17105-2649

Rhode Island

Sheldon Whitehouse, Director, Leo R. McAloon, Jr., Associate Director, Valerie Voccio, Administrator, Real Estate, Division of Licensing & Consumer Protection, Real Estate Section, 233 Richmond St., Suite 230, Providence 02903-4237

South Carolina

Henry L. Jolly, Commissioner, South Carolina Real Estate Commission, Capitol Center-AT&T Bldg., 1201 Main St., Suite 1500, Columbia 29201

South Dakota

Larry G. Lyngstad, Executive Director, Real Estate Commission, Box 490, Pierre 57501

Tennessee

Bruce E. Lynn, Executive Director, Tennessee Real Estate Commission, 500 James Robertson Parkway, 1st Floor, Nashville 37243-1151

Texas

Wallace Collins, Administrator, Texas Real Estate Commission, P.O. Box 12188, Austin 78711-2188

Utah

Blaine E. Twitchell, Director, Division of Real Estate, Department of Commerce, Heber M. Wells Bldg., 160 E. 300 S., P.O. Box 45806, Salt Lake City 84145-0806

Vermont

Jean E. Brown, Executive Director, Office of the Secretary of State, Vermont Real Estate Commission, 109 State St., Montpelier 05609-1106

Virginia
Bonnie S. Salzman, Director, Department of Commerce, Secretary, Virginia Real Estate Board, 3600 W. Broad St., Richmond 23230

Washington
Syd Beckett, Program Administrator, Department of Licensing, Real Estate and Escrow, P.O. Box 9012, Olympia 98504

West Virginia
Richard E. Strader, Executive Director, West Virginia Real Estate Commission, 1033 Quarrier St., Suite 400, Charleston 25301

Wisconsin
Cletus J. Hansen, Director, Bureau of Direct Licensing and Real Estate, Wisconsin Department of Regulation and Licensing, 1400 E. Washington Ave., P.O. Box 8935, Madison 53708

Wyoming
Wyoming Real Estate Commission, Barrett Bldg., Cheyenne 82002

CANADA

British Columbia
Robert J. Hobart, Superintendent of Real Estate, Suite 1900, 1050 W. Pender St., Vancouver, B.C. V6E 3S7

Manitoba
J.W. Storsley, Registrar, Real Estate Brokers Act, Manitoba Securities Commission, Department of Consumer and Corporate Affairs, Room 1118, 405 Broadway Ave., Winnipeg, Manitoba R3C 3L6

Ontario
Gordon J. Randall, Registrar of Real Estate & Business Brokers Act and Condominium Act, Ministry of Consumer and Commercial Relations, 3rd Floor, 555 Yonge St., Toronto, Ontario M7A 2H6

Courtesy of The Real Estate Board of New York, Inc.

Areas of Plane Surfaces

Form	Name	Area
	Triangle	$\dfrac{\text{Altitude} \times \text{Base}}{2}$
	Trapezium irregular quadrilateral	Divide into two triangles and compute as above
	Parallel-ogram	Either parallel side $\times$ altitude
	Trapezoid	½ sum of parallel sides $\times$ altitude
	Regular Polygon	½ sum of all sides $\times$ inside radius
	Circle	$\pi = 3.1416$ πr^2 or .7854 d² or .0796 cir.²
	Sector of Circle	$\dfrac{A^\circ}{360^\circ} \times \pi r^2$ or length of arc $\times$ ½ radius
	Segment of Circle	$\dfrac{r^2}{2}\left(\dfrac{\pi A^\circ}{180} - \sin A^\circ\right)$ or subtract triangle from sector
	Ellipse	Major axis $\times$ minor axis $\times$ .7854
	Parabola	Base $\times$ ⅔ altitude

Useful Rules

To Find Circumference

Multiply diameter by	3.1416
Or divide diameter by	0.3183

To Find Diameter

Multiply circumference by	0.3183
Or divide circumference by	3.1416

To Find Radius

Multiply circumference by	0.15915
Or divide circumference by	6.28318

To Find Side of an Inscribed Square

Multiply diameter by	0.7071
Or multiply circumference by	0.2251
Or divide circumference by	4.4428

To Find Side of an Equal Square

Multiply diameter by	0.8862
Or divide diameter by	1.1284
Or multiply circumference by	0.2821
Or divide circumference by	3.545

Square

A side multiplied by 1.4142 equals diameter of its circumscribing circle.
A side multiplied by 4.443 equals circumference of its circumscribing circle.
A side multiplied by 1.128 equals diameter of an equal circle.
A side multiplied by 3.547 equals circumference of an equal circle.

To Find the Area of a Circle

Multiply circumference by one-quarter of the diameter.	
Or multiply the square of diameter by	0.7854
Or multiply the square of circumference by	0.07958
Or multiply the square of ½ diameter by	3.1416

To Find the Surface of a Sphere or Globe

Multiply the diameter by the circumference.	
Or multiply the square of diameter by	3.1416
Or multiply four times the square of radius by	3.1416

To Find the Cubic Inches (Volume) in a Sphere or Globe

Multiply the cube of the diameter by .5236.

Signs and Symbols

÷ geometrical proportion

≡ identical with

± plus or minus

∠ angle

∟ right angle

⊏ or > greater than

⊐ or < less than

⊥ perpendicular

~ difference

∫ integration

≑ equivalent

: : proportion

-: difference, excess

∴ therefore

∵ because

∞ infinity

∝ varies as

√ radical

° degree

′ minute or foot

″ second or inch

—w— water line

—G— gas line

—·—·— center line

—x—x— fence line

L^s lengths

L^l lineal foot

☑ ⏧ per square foot

⌀ diameter

ℙ plate

₵ center line

P- direction of pressure

$\frac{\text{A} \quad \text{A}}{\text{or}}$
⌐A   A⌐   indicates cross section of a drawing

▨ indicates exposed surface of a cross section

pounds after a number, number before a number

⊡ stadia station

△ triangulation station

⊙ transit traverse station

◐ indicates elevation point

3½″ ↔ dimension line, number indicates distance between lines

⇒ indicates that a section of a drawing, identical to the sections on either side of the symbol, has been omitted to reduce size

20″ ◣ 5″ indicates dimensions of rise and span of a roof pitch

Measures

The English System

Linear Measure

12 inches	=	1 foot
3 feet	=	1 yard
5.5 yards	=	1 rod
40 rods	=	1 furlong
8 furlongs	=	1 mile

Square Measure

144 square inches	=	1 square foot
9 square feet	=	1 square yard
43,560 square feet	=	1 acre
640 acres	=	1 square mile

Cubic Measure

1,728 cubic inches	=	1 cubic foot
27 cubic feet	=	1 cubic yard
128 cubic feet	=	1 cord
24.75 cubic feet	=	1 perch

Board Measure

1 board foot	=	144 cubic inches
1 board foot	=	1" x 1' x 1'
1 ton round timber	=	40 cubic feet
1 ton hewn timber	=	40 cubic feet

Measure of Angles and Arcs

60 seconds	=	1 minute
60 minutes	=	1 degree
90 degrees	=	1 quadrant
360 degrees	=	1 full circle

Nautical Measure

1.852 kilometers	=	1 nautical mile
1.150779 statute mile	=	1 nautical mile
6,076.11549 feet	=	1 nautical mile
1 nautical mile per hour	=	1 knot
6 feet	=	1 fathom
120 fathoms	=	1 cable length

Surveyor's or Land Measure

1 link = 7.92 inches
1 rod (or pole) = 25 links = 16½ feet
1 chain = 100 links = 4 rods = 66 feet
1 furlong = 40 rods = 10 chains = 1/8 mile
1 mile = 320 rods = 80 chains = 5,280 feet
1 acre = 160 square rods = 43,560 square feet
1 square mile = 640 acres

Engineer's Chain

12 inches	=	1 link
100 links or 100 feet	=	1 chain
52.8 chains	=	1 mile

Dry Measure—*Grain, Fruit, etc.*

2 pints (pt.)	=	1 quart (qt.)	=	67.20 cu. in.	=	1.1012 liter (l.)
8 quarts	=	1 peck (pk.)	=	537.61 cu. in.	=	8.8096 l.
4 pecks	=	1 bushel (bu.)	=	2150.42 cu. in.	=	35.2383 l.
Imperial dry quart	=	1.0320 U.S. dry quarts				

Legal avoirdupois weight as fixed by U.S. government of 1 bushel (bu.) of:

          wheat = 60 lb.
          barley = 48 lb. (varies from 32 to 50 lb. in various states)
          oats = 32 lb.
          rye = 56 lb.
          corn = varies from 52 to 56 lb. in various states
   Indian corn = 56 lb.
      potatoes = 60 lb. (North Carolina and West Virginia, 56 lb.)

Liquid Measure

4 gills (gi.)	= 1 pint (pt.)	= 28.875 cu. in.	= 0.4732 liter (l.)
2 pints	= 1 quart (qt.)	= 57.75 cu. in.	= 0.9463 l.
4 quarts	= 1 gallon (gal.)	= 231 cu. in.	= 3.7853 l.
31½ gallons	= 1 barrel		

The Metric System

Measures of Length

10 millimeters (mm.)	= 1 centimeter	cm.
10 centimeters	= 1 decimeter	dm.
10 decimeters	= 1 meter	m.
10 meters	= 1 dekameter	Dm.
10 dekameters	= 1 hektometer	Hm.
10 hektometers	= 1 kilometer	Km.

1 meter = $\begin{cases} 39.37 \text{ inches} \\ 3.28083 \text{ feet} \\ 1.0936 \text{ yards} \end{cases}$

1 centimeter = 0.3937 inch

1 millimeter = $\begin{cases} 0.03937 \text{ inch, or} \\ \text{approximately} \\ 1/25 \text{ in.} \end{cases}$

1 kilometer = 0.62137 mile
1 foot = 0.3048 meter
1 inch = $\begin{cases} 2.54 \text{ centimeters} \\ 25.4 \text{ millimeters} \end{cases}$
1 yard = 0.9144 meters
1 rod = 5.029 meters
1 mile = 1.6093 kilometers

The Metric System (continued)

Measures of Surface

Myriameter	10,000 meters	6.2137 miles
Kilometer	1,000 meters	0.62137 miles
Hectometer	100 meters	328 feet 1 inch
Dekameter	10 meters	393.7 inches
Meter	1 meter	39.37 inches
Decimeter	0.1 meter	3.937 inches
Centimeter	0.01 meter	0.3937 inch
Millimeter	0.001 meter	0.0394 inch

1 square meter = $\begin{cases} 10.764 \text{ square feet} \\ 1.196 \text{ square yards} \\ 1 \text{ centiare} \end{cases}$

1 square centimeter = 0.155 square inch

1 square millimeter = 0.00155 square inch

1 square yard = 0.836 square meter

1 square foot = 0.0929 square meter

1 square inch = $\begin{cases} 6.452 \text{ square centimeters} \\ 645.2 \text{ square millimeters} \end{cases}$

1 square rod = 25.29 square meters

1 acre = 0.4046 hectares

1 square mile = 259 hectares

Cuerda	3,930.40 square meters	0.97123 acres
Hectare	10,000 square meters	2.471 acres
Are	100 square meters	119.6 square yards
Centiare	1 square meter	1,550 square inches

Measures of Volume and Capacity

1 cubic meter = $\begin{cases} 35.314 \text{ cubic feet} \\ 1.308 \text{ cubic yards} \\ 264.2 \text{ gallons (231 cubic inches)} \end{cases}$

1 cubic decimeter = $\begin{cases} 61.023 \text{ cubic inches} \\ 0.0353 \text{ cubic feet} \end{cases}$

1 cubic centimeter = 0.061 cubic inch

1 liter = $\begin{cases} 1 \text{ cubic decimeter} \\ 61.023 \text{ cubic inches} \\ 0.0353 \text{ cubic foot} \\ 1.0567 \text{ quarts (U.S.)} \\ 0.2642 \text{ gallon (U.S.)} \\ 2.202 \text{ lbs. of water at } 62°F. \end{cases}$

1 cubic yard = 0.7645 cubic meter

1 cubic foot = $\begin{cases} 0.02832 \text{ cubic meter} \\ 28.317 \text{ cubic decimeters} \\ 28.317 \text{ liters} \end{cases}$

1 cubic inch = 16.393 cubic centimeters

Cord	3.625	steres
Liquid quart, U.S.	0.9463	liter
Dry quart, U.S.	1.101	liters
Quart, imperial	1.136	liters
Gallon, U.S.	3.785	liters
Gallon, imperial	4.546	liters
Peck, U.S.	8.810	liters
Peck, imperial	9.092	liters
Bushel, U.S.	35.24	liters
Bushel, imperial	36.37	liters

The Metric System (continued)

Measures of Weight

1 gram	=	15.432 grains	1 grain	=	0.0648 gram	
1 kilogram	=	2.2046 pounds	1 ounce avoirdupois	=	28.35 grams	

1 metric ton = $\begin{cases} 0.9842 \text{ ton of } 2240 \text{ lbs.} \\ 19.68 \text{ hundred-weights (cwt.)} \\ 2204.6 \text{ lbs.} \end{cases}$

1 grain	=	0.0648 gram
1 ounce avoirdupois	=	28.35 grams
1 ounce Troy	=	31.103 grams
1 pound, avoirdupois	=	0.4536 kilogram
1 pound, Troy	=	0.3732 kilogram
1 ton, long	=	1.0160 metric tons
1 ton, short	=	0.9072 metric ton

Miscellaneous

1 kilogram per meter	=	0.6720	pounds per foot
1 gram per square millimeter	=	1.422	pounds per square inch
1 kilogram per square meter	=	0.2084	pounds per square foot
1 kilogram per cubic meter	=	0.0624	pounds per cubic foot
1 degree centigrade	=	1.8	degrees Fahrenheit
1 pound per foot	=	1.488	kilograms per meter
1 pound per square foot	=	4.882	kilograms per square meter
1 pound per cubic foot	=	16.02	kilograms per cubic meter
1 degree Fahrenheit	=	0.5556	degrees centigrade
1 calorie (French Thermal Unit)	=	3.968	Btu (British Thermal Unit)

1 horse power = $\begin{cases} 33{,}000 & \text{foot pounds per minute} \\ 746 & \text{watts} \end{cases}$

1 watt (unit of electrical power) = $\begin{cases} 0.00134 & \text{horse power} \\ 44.22 & \text{foot pounds per minute} \end{cases}$

1 kilowatt = $\begin{cases} 1{,}000 & \text{watts} \\ 44{,}220 & \text{foot pounds per minute} \\ 1.34 & \text{horse power} \end{cases}$

Conversion Factors for Measurement of Irrigation Water

1 second-foot = 1 cubic foot per second = 450 gallons per minute = about 1 acre-inch per hour.

1 cubic foot of water = 7.48 gallons.

A body of water under a head of 4 inches delivers through a hole 1 inch square 1/50 of a second-foot.

Legal miner's inch (California statutes, 1901) = 1 1/2 cubic feet per minute, measured under a 6-inch pressure, and is equivalent to a flow of 11 1/4 gallons per minute, or 1/40 cubic foot per second.

In practice, a miner's inch = 9 gallons per minute = 1/50 cubic foot per second.

1 acre-inch = 27,152 gallons, and will be supplied by a flow of 1 miner's inch in 50.4 hours.

Conversion Factors (continued)

Formula for Measuring Irrigation Water

1. Water measurement unit—cubic feet per second or second-feet.

$$\frac{\text{Number second-feet} \times \text{hours run}}{\text{Number acres}} = \begin{array}{l}\text{Acre-inches or inches}\\\text{depth on whole area.}\end{array}$$

2. Water measurement unit (Southern California)—miner's inch, 1/50 second-foot or 9 gallons per minute.

$$\frac{\text{Number miner's inches} \times \text{hours run}}{50 \times \text{number acres}} = \text{Acre-inches.}$$

3. Water measurement unit—statutory inches (1/40 second-foot or 11 1/4 gallons per minute).

$$\frac{\text{Number miner's inches} \times \text{hours run}}{40 \times \text{number acres}} = \text{Acre-inches.}$$

4. Pump—Gallons per minute.

$$\frac{\text{Gallons per minute} \times \text{hours run}}{450 \times \text{number acres}} = \text{Acre-inches.}$$

Water Measure

1 cubic foot = 7.4805 gallons
1 cubic foot = 62.42 pounds
1 gallon = 8.355 pounds

1 cubic foot per second = 50 miner's inches in Idaho, Kansas, Nebraska, New Mexico, and Southern California.
1 cubic foot per second = 40 miner's inches in Arizona, Montana, Oregon, and Northern California.

Selected Conversions *to* Metric Measures

Symbol	When you know	Multiply by	To find	Symbol
		LENGTH		
in.	inches	2.540	centimeters	cm
ft.	feet	30.480	centimeters	cm
yd.	yards	0.9144	meters	m
mi.	miles	1.6093	kilometers	kn
		AREA		
in.^{2}	square inches	6.542	sq. centimeters	cm^2
ft.^{2}	square feet	0.0929	sq. meters	m^2
yd.^{2}	square yards	0.836	sq. meters	m^2
mi.^{2}	square miles	2.590	sq. kilometers	km^2
	acres	0.4046	hectares	ha

Selected Conversions to Metric Measures (continued)

Symbol	When you know	Multiply by	To find	Symbol
MASS (weight)				
oz.	ounces	28.35	grams	g
lb.	pounds	0.4536	kilograms	kg
	short tons (2000 lbs.)	0.9072	tonnes (1000 kg)	t
CÁPACITY (liquid measure)				
fl. oz.	fluid ounces	29.573	milliliters	ml
pt.	pints	0.4732	liters	l
qt.	quarts	0.9463	liters	l
gal.	gallons	3.7853	liters	l
CAPACITY (dry measure)				
pt.	pints	0.5506	liters	l
qt.	quarts	1.1012	liters	l
gal.	gallons	4.545	liters	l
pk.	pecks	0.009	cubic meters	m^3
bu.	bushels	0.036	cubic meters	m^3
VOLUME				
$in.^3$	cubic inches	16.393	cubic centimeters	cm^3
$ft.^3$	cubic feet	0.028	cubic meters	m^3
$yd.^3$	cubic yards	0.765	cubic meters	m^3
TEMPERATURE (exact)				
°F	Fahrenheit	5/9 (after subtracting 32)	Celsius	°C

Selected Conversions *from* Metric Measures

Symbol	When you know	Multiply by	To find	Symbol
		LENGTH		
mm	millimeters	0.0394	inches	in.
cm	centimeters	0.3937	inches	in.
m	meters	3.937	feet	ft.
m	meters	1.0936	yards	yd.
km	kilometers	0.62137	miles	mi.
		AREA		
cm^2	sq. centimeters	0.155	sq. inches	$in.^2$
m^2	sq. meters	1.196	sq. yards	$yd.^2$
km^2	sq. kilometers	0.386	sq. miles	$mi.^2$
ha	hectares ($10,000\ m^2$)	2.471	acres	
		MASS (weight)		
g	grams	0.035	ounces	oz.
kg	kilograms	2.2046	pounds	lb.
t	tonnes (1000 kg)	1.1023	short tons (2000 lbs.)	
		CAPACITY (liquid measure)		
ml	milliliters	0.0338	fluid ounces	fl. oz.
l	liters	2.1134	pints	pt.
l	liters	1.0567	quarts	qt.
l	liters	0.2642	gallons	gal.
		CAPACITY (dry measure)		
l	liters	1.8162	pints	pt.
l	liters	0.9081	quarts	qt.
l	liters	0.2270	gallons	gal.
m^3	cubic meters	111.1111	pecks	pk.
m^3	cubic meters	27.7778	bushels	bu.
		VOLUME		
cm^3	cubic centimeters	0.00006	cubic inches	$in.^3$
m^3	cubic meters	35.7143	cubic feet	$ft.^3$
m^3	cubic meters	1.3072	cubic yards	$yd.^3$
		TEMPERATURE (exact)		
°C	Celsius	9/5 (then add 32)	Fahrenheit	°F

Energy Conversion Factors

The common unit of energy measure is the British thermal unit (Btu), which is the unit used to calculate and compare energy costs and savings. To convert between the common energy units, use the factors in this table.

To Convert	Into	Multiply By
Barrels, oil	gallons	42.0
Cubic feet, natural gas	therms	0.01
Cubic feet, natural gas	Btus	1,020
Gallons, No. 2 oil	Btus	138,000*
Gallons, No. 4 oil	Btus	145,000*
Gallons, No. 5 oil	Btus	148,000*
Gallons, No. 6 oil	Btus	150,000*
Gallons, kerosene	Btus	135,000*
Gallons, gasoline	Btus	125,000*
Gallons, diesel oil	Btus	138,700*
Horsepower-hours	Btus	2,544
Horsepower-hours	kWhs	0.7457
Horsepower	Btu/min	42.4176
Horsepower (boiler)	Btu/hr	33,479
Kilowatt-hours	Btus	3,413
mCF natural gas	Btus	1,000,000
Short ton, eastern steam coal	Btus	23,100,000*
Short tons, western coal	Btus	21,000,000*
Short tons, anthracite coal	Btus	25,400,000*
Short tons, bituminous steam coal	Btus	21,600,000*
Short tons, lignite, brown coal	Btus	14,000,000*
Steam, saturated (lbs.)	Btus	970
Therms, natural gas	cubic feet	100
Therms, natural gas	Btus	100,000
Tons, refrigeration	Btus/hr	12,000

*These are average values. Since exact Btu content varies with type and source, contact supplier when extreme accuracy is essential.

Conversion of Chains to Rods and Feet

Chains	Rods	Feet	Chains	Rods	Feet	Chains	Rods	Feet
1	4	66	15	60	990	28	112	1848
2	8	132	16	64	1056	29	116	1914
3	12	198	17	68	1122	30	120	1980
4	16	264	18	72	1188	31	124	2046
5	20	330	19	76	1254	32	128	2112
6	24	396	20	80	1320	33	132	2178
7	28	462	21	84	1386	34	136	2244
8	32	528	22	88	1452	35	140	2310
9	36	594	23	92	1518	36	144	2376
10	40	660	24	96	1584	37	148	2442
11	44	726	25	100	1650	38	152	2508
12	48	792	26	104	1716	39	156	2574
13	52	858	27	108	1782	40	160	2640
14	56	924						

Cubic Computation

See sketch on facing page.

	Cubic Feet
Basement — 28′ × 26′ × 7′	5,096
Main Portion of Building — 28′ × 26′ × 19′	13,832
Attic — 28′ × 26′ × 4.5′	3,276
°Open Porch — $\dfrac{8' \times 26' \times 12'}{3}$	832
Bay Window — 2.5′ × 7′ × 8′	140
Dormer — $\dfrac{4' \times 8' \times 5'}{2}$	80
	Total 23,256

°If enclosed, divisor should be 2. If enclosed, finished, and heated, consider as part of the house and use actual cube.

Cubic Contents Computation

Illustrative Drawing
See computation on previous page.

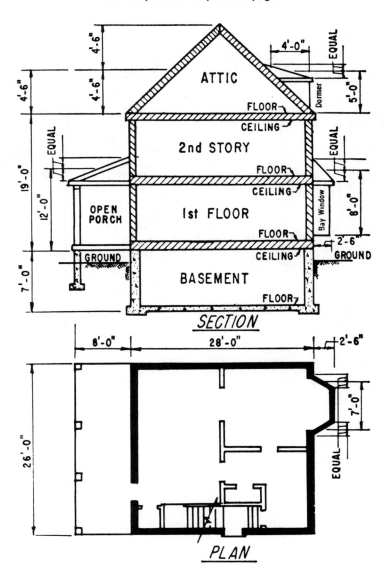

House Cross Section

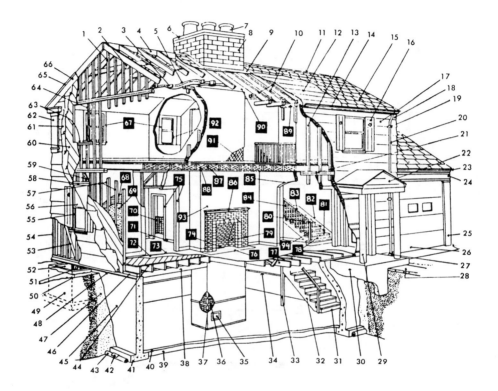

1. Gable stud
2. Collar beam
3. Ceiling joist
4. Ridge board
5. Insulation
6. Chimney cap
7. Chimney pots
8. Chimney
9. Chimney flashing
10. Rafters
11. Ridge
12. Roof boards
13. Stud
14. Eave gutter
15. Roofing
16. Blind or shutter
17. Bevel siding
18. Downspout gooseneck
19. Downspout strap
20. Downspout leader
21. Double plate
22. Entrance canopy
23. Garage cornice
24. Frieze
25. Door jamb
26. Garage door
27. Downspout shoe
28. Sidewalk
29. Entrance post
30. Entrance platform
31. Stair riser

32. Stair stringer
33. Girder post
*34. Chair rail
35. Cleanout door
36. Furring strips
37. Corner stud
38. Girder
39. Gravel fill
40. Concrete floor
41. Foundation footing
42. Paper strip
43. Drain tile
*44. Diagonal subfloor
45. Foundation wall
46. Sill
47. Backfill
48. Termite shield
49. Areaway wall
50. Grade line
51. Basement sash
52. Areaway
53. Corner brace
54. Corner stud
55. Window frame
56. Window light
57. Wall studs
58. Header
59. Window cripple
*60. Wall sheathing
61. Building paper
62. Pilaster
63. Rough header

64. Window stud
65. Cornice moulding
66. Frieze board
67. Window casing
68. Lath
69. Insulation
70. Wainscoting
71. Baseboard
72. Building paper
73. Finish floor
74. Ash dump
75. Door trim
76. Fireplace hearth
77. Floor joists
78. Stair riser
79. Fire brick
80. Newel cap
81. Stair tread
82. Finish stringer
83. Stair rail
84. Balusters
85. Plaster arch
86. Mantel
87. Floor joists
88. Bridging
89. Lookout
90. Attic space
91. Metal lath
92. Window sash
93. Chimney breast
94. Newel

* These items are only found in older homes.

U.S. Public Survey Diagram

Four Townships

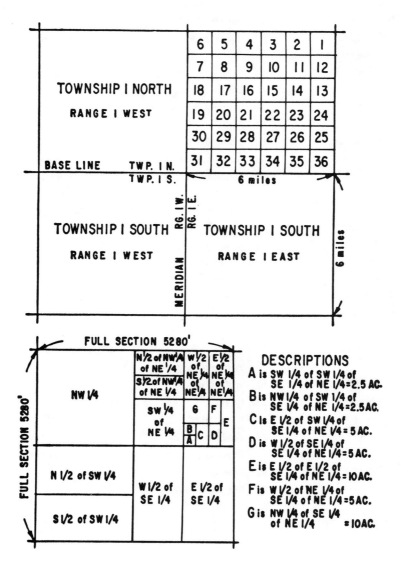

Roof Types

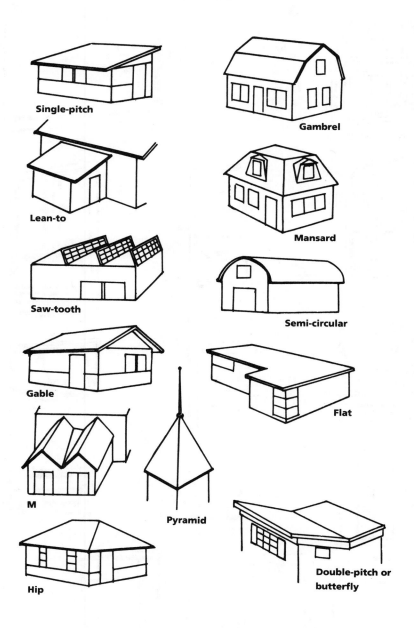

Single-pitch

Gambrel

Lean-to

Mansard

Saw-tooth

Semi-circular

Gable

Flat

M

Pyramid

Hip

Double-pitch or butterfly

Window Types

Double-hung

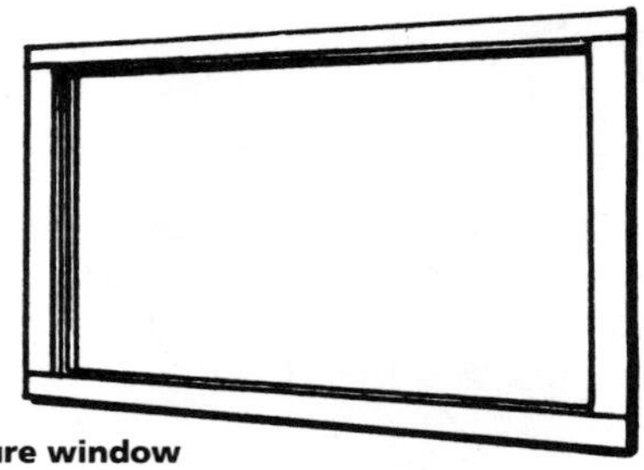

Picture window

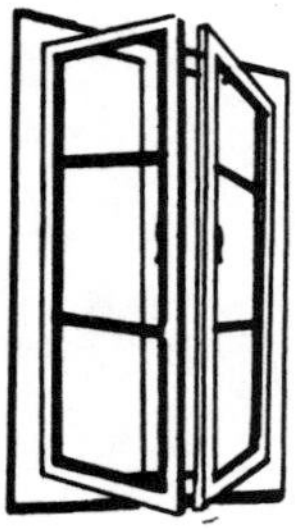

Casement

Projected intermediate

Intermediate combination

Manual awning

Jalousie

Basement

Traverse

Circle head

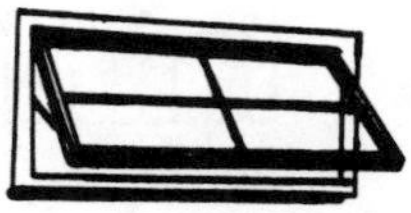

Transom

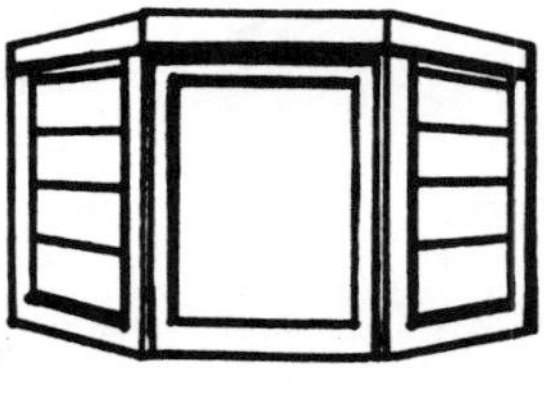

Fixed bay

Fixed bow

Brick Masonry Bonds

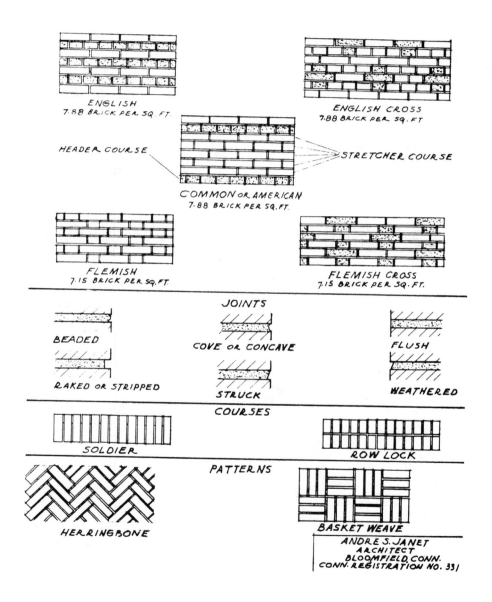

ENGLISH
7.88 BRICK PER SQ. FT.

ENGLISH CROSS
7.88 BRICK PER SQ. FT

HEADER COURSE

STRETCHER COURSE

COMMON OR AMERICAN
7.88 BRICK PER SQ. FT.

FLEMISH
7.15 BRICK PER SQ. FT.

FLEMISH CROSS
7.15 BRICK PER SQ. FT.

JOINTS

BEADED

COVE OR CONCAVE

FLUSH

RAKED OR STRIPPED

STRUCK

WEATHERED

COURSES

SOLDIER

ROW LOCK

PATTERNS

HERRINGBONE

BASKET WEAVE

ANDRE S. JANET
ARCHITECT
BLOOMFIELD, CONN.
CONN. REGISTRATION NO. 331

493

Masonry Arches

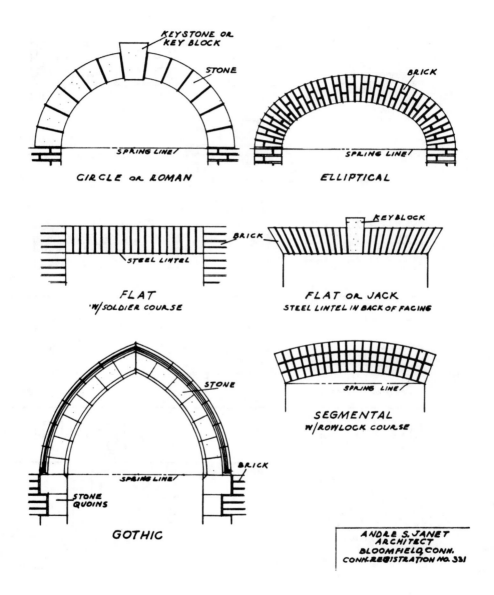

KEYSTONE OR KEY BLOCK

STONE

SPRING LINE

CIRCLE OR ROMAN

BRICK

SPRING LINE

ELLIPTICAL

BRICK

STEEL LINTEL

FLAT
W/SOLDIER COURSE

KEYBLOCK

BRICK

FLAT OR JACK
STEEL LINTEL IN BACK OF FACING

STONE

SPRING LINE

SEGMENTAL
W/ROWLOCK COURSE

STONE

BRICK

SPRING LINE

STONE QUOINS

GOTHIC

ANDRE S. JANET
ARCHITECT
BLOOMFIELD, CONN.
CONN. REGISTRATION NO. 331

494

Door Framing

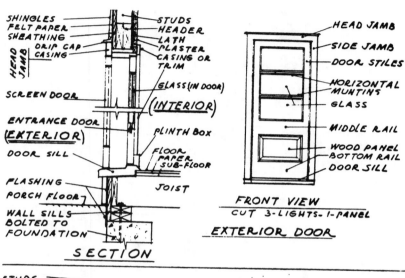

SHINGLES
FELT PAPER
SHEATHING
DRIP CAP
CASING
HEAD JAMB

STUDS
HEADER
LATH
PLASTER
CASING OR TRIM

GLASS (IN DOOR)
(INTERIOR)

SCREEN DOOR

ENTRANCE DOOR
(EXTERIOR)

PLINTH BOX

DOOR SILL

FLOOR
PAPER
SUB-FLOOR

FLASHING
PORCH FLOOR

JOIST

WALL SILLS
BOLTED TO
FOUNDATION

SECTION

HEAD JAMB
SIDE JAMB
DOOR STILES
HORIZONTAL MUNTINS
GLASS
MIDDLE RAIL
WOOD PANEL
BOTTOM RAIL
DOOR SILL

FRONT VIEW
CUT 3-LIGHTS-1-PANEL

EXTERIOR DOOR

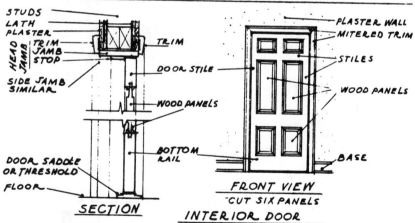

STUDS
LATH
PLASTER
TRIM
JAMB
STOP
HEAD JAMB

TRIM

DOOR STILE

SIDE JAMB
SIMILAR

WOOD PANELS

BOTTOM RAIL

DOOR SADDLE
OR THRESHOLD

FLOOR

SECTION

PLASTER WALL
MITERED TRIM

STILES

WOOD PANELS

BASE

FRONT VIEW
CUT SIX PANELS

INTERIOR DOOR

ANDRES JANET
ARCHITECT
BLOOMFIELD CONN.
CONN. REGISTRATION NO. 331

Roof and Wall Framing

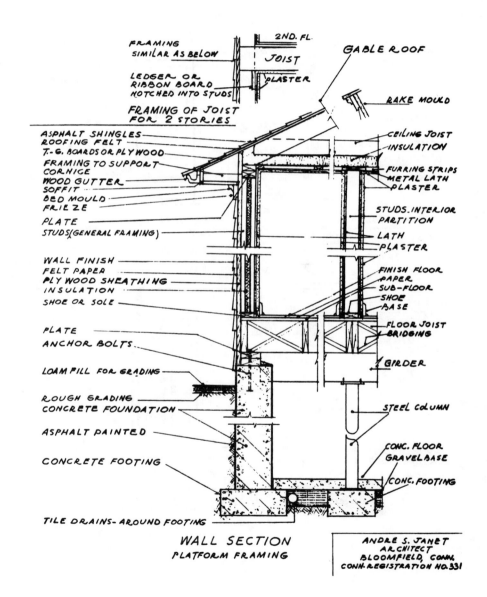

FRAMING SIMILAR AS BELOW

2ND. FL.

JOIST

PLASTER

LEDGER OR RIBBON BOARD NOTCHED INTO STUDS

FRAMING OF JOIST FOR 2 STORIES

GABLE ROOF

RAKE MOULD

ASPHALT SHINGLES
ROOFING FELT
T.-G. BOARDS OR PLYWOOD
FRAMING TO SUPPORT CORNICE
WOOD GUTTER
SOFFIT
BED MOULD
FRIEZE
PLATE
STUDS (GENERAL FRAMING)

CEILING JOIST
INSULATION

FURRING STRIPS
METAL LATH
PLASTER

STUDS. INTERIOR PARTITION

LATH
PLASTER

WALL FINISH
FELT PAPER
PLYWOOD SHEATHING
INSULATION
SHOE OR SOLE

FINISH FLOOR
PAPER
SUB-FLOOR
SHOE
BASE

PLATE
ANCHOR BOLTS

LOAM FILL FOR GRADING

ROUGH GRADING
CONCRETE FOUNDATION

ASPHALT PAINTED

CONCRETE FOOTING

FLOOR JOIST
BRIDGING

GIRDER

STEEL COLUMN

CONC. FLOOR
GRAVEL BASE

CONC. FOOTING

TILE DRAINS- AROUND FOOTING

WALL SECTION
PLATFORM FRAMING

ANDRE S. JANET
ARCHITECT
BLOOMFIELD, CONN.
CONN. REGISTRATION NO. 331

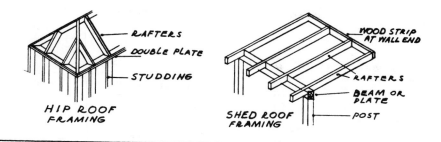

RAFTERS
DOUBLE PLATE
STUDDING

HIP ROOF FRAMING

WOOD STRIP AT WALL END
RAFTERS
BEAM OR PLATE
POST

SHED ROOF FRAMING

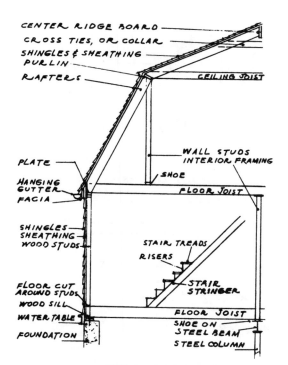

CENTER RIDGE BOARD
CROSS TIES, OR COLLAR
SHINGLES & SHEATHING
PURLIN
RAFTERS
CEILING JOIST

PLATE
HANGING GUTTER
FACIA

WALL STUDS INTERIOR FRAMING
SHOE
FLOOR JOIST

SHINGLES
SHEATHING
WOOD STUDS

STAIR TREADS
RISERS
STAIR STRINGER

FLOOR CUT AROUND STUDS
WOOD SILL
WATER TABLE
FOUNDATION

FLOOR JOIST
SHOE ON STEEL BEAM
STEEL COLUMN

WALL SECTION
BRACED FRAMING
GAMBREL ROOF

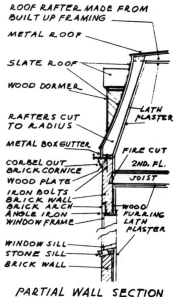

ROOF RAFTER MADE FROM BUILT UP FRAMING
METAL ROOF

SLATE ROOF

WOOD DORMER

RAFTERS CUT TO RADIUS

METAL BOX GUTTER

CORBEL OUT BRICK CORNICE
WOOD PLATE
IRON BOLTS
BRICK WALL
BRICK ARCH
ANGLE IRON
WINDOW FRAME

WINDOW SILL
STONE SILL
BRICK WALL

LATH PLASTER

FIRE CUT
2ND. FL.
JOIST

WOOD FURRING
LATH PLASTER

PARTIAL WALL SECTION
MANSARD ROOF

ANDRE S. JANET
ARCHITECT
BLOOMFIELD, CONN
CONN. REGISTRATION No. 331

Interior Trim

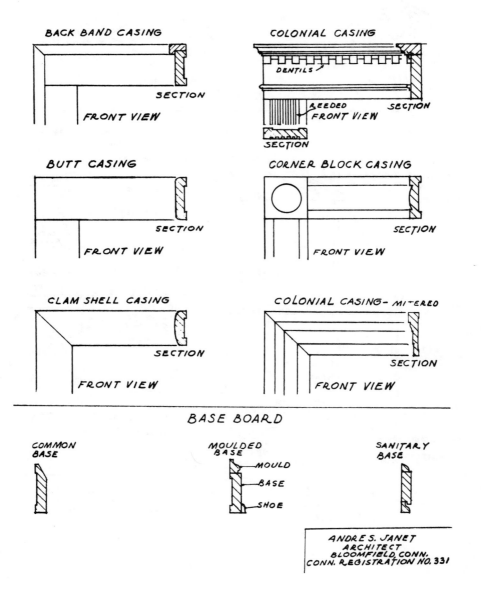

BACK BAND CASING
SECTION
FRONT VIEW

COLONIAL CASING
DENTILS
REEDED
FRONT VIEW
SECTION
SECTION

BUTT CASING
SECTION
FRONT VIEW

CORNER BLOCK CASING
SECTION
FRONT VIEW

CLAM SHELL CASING
SECTION
FRONT VIEW

COLONIAL CASING - MITERED
SECTION
FRONT VIEW

BASE BOARD

COMMON BASE

MOULDED BASE
MOULD
BASE
SHOE

SANITARY BASE

ANDRE S. JANET
ARCHITECT
BLOOMFIELD, CONN.
CONN. REGISTRATION NO. 331

498

Window Framing—Casement

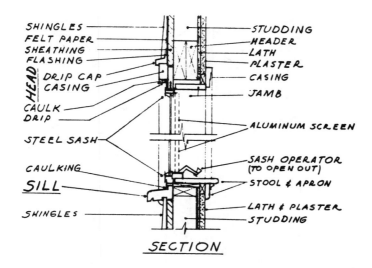

SHINGLES
FELT PAPER
SHEATHING
FLASHING
DRIP CAP
CASING
CAULK
DRIP

HEAD

STEEL SASH

CAULKING

SILL

SHINGLES

STUDDING
HEADER
LATH
PLASTER
CASING
JAMB

ALUMINUM SCREEN

SASH OPERATOR
(TO OPEN OUT)
STOOL & APRON

LATH & PLASTER
STUDDING

SECTION

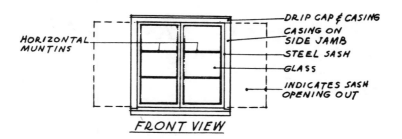

HORIZONTAL
MUNTINS

DRIP CAP & CASING
CASING ON
SIDE JAMB
STEEL SASH
GLASS
INDICATES SASH
OPENING OUT

FRONT VIEW

ANDRE S. JANET
ARCHITECT
BLOOMFIELD, CONN.
CONN. REGISTRATION NO. 331

Window Framing—Double-Hung—Metal

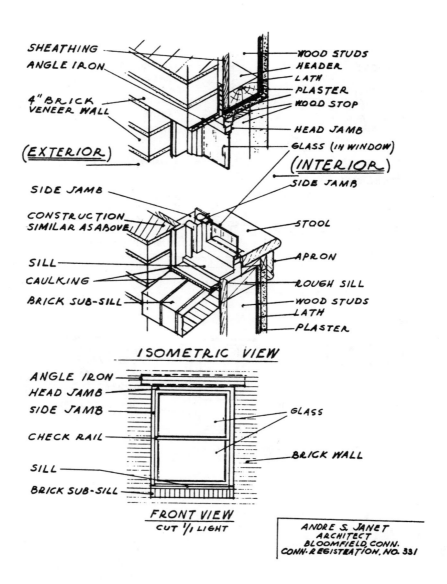

SHEATHING
ANGLE IRON
4" BRICK VENEER WALL
(EXTERIOR)
WOOD STUDS
HEADER
LATH
PLASTER
WOOD STOP
HEAD JAMB
GLASS (IN WINDOW)
(INTERIOR)
SIDE JAMB

SIDE JAMB
CONSTRUCTION SIMILAR AS ABOVE
SILL
CAULKING
BRICK SUB-SILL
STOOL
APRON
ROUGH SILL
WOOD STUDS
LATH
PLASTER

ISOMETRIC VIEW

ANGLE IRON
HEAD JAMB
SIDE JAMB
CHECK RAIL
SILL
BRICK SUB-SILL
GLASS
BRICK WALL

FRONT VIEW
CUT 1/1 LIGHT

ANDRE S. JANET
ARCHITECT
BLOOMFIELD, CONN.
CONN. REGISTRATION, NO. 331

500

Window Framing—Double-Hung—Wood

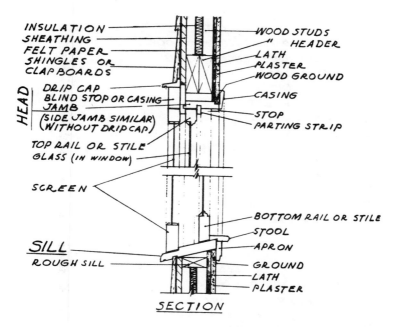

INSULATION
SHEATHING
FELT PAPER
SHINGLES OR
CLAPBOARDS

WOOD STUDS
HEADER
LATH
PLASTER
WOOD GROUND

HEAD

DRIP CAP
BLIND STOP OR CASING
JAMB
(SIDE JAMB SIMILAR)
(WITHOUT DRIP CAP)

CASING

STOP
PARTING STRIP

TOP RAIL OR STILE
GLASS (IN WINDOW)

SCREEN

BOTTOM RAIL OR STILE
STOOL
APRON

SILL
ROUGH SILL

GROUND
LATH
PLASTER

SECTION

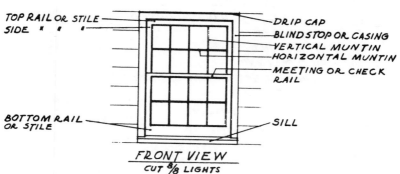

TOP RAIL OR STILE
SIDE " " "

DRIP CAP
BLIND STOP OR CASING
VERTICAL MUNTIN
HORIZONTAL MUNTIN
MEETING OR CHECK
RAIL

BOTTOM RAIL
OR STILE

SILL

FRONT VIEW
CUT ⁸⁄₈ LIGHTS

ANDRE S. JANET
ARCHITECT
BLOOMFIELD, CONN.
CONN. REGISTRATION NO. 331

501

Electrical Symbols

⊖	DUPLEX CONVENIENCE — FLOOR
⊖	DUPLEX CONVENIENCE — WALL
⊖w.p.	WATER PROOF
©	CLOCK OUTLET
Ⓕ	FAN OUTLET
⊖	RANGE OUTLET
◑	SPECIAL PURPOSE
⊖Ⓡ	RADIO & CONVENIENCE
▣	PUSH BUTTON
▭	BUZZER
▭	BELL
◇	ANNUNCIATOR
▣	DOOR OPENER
▣	MAID SIGNAL

FIXTURES

○	CEILING HUNG
○pc	CEILING HUNG — PULL CHAIN
⊘	CLOSET, WITH SWITCH ON DOOR JAMB
▣	RECESSED OR CEILING MOUNTED
⬦	INDIRECT — CEILING MOUNTED
–○	WALL BRACKET
–Ⓝ	NITE LIGHT
–Ⓟ	PILOT LIGHT
▬	ULTRA-VIOLET GERMICIDAL LAMP
▭	FLUORESCENT
═	SINGLE ROW SLIMLINE
☰	THREE ROW SLIMLINE
⊥	FLUORESCENT, WITH STEMS
	CORNICE LIGHTING
	COVE LIGHTING

ANDRE S. JANET
ARCHITECT
BLOOMFIELD, CONN.
CONN. REGISTRATION NO. 331

SWITCHES

S	SINGLE POLE
S_2	DOUBLE POLE
S_3	THREE WAY
S_4	FOUR WAY

WIRING

————	BRANCH CIRCUIT — CONCEALED IN CEILING
— · —	" " — " IN FLOOR
- - - - -	" " — EXPOSED
—///—	" " — 3 WIRE
—//—//—	" " — 4 WIRE
——▶—▶	HOME RUN TO PANELBOARD

WIRING PLATES

WATER PROOF DUPLEX
CONVENIENCE OUTLET

AUTOMATIC
DOOR SWITCH

GROUNDING TYPE
4-WIRE

RANGE OUTLET

GROUNDING TYPE
3-WIRE

CLOCK HANGER

ANDRE S. JANET
ARCHITECT
BLOOMFIELD CONN.
CONN. REGISTRATION NO. 331

Plumbing Symbols

PLAN VIEWS

BATH TUBS

4'-0" x 4'-1" x 16"
RECESSED

3'-3" x 3'-8" x 12"
SHOWER OR FOOT

4'-0" x 4'-1" x 16"
CORNER

4'-6" TO 6'-0" x 16"
RECESSED

ROLL RIM.

LAVATORIES

FLAT TOP FOR
COUNTER

LOW BACK
PEDESTAL OR LEGS

SHELF BACK
WALL HUNG

ANGLE
WALL HUNG

SHOWERS

BAKED ENAMEL CABINET
PLASTIC CURTAIN

BUILT-IN WALL
GLASS DOOR

URINALS

FLOOR
TYPE

WALL
HUNG

TROUGH
TYPE

PEDESTAL
TYPE

WATER CLOSETS

LOW TANK
WALL HUNG

FLUSH VALVE
FLOOR OR
WALL HUNG

BIDET

KITCHEN EQUIPMENT

FLAT RIM SINK

SINK & TRAY COMBINATION

LAUNDRY TRAYS
SINGLE — DOUBLE

CABINET UNIT. WITH
DISHWASHER.
D.W

MISCELLANEOUS

AUTOMATIC WASHER

AUTOMATIC DRYER

COUNTER UNIT
WATER HEATER

WATER HEATER

ANDRE S. JANET
ARCHITECT
BLOOMFIELD. CONN.
CONN. REGISTRATION NO. 331

Overview of Tax Considerations*

I. Tax rates

  A. Ordinary income

  1. The maximum tax rate for married taxpayers filing jointly in 1991 was 31%.

  2. The maximum tax rate for corporations in 1991 was 39%.

  B. Capital gain

  1. Capital gain (or loss) from the sale of real estate is currently taxed at the same rate as ordinary income.

  2. Prior to the Tax Reform Act of 1986, there was a 60% capital gain exclusion.

II. Depreciation allowance

  A. Real property

  1. Improvements (not land) can be depreciated.

  2. Nonresidential real estate is depreciated over 31.5 years using straight-line depreciation.

  3. Residential real estate is depreciated over 27.5 years using straight-line depreciation.

  4. Note that the depreciation allowed for tax purposes is unrelated to the actual depreciation in property value.

  5. Prior to 1986 real property could be depreciated over 19 years.

  B. Personal property

  1. Personal property includes furniture, trade fixtures and equipment that is not real property.

  2. Personal property can be depreciated over a shorter period (7 years) than real property.

III. Tax credits

    A. Tax credits reduce the investor's tax liability, dollar for dollar.

    B. A 20% tax credit is available for the rehabilitation of certified historic structures.

    C. A 10% credit is available for properties originally placed in service before 1936.

    D. Tax credits are also available for the purchase or renovation of low-income housing.

IV. Other considerations

    A. Income (loss) from rental real estate may be classified as "passive income" (loss).

    B. Passive losses (from negative taxable income) *cannot* normally be used to offset wages, interest, and dividend income.

    C. Passive losses can be used to offset passive income from other real estate investments or the same investment in future years.

    D. Passive losses can also offset capital gain from the sale of property.

Note: The above discussion is only intended to convey very general aspects of the tax law so that the motivations of tax-oriented investors can be appreciated.

* This addendum, which is based on the Tax Reform Act of 1986, is subject to change and should not be relied upon for tax decisions.

Summary of 1986 Tax Law Changes

	OLD	NEW
Maximum tax rate	50%	28% (33% for phased income)
Capital gains exclusion	60%	None
Depreciation		
Residential	19 yrs. ACRS (175% db)	27.5 yrs. sl
Nonresidential	19 yrs. ACRS (175% db)	31.5 yrs. sl
Personal property (furniture & fixtures)	5 yrs. ACRS (150% db)	7 yrs. (200% db)
Depreciation recapture applied only if ACRS used		
Residential	Excess depreciation	N/A
Nonresidential	All depreciation	N/A
Tax credits		
Personal property	10%	None
Rehab		
Certified Historic Site	25%	20%
Other	15% or 20% (depending on age; nonresidential only)	10% (if placed in service before 1936; can be residential or nonresidential)
Passive loss limitations	None	Limited to passive income ($25,000 more allowed for "active participants" in rental real estate)

ACRS - Accelerated cost recovery system
db - declining balance
sl - straight-line

Note: This is a very general summary for discussion purposes only. It is not complete. Consult your tax accountant before making any decisions based on this information.

Types of Range Vegetation

annuals. A type of range vegetation in which annual forbs or annual grasses constitute the dominant vegetation. Abandoned lands often fall into this class.

barren. A type of range that includes all areas on which there is naturally no vegetation such as intermittent lake beds, saline flats, active sand dunes, shale, rock slides, and lava flows. Areas that have been denuded should not be confused with areas that are naturally barren, nor should areas containing annuals for part of the year be classified under this type of range.

broad-leaved trees. A type of range vegetation including all deciduous trees such as aspen, cottonwood, birch, and alder.

browse shrub. A type of range that includes foothills and mountain ranges where browse, except sage-brush, is predominant; usually occupies the transition zone of the lower foothills or mountain slopes.

conifer. Any of an order of trees or shrubs that bear cones—e.g., evergreens, pines; as range vegetation includes all range lands dominated by coniferous timber with supporting grasses, forbs, or browse.

creosote bush. A type of range where creosote (Corvillea) is the predominant vegetation.

desert shrub. A general type of range that includes areas where desert shrubs dominate; includes black-bush (*coleogyne*), coffee berry (*simmondsia*), cat's claw (*acacia* and *mimosa*), gray molly (*kochia*), hopsage (*grayia*), horse brush (*tetradymia*), and little rabbit brush (*crysothamnus stenophyllus*), but so few pure types of each that a separate type is not justified.

grassland. A type of range that includes all grasslands other than meadow; perennial grasses predominate although forbs and browse may be present.

greasewood. Areas where greasewood (*sarcobatus*) is the predominant vegetation.

half shrub. Semiwoody perennials of low stature such as *aplopappus, gutierrezia, artemisia frigida,* and *eriogonum wrightii*; plants commonly consist of woody caudex which produce herbaceous stems that die back annually.

meadow. A type of range that includes areas where sedges, rushes, and mesic grasses predominate; usually remains wet or moist throughout the summer.

mesquite. Areas where various species of mesquite (*prosopis*) predominate.

perennial forb. Areas where perennial forbs predominate. There is little vegetation of the true forb type because forb cover is usually tempo-rary in nature and is soon replaced by a permanent type of vegetation if the disturbing factor is removed.

pinon juniper. A type of range that includes pinon, juniper, and digger pine.

sagebrush. Areas where species of sagebrush predominate.

saltbrush. Areas where various salt desert shrubs such as *atriplex* predominate.

waste. All vegetated areas that have insufficient value to be used economically due to inaccessibility, density of timber, or sparseness of forage. Large areas of sparse forage that are not located near a better type are classified as waste (for grazing) because it is impractical to run stock over a large area to get to a small amount of feed.

winter fat. Areas where winter fat (*eurotia*) constitutes the predominant vegetation.

Types of Soil

acid soil. A soil that has an acid reaction; more particularly, a soil that has a preponderance of hydrogen ions over hydroxyl ions in the soil solution. A pH of 7 represents the neutral point in a soil solution, so any value below 7 is acid.

adobe. Describes a soil that cracks deeply upon drying and breaks into irregular, but roughly cubical, blocks; usually heavy-textured and high in colloidal clay.

aeloian soil. Soil developed from material transported and deposited by the wind.

alkaline soil. A soil that is alkaline in reaction; the opposite of acid; has a pH above 7.

alluvial soil. An azonal soil formed from materials (alluvion) transported by flowing water; an unstable soil.

azonal soil. An insufficiently developed soil lacking a definite soil profile.

bog soil. An intrazonal group of marshy or swampy soils underlain with peat; common to humid or subhumid climates.

calcareous soil. A soil containing carbonate of calcium (limestone).

catena. A group of soils within one zonal region developed from similar parent material but different in solum characteristics owing to differences in relief and/or drainage.

chernozem. A zonal group of soils with a deep, dark-colored to nearly black surface horizon, rich in organic material, which grades into lighter-colored soils and finally into a layer of lime accumulation; developed under tall and mixed grasses in a temperate-to-cool, subhumid climate.

clay. Small mineral soil grain, less than 0.005 millimeter in diameter; plastic when moist, but hard when baked or fired.

clay loam. Describes a soil that contains a moderate amount of fine material mixed with coarser soil grains. When the moist soil is pressed between the thumb and finger, it will form a "ribbon" that will break easily. The moist soil is plastic and will form a cast that will bear much handling. When kneaded by hand it does not crumble readily, but tends to form a heavy, compact mass.

claypan. A dense, heavy soil horizon underlying the upper part of the soil which, because of the characteristics of clay, interferes with water movement and root development.

coarse-textured soil. A soil that contains a preponderance of soil grains larger than 0.25 millimeter; includes sandy loams, gravelly sandy loams, and loamy sands.

colluvial soil. Soil material found at the base of a steep hill or slope which has been transported by gravity or water.

desert soil. A zonal group of soils with a light-colored surface soil usually underlain by calcareous material and frequently by hardpan; developed under extremely scant shrub vegetation in areas with warm-to-cool arid climates.

drouthy soil. A loose-textured soil with poor water-holding capacity due to such conditions as a sand or gravel subsoil.

fine sandy loam. A soil with a fine sandy loam texture containing much sand but enough silt and clay to make it coherent. The sands contain 50% or more fine sands, or less than 25% fine gravel, coarse, and medium sand. Thus the fine sandy loam type contains a larger percentage of fine sand than does the sandy loam type.

fine-textured soil. A soil that contains a high percentage of fine particles 0.005 millimeter in diameter or less. Such soils are also referred to as *clays*.

glacial soil. Parent material of soil that has been moved and redeposited by glacial activity.

gumbo soil. A silty, fine-textured soil which becomes very sticky when wet and has a greasy appearance.

hardpan. A layer of silt, clay, or other soil material cemented together; a hardened soil horizon that will not dissolve to any appreciable extent in water. The soil may have any texture and be compacted or cemented by iron oxide, organic material, silica, calcium carbonate, or other substances.

heavy soil. Sometimes used to describe a clay soil. *See also* clay; fine-textured soil.

immature soil. A young or imperfectly developed soil; one lacking individual horizons.

impervious soil. Describes a soil that does not allow the passage of water, air, or plant roots.

lacustrine soil. Soils formed from materials deposited by the waters of lakes and ponds; usually fine-textured and heavy.

light-textured soils. Sometimes used to describe a sandy or coarse-textured soil.

loam. A soil with a mixture of different grades of sand, silt, and clay in such proportions that the characteristics of no single soil predominates; mellow with a gritty feel and slightly plastic when moist. If squeezed when dry, it will form a cast that will require careful handling; if squeezed when wet, the cast can be handled freely without breaking. *See also* clay loam; fine sandy loam; sandy loam; silt clay loam; silt loam.

loess. Wind-blown material; differs from till and water sediment in that it is uniformly silty.

marine soil. A soil formed from materials deposited by the oceans and seas and later exposed by upward movement of the terrain; e.g., the coastal plain soils of Maryland and Virginia.

medium-textured soil. Sometimes used to describe loams, fine sandy loams, and clay loams.

mellow. Describes soil that is easily worked due to its friability and loamy characteristics.

muck. Fairly well-decomposed organic soil material that is relatively high in mineral content, dark in color, and accumulated under poor drainage conditions.

neutral soil. A soil that is not significantly acid or alkaline, which is a desirable condition; has a pH between 6.6 and 7.3.

organic soil. Describes any soil that is predominantly organic material.

peat soil. Unconsolidated soil material consisting largely of undecomposed or slightly decomposed organic matter accumulated under excessively moist conditions.

pedalfers soil. A soil in which there has been a shifting of alumina and iron oxide downward in the soil profile but with no horizon of carbonate accumulation.

pedocal soil. A soil with an horizon of accumulated carbonates in the soil profile.

phase soil. The part of a soil unit or soil type that differs slightly from the characteristics normal for the soil type. These minor variations, which may be of great importance, are mainly in external characteristics such as relief, stoniness, or accelerated erosion.

podzol. A zonal group of soils with an organic mat and a thin organic-mineral layer above a gray leached layer which rests upon an alluvial dark brown horizon; developed under coniferous or mixed forest or under vegetation in a temperate-to-cold, moist climate.

prairie soils. A zonal group of soils with a dark brown or grayish brown surface horizon, grading through brown soil to lighter-colored parent material at two to five feet; developed under tall grasses in a temperate, relatively humid climate. The term has a restricted meaning in soil science and is not applied to all dark-colored soils of the treeless plains, but only to those in which carbonates have not been concentrated in any part of the profile by soil-forming processes.

primary soil. A soil formed in place from the weathering of the underlying rock and minerals.

recent soil. A secondary soil of such recent deposition that the weathering or aging processes have made little or no change in the profile.

residual soil. Soil formed in place by the weathering of mineral material, i.e., by the disintegration and decomposition of rock in place.

saline soil. A soil that contains enough common alkali salts to affect plant growth adversely.

sandy loam. A soil containing much sand and enough silt and clay to make it somewhat coherent; the sand grains can be felt; forms a weak cast when dry and squeezed by hand.

secondary soil. A soil that has been transported by water or wind and has been redeposited; alluvial soil.

silt clay loam. A soil that is made up of moderate amounts of fine grades of sand and moderate amounts of clay but is more than 50% silt and clay, containing more clay than silt loam; cloddy when dry and when wet tends to "ribbon" if squeezed between finger and thumb.

silt loam. A soil made up of moderate amounts of the fine grades of sand, small amounts of clay, and one half or more silt; cloddy when dry but smooth when wet and will not "ribbon."

transported soil. Secondary soil; soil that has been moved and redeposited by water or wind.

upland soil. Soils developed through the disintegration and decomposition of rocks in place and the weathering of the resulting debris; primary soil usually occupying hilly to mountainous terrain.

Bibliography

Books

Abrams, Charles. *The Language of Cities: A Glossary of Terms*. Viking Penguin, Inc., 1971.

Akerson, Charles B. *The Appraiser's Workbook*. Chicago: American Institute of Real Estate Appraisers, 1985.

_____ . *Capitalization Theory and Techniques: Study Guide*. Rev. ed. Chicago: American Institute of Real Estate Appraisers, l984.

Albritton, Harold D. *Controversies in Real Property Valuation: A Commentary*. Chicago: American Institute of Real Estate Appraisers, l982.

Alexander, Ian. *Office Location and Public Policy*. New York: Chancer Press, 1979.

American Association of State Highway Officials. *Acquisitions for Right of Way*. Washington, D.C.: American Association of State Highway Officials, 1962.

American Institute of Real Estate Appraisers. *The Appraisal of Rural Property*. Chicago: American Institute of Real Estate Appraisers, l983.

_____ . *Appraisal Thought: A 50-Year Beginning*. Chicago: American Institute of Real Estate Appraisers, 1982.

_____ . *Appraising Residential Properties*. Chicago: American Institute of Real Estate Appraisers, 1988.

_____ . *Forecasting: Market Determinants Affecting Cash Flows and Reversions*. Research Series Report 4. Chicago: American Institute of Real Estate Appraisers, 1989.

_____ . *Impacts of Regulation on the Appraisal Industry*. Research Series Report 2. Chicago: American Institute of Real Estate Appraisers, 1987.

_____ . *Readings in Highest and Best Use*. Chicago: American Institute of Real Estate Appraisers, 1981.

_____ . *Readings in the Income Approach to Real Property Valuation, Volume I.* Chicago: American Institute of Real Estate Appraisers, 1977.

_____ . *Readings in the Income Capitalization Approach to Real Property Valuation, Volume II.* Chicago: American Institute of Real Estate Appraisers, 1985.

_____ . *Readings in Market Research for Real Estate.* Chicago: American Institute of Real Estate Appraisers, l985.

_____ . *Readings in Real Property Valuation Principles, Volume I.* Chicago: American Institute of Real Estate Appraisers, 1977.

_____ . *Readings in Real Property Valuation Principles, Volume II.* Chicago: American Institute of Real Estate Appraisers, 1985.

_____ . *Real Estate Market Analysis and Appraisal.* Research Series Report 3. Chicago: American Institute of Real Estate Appraisers, 1988.

Andrews, Richard B. *Urban Land Economics and Public Policy.* New York: Free Press, 1971.

Andrews, Richard N. L. *Land in America.* Lexington, Mass.: D.C. Heath, l979.

Appraisal Institute. *The Appraisal of Real Estate.* 10th ed. Chicago: Appraisal Institute, 1992.

_____ . *Measuring the Effects of Hazardous Materials Contamination on Real Estate Values: Techniques and Applications.* Chicago: Appraisal Institute, 1992.

Arnold, Alvin L. and Jack Kusnet. The Arnold Encyclopedia of Real Estate. Boston, Mass.: Warren, Gorham & Lamont, Inc., 1978.

Babcock, Frederick M. *The Valuation of Real Estate.* New York: McGraw-Hill, 1932.

Barlowe, Raleigh. *Land Resource Economics.* 4th ed. Englewood Cliffs, N.J.: Prentice-Hall, 1986.

Bierman, Harold Jr., and Seymour Smidt. *The Capital Budgeting Decision.* 6th ed. New York: Macmillan, l984.

Bish, Robert L. and Hugh O. Nourse. *Urban Economics and Policy Analysis.* New York: McGraw-Hill, 1975.

Bloom, George F., Arthur M. Weimer, and Jeffrey D. Fisher. *Real Estate.* 8th ed. New York: Wiley, 1982.

Bonbright, James C. *The Valuation of Property.* Vols. 1 and 2. New York: McGraw-Hill, l937.

Bongiorno, Benedetto and Robert R. Garland. *Real Estate Accounting and Reporting Manual.* Boston, Mass.: Warren, Gorham & Lamont, Inc., 1983.

Burton, James H. *Evolution of the Income Approach.* Chicago: American Institute of Real Estate Appraisers, l982.

Byrne, Therese E. *A Guide to Real Estate Information Sources.* 1980.

Carn, Neil, Joseph Rabianski, Maury Seldin, and Ronald L. Racster. *Real Estate Market Analysis: Applications and Techniques.* Englewood Cliffs, N.J.: Prentice-Hall, 1988.

Cartwright, John M. *Glossary of Real Estate Law.* The Lawyers Cooperative Publishing Co., 1972.

Clapp, John M. *Handbook for Real Estate Market Analysis.* Englewood Cliffs, N.J.: Prentice-Hall, 1987.

Clark, Louis E., Jr. and F. M. Treadway, Jr. *Impact of Electric Power Transmission Line Easements on Real Estate Value.* Chicago: American Institute of Real Estate Appraisers, 1972.

Conroy, Kathleen. *Valuing the Timeshare Property.* Chicago: American Institute of Real Estate Appraisers, 1981.

Davies, Pearl Janet. *Real Estate in American History.* Washington, D.C.: Public Affairs Press, 1958.

Desmond, Glenn M. and Richard E. Kelley. *Business Valuation Handbook.* Llano, Calif: Valuation Press, 1988.

Dilmore, Gene. *Quantitative Techniques in Real Estate Counseling.* Lexington, Mass.: D.C. Heath, 1981.

Dombal, Robert W. *Appraising Condominiums: Suggested Data Analysis Techniques.* Chicago: American Institute of Real Estate Appraisers, 1981.

Eaton, James D. *Real Estate Valuation in Litigation.* Chicago: American Institute of Real Estate Appraisers, 1982.

Financial Accounting Standards Board. *FASB Statement No. 66, Accounting for Sales of Real Estate.* Norwalk, Conn.: Financial Accounting Standards Board, 1982.

_____ . *FASB Statement No. 67, Accounting for Costs and Initial Rental Operations of Real Estate Projects.* Norwalk, Conn.: Financial Accounting Standards Board, 1982.

Friedman, Edith J., ed. *Encyclopedia of Real Estate Appraising.* 3rd ed. Englewood Cliffs, N.J.: Prentice-Hall, 1978.

Friedman, Jack P. et al. *Dictionary of Real Estate Terms.* New York: Barron, 1987.

Gale Research Inc. *Encyclopedia of Associations,* 26th ed. Detroit: Gale Research Inc., 1992.

Gibbons, James E. *Appraising in a Changing Economy: Collected Writings of James E. Gibbons.* Chicago: American Institute of Real Estate Appraisers, 1982.

Gimmy, Arthur E. and Martin E. Benson. *Golf Courses and Country Clubs: A Guide to Appraisal, Market Analysis, and Financing.* Chicago: Appraisal Institute, 1992.

Gimmy, Arthur E. and Michael G. Boehm. *Elderly Housing: A Guide to Appraisal, Market Analysis, Development and Financing.* Chicago: American Institute of Real Estate Appraisers, 1988.

Gimmy, Arthur E. and Brian B. Woodworth. *Fitness, Racquet Sports, and Spa Projects: A Guide to Appraisal, Development, and Financing.* Chicago: American Institute of Real Estate Appraisers, 1989.

Graaskamp, James A. *Graaskamp on Real Estate.* Stephen P. Jarchot, ed. Washington, D.C.: Urban Land Institute, 1991.

_____ . *A Guide to Feasibility Analysis.* Chicago: Society of Real Estate Appraisers, 1970.

Greer, Gaylon E. *The Real-Estate Investment Decision.* Lexington, Mass.: D.C. Heath, 1979.

Gross, Jerome S., comp. *Webster's New World Illustrated Encyclopedia Dictionary of Real Estate.* 3rd ed. New York: Prentice-Hall, 1987.

Haggett, Peter. *Locational Analysis in Human Geography.* New York: St. Martin's, 1965.

Harris, Cyril M., ed. *Dictionary of Architecture and Construction.* New York: McGraw-Hill, 1975.

Harris, Jack C., PhD and Jack P. Friedman, PhD. *Barron's Real Estate Handbook.* Woodbury, N.Y.: Barron's Educational Series, 1984.

Harrison, Henry S. *Houses—The Illustrated Guide to Construction, Design and Systems.* Rev. ed. Chicago: Realtors National Marketing Institute, 1990.

Heilbroner, Robert L. *The Worldly Philosophers.* Rev. ed. New York: Simon and Schuster, 1964.

Himstreet, William C. *Communicating the Appraisal: The Narrative Report.* Chicago: Appraisal Institute, 1991.

Hoover, Edgar M. *The Location of Economic Activity.* New York: McGraw-Hill, 1963.

Institute on Planning, Zoning, and Eminent Domain. *Proceedings.* Albany, N.Y.: Matthew Bender. Series began in 1959.

International Association of Assessing Officers. *Property Appraisal and Assessment Administration.* Chicago: International Association of Assessing Officers, 1990.

_____ . *Property Assessment Valuation.* Chicago: International Association of Assessing Officers, 1977.

Jevons, W. Stanley. *The Theory of Political Economy.* 5th ed. New York: Augustus M. Kelley, 1965.

Kahn, Sanders A. and Frederick E. Case. *Real Estate Appraisal and Investment.* 2nd ed. New York: Ronald Press, 1977.

Keune, Russell V., ed. *The Historic Preservation Yearbook.* Bethesda, Md.: Adler and Adler, 1984.

Kinnard, William N., Jr. *Income Property Valuation: Principles and Techniques of Appraising Income-Producing Real Estate.* Lexington, Mass.: D.C. Heath, 1971.

Kinnard, William N., Jr., ed. *1984 Real Estate Valuation Colloquium: A Redefinition of Real Estate Appraisal Precepts and Practices.* Boston, Mass.: Oelgeschlager, Gunn & Hain in association with the Lincoln Institute of Land Policy, 1986.

Kinnard, William N., Jr. and Byrl N. Boyce. *Appraising Real Property.* Lexington, Mass: D.C. Heath, 1984.

Kinnard, William N., Jr., Stephen D. Messner, and Byrl N. Boyce. *Industrial Real Estate.* 4th ed. Washington, D.C.: Society of Industrial Realtors, 1979.

Klink, James J. *Real Estate Accounting and Reporting: A Guide for Developers, Investors and Lenders.* New York: John Wiley & Sons, Inc., 1980.

Kratovil, Robert and Raymond J. Werner. *Real Estate Law.* 8th ed. Englewood Cliffs, N.J.: Prentice-Hall, 1983.

Levine, Mark Lee. *Real Estate Appraisers' Liability.* New York: Clark Boardman Callaghan, 1991.

Love, Terrence L. *The Guide to Appraisal Office Policies and Procedures.* Chicago: Appraisal Institute, 1991.

Mason, James J., ed. and comp. *American Institute of Real Estate Appraisers Financial Tables.* Chicago: American Institute of Real Estate Appraisers, 1981.

R.S. Means, Inc. *Means Illustrated Construction Dictionary.* New unabr. ed. Kingston, Mass.: R.S. Means, Inc., 1991.

Mills, Arlen C. *Communicating the Appraisal: The Individual Condominium or PUD Unit Appraisal Report.* Chicago: American Institute of Real Estate Appraisers, 1988.

————. *Communicating the Appraisal: The Uniform Residential Appraisal Report.* Chicago: American Institute of Real Estate Appraisers, 1988.

Mills, Arlen C. and Dorothy Z. *Communicating the Appraisal: The Small Residential Income Property Appraisal Report.* Chicago: Appraisal Institute, 1990.

National Cooperative Highway Research Program. *Reports.* Washington, D.C.: National Academy of Sciences Highway Research Board, 1966-1979.

North, Lincoln W. *The Concept of Highest and Best Use.* Winnipeg, Manitoba: Appraisal Institute of Canada, 1981.

Noyes, C. Reinold. *The Institution of Property.* London: Longmans, Green and Company, 1936.

Olin, Harold B., John L. Schmidt, and Walter H. Lewis. *Construction—Principles, Materials & Methods.* 4th ed. Chicago: Institute of Financial Education and Interstate Printers and Publishers, 1980.

O'Mara, Paul W. *Residential Development Handbook.* Washington, D.C.: Urban Land Institute, 1978.

Perin, Constance. *Everything in Its Place: Social Order and Land Use in America.* Princeton, N.J.: Princeton University Press, 1977.

Ratcliff, Richard U. *Modern Real Estate Valuation: Theory and Application.* Madison, Wis.: Democrat Press, 1965.

_____ . *Urban Land Economics.* New York: Greenwood, 1972.

Reilly, John W. *The Language of Real Estate.* 3rd ed. Chicago: Real Estate Education Co., 1989.

Reynolds, Judith. *Historic Properties: Preservation and the Valuation Process.* Chicago: American Institute of Real Estate Appraisers, 1982.

Ring, Alfred A. and James H. Boykin. *The Valuation of Real Estate.* 3rd ed. Englewood Cliffs, N.J.: Prentice-Hall, 1986.

Ring, Alfred A. and Jerome Dasso. *Real Estate Principles and Practices.* 10th ed. Englewood Cliffs, N.J.: Prentice-Hall, 1985.

Roca, Ruben A. *Market Research for Shopping Centers.* New York: International Council of Shopping Centers, 1980.

Rohan, Patrick J. and Melvin A. Reskin. *Condemnation Procedures and Techniques; Forms.* Albany, N.Y.: Matthew Bender, 1968 (looseleaf service).

Roll, Eric. *A History of Economic Thought.* 3rd. ed. Englewood Cliffs, N.J.: Prentice-Hall, 1964.

Rosenberg, Jerry M. *Dictionary of Banking and Finance.* New York: John Wiley & Sons, Inc., 1982.

Rushmore, Stephen. *Hotels and Motels: A Guide to Market Analysis, Investment Analysis, and Valuations.* Chicago: Appraisal Institute, 1992.

_____ . *The Computerized Income Approach to Hotel-Motel Market Studies and Valuations.* Chicago: Appraisal Institute, 1990.

Sackman, Julius L. and Patrick J. Rohan. *Nichols' Law of Eminent Domain.* 3rd rev. ed. Albany, N.Y.: Matthew Bender, 1973 (looseleaf service).

Sahling, Leonard. *Real Estate Economics Special Report.* "Rent or Buy: A Market Analysis." New York: Merrill Lynch, 1990.

Samuelson, Paul A. and William D. Nordhaus. *Economics.* 13th ed. New York: McGraw-Hill, 1989.

Schmutz, George L. *The Appraisal Process.* North Hollywood, Calif., 1941.

_____ . *Condemnation Appraisal Handbook.* Rev. and enl. by Edwin M. Rams. Englewood Cliffs, N.J.: Prentice-Hall, 1963.

Schwanke, Dean. *Smart Buildings and Technology-Enhanced Real Estate, Volume I.* Washington, D.C.: Urban Land Institute, 1976.

Seldin, Maury and James H. Boykin. *Real Estate Analyses.* Homewood, Ill.: American Society of Real Estate Counselors and Dow Jones-Irwin, 1990.

Shenkel, William M. *Modern Real Estate Appraisal.* New York: McGraw-Hill, 1978.

Sirmans, C.F. and Austin J. Jaffe. *The Complete Real Estate Investment Handbook: A Professional Investment Strategy.* 4th ed. New York: Prentice-Hall, 1988.

Smith, Halbert C. and Jerry D. Beloit. *Real Estate Appraisal.* 2nd ed. Columbus, Ohio: Century VII Publishing Company, 1987.

Smith, Halbert C., Carl J. Tschappat, and Ronald L. Racster. *Real Estate and Urban Development.* 3rd ed. Homewood, Ill.: Richard D. Irwin, 1981.

Talamo, John. *The Real Estate Dictionary.* Boston, Mass.: Laventhol & Horwath/Financial Publishing Co., 1984.

United States Department of Commerce, Bureau of Census. *Statistical Abstract of the United States, 1990.* Washington, D.C.: U.S. Government Printing Office, 1990.

Urban Land Institute. *Shopping Center Development Handbook.* Washington, D.C.: Urban Land Institute, 1985.

Vane, Howard R. and John L. Thompson. *Monetarism—Theory, Evidency and Policy.* New York: Halsted, 1979.

Ventolo, William L. and Martha R. Williams. *Fundamentals of Real Estate Appraisal.* 5th ed. Chicago: Real Estate Education Co., 1990

Vernor, James D., ed. *Readings in Market Research for Real Estate.* Chicago: American Institute of Real Estate Appraisers, 1985.

Vernor, James D. and Joseph Rabianski. *Shopping Center Appraisal and Analysis.* Chicago: Appraisal Institute, 1993.

Weinberg, Norman, Paul J. Colletti, William A. Colavito, and Frank A. Melchior. *Guide to the New York Real Estate Salespersons Course.* New York: John Wiley & Sons, Inc., 1983.

Wendt, Paul F. *Real Estate Appraisal Review and Outlook.* Athens: University of Georgia Press, 1974.

West, Bill W. and Richard L. Dickinson. *Street Talk in Real Estate.* California: Unique Publishing, 1987.

White, John Robert. *Real Estate Valuing, Counseling, Forecasting: Selected Writings of John Robert White.* Chicago: American Institute of Real Estate Appraisers, 1984.

Witherspoon, Robert E., Jon P. Abbett, and Robert M. Gladstone. *Mixed-Use Developments: New Ways of Land Use.* Washington, D.C.: Urban Land Institute, 1976.

Wolf, Peter. *Land in America: Its Value, Use, and Control.* New York: Pantheon, 1981.

Dictionaries and Sources of Information on Computers

Arck Publications, Inc. *Small Business Computers.* Arck Publications, Inc., 1984

Freedman, Alan. *Electronic Computer Glossary.* Point Pleasant, Penn.: The Computer Language Co., 1993.

Microsoft Press. *Microsoft Press Computer Dictionary.* Redmond, Wash.: Microsoft Corporation, 1991.

Nader, Jonar. *Prentice-Hall's Illustrated Dictionary of Computing.* Englewood Cliffs, N.J.: Prentice- Hall, 1992.

Pfaffenberger, Bryan. *Que's Computer User's Dictionary.* Carmel, Ind.: Que Corporation, 1990.

Prentice-Hall. *Webster's New World Dictionary of Computing.* Englewood Cliffs, N.J.: Prentice-Hall, 1992

Building Cost Manuals

Boeckh Building Valuation Manual. Milwaukee: American Appraisal Co., 1967. 3 vols.
Vol. 1—*Residential and Agricultural;* Vol. 2—*Commercial;* Vol. 3—*Industrial and Institutional.* Uses 1967 cost database and includes wide variety of building models. Built up from unit-in-place costs converted to cost per square foot of floor or ground area. *Boeckh Building Cost Modifier* is published bimonthly for updating with current modifiers.

Building Construction Cost Data. Duxbury, Mass.: Robert Snow Means Co., annual.
Lists average unit prices on many building construction items for use in engineering estimates. Components arranged according to uniform system adopted by the American Institute of Architects, Associated General Contractors, and Construction Specifications Institute.

Dodge Building Cost Calculator & Valuation Guide. New York: McGraw-Hill Information Systems Co. (looseleaf service, quarterly supplements).
Lists building costs for common types and sizes of buildings. Local cost modifiers and historical local cost index tables included. Formerly *Dow Building Cost Calculator.*

Marshall Valuation Service. Los Angeles: Marshall and Swift Publication Co. (looseleaf service, monthly supplements).
Cost data for determining replacement costs of buildings and other improvements in the United States and Canada. Includes current cost multipliers and local modifiers.

Residential Cost Handbook. Los Angeles: Marshall and Swift Publication Co. (looseleaf service, quarterly supplements).
Presents square-foot method and segregated-cost method. Local modifiers and cost-trend modifiers included.

Sources of Operating Costs and Ratios

Only a few published sources are cited below. Attention is directed to the first item listed.

Robert Morris Associates. *Sources of Composite Financial Data—A Bibliography*. 3rd ed. Philadelphia, 1971.

> An annotated list of 98 nongovernment sources, arranged in manufacturing, wholesaling, retail, and service categories. Subject index to specific businesses. Publishers' names and addresses included for each citation.

Building Owners and Managers Association International. *Downtown and Suburban Office Building Experience Exchange Report*. Washington, D.C.

> Published annually since 1920. Includes analysis of expenses and income quoted in cents per square foot as well as national, regional, and selected city averages.

Dun & Bradstreet, Inc. *Key Business Ratios in 125 Lines*. New York.

> Published annually. Contains balance sheet and profit-and-loss ratios.

Hotel Association of New York City, Inc. *A Uniform System of Accounts for Hotels*. 8th ed. New York: Hotel Association of New York City, Inc., 1986.

Institute of Real Estate Management. *Income/Expense Analysis: Apartments, Condominiums & Cooperatives*. Chicago.

> Published annually since 1954. Data arranged by building type, then by national, regional, metropolitan, and selected city groupings. Operating costs listed per room, per square foot, etc. Formerly *Apartment Building Experience Exchange*.

_____ . *Income/Expense Analysis: Suburban Office Buildings*. Chicago.

> Published annually since 1976. Data analyzed on the basis of gross area and gross and net rentable office areas. Includes dollar-per-square-foot calculations; national, regional, and metropolitan comparisons; and detailed analyses for selected cities.

National Retail Merchants Association, Controllers' Congress. *Department Store and Specialty Store Merchandising and Operating Results*. New York.

> Published annually since 1925. Merchandise classification base used since 1969 edition (1968 data). Includes geographical analysis by Federal Reserve districts. Known as the "MOR" report.

_____ . *Financial and Operating Results of Department and Specialty Stores*. New York.

> Published annually since 1963. Data arranged by sales volume category. Known as the "FOR" report.

Pannell Kerr Forster. *Clubs in Town & Country*. Houston.

> Published annually since 1953. Lists income-expense data and operating ratios for city and country clubs. Geographical data broken down into four U.S. regions.

_____. *Trends in the Hotel Industry.* Houston.

>Published annually since 1937. Lists income-expense data and operating ratios for transient and resort hotels and motels. Geographical data broken down into five U.S. regions.

Smith Travel Research. *Lodging Outlook.* Gallatin, Tenn.

>Tracks number of lodging units in the United States and compiles statistics on occupancy, average room rate, and other operating characteristics of thousands of hotels and motels.

Urban Land Institute. *Dollars and Cents of Shopping Centers.* Washington, D.C.

>First issued in 1961 and revised every three years. Includes income and expense data for neighborhood, community, and regional centers as well as statistics for specific tenant types.

Periodicals

American Right of Way Proceedings. American Right of Way Association, Los Angeles.

>Annual. Papers presented at national seminars.

Appraisal Institute Magazine. Appraisal Institute of Canada, Winnipeg, Manitoba.

>Quarterly. General and technical articles on appraisal and expropriation in Canada. Includes information on institute programs, news, etc.

The Appraisal Journal. Appraisal Institute, Chicago.

>Quarterly. Periodical created in 1993 from the merger of *The Appraisal Journal* and *The Real Estate Appraiser.* Provides valuable, timely information pertinent to residential, industrial, rural, and commercial real estate valuation.

Appraiser News. Appraisal Institute, Chicago.

>Monthly news bulletin covering current events and trends in appraisal practice.

Buildings. Stamats Communications, Inc., Cedar Rapids, Iowa.

>Monthly. Journal of building construction and management.

Editor and Publisher Market Guide. Editor and Publisher, New York.

>Annual. Standardized market data for more than 1,500 areas in the United States and Canada, including population estimates for trading areas. List of principal industries, transportation, climate, chain store outlets, etc.

Emerging Trends in Real Estate. Real Estate Research Corp., Atlanta, Ga.., and New York.

>Annual.

Environmental Watch. Appraisal Institute, Chicago.

>Quarterly. Published since 1988. Up-to-date information on environmental issues affecting real estate appraisal.

Home Sales. National Association of Realtors, Washington, D.C.
> Monthly. Reports sales of existing and new single-family homes and residential condominium and cooperative units.

Income Property Rates. Crittenden Publishing, Inc., Novato, Calif.
> Weekly. Rates and terms on funding for income properties.

Journal of the American Real Estate and Urban Economics Association. Bloomington, Ind.
> Quarterly. Focuses on research and scholarly studies of current and emerging real estate issues.

Journal of the American Society of Farm Managers and Rural Appraisers. Denver.
> Semiannual. Includes appraisal articles.

Journal of Property Management. Institute of Real Estate Management, Chicago.
> Bimonthly. Covers a broad range of property investment and management issues.

The Journal of Real Estate Research. American Real Estate Society, Cleveland.
> Quarterly. Includes articles relating to real estate brokerage.

Just Compensation. Sherman Oaks, Calif.
> Monthly. Reports on condemnation cases.

Land Economics. University of Wisconsin, Madison.
> Quarterly. Devoted to the study of economics and social issues. Includes reports on university research and trends in land utilization. Frequently publishes articles on developments in other countries.

MarketSource. Appraisal Institute, Chicago.
> Quarterly. Published since 1991. Data on key rates, economic trends, and real estate financing and market conditions.

Mobility. Employee Relocation Council. Washington, D.C.
> Monthly.

The following periodicals on debenture and equity investment are published by Moody's Investors Service, Inc., New York.

Moody's Bank and Finance News Reports.
> Twice weekly.

Moody's Bond Record.
> Monthly.

Moody's Bond Survey.
> Weekly.

Moody's Commercial Paper Record.
> Monthly.

Moody's Dividend Record.
> Twice weekly.

Moody's Handbook of Common Stocks.
> Quarterly.

Moody's Handbook of Over-the-Counter Stocks.
> Quarterly.

Moody's Industrials.
> Twice weekly.

Moody's Investors Fact Sheets.
> Irregular.

Moody's Municipals and Governments.
> Twice weekly.

Moody's Over-the-Counter Industrials.
> Weekly.

Moody's Public Utilities.
> Twice weekly.

Moody's Transportation.
> Twice weekly.

National Real Estate Review. National Association of Realtors, Washington, D.C.
> Annual. Includes information on office, industrial, retail, multifamily, and hotel real estate.

Property Tax Journal. International Association of Assessing Officers, Chicago.
> Quarterly. Includes articles on property taxation and assessment administration.

The Quarterly Byte. Appraisal Institute, Chicago.
> Quarterly. Addresses use of computers in appraising.

Real Estate Finance. Crittenden Publishing, Inc., Novato, Calif.
> Weekly. Real estate finance information.

Real Estate Issues. American Society of Real Estate Counselors, Chicago.
> Semiannual.

Real Estate Law Journal. Warren, Gorham and Lamont, Inc., Boston.
> Quarterly. Publishes articles on legal issues and reviews current litigation of concern to real estate professionals.

Real Estate Report. Real Estate Research Corp., Atlanta, Ga., and New York.
> Quarterly.

Right of Way. American Right of Way Association, Los Angeles.
> Bimonthly. Articles on all phases of right-of-way activity—e.g., condemnation, negotiation, pipelines, electric power transmission lines, and highways. Includes association news.

Small Business Reporter. Bank of America, San Francisco.
> Irregular. Each issue devoted to a specific type of small business—e.g, coin-operated laundries, greeting card shops, and restaurants.

The following periodicals on debenture and equity investment are published by Standard and Poor's Corporation, New York.

Standard and Poor's Bond Guide.
> Monthly.

Standard and Poor's Bond Record.
> Twice weekly.

Standard and Poor's Commercial Paper Ratings Guide.
> Monthly.

Standard and Poor's Daily Stock Price Record: American Exchange.
> Quarterly.

Standard and Poor's Daily Stock Price Record: N.Y. Stock Exchange.
> Quarterly.

Standard and Poor's Daily Stock Price Record: Over-the-Counter Exchange.
> Quarterly.

Standard and Poor's Dividend Record.
> Daily and quarterly.

Standard and Poor's Earnings Forecaster.
> Weekly.

Standard and Poor's Outlook.
> Weekly.

Standard and Poor's Registered Bond Interest Record.
> Weekly.

Standard and Poor's Stock Guide.
> Monthly.

Standard and Poor's Stock Summary.
> Monthly.

Survey of Buying Power. Sales Management, New York.

> Annual. Includes population totals and characteristics and income and consumption data presented in national, regional, metropolitan area, county, and city categories. Separate section for Canadian information. Population estimates between decennial censuses.

Survey of Current Business. U.S. Bureau of Economic Analysis, U.S. Department of Commerce, Washington, D.C.

> Monthly. Includes statistical and price data. Biennial supplement, *Business Statistics.*

Urban Land. Urban Land Institute, Washington, D.C.

> Monthly. Publishes articles relating to urban land use and real estate development.

Valuation. American Society of Appraisers, Washington, D.C.

> Three issues per year. Articles on real property valuation and the appraisal of personal and intangible property. Includes society news. Previously published as *Technical Valuation.*